THE NEO-BABYLONIAN EMPIRE AND BABYLON IN THE LATTER PROPHETS

HARVARD SEMITIC MUSEUM PUBLICATIONS

Lawrence E. Stager, General Editor
Michael D. Coogan, Director of Publications

HARVARD SEMITIC MONOGRAPHS

edited by
Peter Machinist

Number 59

THE NEO-BABYLONIAN EMPIRE AND BABYLON IN THE LATTER PROPHETS

by
David Stephen Vanderhooft

David Stephen Vanderhooft

THE NEO-BABYLONIAN EMPIRE AND BABYLON IN THE LATTER PROPHETS

Scholars Press
Atlanta, Georgia

THE NEO-BABYLONIAN EMPIRE AND BABYLON IN THE LATTER PROPHETS

by
David Stephen Vanderhooft

Library of Congress Cataloging-in-Publication Data

Vanderhooft, David Stephen.
The Neo-Babylonian empire and Babylon in the latter prophets / David Stephen Vanderhooft.
p. cm. — (Harvard Semitic museum publications) (Harvad Semitic monographs ; no. 59)
Includes bibliographical references and index.
ISBN 0-7885-0579-3 (cloth : alk. paper)
1. Babylonia—History. 2. Bible. O.T. Prophets—History of Biblical events. I. Title. II. Series. III. Series: Harvard Semitic monographs ; no. 59.
DS73.9.V36 1999
935—dc21
99-38843
CIP

08 07 06 05 04 03 02 01 00 99 5 4 3 2 1

Printed in the United States of America
on acid-free paper

CONTENTS

ACKNOWLEDGMENTS vii

ABBREVIATIONS ix

INTRODUCTION 1

CHAPTER 1. INTO THE ETERNAL SHADOW OF BABYLON
NEO-BABYLONIAN IDEAS OF IMPERIAL RULE IN THE ROYAL INSCRIPTIONS

1.1 Introduction 9
1.2 The Form of the Texts 13
1.3 The Titulary 16
1.4 The Absence of Imperial Rhetoric in the Inscriptions of Nabopolassar 23
1.5 The Evolution of Babylonian Imperial Ideas: Nebuchadnezzar 33
1.5.1 The King's Call and Language of Imperial Hegemony 34
1.5.2 Nebuchadnezzar as Protector of Humanity 41
1.5.3 Babylon as Center of the World 45
1.5.4 The King's Enemies 49
1.5.5 Precedents and Summary 50
1.6 Nabonidus's Reformulation 51

CHAPTER 2. BABYLONIAN IMPERIAL ADMINISTRATION IN THE LEVANT

2.1 Introduction 61
2.2 The Contraction of Assyria and Egypt's Rise in the Southern Levant 63
2.2.1 The Contraction of Assyria 64
2.2.2 Egypt's Rise in the Southern Levant 69
2.3 Nebuchadnezzar's Arrival in the Levant 81

2.4 Nebuchadnezzar's Empire 89
2.4.1 Administrative Geography 90
2.4.1.1 Territorial Divisions in the Empire 90
2.4.1.2 Imperial Officials 99
2.4.1.3 The Case of Judah 104
2.4.1.4 Deportation 110
2.4.2. Economic Geography 112

CHAPTER 3. BABYLON IN THE LATTER PROPHETS

3.1 Introduction 115
3.2 Micah 4:10 117
3.3 The Foreign Nation Oracles in the First Isaiah 123
3.3.1 Isaiah 13 124
3.3.2 Isaiah 14:1-23 128
3.3.3 Isaiah 21:1-10 129
3.4 Jeremiah 135
3.4.1 The Foe From the North 136
3.4.2 The Babylonian King and His Administration 149
3.5 Habakkuk 1-2 152
3.6 Ezekiel 163
3.6.1 Ezekiel 17 164
3.6.2 Ezekiel 21:23-29 167
3.7 Second Isaiah 169
3.7.1 Isaiah 40:18-20 172
3.7.2 Isaiah 46:1-2 175
3.7.3 Isaiah 47 181
3.8 Jeremiah 50:1-51:58 188
3.8.1 Descriptions of Babylon 190
3.8.2 The Fall of Babylon 193

CHAPTER 4. SUMMARY AND CONCLUSIONS 203

BIBLIOGRAPHY 211

INDEX OF TEXTUAL CITATIONS 233

GENERAL INDEX 241

ACKNOWLEDGMENTS

The present monograph was submitted originally as a doctoral dissertation to the Department of Near Eastern Languages and Civilizations at Harvard University in May 1996. It is published here in revised and updated form. It is a pleasure for me to acknowledge those persons and institutions who have offered their guidance and support. Peter Machinist served as dissertation director and subsequently as volume editor for the Harvard Semitic Monographs series. From the inception of the project he has provided patient counsel and incisive commentary, and his influence will be clear throughout the volume. His brilliant comparative work on Mesopotamia and Israel will continue to serve as a model for me. Lawrence Stager, General Editor for the Harvard Semitic Museum, served as a dissertation advisor. He has taught me much about the material culture of the ancient Near East and has strongly influenced my thinking as an historian. I am thankful for his unfailing support and his constructive criticisms at every stage. Steven Cole also served on the dissertation committee, and his comments and demand for precision benefited the overall project. I am much indebted to these three scholars.

From the beginning of my graduate studies I have had the good fortune to benefit from conversations with Baruch Halpern, a superb comparativist, an excellent mentor, and a friend. I am also grateful to my teachers at Harvard and elsewhere who have offered guidance and training, including Frank Moore Cross, Jo Ann Hackett, Theodore Hiebert, John Huehnergard, James Kugel, and Saul Olyan. Michael Coogan, Director of Publications for the Harvard Semitic Museum, edited the manuscript with great care and deserves thanks. Philip King, my esteemed colleague, offered encouragement and invaluable advice on substantive issues throughout the revision process. I was fortunate to discuss and refine some of my ideas with Nadav Na'aman in the summer of 1998. Walter Hannam read the camera-ready manuscript and made numerous corrections and astute observations which improved the volume. Leigh Andersen of Scholars Press provided prompt and expert advice on preparing the manuscript for publication. Of course, none of the individuals singled out here should be held responsible for the errors or shortcomings which remain.

The Social Sciences and Humanities Research Council of Canada and the Mrs. Giles Whiting Foundation provided support during the dissertation phase. Most recently, Boston College furnished a subvention grant to offset the costs of publication. I am grateful to Donald Dietrich, the Theology Department chair; Patricia De Leeuw, Associate Dean; and Michael Smyer, Dean and Associate Vice President for Research, for their aid in this matter.

I would also like to thank all of the members of my family for their support over the years. Chris Vanderhooft alleviated many small burdens early on in the process. My mother, always a willing partner in conversation, has been unwavering in her encouragement of my academic career, even in difficult times. For this and much more I thank her. My father, and Johanna and Siebe Dykstra will not see the study come to press, but they were nevertheless instrumental in preparing me to write it. Jordan, Megan, and Adrienne arrived to offer assistance, although that resulted at least once in the need to extract an upside down diskette from the A drive. I thank the three of them for their patience and love. Finally, I dedicate this study, with admiration and love, to Shannon.

David Vanderhooft
Lexington, Massachusetts
Spring, 1999

ABBREVIATIONS

AASOR	Annual of the American Schools of Oriental Research
AB	Anchor Bible
ABD	D. N. Freedman, ed., *The Anchor Bible Dictionary*
ADAJ	*Annual of the Department of Antiquities of Jordan*
AfO	*Archiv für Orientforschung*
AHw	W. von Soden, *Akkadisches Handwörterbuch*
AJA	*American Journal of Archaeology*
AJSL	*American Journal of Semitic Languages and Literatures*
ALBO	Analecta lovaniensia biblica et orientalia
ANEP	J. B. Pritchard, ed., *The Ancient Near East in Pictures*, 2d ed.
ANET	J. B. Pritchard, ed., *Ancient Near Eastern Texts*, 3d ed.
AnOr	Analecta Orientalia
AnSt	*Anatolian Studies*
AOAT	Alter Orient und Altes Testament
AoF	*Altorientalische Forschungen*
AOS	American Oriental Society
ARE	J. H. Breasted, ed., *Ancient Records of Egypt*
ArOr	*Archív orientální*
AS	Assyriological Studies
ASOR	American Schools of Oriental Research
ATANT	Abhandlungen zur Theologie des Alten und Neuen Testaments
BA	*Biblical Archaeologist*
BAR	*Biblical Archaeology Review*
BASOR	*Bulletin of the American Schools of Oriental Research*
BDB	F. Brown, S. R. Driver, and C. A. Briggs, *Hebrew and English Lexicon of the Old Testament*
BETL	Bibliotheca ephemeridum theologicarum lovaniensium
BHLT	Grayson, *Babylonian Historical Literary Texts*

BHS	*Biblia Hebraica Stuttgartensia*
BHT	Sidney Smith, *Babylonian Historical Texts Relating to the Capture and Downfall of Babylon*
BIWA	R. Borger, *Beiträge zum Inschriftenwerk Assurbanipals*
Bib	*Biblica*
BibOr	Biblica et Orientalia
BKAT	Biblischer Kommentar: Altes Testament
BN	*Biblische Notizen*
BO	*Bibliotheca orientalis*
BRM	Babylonian Records in the Library of J. Pierpont Morgan
BSOAS	*Bulletin of the School of Oriental and African Studies*
BTT	A. R. George, *Babylonian Topographical Texts*
BWANT	Beiträge zur Wissenschaft vom Alten und Neuen Testament
BZAW	Beihefte zur *Zeitschrift für die alttestamentliche Wissenschaft*
CAD	*Chicago Assyrian Dictionary*
CAH	*Cambridge Ancient History*
CBQ	*Catholic Biblical Quarterly*
CCK	D. J. Wiseman, *Chronicles of the Chaldean Kings*
CH	Codex Hammurapi
CIS	*Corpus Inscriptionum Semiticarum*
CMHE	F. M. Cross, Jr., *Canaanite Myth and Hebrew Epic*
CT	Cuneiform Texts from Babylonian Tablets
DN	Divine Name
EI	*Eretz-Israel*
ETL	*Ephemerides theologicae lovanienses*
GAG	W. von Soden, *Grundriss der akkadischen Grammatik*
GKC	*Gesenius' Hebrew Grammar*, ed. E. Kautsch, trans. A. E. Cowley
GN	Geographical Name
GM	*Göttinger Miszellen*
HALAT	*Hebräisches und aramäisches Lexikon zum Alten Testament*
HAR	*Hebrew Annual Review*
HB	Hebrew Bible
HSM	Harvard Semitic Museum
HUCA	*Hebrew Union College Annual*
IBHS	B. Waltke and M. O'Connor, *Introduction to Biblical*

	Hebrew Syntax
IEJ	*Israel Exploration Journal*
IOS	*Israel Oriental Studies*
JANES	*Journal of the Ancient Near Eastern Society* (of Columbia University)
JAOS	*Journal of the American Oriental Society*
JARCE	*Journal of the American Research Center in Egypt*
JBL	*Journal of Biblical Literature*
JCS	*Journal of Cuneiform Studies*
JESHO	*Journal of the Economic and Social History of the Orient*
JHS	*Journal of Hellenic Studies*
JNES	*Journal of Near Eastern Studies*
Joüon	P. Joüon, *A Grammar of Biblical Hebrew*, trans. and rev. by T. Muraoka
JPOS	*Journal of the Palestine Oriental Society*
JQR	*Jewish Quarterly Review*
JSOT	*Journal for the Study of the Old Testament*
JSOTSup	Journal for the Study of the Old Testament, Supplements
KAI	H. Donner and W. Röllig, ed., *Kanaanäische und aramäische Inschriften*
Leš	*Lešonénu*
LIH	L. W. King, *The Letters and Inscriptions of Hammurabi*
MDOG	Mitteilungen der deutschen Orientgesellschaft
MVAG	Mitteilungen der vorderasiatisch-ägyptischen Gesellschaft
NA	Neo-Assyrian
NABU	*Nouvelles assyriologiques brèves et utilitaires*
NAPR	*North Akkad Project Reports*
NB	Neo-Babylonian
NEAEHL	*New Encyclopedia of Archaeological Excavations in the Holy Land*, ed. E. Stern.
OBO	Orbis Biblicus et Orientalis
OIP	Oriental Institute Publications
OLA	Orientalia Lovaniensia Analecta
Or	*Orientalia*
OTL	Old Testament Library
PKB	J. A. Brinkman, *A History of Post-Kassite Babylonia*
RA	*Revue d'assyriologie et d'archéologie orientale*
RAI	Rencontre Assyriologique Internationale
RB	*Revue biblique*

RIMB 2	G. Frame, *Rulers of Babylonia from the Second Dynasty of Isin to the End of Assyrian Domination (1157-612 B.C.)*
RLA	*Reallexikon der Assyriologie*
SAA	State Archives of Assyria
SAAB	*State Archives of Assyria Bulletin*
SAAS	State Archives of Assyria Studies
SANE	Sources from the Ancient Near East
SBAW	Sitzungsberichte der bayerischen Akademie der Wissenschaften
SBLDS	Society of Biblical Literature Dissertation Series
SBLMS	Society of Biblical Literature Monograph Series
ScrHier	Scripta Hierosolymitana
TA	*Tel Aviv*
TCS	Texts from Cuneiform Sources
TDOT	*Theological Dictionary of the Old Testament*
TWAT	*Theologisches Wörterbuch zum alten Testament*
UF	*Ugarit-Forschungen*
UT	Cyrus Gordon, *Ugaritic Textbook*
VAB	Vorderasiatische Bibliothek
VS	Vorderasiatische Schriftdenkmäler
VT	*Vetus Testamentum*
VTSup	Vetus Testamentum, Supplements
WHJP	World History of the Jewish People
WO	*Welt des Orients*
WVDOG	Wissenschaftliche Veröffentlichungen der deutschen Orientgesellschaft
YNER	Yale Near Eastern Researches
YNES	Yale Near Eastern Studies
YOS	Yale Oriental Series
YOR	Yale Oriental Series Researches
ZA	*Zeitschrift für Assyriologie*
ZAW	*Zeitschrift für die alttestamentliche Wissenschaft*
ZDMG	*Zeitschrift der deutschen morgenländischen Gesellschaft*
ZDPV	*Zeitschrift des deutschen Palästina-Vereins*

INTRODUCTION

As a discipline, biblical studies has often turned to Mesopotamian civilization to clarify the origin or meaning of biblical language, themes, and institutions; it has also devoted special attention to particular Mesopotamian rulers who are credited in the biblical record with decisive political intervention in Syria-Palestine. Such attention is in some measure justified by the Hebrew Bible (hereafter HB), which recognizes Mesopotamia as the source of cultural innovations (Nimrod [Gen 10:8-9]; Tower of Babel [Gen 11:1-9]) and identifies Mesopotamian rulers, Sennacherib for example, as dangerous aggressors. Nevertheless, the tendency to view Mesopotamian civilization primarily as illustrative of matters biblical deprecates the value of comparative research, which risks degenerating into the procedure Samuel Sandmel derisively labeled "parallelomania."[1] I will reverse the usual focus within biblical studies and ask, in connection with the period of the Neo-Babylonian dynasty (c. 605-539 B.C.E.), not simply how imperial Babylon influenced Judah or particular biblical writers, but rather how the biblical texts illuminate the phenomenon of Babylonian imperialism.

---

[1] For a critique of the assumptions underlying the search for parallels to illuminate the Bible, even in less extreme formulations, see S. Sandmel, "Parallelomania," *JBL* 81 (1962): 1-13. The opposite procedure, to prove that biblical ideas and institutions were essentially derivative of Babylonian ones, was taken to its extreme in the early part of the century in the so-called Pan-Babylonian movement. For a good review of the work that emerged from this movement, see K. Johanning, *Der Bibel-Babel Streit: Eine Forschungsgeschichtliche Studie*, Europäische Hochschulschriften Reihe 23, Bd 343 (Frankfurt: Peter Lang, 1988); R. G. Lehmann, *Friedrich Delitzsch und der Babel-Bibel-Streit*, OBO 133 (Freiburg: Universitätsverlag; Göttingen: Vandenhoeck and Ruprecht, 1994); and more briefly M. T. Larsen, "The 'Babel/Bible' Controversy and its Aftermath," in *Civilizations of the Ancient Near East*, ed. J. M. Sasson et al. (New York: Macmillan, 1995), 1.95-106; and H. B. Huffmon, "*Babel und Bibel*: The Encounter between Babylon and the Bible," *Michigan Quarterly Review* 22 (1983): 309-20.

In broad terms, the present study seeks to clarify the character and functions of the Neo-Babylonian empire in its relationship to subjugated populations, and in particular to the population of Judah. Two related questions frame the discussion: 1) How did the Babylonians conceive and implement their role as imperial rulers? 2) Can the responses of subject populations to these conceptions and implementations furnish independent evidence about the empire? In other words, this study investigates Babylonian imperialism from two complementary perspectives: from native sources, which project the Babylonian imperial self-portrait, and from the writings of the biblical prophets, which provide a portrait from the perspective of a subjugated population.

Such a comparative approach is not new. The most direct influence on its formulation here is the essay by P. Machinist entitled, "Assyria and its Image in the First Isaiah." Machinist articulated, for the Neo-Assyrian period, the types of questions to which the present study attempts to formulate answers:

> What did the Neo-Assyrian empire look like to others, especially its contemporaries? How do such views, when measured against those of the Assyrians themselves, help us to understand the empire—the ways it functioned, the ways it related to the outside?[2]

The influence of Machinist's formulation on the present discussion will become clear below, where it offers a point of departure for the analysis of the prophetic descriptions of Babylon in chapter three. The major difference with respect to the Neo-Babylonian empire, in contrast to the Neo-Assyrian, is that there is still work to do in articulating what the Babylonian imperial ideas and practices were. A significant part of the present discussion is therefore devoted to this task. The first chapter attempts to clarify what imperial ideas emerge from analysis of the Neo-Babylonian royal inscriptions, while the second investigates the procedures by which the Babylonians maintained their imperial rule. The third chapter investigates how the Latter Prophets portray Babylon.

Analysis of the Neo-Babylonian royal inscriptions has for the most part focused on clarification of specific historical or religious problems to which the texts make incidental reference. The inscriptions, however, can also elucidate Babylonian ideas about empire, even if

---

[2] P. Machinist, "Assyria and Its Image in the First Isaiah," *JAOS* 103 (1983): 719.

these ideas must be described at a relatively high level of abstraction in the absence of any systematic treatment of the topic by the Babylonians.[3] This assertion, that the royal inscriptions provide clarification of the imperial worldview, derives from observations about the royal inscriptions such as the following by A. L. Oppenheim:

> [I]n their substance . . . [the royal inscriptions] reflect a dialogue that took place continuously at the court of the king between the ruler and those who helped him determine the policies of the realm and [who helped him] reconcile political and economic realities with the traditional aspirations of Mesopotamian rule over an ever-expanding empire.[4]

It should repay investigation to penetrate the traditional language of the royal inscriptions to determine how it encodes the imperial assumptions of the authors. It is also important to ask whether any development in these imperial ideas is discernible in the royal inscriptions composed under the different kings of the Neo-Babylonian dynasty. For although a relatively stable program was presented and sustained during the long reign of Nebuchadnezzar II, various other kings of the dynasty expressed different aspirations, as we shall see, suggesting that ideas pertaining to imperial rule were not uniform during the course of the dynasty. Finally, it will be useful where possible to contrast the ideas about imperial rule in the Babylonian royal inscriptions with those of the Neo-Assyrian kings, and to investigate the degree of continuity between them.

The second chapter analyzes in more concrete terms the contours of Babylonian imperial rule in the western part of the empire, particularly in the southern Levant. Here the evidence is admittedly not

---

[3] For a discussion of the problem of "self-consciousness" in the Mesopotamian literary tradition, and the apparent absence of treatises designed to lay out "the formal exposition of principles and their proofs," see P. Machinist, "On Self-Consciousness in Mesopotamia," in *The Origins and Diversity of Axial Age Civilizations*, ed. S. N. Eisenstadt (Albany, N.Y.: State University of New York Press, 1986), 183-202.

[4] A. L. Oppenheim, "Neo-Assyrian and Neo-Babylonian Empires," in *Propaganda and Communication in World History*, vol. 1, *The Symbolic Instrument in Early Times*, ed. H. D. Lasswell, D. Cerner, and H. Speier (Honolulu: University Press of Hawaii, An East-West Center Book, 1979), 118. Efforts to understand the imperial ideas of the Assyrian kings through analysis of their royal inscriptions is quite developed; see below, chapter 1, n. 12 for some references. The Babylonian inscriptions, for reasons to be discussed, have received less attention in this regard.

as full as the historian might like. Nevertheless, it allows one to rule out certain theories about imperial practice, and thus to clarify further how the empire functioned and how it did not. The particular focus is on imperial procedures of the Babylonians in the west under Nebuchadnezzar II, who was by all accounts the principal architect of the empire. The imperial administrative and economic geography can be better understood on the basis of renewed investigation of several of Nebuchadnezzar's royal inscriptions (including an unpublished fragment of his Etemenanki inscription), and also on the basis of newer archeological excavations in the southern Levant. Data from excavations, although discussed here selectively, provide an important balance to reconstructions of the imperial bureaucracy derived from textual sources. The analysis of Judah's status under Babylonian domination can also illuminate the imperial system in the west. It will be helpful as well to inquire about the problem of continuity between the Babylonian imperial bureaucracy and the earlier Assyrian one; this corresponds to the investigation, in chapter one, of imperial ideas in the royal inscriptions. To anticipate, it appears that both the imperial objectives and the bureaucratic system of the Babylonians differed in important ways from those of the Assyrians.

In chapter three, attention focuses on the writings of the Latter Prophets, that corpus within the HB in which Babylonian ideas about empire and the mechanisms for sustaining it were subjected to the most scrutiny and criticism. The decision to focus on the Latter Prophets is in part one of expedience. The large volume of texts in the HB that deal in some way with Babylon or Babylonia precludes systematic analysis of them all in the present context.[5] The prophetic corpus is more manageable in extent—although even within it selection will be necessary—and it has the virtue of containing a large body of material that is contemporaneous with the Neo-Babylonian dynasty. It is not merely manageable and contemporaneous, however; the prophetic texts also reflect explicitly and self-consciously on the character and the fate of the empire, and it is this reflection in the disparate texts that makes comparison between them particularly fruitful.

---

[5] For example, this study does not treat the problem of the literary relationship between the creation stories in Genesis and the Babylonian epic *Enūma Eliš*, or the relationship between the flood narrative of Genesis 6 and the accounts of a primordial deluge in Gilgamesh XI and *Atra-ḫasis*. Nor does it treat the much later traditions about the Babylonian court preserved in Daniel, which derive from the Hellenistic period.

Any empire is concerned by definition with the domination of conquered people. The perspective of the conquered, however, is often harder to obtain than that of the conquerors. The reverse is true of Judah and Babylon, since in this case the vanquished wrote the history; that is to say, the biblical writers, and the prophets in particular, produced perhaps the most influential portrait of Babylon to survive antiquity. Not until the recovery of the Babylonian perspective during the last 150 years has it been possible to gain even a partial understanding of the imperial phenomenon from native texts. Nevertheless, comparative study has continued to focus on illuminating biblical ideas or particular events on the basis of Babylonian evidence. An inversion of this perspective, however, makes it possible to use contemporary prophetic ideas about empire to gain a fuller understanding of Babylonian imperialism as it was perceived by a subjugated community.

I have used the terms "empire" and "imperialism" above, and a few words are required to explain how I understand them. For the most part, no theoretical definition of the terms is presumed. That is to say, I subscribe to a functional definition of the sort that M. Larsen succinctly expressed in his review of Mesopotamian imperial traditions:

> Empire is a relationship between a ruling and controlling power and one or more subjugated and dominated peoples. . . . an empire [may] be defined as a supernational system of political control, and such a system may have either a city-state or a territorial state as its center.[6]

This is naturally something of a catch-all definition, and debate persists about the applicability of the terms to the circumstances of Mesopotamian hegemony beyond the heartland. Lamprichs, for example, has recently argued that the multivalence of the term imperialism, as well as its various theoretical applications for modeling European history of the nineteenth and twentieth centuries, renders its usage problematic even for the Neo-Assyrian context.[7] It is unnecessary here fully to reprise the debate, but a brief discussion will highlight the usefulness of Larsen's definition.

---

[6] M. T. Larsen, "The Tradition of Empire in Mesopotamia," in *Power and Propaganda: A Symposium on Ancient Empires*, Mesopotamia 7 (Copenhagen: Akademisk Forlag, 1979), 91.

[7] R. Lamprichs, *Die Westexpansion des neuassyrischen Reiches: Eine Strukturanalyse*, AOAT 239 (Kevelaer: Butzon & Bercker; Neukirchen-Vluyn: Neukirchener, 1995), 5-16, 23-24.

There were very few occasions when a unified political power centered in Babylon exerted significant extraterritorial influence. One such period was under the first dynasty of Babylon, during the reign of Hammurapi, although the scope and cohesion of Babylon's power in that period remain subjects for study.[8] Another period of such influence was during the reign of Nebuchadnezzar II. From the Babylonian point of view, therefore, the expansionist, imperial circumstances of the sixth century were not normative. The Babylonians thus exerted considerable intellectual and administrative efforts to justify the domination of subject populations, and pressed into service for this purpose traditional ideas about kingship and the organization of the state. Whether one calls this new expansionist reality "empire," and characterizes the ideas and procedures generated to sustain it by the adjective "imperial," or whether another designation is used, such as Lamprich's "expansive Herrschafts-system," does not change the novelty of the situation or the fact that it was, at base, focused on domination and exploitation of non-Babylonian populations for the benefit of a ruling elite. Furthermore, since intellectual and bureaucratic arrangements will naturally develop somewhat differently in any particular manifestation of imperialism, a broad definition of the phenomenon is required for the purpose of comparative study.

As the foregoing discussion indicates, the present study is not conceived in the first place as an exhaustive analysis of the political history of the Neo-Babylonian dynasty.[9] Political history is important to the discussion, but it is pursued selectively rather than comprehensively to clarify issues concerning the Babylonian imperial worldview and administration in relation to the populations of the southern Levant. Similarly, the exegesis of biblical passages in chapter three is not exhaustive. The focus is rather on what representative biblical texts say about Babylon and how they say it, and the value of this information for understanding the empire.

The goal of the present discussion, then, is to provide a more satisfactory interpretation of the character and functions of the Neo-Babylonian empire in its interaction with the populations that came under its sway. Considerable efforts have been devoted to accomplishing

---

[8] See, e.g., C. J. Gadd, "Hammurabi and the End of His Dynasty," in *CAH*, rev. ed., vol. 2, ch. 5 (Cambridge: Cambridge University Press, 1965).

[9] For a more concerted effort in this vein, see E. von Voigtlander, "A Survey of Neo-Babylonian History" (Ph.D. diss., University of Michigan, Ann Arbor, 1963).

such an analysis of the Neo-Assyrian empire.[10] Through renewed investigation of Neo-Babylonian cuneiform sources, archeology, and the perspectives about Babylon contained in the biblical prophetic writings, new observations emerge about the last Mesopotamian empire and the populations that it dominated.

[10] From the point of view of Judean history and the biblical literature, see, for example, M. Cogan, *Imperialism and Religion: Assyria, Israel and Judah in the Eighth and Seventh Centuries* B.C.E., SBLMS 19 (Missoula: Scholars, 1974); and, with updated bibliography, idem, "Judah Under Assyrian Hegemony: A Re-examination of Imperialism and Religion," *JBL* 112 (1993): 403-14.

CHAPTER 1

INTO THE ETERNAL SHADOW OF BABYLON

NEO-BABYLONIAN IDEAS OF IMPERIAL RULE IN THE ROYAL INSCRIPTIONS

1.1 Introduction

The royal inscriptions are a principal source of information about the Neo-Babylonian[1] dynasty, which ruled Babylonia and much of the Near East from 626-539 B.C.E. These inscriptions,[2] however, also create problems for the historian. The Babylonian scribes, unlike their counterparts in the Assyrian empire, were uninterested in documenting

---

[1] The term "Neo-Babylonian" (NB) has both chronological and linguistic application. Chronologically, it refers to the era of the dynasty inaugurated by Nabopolassar in 626 that ruled Babylonia until 539. Linguistically, "Neo-Babylonian" refers to an Akkadian dialect characteristic of the Babylonian region from roughly the end of the second millennium until about the mid-sixth century (*CAD* Ḫ vi). W. von Soden uses the designation "Neubabylonisch" (nB) to characterize the language of the period between 1000 and 625, and "Spätbabylonisch" (spB) for the period after 625; for von Soden, spB thus includes the royal inscriptions of the Neo-Babylonian kings (*GAG* §2 g-h). *CAD* uses Neo-Babylonian (NB) for the period between 1000 and the end of the Neo-Babylonian dynasty (539), Late Babylonian (LB) for texts of Achaemenid or later date. I will similarly use "Late Babylonian" to refer only to the language of the period after the Neo-Babylonian dynasty. A complication in the literature and lexica is that von Soden uses the designation "Jungbabylonisch" (jB), the *CAD* "Standard Babylonian" (SB), to refer to the Akkadian "literary" dialect of the first millennium. I will refer to the language of the royal inscriptions as Neo-Babylonian, rather than Standard Babylonian, for the sake of simplicity.

[2] S. Langdon, *Die neubabylonischen Königsinschriften*, trans. R. Zehnpfund, VAB 4 (Leipzig: J. C. Hinrichs, 1912 [hereafter VAB 4]); P.-R. Berger, *Die neubabylonischen Königsinschriften: Königsinschriften des ausgehenden babylonischen Reiches (625-539 a. Chr.)*, AOAT 4/1 (Kevelaer: Butzon & Bercker; Neukirchen-Vluyn: Neukirchener, 1973). On the typology of Akkadian royal inscriptions generally, see especially A. K. Grayson, "Assyria and Babylonia," *Or* n.s. 49 (1980): 140-94, and J. Renger, "Königsinschriften B. Akkadisch," *RLA* 6 (1980-1983): 65-77.

the relationship between the kings of Babylon and the many other peoples within the empire.[3] Although there are a few exceptions, the royal inscriptions[4] do not focus on political relationships, military encounters, or the heroic deeds of the Babylonian kings in battle.[5] Not

---

[3] This fact is generally recognized; see, e.g., S. Langdon, *Building Inscriptions of the Neo-Babylonian Empire; Part I, Nabopolassar and Nebuchadnezzar* (Paris: E. Laroux, 1905), introduction; A. L. Oppenheim, *Ancient Mesopotamia: Portrait of a Dead Civilization*, 2d rev. ed. completed by E. Reiner (Chicago: University of Chicago Press, 1979), 149; Grayson, "Assyria and Babylonia," 160; Renger, "Königsinschriften," 70.

[4] The following conventions are adopted for the citation of the Neo-Babylonian royal inscriptions: when an inscription has been published in VAB 4, the page number (if line numbers are cited), the inscription number in parentheses, column number (if necessary), and line numbers will be cited. Easy access to more recent publication and bibliographic information is available in Berger, *Königsinschriften*, and his numbering will be added for ease of reference after the VAB 4 inscription number, preceded by an "=" sign. E.g., VAB 4 60 (Npl 1=Zyl III,1) i 1 would be: Vorderasiatische Bibliothek volume 4, page 60 (Nabopolassar text number 1 = Berger's Nabopolassar Zylinder III,1) column i line 1. Where texts have not been published by Langdon, their standard publication information, together with Berger's designation if it exists, will be provided: e.g., YOS 1 45 (=Nbn Zyl II,7). All transliterations have been updated where necessary on the basis of published copies, although no effort has been made to cite all variant orthographies where multiple exemplars of an inscription are extant. Improvements of readings in VAB 4 are not usually noted, and all translations are my own unless otherwise indicated. Assyriological abbreviations that are not given in the list contained in the front matter (pages ix-xii) follow those in *CAD* Š/3.

[5] We hear about only a few battles in the royal inscriptions; one that scholars often point to is Nebuchadnezzar's report of the removal of enemies from the Lebanon in his Wadi Brisa inscription. It is probable that this was a military campaign; the text reads: *i-na e-mu-qu* ^{d}AG *ù* ^{d}AMAR.UTU EN.EN-*e-a a-na* KUR *la-ab-na-nu a-na* [xxx]⸢*a*⸣ *ú-sa-ad-di-ru* [. . .] *na-ka-ar-šu e-li-iš ù ša-ap-li-iš as-su-uḫ-ma*, "by the strength of Nabû and Marduk, my lords, to the land of Lebanon in order to [. . .] I organized [. . .] its enemy everywhere [lit. above and below] I uprooted" (WVDOG 5 pl. 39:26-30; cf. Oppenheim, *ANET*, 307). Nebuchadnezzar's inscriptions also occasionally mention that he subdued all rebels by traversing difficult regions and routes, an archaic motif (see, e.g., VAB 4 [Nbk 15=St. Tfl. X] ii 17-23). The fragmentary tablet edited in VAB 4 206 (Nbk 48=Tontafel Frg. II,1) refers to a campaign in Nebuchadnezzar's thirty-seventh year against Egypt, but it is not a conventional royal inscription (for a copy see D. J. Wiseman, *The Chronicles of the Chaldean Kings (625-556 B.C.)* [London: British Museum, 1956], pls. XX and XXI [hereafter Wiseman, *CCK*]; for a partial translation, see Oppenheim, *ANET*, 308). The "historical epic" of Nabonidus (W. G. Lambert, "A New Source for the Reign of Nabonidus," *AfO* 22 [1968]: 1-8) also mentions campaigns against the west, but this inscription is also not a conventional commemorative royal inscription; on the text's classification as an historical epic, see now P. Machinist and H. Tadmor, "Heavenly Wisdom," in *The Tablet and the*

one of the Neo-Babylonian royal inscriptions contains a narrative that recounts the specific circumstances of a military encounter: they possess no discussions of strategy or battle scenarios; only one inscription mentions foreign captives;[6] and they do not mention sieges or the installation of compliant rulers. The texts that refer to past events come from the reign of Nabonidus (e.g., VAB 4 [Nbn 8]), who at least occasionally emulated the inscriptions of the Sargonid kings of Assyria, especially those of Assurbanipal.[7] After Nabopolassar, the royal inscriptions sometimes schematically list the commodities and building materials that flowed into Babylonia, and, much more rarely, foreign subjects. The scribes include this information, however, only if it contributes to the description of the building projects.

Moreover, this characteristically apolitical perspective of the Babylonian royal inscriptions had a long history. It was characteristic of royal inscriptions already in the Old Babylonian period (with exceptions from Mari and Eshnunna), and, as Brinkman notes, from the end of the Kassite period until "the eighth century, Babylonian official records—such as royal inscriptions and chronicles—exhibit profound disinterest in most military or political events."[8] This situation changed with the Babylonian chronicles, which begin to record such events by the reign of Nabonassar (747-734 B.C.E.),[9] but it never really did change in the royal inscriptions. Consequently, the historiographical principles of the scribes of the royal inscriptions remain opaque, as Oppenheim notes,[10] and it is thus difficult to coax data from these texts that are relevant for reconstructing political history.

Scroll: Near Eastern Studies in Honor of William W. Hallo, ed. M. Cohen, D. Snell, and D. Weisberg (Bethesda, Md.: CDL, 1993), 150.

[6] Nabonidus mentions 2,850 captives from Ḫumê (Cilicia) in VAB 4 284 (Nbn 8=Stl. Frgm. XI) ix 31-32. On the identification of Ḫumê, see W. F. Albright, "Cilicia and Babylonia under the Chaldean Kings," *BASOR* 120 (1950): 22-25.

[7] B. Landsberger, "Die Basaltstele Nabonids von Eski-Harran," in *Halil Edhem Hâtira Kitabi*, vol. I (Ankara: Türk Tarih Kurumu Basimevi, 1947); H. Tadmor, "The Inscriptions of Nabunaid: Historical Arrangement" in *Studies in Honor of Benno Landsberger*, ed. H. Güterbock and T. Jacobsen, AS 16 (Chicago: University of Chicago Press, 1965), 353 and n. 16; Renger, "Königsinschriften," 70 § 9C; P.-A. Beaulieu, *The Reign of Nabonidus King of Babylon, 556-539 B.C.*, YNER 10 (New Haven: Yale University Press, 1989), 2, 143.

[8] J. A. Brinkman, *A Political History of Post-Kassite Babylonia, 1158-722 B.C.*, AnOr 43 (Rome: Pontifical Biblical Institute, 1968), 316 (hereafter Brinkman, *PKB*).

[9] TCS 5 chron 1.

[10] Oppenheim, *Ancient Mesopotamia*, 144-53.

If we approach this problem of the apolitical character of the royal inscriptions from a different angle, however, other results emerge. Historical analysis of the royal inscriptions has focused mainly on establishing their chronology and on illuminating particular political events (e.g., Nebuchadnezzar's campaigns to the Levant) or religious ideas (e.g., Nabonidus's exaltation of Sîn). It is possible, however, to look at the problem in a way that will clarify the ideas that shaped the relationship between the empire and its subject populations. If the royal inscriptions infrequently give specific data about political history, can they nevertheless illuminate broader Babylonian ideas about imperial rule and the evolution of those ideas? Do these texts clarify how the Neo-Babylonian kings and their coteries conceived their roles as rulers and as overseers of a far-flung empire, or how they projected that conception at home and abroad? The answer, I think, is yes. My hypothesis is that both the self-conscious manipulation of conventional literary formulae and the inclusion of atypical information in these inscriptions clarify the outlines of Babylonian ideas about imperial rule.

Admittedly, much in the language and substance of the Neo-Babylonian royal inscriptions is not unique to them. The indebtedness of the royal scribes to literary traditions of the past is readily evident, as we will see. In addition, the texts were not intended to be read as straightforward political propaganda: like many other Mesopotamian royal inscriptions, they were often not deposited in locations accessible to human viewers, which suggests that they were intended for a divine audience, or for future rulers who might uncover them. Despite this, the inscriptions reflect a dialectic between such traditional language and the mundane matters of insuring the political and economic viability of the empire, as Oppenheim argued.[11] Thus, if it is the Babylonian chronicle series, administrative tablets, and non-cuneiform sources (principally the HB and the Greek historians) that clarify Babylonian military and administrative *procedures* in the periphery of the empire (see chapter two), it is only the royal inscriptions that furnish a fuller view of the *ideas* about imperial rule. The challenge, then, is to clarify what is uniquely Neo-Babylonian in the formulation and expression of these ideas.[12]

---

[11] See the quotation from Oppenheim in the Introduction above (p. 3).

[12] Precisely this sort of effort has been directed toward the Neo-Assyrian royal inscriptions, where, admittedly, the overtly political character of the texts is more pronounced. But even in the Assyrian case, as M. Liverani noted in his programmatic essay, there is a risk "of not quite bringing out the distinctive

1.2 The Form of the Texts

To understand the royal inscriptions requires an appreciation of their form. The following comments provide a rough sketch. In the first and still largest edition of the Neo-Babylonian royal inscriptions, Stephen Langdon reconstructed a basic typology. He argued that their literary prototype existed already in third-millennium Sumerian texts, and called the first and most basic type met with in the Neo-Babylonian corpus "contemporary documents of the first class."[13] This type opens with the royal titulary, the final element of which is usually the independent first person pronoun *anāku*, "I," used predicatively. There follows a temporal clause beginning with the conjunction *inūma* (or *inu*[*m*]), "when," that typically narrates the king's commission by his patron gods and, occasionally, obstacles that the king overcame. A third section begins with an adverb, *inūmīšu*, "at that time," and describes the principal building project that the inscription commemorates. A prayer or hymn of variable length and complexity usually concludes the text. Sometimes this prayer or hymn is directed to the architectural object that is the subject of the *inūmīšu* section, with a request that the building

characteristics of the Assyrian imperialism," and instead simply noting its conformity to general notions of imperial ideologies ("The Ideology of the Assyrian Empire," in *Power and Propaganda, A Symposium on Ancient Empires*, ed. M. T. Larsen, Mesopotamia 7 [Copenhagen: Akademisk Forlag, 1979], 303). The problem, as Machinist stated it in his recent overview of the Assyrian promulgation of the idioms of sovereignty, is that even the Assyrian royal inscriptions "provide . . . no systematic treatise, no effort at an argumentative presentation of issues. . . . We must rather glean the attitudes from a much more random occurrence of laconic phrases" ("Assyrians on Assyria in the First Millennium B.C.," in *Anfänge politischen Denkens in der Antike, die nahöstlichen Kulturen und die Griechen*, ed. K. Raaflaub and E. Müller-Luckner [Munich: R. Oldenbourg, 1993], 103). See also the study of H. Tadmor, "History and Ideology in the Assyrian Royal Inscriptions," in *Assyrian Royal Inscriptions: New Horizons in Literary, Ideological, and Historical Analysis*, ed. F. M. Fales, Orientis Antiqui Collectio 17 (Rome: Instituto per l'oriente, 1981), 13-33; and idem, "Propaganda, Literature, Historiography: Cracking the Code of the Assyrian Royal Inscriptions," in *Assyria 1995*, ed. S. Parpola and R. M. Whiting (Helsinki: Neo-Assyrian Text Corpus Project, 1997), 325-38. The same problems pertain in the Babylonian situation, but this should not preclude investigation.

[13] VAB 4, p. 6; see further Berger, *Königsinschriften*, 92; and E. Reiner, *"Your Thwarts in Pieces, Your Mooring Rope Cut": Poetry from Babylonia and Assyria*, Michigan Studies in the Humanities 5 (Ann Arbor: Horace B. Rackham School of Graduate Studies, 1985), 1-16.

intercede on behalf of the king before the patron deity (frequently Marduk). Alternatively, or in addition, the hymn may be directed to the deity proper. Langdon argued that the scribes composed documents of this first type contemporaneously with the building project commemorated in the *inūmīšu* section.

A prototypical example of this first type comes from Nabopolassar (626-605), the founder of the Neo-Babylonian dynasty. The inscription is on a barrel-shaped clay cylinder, by far the most common form of these texts,[14] which H. Rassam excavated at Sippar in 1881:

> Nabopolassar, the mighty king, king of Babylon, king of the land of Sumer and Akkad, the one who establishes the foundations of the land, the exalted prince, the one longed for by Nabû and Marduk, favorite of Šamaš, beloved of Aya, hero of heroes, whom the terrifying Erra allows to obtain his desire, the pious, the reverent, who always seeks the divine rules of the great gods, the king whose deeds surpass those of the kings his fathers, am I (*anāku*) (i 1-20).
>
> When (*inūma*) Šamaš,[15] the great lord, went by my side I killed the Subarian; I turned the land of my enemies into tells and ruins (i 21-ii 4).
>
> At that time (*inūmīšu*), for Bēlet-Sippar, the lofty princess my queen, I built anew E-edinna, the temple of her[16] well-being, and made it shine like daylight (ii 5-10).

---

[14] On the history and use of clay cylinders, see R. S. Ellis, *Foundation Deposits in Ancient Mesopotamia*, YNER 2 (New Haven: Yale University Press, 1968), 110-13.

[15] Spelled *Ša-aš-šu*, and without the divine determinative; see K. L. Tallqvist, *Akkadische Götterepitheta* (Helsinki: Societas Orientalis Fennica, 1938; repr., New York: Georg Olms, 1974), 453 (page references are to the reprint edition). The mention of Šamaš rather than Marduk as the royal protector is no doubt determined by the fact that the text comes from Sippar, one of two primary cult centers of Šamaš, the other being Larsa.

[16] The text has "his": *ana bēlet Sippar . . . E-edinna bīt tapšuḫtišu*. Short final vowels were generally not pronounced in the Neo-Babylonian dialect, and frequently the final vowel in the orthography is not historically justified. This explains the orthography with *-šu* here when the antecedent is feminine: only the [*š*] was pronounced. For this phenomenon, see J. P. Hyatt, *The Treatment of Final Vowels in Early Neo-Babylonian*, YOR 23 (New Haven: Yale University Press, 1941), 16-17; and *GAG* §§ 42k nn. 5 and 9, 63e, and 192b; for other examples and discussion of the phenomenon in the Neo-Babylonian royal inscriptions, see also Landsberger, "Basaltstele," 133, n. 3; and C. J. Gadd, "The Harran Inscriptions of Nabonidus," *AnSt* 8 (1958): H 1, B ii 6-7, and p. 55; for an update of Hyatt's data,

> Therefore (*ana šattim*),[17] O Bēlet-Sippar, surpassing mistress, when I have completed this temple and you have taken up residence in it, establish me, Nabopolassar, the king your provider, for eternity like the brickwork of Sippar and Babylon; prolong my kingship to far-off days (ii 11-22).[18]

While this text fits Langdon's definition of the first inscription type very well, many others do not. As the need to include more information arose, the scribes modified the form and content of the first type. Langdon therefore identified a second type and labeled it "redacted contemporary documents, or documents of the second class."[19] In these texts, which appear first in the reign of Nebuchadnezzar II (605-562), the second, or *inūma*, section is often expanded considerably to include summaries of previous royal building activities before the principal account in the *inūmīšu* section. As Langdon noted, the scribes often culled these summaries directly from texts of the first class.[20] Prime examples of this type are the cylinders CT 37 pls. 5-20 (=Nbk Zyl III,6) and PBS 15 79 (=Nbk Zyl III,8), in which the *inūma* sections recount earlier building projects at length and comprise respectively 150 of 192 lines and 247 of 288 lines. Although Langdon's two types account for many of the royal inscriptions, a number of exceptions remain, and the texts of Nabonidus frequently diverge substantially, as we will show below.

Berger produced the most systematic review of Langdon's typology. In Berger's revised view, there are three formulaic parts

---

see S. W. Cole, *The Early Neo-Babylonian Governor's Archive from Nippur*, OIP 114 (Chicago: The Oriental Institute of the University of Chicago, 1996), 10-12.

[17] On the syntax of *ana šattim* in royal inscriptions, see J. G. Westenholz, "Akkadian 'Therefore': An Example of Morpheme Substitution Among Pronouns," *Or* n.s. 54 (1985): 321-26.

[18] VAB 4 64-66 (Npl 3=Zyl II,2).

[19] VAB 4, p. 7.

[20] This is why Ellis argued that some cylinders were not found in the cities whose buildings they were intended to commemorate: the scribes kept duplicate texts on hand in various centers to quote their building summaries in new texts (Ellis, *Foundation Deposits*, 112-13). Langdon similarly argued that it was important for the scribes to have building summaries available for consultation and quotation as the number of building projects and commemorative inscriptions grew. Beaulieu, on the other hand, has argued that duplicate texts from one project could be deposited in different but contemporaneous building projects in other cities because the projects "were thought to be closely related to one another" (*Reign of Nabonidus*, 19). This conclusion does not seem likely.

common to all the inscriptions except a few from Nabonidus: the titulary, the report section, and the hymn.[21] He thus includes everything that is not part of the titulary or hymn under one rubric: the report section. Patterns do emerge within these parts, with the greatest variation in the report section. The *inūma–inūmīšu* type, Langdon's first, occurs frequently, but many other coordinating formulae appear as well, and these do not fall into clear categories beyond Berger's broad tripartite division. His revision of Langdon's typology is thus simpler and more generally applicable.

With this broad outline of the form of the inscriptions in place, it is possible to proceed to a discussion of what information in them illuminates Babylonian ideas of imperial rule.

1.3 The Titulary

The titulary of the Neo-Babylonian kings, tabulated by Berger on the basis of inscriptions known up to about 1970,[22] largely conforms to preceding Babylonian patterns. It is subject to wide variation in length, but normally consists of the following elements: personal name (PN), titles (normally including *šar Bābili*, "king of Babylon"), epithets, filiation, and pronoun (*anāku*).[23] The royal titles and epithets are potential indicators of the imperial self-consciousness of the Neo-Babylonian kings.

The Babylonian scribes were fond of archaic royal titles and epithets. Berger listed a number of common archaic titles that appear in the Neo-Babylonian inscriptions:[24] *iššakku*, "(city) ruler," a royal title which goes back to Sargonic times;[25] *šakkanakku*, "viceroy," which occurs as a royal title by the Ur III period;[26] and *šar māt Šumeri u Akkadî*, "king of the land of Sumer and Akkad," which first appears in inscriptions of Ur-Nammu in the Ur III period, and is the most

---

[21] Berger, *Königsinschriften*, 84.

[22] Ibid., 72-82, 84.

[23] For exceptions to the pattern PN . . . *anāku*, see W. L. Moran, "Notes on the New Nabonidus Inscriptions," *Or* n.s. 28 (1959): 131.

[24] Berger, *Königsinschriften*, 92.

[25] M.-J. Seux, *Épithètes royales akkadiennes et sumériennes* (Paris: Letouzey et Ané, 1967), 110-16.

[26] *CAD* Š/1 176, s.v. *šakkanakku*; see also Brinkman, *PKB*, n. 1976.

geographically inclusive.[27] The title *šar Bābili*, "king of Babylon," nearly universal in the Neo-Babylonian inscriptions, is also early, going back to the second millennium.[28] This use of archaic titles is not unusual, but together with a special interest in titles that originated with Hammurapi in the Old Babylonian period, it illuminates specific ways in which the scribes portrayed the Neo-Babylonian kings as bearers of an ancient Babylonian royal tradition.[29] The following royal epithets appeared first in the inscriptions of Hammurapi and subsequently only in inscriptions of Babylonian kings; they thus occur in the Neo-Babylonian titulary, but not in the Assyrian: *ašru*, "humble,"[30] *bābil igisê rabûtim ana* X, "who brings expensive gifts to X (=temples and gods, or both),"[31] *emqu*, "wise,"[32] *etel šarrī*, "prince of kings,"[33] *mugarrini karê*

[27] For this title in particular and the archaic titles in general, see W. W. Hallo, *Early Mesopotamian Royal Titles: A Philologic and Historical Analysis*, AOS 43 (New Haven: American Oriental Society, 1957).

[28] Hammurapi's royal inscriptions often use the title LUGAL KÁ.DINGIR.RA.KI, "king of Babylon"; see, e.g., *LIH* no. 57: 3; and no. 95: 3.

[29] Numerous royal inscriptions of Hammurapi were recopied in the Neo-Babylonian script in the first millennium. Several Old-Babylonian royal inscriptions, including *LIH* nos. 59 and 96, are known only from Neo-Babylonian copies. The Neo-Babylonian scribes also copied the Laws of Hammurapi. For a list of the NB/LB versions of the Laws, with bibliography, see R. Borger, *Babylonisch-Assyrische Lesestücke*, 2d ed., AnOr 54 (Rome: Pontifical Biblical Institute, 1979), 1:2-4, under the sigla C, W, Z, and s. The first of these, published in copy in E. Bergmann, *Codex Ḫammurabi: Textus Primigenius*, 3d ed. (Rome: Pontifical Biblical Institute, 1953), 52, contains the prologue to the Laws, in which a long list of Hammurapi's royal epithets appears. The copy is Neo-Babylonian and demonstrates that scribes of the period knew Hammurapi's titulary intimately. More will be said about their familiarity with the Laws below.

[30] Seux, *Épithètes royales*, 366. There are two NA exceptions, Aššur-uballiṭ I (AOB 1 38 2:3) and Esarhaddon (Borger Esarh. 12 Ep. 1:17). The latter, however, is an inscription intended for Babylon in which Babylonian titles and language are widely used. Esarhaddon frequently imitated Babylonian inscriptions when commemorating building projects in Babylonia; see, B. N. Porter, *Images, Power, and Politics: Figurative Aspects of Esarhaddon's Babylonian Policy* (Philadelphia: American Philosophical Society, 1993), 44.

[31] Hammurapi uses only *bābil ḫegallim ana Ekišnugal*, "who brings abundance to Ekišnugal," but the parallel to the Neo-Babylonian phrase is exact; and this use of the active participle *bābilu* in the titulary is shared only by Hammurapi and the NB kings; see Seux, *Épithètes royales*, 46.

[32] Ibid., 82. *rubû emqu*, "wise prince" is also a characteristically Neo-Babylonian title (ibid., 252). It is used twice by Esarhaddon, but in nearly identical inscriptions, one intended for Nippur and the other for Uruk (Borger Esarh. 70 §39; 74 §47: 24).

[33] Seux, *Épithètes royales*, 91.

bitrûtim, "who stores barley in immense piles,"[34] *muštālu*, "judicious one,"[35] *muštēmiqu* "suppliant,"[36] *muṭaḫḫid* X, "who makes abundant X" (for temples/gods),[37] *qarrād qarrādī*, "hero of heroes,"[38] and *šar mīšarim*, "king of justice."[39] There were, in addition to Hammurapi, other Babylonian kings who influenced the Neo-Babylonian royal titulary. One important figure was Nebuchadnezzar I of the Second Dynasty of Isin (1125-1104 B.C.E.).[40] The inscriptions of Nebuchadnezzar I inaugurated numerous royal epithets in the Babylonian literary tradition. These include the following examples, which are used subsequently in the Neo-Babylonian titulary, but not in the Assyrian one: *mukīn išdī mātim*, "the one who establishes the foundations of the land,"[41] *mušte᾿ʾû ašrāt* DN, "the one who constantly

---

[34] Ibid., 96; only Hammurapi (CH iii 21) and Nebuchadnezzar.

[35] Seux, *Épithètes royales*, 171. It is also used as an adj. in the NB titulary: *rēʾûm muštālu* "judicious shepherd" (ibid., 246); and *rubû muštālu* "judicious prince" (ibid., 253).

[36] Ibid., 171; only Hammurapi and Nebuchadnezzar.

[37] Ibid., 351-52, exceptions occur in the inscriptions of Esarhaddon (Borger Esarh. 92 §63 7), and probably Assurbanipal ([*mu-ṭa-a*]*ḫ-ḫi-du sat*-[*tuk-ki*], Bauer Asb. 42 Sm 671 20).

[38] Seux, *Épithètes royales*, 231; only Hammurapi and Nabopolassar.

[39] Ibid., 316-17. Assurbanipal is also referred to as *rāʾim kitti šar mīšari*, "who loves truth, king of justice," in several administrative texts (ibid., 237).

[40] The influence of Nebuchadnezzar I was recognized already by Hinke in his publication of an important *kudurru* from that king's reign (W. J. Hinke, *A New Boundary Stone of Nebuchadrezzar I from Nippur*, Babylonian Expedition of the University of Pennsylvania. Series D., Researches and Treatises; vol. 4 [Philadelphia: University of Pennsylvania, 1907], 124-25); see recently V. A. Hurowitz, *Divine Service and Its Rewards: Ideology and Poetics in the Hinke Kudurru*, Beer-Sheva Studies by the Department of Bible and Ancient Near East, 10 (Beer-Sheva, Israel: Ben-Gurion University of the Negev, 1997), 51, n. 56. For a discussion of the reign and titulary of Nebuchadnezzar I, see Brinkman, *PKB*, 104-16.

[41] Ibid., 131. Also used once by Sargon II, but in an inscription that, according to H. Tadmor, virtually plagiarizes a text of the Babylonian king Merodach-baladan II (C. J. Gadd, "Inscribed Barrel Cylinder of Marduk-apla-iddina II," *Iraq* 15 [1953]; Tadmor, "Propaganda, Litarature, Historiography," 333-34). Nebuchadnezzar I's use of the epithet may ultimately derive from the time of Hammurapi, who calls himself *mukīn išdī Sipparim*, "the one who established the foundations of Sippar" (Seux, *Épithètes royales*, 132).

seeks the sanctuaries of DN,"[42] *mutnennû*, "the pious one,"[43] and *kanšu*, "the submissive one."[44]

A better understanding of the Neo-Babylonian titulary emerges through comparison with the titulary of the Neo-Assyrian kings who ruled Babylonia and composed inscriptions for projects in that region (Sargon II, Esarhaddon, Assurbanipal, Šamaš-šuma-ukīn, and Aššur-etel-ilāni).[45] In these inscriptions the Assyrian kings adopted several typically Babylonian epithets together with their regular Assyrian titulary. Sargon uses the three most common epithets, *šar Bābili*, "king of Babylon,"[46] *šakkanak Bābili*, "viceroy of Babylon," and *šar māt Šumeri u Akkadî*, "king of the land of Sumer and Akkad,"[47] as well as *zānin Esagil u Ezida*, "caretaker of Esagil and Ezida."[48] Sennacherib claims no Babylonian royal epithets, an indication of his ill-feeling toward Babylonia.[49] Esarhaddon, by far the most ambitious in his use of

---

[42] Ibid., 323-25.

[43] Ibid., 172. The use of *mutnennû* alone as a substantive is characteristically Babylonian, and in the titularies of Nebuchadnezzar II, Neriglissar, and Nabonidus, it always follows *emqu*, "wise" (ibid. 82, n. 40). *mutnennû* is used by the Assyrian kings, but only as an adjective to qualify other titles such as *rēšu*, *rē'û*, or *šakkanakku*.

[44] Ibid., 131; used once by Esarhaddon in a text for Babylon (Borger Esarh. 12 §11 Ep. 1. 17).

[45] The Babylonian inscriptions of the Neo-Assyrian kings (with some exceptions) have now been reedited by G. Frame, *Rulers of Babylonia From the Second Dynasty of Isin to the End of Assyrian Domination (1157-612 BC)*, RIMB 2 (Toronto: University of Toronto Press, 1995). These inscriptions are often written in the contemporary Babylonian script, rather than Assyrian, and occasionally even in the archaizing Babylonian script (beginning under Esarhaddon), which proves that Babylonian scribes were composing these texts for their Assyrian lords. For the Babylonian policy of Esarhaddon, see now Porter, *Images*; and G. Frame, *Babylonia 689-627 B.C.: A Political History*, Nederlands Historisch-Archaeologisch Instituut te Istanbul 69 (Istanbul: Nederlands Historisch-Archaeologisch Instituut, 1992), 67-78; earlier also Grayson, "Assyria and Babylonia," 162; and J. A. Brinkman, *Prelude to Empire: Babylonian Society and Politics, 747-626 B.C.* Occasional Publications of the Babylonian Fund, 7 (Philadelphia: University Museum, 1984), 70-76.

[46] LUGAL TIN.TIR.KI (UVB 1 56).

[47] On the significance of these three, see Seux, *Épithètes royales*, 14, and n. 2.

[48] First attested with Hammurapi and used also in the Kassite era; see Seux, *Épithètes royales*, 444.

[49] Neither do Sennacherib's successors ascribe any specifically Babylonian epithets to him when, in their Babylonian inscriptions, they mention him as their ancestor (so also A. K. Grayson, "Chronicles and the Akītu-Festival," in *Actes de la 17e RAI*, ed. A. Finet [Ham-sur-Heure, Belgium: Comité belge de recherches en Mesopotamie, 1970], 168). Sennacherib is called only *šarru rabû*, *šarru dannu*, *šar*

Babylonian epithets (because he was the most ambitious builder there) adopts the usual epithets *šar Bābili*,[50] *šakkanak Bābili*,[51] and *šar māt Šumeri u Akkadî*,[52] as well as *nibīt Marduk*, "one chosen by Marduk."[53] In several of his cylinder inscriptions commemorating the renovation of the Eanna temple at Uruk, Esarhaddon claims other Babylonian epithets:[54] *mušte"û ašrāti ilāni rabûti*, "who always seeks the sanctuaries of the great gods,"[55] *pāliḫ bēl bēlē*, "who reveres the lord of lords (i.e., Marduk)," *ēpiš Esagil u Bābili*, "who built Esagil and Babylon," *zānin Ezida*, "caretaker of Ezida," *muddiš Eanna*, "who renovated Eanna," and *mušaklil ešrēti (kullat) māḫāzī*, "who completes the sanctuaries of (all) the cult centers." As noted above, Esarhaddon's scribes also assign him epithets that Hammurapi had introduced into the Babylonian tradition, including *ašru*, *emqu*, *muṭaḫḫidu*, and *kanšu*. Assurbanipal, although he had many inscriptions written for Babylonia, does not usually adopt Babylonian epithets in them.[56] When Assurbanipal's Babylonian inscriptions give the name of his father Esarhaddon, however, they always note Esarhaddon's principal Babylonian epithets. The last Neo-Assyrian king who had inscriptions composed for Babylonia, Aššur-etel-ilāni, did not claim Babylonian royal epithets either. We may also note that whenever a king, including Šamaš-šuma-ukīn, mentions his Sargonid forebears who also ruled Babylonia, he never changes the epithets that a particular king had claimed, although occasionally one or more is left out. In sum, the Assyrian use of Babylonian epithets, apart from Esarhaddon's, is limited to a few common ones, and these are never the only epithets used.

The Assyrian kings invariably also list one or more additional epithets before their adopted Babylonian royal epithets. The Assyrian

---

kiššati, and *šar māt Aššur*, epithets we will discuss below. For discussions of Sennacherib's hostile attitude toward Babylon, see J. A. Brinkman, "Sennacherib's Babylonian Problem: An Interpretation," *JCS* 25 (1973): 89-95; and, differently, P. Machinist, "The Assyrians and Their Babylonian Problem," *Wissenschaftskolleg zu Berlin Jahrbuch* (1984-85): 353-64.

[50] MAN KÁ.DIŠ.(DIŠ) (Borger Esarh. 30 §13 etc.).

[51] GÌR.NÍTA TIN.TIR.KI (Borger Esarh. 30 §18 7).

[52] For references, see Seux, *Épithètes royales*, 303.

[53] Borger, Esarh. 73 §47 9.

[54] For the texts, see ibid., 75 §48 6-9; and 77 §50.

[55] *mušte"û ašrāt* DN is characteristic of the Babylonian tradition, going back to Nebuchadnezzar I, but it is used occasionally by Esarhaddon and Assurbanipal, and once by Shalmaneser III; see Seux, *Épithètes royales*, 323-25.

[56] He does, however, use *zānin Esagil*, "caretaker of Esagil" (RIMB 2 200 13; 218 8).

epithets include *šar māt Aššūr*, "king of the land of Assyria," *šarru rabû*, "great king," *šarru dannu*, "mighty king," *šar kiššati*, "king of the universe," and *šar kibrāt erbetti*, "king of the four corners."[57] Of these, *šarru rabû* came into common use in the international political vernacular of the fourteenth through thirteenth centuries (although it is attested earlier) and remained in use after that almost exclusively in the Assyrian tradition.[58] The epithet *šar kiššati* is an archaic one going back to Sargon of Akkad; it is ubiquitous in Neo-Assyrian royal inscriptions.[59] The other two epithets, *šarru dannu* and *šar kibrāt erbetti*, were common in royal inscriptions in the third through first millennia,[60] but they are exceedingly rare in the Neo-Babylonian period. Of the Neo-Babylonian kings, only Nabonidus uses all four epithets just mentioned: *šarru rabû*, *šarru dannu*, *šar kiššati*, and *šar kibrāt erbetti*. They occur in the cylinder describing his plan to rebuild the Eḫulḫul temple in Ḫarran and the Ebabbar temple in Sippar.[61] Tadmor, following Landsberger, argued that Nabonidus's scribes modeled this inscription on one or more texts of Assurbanipal.[62] The only one of the four epithets

---

[57] These five constitute the base upon which the rest of the Assyrian titulary is founded; see Seux, *Épithètes royales*, 13 and n. 2.

[58] Ibid., 298-301.

[59] Ibid., 308-12; for the general Neo-Assyrian conception of kingship reflected in the titulary, see, e.g., P. Garelli, "La conception de la royauté en Assyrie," in *Assyrian Royal Inscriptions: New Horizons in Literary, Ideological, and Historical Analysis*, ed. F. M. Fales, Orientis Antiqui Collectio 17 (Rome: Instituto per l'Oriente, 1981), 1-5.

[60] For their early use, see Hallo, *Early Mesopotamian Royal Titles*.

[61] VAB 4 218 (Nbn 1=Zyl III,2). *šar kiššati* also occurs in a brick inscription of Nabonidus, VAB 4 (Nbn 14=Backst. B I,2); see now C. B. F. Walker, *Cuneiform Brick Inscriptions* (London: British Museum Publications, 1981), 93. In fact, there is one occurrence of the epithet *šar kiššati* for Nabopolassar and two for Nebuchadnezzar, according to Seux; these titles occur, however, in the colophons of administrative tablets, not royal inscriptions (*Épithètes royales*, 312). The Nabopolassar text reads: "22 Sivan, year 17, Nabopolassar, king of the universe" (^{md}AG.A.PAB LUGAL ŠÚ; see J. N. Strassmeier, "Inschriften von Nabopalassar," *ZA* 4 [1889]: 144, no. 15, rev. 9). One Nebuchadnezzar text reads: "king of the universe" (LUGAL KI.ŠÁR.RA; Bezold, Cat. Vol. 3, 1000, K 9288); and the other, from Dilbat: Nebuchadnezzar, "king of Babylon, king of the universe" (LUGAL TIN.TIR.KI LUGAL *kiš-ša-tu*$^!$, Ni 2577, cited in *RLA* 2, 219, s.v. "Dilbat").

[62] VAB 4 (Nbn 1=Zyl III,2); Landsberger, "Basaltstele," 147-49; Tadmor, "Inscriptions of Nabunaid," 353; Tadmor is followed in turn by Berger, *Königsinschriften*, 96; and Beaulieu, *Reign of Nabonidus*, 143, 214. For another concrete example of Assyrian influence on the composition of this inscription, note the use of the characteristically Assyrian ritual for consecration of new structures: the mixing of oil, honey, and other liquids into the brick mortar (*šallaru*) (VAB 4

used in the royal inscriptions of the other Neo-Babylonian kings is *šarru dannu*, used three times by Nabopolassar.[63] In view of the ancient pedigree of these titles it is curious that the Neo-Babylonian kings avoided them almost entirely. A possible explanation for the avoidance of *šar kiššati* and *šar kibrāt erbetti* is that the Neo-Babylonian titulary is generally reticent in claiming epithets that implied rule beyond Babylonia or that were militaristic in tone.[64] This explanation, however, would hardly apply to *šarru rabû* or *šarru dannu*. The glaring instance where Nabonidus uses all of them—in a text exhibiting the influence of an Assyrian model—gives a clue about their avoidance. The other Neo-Babylonian kings, perhaps, did not favor these epithets because the Neo-Assyrian kings, even in their Babylonian inscriptions, had so favored them as the basis for their imperial theory.[65]

What conclusions follow from this discussion of the Neo-Babylonian titulary? First, it is self-consciously Babylonian, and is especially indebted to several illustrious forebears: Hammurapi, Nebuchadnezzar I (to a lesser degree), and sometimes even to the

---

222 [Nbn 1=Zyl III,2] ii 5). Ellis suggested that there is another example of this ritual described in an inscription of Nabopolassar, which says that Nebuchadnezzar, the crown prince, carried clay (*ṭiddu*) that was mixed with aromatics (VAB 4 62 [Npl 1=Zyl III,1] iii 1-5; see Ellis, *Foundation Deposits*, 29-31). In that instance, however, the clay (*ṭiddu*) did not contain honey, and the text does not specify that the aromatics were mixed into the mortar (*šallaru*) as the inscriptions of Nabonidus and the Assyrian kings always do (see *CAD* Š/1 247, s.v. *šallaru* A a). The Nabopolassar text does not reflect the Assyrian ritual, whereas that of Nabonidus does.

[63] VAB 4 64 (Npl 3=Zyl II,2) i 2; BRM 4 51 (=YOS 9 84=Zyl II,3) i 2; and Grayson, *BHLT*, 82 ii 14. The last occurs in direct address to the king by an Assyrian; the irony was noted by H. Tadmor, "Nabopolassar and Sin-shum-lishir in a Literary Perspective," in *Festschrift für Rykle Borger zu seinem 65. Geburtstag am 24. Mai 1994: tikip santakki mala bašmu*, ed. S. M. Maul, Cuneiform Monographs 10 (Groningen: Styx, 1998), 356.

[64] For an overview of royal titles pertaining to rule over the world, see Seux, *Épithètes royales*, 26-27; virtually none of these occurs in the Neo-Babylonian titulary. A notable exception occurs again in a text of Nabonidus that dates from his tenth year, the period when he was in Teima and had subdued the northern Arabian peninsula: *kāšidu šadî elûtim*, "conqueror of lofty mountains," (VAB 4 234 [Nab 3=Zyl III,1] i 10). There are a few other exceptions in Nabonidus's titulary, as we will see.

[65] For these epithets as reflections of the Assyrian expansionist theory, see among others Garelli, "Conception de la royauté"; and Machinist, "Assyrians on Assyria," 85. H. Tadmor has recently arrived independently at the same conclusion; see his study "Nabopolassar and Sin-shum-lishir," 356.

dynasty of Sargon of Agade.[66] On the other hand, the Babylonian scribes generally avoided several common, archaic Babylonian epithets that the Assyrian kings had often used, as well as specifically Assyrian epithets. Second, except for several of the above-mentioned inscriptions of Nabonidus (which we will explore further below), the Neo-Babylonian titulary contains few royal epithets referring to rule over the world. The titulary focuses more specifically on the king's role as ruler of Babylon and as servant of the Babylonian patron deities and their temples.[67] The notion of rulership over the "whole inhabited earth" does indeed emerge in the royal inscriptions after Nabopolassar, but the titulary proper almost never expresses it. This contrasts sharply with the Neo-Assyrian royal inscriptions, including those which commemorated building projects in Babylonia and which reflect Babylonian form and style: the Neo-Assyrian titulary almost invariably emphasizes the king's role as ruler of the world.

1.4 The Absence of Imperial Rhetoric in the Inscriptions of Nabopolassar

When the historian moves from the general Neo-Babylonian titulary to the inscriptions of the dynasty's first king, Nabopolassar, he wants to know what attitudes Nabopolassar's inscriptions communicate about the role of the king vis-à-vis the non-Babylonian world. Here the king's report of his commission or call to rule offers evidence. When it is present in Nabopolassar's inscriptions, the call to rule usually follows the titulary and the introductory conjunction *inūma*, "when." The call contains several types of information. First, it dilineates the basic responsibilities of the Babylonian king.[68] As Nabopolassar's inscriptions phrase it, the gods designated the king *ana*

---

[66] Thus perhaps the epithet *muttarû tenēšēti*, "guardian of mankind," used by Nebuchadnezzar II, but already attested as *muttarû ṣābī* GN, "guardian of the troops/people of GN," in the reign of Narām-Sîn (Seux, *Épithètes royales*, 263; see also *CAD* A/2 314, s.v. *arû*).

[67] Garelli notes that the Old Babylonian titulary, although it did use militaristic epithets, did not emphasize them, but focused instead on the king as "the shepherd of his people" ("Conception de la royauté," 2). The common use of militaristic epithets in the Old Babylonian titulary is nevertheless not shared by the Neo-Babylonian kings.

[68] For a succinct survey of the Babylonian king's responsibilities, see A. K. Grayson, "Mesopotamia, History of (Babylonia)," in *ABD*, ed. D. N. Freedman (Garden City, N.Y.: Doubleday, 1992), 4:767.

bēlūt māti, "for rulership of the land,"[69] and *ana zanān māḫāzī uddušu ešrēti*, "to provide for cult centers (and) to renew shrines."[70] In fact it is the demands of the latter phrase in particular that define the king's role in these texts. A hortatory passage at the end of one of Nabopolassar's inscriptions says this explicitly: it exhorts future kings to revere the gods and their sanctuaries rather than to put their trust in military might.[71]

Uniquely in Nabopolassar's reign, four (possibly five) of the seven extant cylinders attributed to him also declare in the *inūma* section that the king either repulsed the Assyrians from Akkad (Babylonia)[72] or actually destroyed the Assyrians. Nabopolassar's first claim occurs twice in similar language:

> *áš-šu-ru-ú šá i-na zi-ru-ut* DINGIR.MEŠ / *ma-at ak-ka-di-i i-bé-lu-ma / i-na ni-ri-šu ka-ab-tim / ú-šá-az-zi-qu ni-ši ma-a-ti / a-na-ku en-šu pi-is-nu-qu / mu-uš-te-ʾu-ú* EN EN.EN / *i-na e-mu-qi ga-áš-ra-a-tim / šá* ^{d}AG *ù* ^{d}AMAR.UTU EN.MEŠ-*e-a / ul-tu ma-at ak-ka-di-i še-ep-šu-nu ap-ru-us-ma / ni-ir-šu-nu ú-ša-ad-di-im*
>
> The Assyrian who because of the wrath of the gods had ruled the land of Akkad and who had oppressed the people of the land with his

---

[69] VAB 4 66 (Npl 4=Zyl I,2) 12.

[70] VAB 4 64 (Npl 2=Zyl II,1) i 6-7.

[71] VAB 4 68 (Npl 4=Zyl I,2) 31-41.

[72] Frame writes the following concerning the use of "Akkad" in the seventh century:

> The terms 'Akkad' and 'Akkadians' often appear in texts from our period, particularly in Assyrian inscriptions. Akkad sometimes refers to the city by that name, sometimes to the land as a whole (as in scholarly reports and some chronicle passages), and sometimes only to the northern part of the land, that is the region originally called Akkad, as opposed to the southern part (ancient Sumer) which was now inhabited mainly by tribal groups. When the Assyrian sources wanted to distinguish the old settled population of the land from the tribal groups, the term people of Akkad or Akkadians was used for the former. For example, in edition A of Assurbanipal's annals we find UN.MEŠ KUR URI.KI KUR *kal-du* KUR *a-ra-mu* KUR *tam-tim*, "the people of Akkad, Chaldea, Aramu, (and) the Sealand," and in an extispicy report from the time of the rebellion of 652-648 *lu-ú* <LÚ.>URI.KI *lu-ú* LÚ *kal-da-a-a lu-ú* LÚ *aḫ-lam-i*, "either Akkad(ians), or Chaldeans, or Aḫlamû (Arameans)." The term 'Akkadians' was employed because this section of the population was imbued with classical Babylonian culture and because it used, or was most familiar with, the Akkadian language, the language of Babylonian civilization for over one thousand years (*Babylonia 689-627 B.C.*, 33).

> heavy yoke—I, the weak, the powerless, who always seek the lord of lords, with the mighty strength of Nabû and Marduk, my lords, I cut off their footsteps from the land of Akkad and threw off their yoke.[73]

The second claim, recorded in two cylinders, is briefer: *su-ba-ru-um a-na-ru* / MA.DA-*su ú-te-er-ru* / *a-na* DU_6 *ù ka-ar-mi*, "I killed the Subarian, I turned his land into tells and ruins."[74]

The two claims are different. The first asserts that Nabopolassar cast off the Assyrian "yoke,"[75] and repulsed the Assyrians from Akkad. The second, using the alternate ethnicon "Subarian" for the Assyrians,[76] boasts of their destruction and the ruination of their land. To these examples from the cylinder inscriptions we may add the account in what Grayson has called the "Nabopolassar-Epic" of the defeat and execution of the Assyrian Sin-šum-lišir, which is included in the description of

---

[73] See the cylinder A Babylon 11 i 28-ii 5, edited by F. N. H. Al-Rawi, "Nabopolassar's Restoration Work on the Wall *Imgur-Enlil* at Babylon," *Iraq* 47 (1985): 1-13; compare VAB 4 68 (Npl 4=Zyl I,2) 17-21; and perhaps BRM 4 pl. 47 (=YOS 9 84=Zyl II,3). The last text might contain a passage like that quoted here, but the text is broken (see Berger, *Königsinschriften*, 33). There may be a forerunner of this statement in a cylinder of Merodach-baladan II which commemorates his reconstruction of the Eanna temple at Uruk. Merodach-baladan's text was apparently composed during his first twelve year reign over Babylonia (721-710), after his participation against the Assyrians at the Battle of Dēr in 721; see Gadd, "Cylinder of Marduk-apla-iddina II," 123-34. The text mentions that the Subarian (here another name for Assyrian) had ruled Akkad because of the wrath of Marduk (ibid., 135 8-9), and that by defeating the Assyrians "he (Merodach-baladan) barred their footsteps from the soil of the land of Akkad" (*ina qaqqar māt Akkadi ušaprisa kibsīšun*, ibid., 135 18).

[74] VAB 4 60 (Npl 1=Zyl III,1) i 29-31; also, partly restored, VAB 4 64 (Npl 2=Zyl II,2) ii 1-4.

[75] The image is no doubt chosen purposefully: the Neo-Assyrian kings frequently used the language of imposing the king's yoke or the yoke of Aššur upon conquered peoples to indicate dominance. Throwing off the yoke was cause for imperial reprisal (for examples, *CAD* N/2 262-63, s.v. *nīru* A 2). Of the Neo-Babylonian kings only Nabonidus uses the image of the yoke (*nīru*) as a metaphor for his rule over foreign peoples (VAB 4 260 [Nbn 6=Zyl II,9] ii 45). Nebuchadnezzar makes the people drag Marduk's chariot pole according to the Etemenanki cylinder (WVDOG 59 46 3.46), although this can also be a pious duty of Babylonians, or even of the king (see for references, *CAD* S 312, s.v. *sirdû* A a). The perspective of outsiders was not so finely nuanced; note Jeremiah's frequent references to the "yoke" (על) of Nebuchadnezzar (e.g., Jer 27:8,11,12; 28:2,4,11).

[76] The two terms have the same referent in Neo-Babylonian usage; see already Langdon's comments in VAB 4, 273, n. 1; also Gadd, "Cylinder of Marduk-apla-iddina II," 127; and Brinkman, *PKB*, n. 922. See also the references below n. 80.

Nabopolassar's rise to power and coronation.[77] There is also a phrase that comes from a brick inscription apparently associated with Nabopolassar's building of Etemenanki, Marduk's ziggurat in Babylon: *māt ayābīya šalālam iqbâm*, "he [Marduk] instructed me to plunder the land of my enemy."[78] The text does not name the Assyrians, but we may presume that they are meant. A more explicit and dramatic statement comes from a unique text published by Gerardi, but which is of uncertain ascription.[79] The text, from a Babylonian king whose name is not preserved on the tablet, contains a declaration of war against an Assyrian king, whose name is likewise not preserved, and against the land of Aššur, also called *māt subarû*, "land of the Subarians."[80] The *casus belli* is Assyria's past crimes against Babylon and spoliation of the Esagil and Ezida temples. If Gerardi is correct in ascribing the tablet to the reign of Nabopolassar,[81] then this inscription provides a dramatic statement of Marduk's commission of the Babylonian king to avenge his city against Assyria: "[Because] of the crimes against Akkad which you committed, Marduk, the great lord, [and the great gods?] shall call [you] to account."[82] This language is entirely absent in the inscriptions of Nabopolassar's successors, as we will see. Even within Nabopolassar's inscriptions there may be a chronological development that the Babylonian chronicle can elucidate.[83]

It is difficult fully to understand this development, however, because of the complexity of the chronological problems associated with the reigns of the kings of Assyria and Babylonia in the 620s.[84] What is

---

[77] Grayson, *BHLT*, 78-85.

[78] WVDOG 59 44 no. 2 (=Backst. B I,6); Berger has argued convincingly that this text is a brick inscription from Babylon; see *Königsinschriften*, 26.

[79] P. Gerardi, "Declaring War in Mesopotamia," *AfO* 33 (1986): 30-38. The text is a Late Babylonian copy of an older inscription, and is not a typical building inscription.

[80] Ibid., 34 obv. 3; and KUR *subartum*, 36 rev. 3.

[81] Since the king is instructed to destroy Nineveh to avenge Babylon (ibid., 36 rev. 5), the text should presumably not postdate the fall of Nineveh in 612 B.C.E., and thus cannot be ascribed to Nebuchadnezzar. It could, however, conceivably date before Nabopolassar.

[82] Ibid., 36 rev. 10-11.

[83] R. Borger, "Der Aufstieg des neubabylonischen Reiches," *JCS* 19 (1965): 59-78; Berger, *Königsinschriften*, 115-117; Al-Rawi, "Imgur-Enlil," 2.

[84] See recently J. Oates, "The Fall of Assyria," in *CAH*, 2d ed., vol. 3, pt. 2, *The Assyrian and Babylonian Empires and Other States of the Near East, from the Eighth to the Sixth Centuries B.C.*, ed. J. A. Boardman et al. (Cambridge: Cambridge University Press, 1991), 166-78; N. Na'aman, "Chronology and History

important for our purposes is that the turmoil in Babylonia immediately after the accession of Nabopolassar (10/IV/626[85]) indicates that the Assyrians maintained a foothold in Babylonia for a number of years. According to the chronicle entry concerning Nabopolassar's first regnal year, Šamaš (of Sippar) and the gods of Shapazzu, in northern Babylonia, entered Babylon, presumably to avoid possible capture by the Assyrians.[86] The two sides fought several indecisive battles in the first and second years of Nabopolassar, although the chronicle makes it clear that the Assyrians continued to hold Nippur into Nabopolassar's third year and could march into Babylonia (Akkad) almost at will.[87] A badly preserved passage in the so-called Nabopolassar Epic also points to early triumphs of Nabopolassar over the Assyrians in Babylonia as a key accomplishment of his reign.[88] The Epic describes the period of Nabopolassar's rise to power and his coronation.[89] There follows mention of a blood bath at Cutha, presumably the result of an otherwise unknown battle, and a description of the execution of an Assyrian official, possibly Sin-šum-lišir, at Nabopolassar's command, and the king's confiscation of the Assyrian's goods.[90] Despite this evidence for early military successes, however, no indication exists that the king had permanently pushed the Assyrians out of Akkad when the Babylonian chronicle breaks off after Nabopolassar's third regnal year (623 B.C.E.). Na'aman has argued from chronological notices in economic texts that Nabopolassar was able finally to capture Nippur and Uruk from the Assyrians only later, perhaps by the end of 620.[91] Even if that date is uncertain, the claim in the cylinders that Nabopolassar expelled the Assyrians from Akkad and threw off their yoke probably dates after the capture of Nippur and Uruk (if Akkad refers here to all Babylonia and

---

in the Late Assyrian Empire (631-619 B.C.)," *ZA* 81 (1991): 243-267, and n. 1 there for earlier literature. For a challenge to Na'aman's thesis, see now S. Zawadski, "A Contribution to the Last Days of the Assyrian Empire," *ZA* 85 (1995): 67-73. The most recent contribution is J. E. Reade, "Assyrian Eponyms, Kings and Pretenders, 648-605 B.C.," *Or* n.s. 67 (1998): 255-65.

[85] TCS 5 chron 2:14.

[86] Ibid., chron 2:19.

[87] Ibid., chron 2:25-32.

[88] Grayson, *BHLT*, 78-79; 82-85.

[89] Ibid., 78-79.

[90] Ibid., 82 ii(?) 10-18; see most recently Tadmor, "Nabopolassar and Sin-shum-lishir," 353-57.

[91] Na'aman, "Chronology and History," 264-65; also Reade, "Assyrian Eponyms," 263; but see Zawadski, "Contribution," 67-73.

not, as traditionally, to the northern region of Babylonia), since before this time the Assyrians maintained a foothold in Babylonia.[92]

Further evidence that Nabopolassar already controlled Nippur when these passages about the expulsion of the Assyrians were written comes from the same two cylinders in which that expulsion is mentioned. The texts state that *adkâmma ummānāt Enlil Šamaš u Marduk*, "I levied for corvée the workmen of Enlil, Šamaš and Marduk."[93] Weissbach argued long ago in his edition of one of the cylinders that this list of deities is a circumlocution for the respective cities of each patron god: Nippur, Sippar and Babylon.[94] As we noted above, Nippur came under Nabopolassar's control only after a protracted struggle against the Assyrians.[95]

When extant portions of the Babylonian chronicle resume in Nabopolassar's tenth year (617), the text reports that the Babylonians had ousted the Assyrians from the regions of Ḫindānu and Sūḫu on the Middle Euphrates. In 617 they defeated the Assyrians at Gablini, also on the Middle Euphrates, and took three towns farther up the river, possibly as far north as the River Baliḫ.[96] The Babylonian military strategy by 617 thus included efforts to control territory along the Middle Euphrates that was still under Assyrian domination. Their successes, even if ephemeral (Sūḫu rebelled by 613: chron 3:31), were a cause for alarm in the West, where Egypt determined by this year (if not earlier) to ally itself to its former enemy, Assyria, and to fight actively against the

---

[92] Berger, *Königsinschriften*, 116; Al-Rawi, "Imgur-Enlil," 2. On the use of the name Akkad in this period, see above n. 72.

[93] A Babylon 11 ii 31 (Al-Rawi, "Imgur-Enlil," 4); and VAB 4 68 (Npl 4=Zyl I,2) i 25.

[94] WVDOG 4 (1904): 22. Compare an inscription of Nebuchadnezzar I that says, ÉRIN-*ni* ^{d}*en-líl* ^{d}UTU *u* ^{d}AMAR.UTU *ú-paḫ-⌈ḫir-ma⌉*, "I assembled the troops of Enlil, Šamaš, and Marduk" for a campaign against Elam (RIMB 2 22, obv. 11). See also the epithet of Nebuchadnezzar II: *muštēšir ba'ulāti Enlil Šamaš u Marduk*, "who keeps in order the subjects of Enlil, Šamaš, and Marduk" (VAB 4 88 [Nbk 9=Zyl III,4] i 3). See also the earlier Babylonian text called "Advice to a Prince," recently reedited by S. Cole (*The Early Neo-Babylonian Governor's Archive*, no. 128), where the archaic right of these cities to be free from tax or corvée duties is already articulated.

[95] The importance of Nabopolassar's seizure of Nippur may also be indicated in the Dynastic Chronicle, which preserves the following fragmentary notice for that king's reign (assuming Grayson's historical reconstruction is correct): . . .] x *en.líl*^{ki} *a-na Bābili*^{ki}, ". . . Nippur to Babylon" (Grayson, *BHLT*, 30 i 24).

[96] TCS 5 chron 3:2-8; on Gablini, see Wiseman, *CCK*, 80; and W. Röllig's recent discussion of the historical background of four Neo-Assyrian tablets from Tell Šēḫ Ḥamad, "Zur historischen Einordnung der Texte," *SAAB* 7 (1993): 129, n. 2.

Babylonians.[97] The court of Josiah in Judah probably also recognized the emerging might of Babylon by this time.[98] Although the Assyrians made several ill-fated attacks into Babylonia later on, little strong evidence survives to show that they controlled territory in Babylonia as late as 617, although the exact date of Nippur's conquest, to repeat, remains uncertain.[99] Nabopolassar's claims that he threw off the Assyrian yoke and ousted the Assyrians from Akkad perhaps come from the second half of his reign, when the king was secure in his rule of Babylonia.

The second claim of the inscriptions quoted above, that Nabopolassar killed the Subarian and ruined his land, may be later than the more restrained claim about repulsing the Assyrians from Akkad. Some associate the second claim with the Median and Babylonian penetration into Assyria and the destruction of Nineveh in 612;[100] and in the years 611 and 610 there is a notice in the chronicle that "the king marched about victoriously in Assyria."[101] Such a reconstruction is plausible, for although the city of Assur had fallen to the Medes in 614, the chronicle suggests that the Babylonians did not arrive in time to participate in the sack.[102] In any case, Nabopolassar's second claim refers explicitly to military penetration into Assyria proper, and might reflect the successes he achieved in the Assyrian heartland in 612 and later.[103] The cylinder inscriptions containing these phrases would then be relatively later than those referring only to the ouster of the Assyrians from Akkad.

What further conclusions may we draw from Nabopolassar's inscriptions about Babylonian relations with the rest of the world? First, the inscriptions indicate that the king employed workmen only from

---

[97] TCS 5 chron 3:10.

[98] A. Malamat, "The Twilight of Judah: In the Egyptian-Babylonian Maelstrom," VTSup 28 (1974): 123-145; idem, "The Kingdom of Judah Between Egypt and Babylon: A Small State Within a Great Power Confrontation," in *Text and Context: Old Testament and Semitic Studies for F.C. Fensham*, ed. W. Classen. JSOTSup 48 (Sheffield: Academic, 1988), 117-29.

[99] See most recently, S. W. Cole, *Nippur in Late Assyrian Times, c. 755-612 B.C.* SAAS 4 (Helsinki: Neo-Assyrian Text Corpus Project, 1996), 79-80.

[100] Berger, *Königsinschriften*, 115; Al-Rawi, "Imgur-Enlil," 2.

[101] TCS 5 chron 3:54, 59.

[102] Ibid., chron 3:27-28. For a similar statement about the failure of the Babylonians to participate in the sack of a foreign city, see also ibid., chron 1 i 36.

[103] This would presumably also be the context for the declaration of war inscription published by Gerardi, if it belongs to Nabopolassar (Gerardi, "Declaring War," 37-38).

Babylonia proper in his building projects, as Langdon already asserted.[104] We have already noted Nabopolassar's use of the workmen/troops (*ummānātu*) of Enlil, Šamaš, and Marduk for corvée, probably a reference to Nippur, Sippar and Babylon. More general phrases occur in his other inscriptions. According to a cylinder describing the rebuilding of Imgur-Enlil, Babylon's inner defense wall, Nabopolassar accomplished the work *in um-ma-nim di-ku-ut ma-ti-ia*, "with the workmen, the levy of my land."[105] Similar language occurs in his Etemenanki cylinder: *um-ma-nim ša-ad-li-a-tim di-ku-ut* MA.DA-*ia lu ú-ša-aš-ši-im*, "the vast range of workmen, the levy of my land, I made carry (tools for brick making)."[106] The Nēmetti-Enlil cylinder has:

> *na-ap-ḫa-ar um-ma-ni-ia tu-up-ši-ik-ku lu e-mi-id* ^{giš}*al-lu* ^{giš}*mar-ri-im lu ú-ša-aš-ši-im ni-ši ma-a-ti e-li-ti ù ša-ap-li-tim ša* ^{d}*na-bi-um ù* ^{d}AMAR.UTU *ṣi-ri-si-⸢na⸣⸢a⸣-na qá-ti-ia ú-ma-al-lu-ú*
>
> I imposed the work-basket on all of my workmen, the hoe and the spade I made the people of the upper and lower land carry —those whose lead rope Nabû and Marduk had placed in my hands.[107]

The phrase "people of the upper and lower land" in this inscription of Nabopolassar is unusual, but it probably does not indicate regions outside Babylonia.[108] These passages, then, confirm the idea that Nabopolassar did not recruit foreign workers for his building projects.

---

104 Langdon, *Building Inscriptions*, 7.

105 Al-Rawi, "Imgur-Enlil," fig. 4 13-14=Zyl I,1.

106 VAB 4 60 (Npl 1=Zyl III,1) ii 2-4.

107 BRM 4 51 14-19 (=YOS 9 84=Zyl II,3).

108 The phrase *nišī māti elīti u šaplīti* is otherwise unattested in the Neo-Babylonian royal inscriptions. Normally, the designations "upper" and "lower" modify *tâmtim*, "sea," and refer to the Mediterranean Sea and Persian Gulf, respectively, in the phrase *tâmtim elītim u šaplītim*. Probably *māti elīti u šaplīti* is a reference to the entire region of Babylonia, i.e., Sumer and Akkad. R. Zadok treats these occurrences of *Mātu-elītu* and *(Mātu-) šaplītu* as two separate GNs of indeterminate location; see *Geographical Names According to New- and Late-Babylonian Texts*, Répertoire géographique des textes cunéiforms 8, Beihefte zum Tübinger Atlas des vorderen Orients B7 (Wiesbaden: L. Reichert, 1985), 227 (hereafter Zadok, Rép. géogr. 8). This is not warranted. Compare the following phrase in an early Neo-Babylonian *kudurru*: [*mu-še*]-*et-bi* GI.DUSU (*tupšikku*) *š*[*a ma*]-*ti* AN.TA (*elīti*) *ù* KI (*šaplīti*) "[who causes to lift?] up the work basket of the upper and lower land" (BBSt No. 5 i 31; for the conjectural restoration of first two signs, see *CAD* M/1 417, s.v. *mātu* 1b; and for the reading [*mā*]*ti* as opposed to [*tâm*]*ti*, see BBSt 26, n. 6). The subject of the phrase is Marduk-zākir-šumi, a governor (*bēl pīḫati*) and the recipient of a royal land grant. The epithet is therefore

A second conclusion derives from Nabopolassar's "call" narratives in the royal building inscriptions. In all of these, the gods commissioned the king to rule over a limited geographical region: Babylonia. Thus the Eḫursagtila[109] and Imgur-Enlil cylinders state: *i-na* KUR *ab-ba-nu-ú iš-ku-na-an-ni a-na re-še-e-tim / a-na be-lu-ut ma-a-ti ù ni-ši-im it-ta-ba ni-bi-ta*, "In the land where I was born he (Marduk) placed me in the highest position, for the rulership of the land and people he designated me."[110] Another example comes from the Nēmetti-Enlil inscription:

> *ì-nu-um* ⸢*ì*⸣-[*lí r*]*a-bi-ú-tim / a-na be-lu-ut ma-a-ti šu-ma-am ṣi-ri-im /* ⸢*ib*⸣*-bu-ú ḫa-aṭ-ṭa à-ri-ik-ti /* ⸢*a*⸣*-na re-te-ed-de-e ni-ši-ia /* ⸢*i*⸣*-qí-pu-ù-ni* ^{giš}*uš-pa-ri-im*[111] *ṣi-ri-im /* [*a*]-⸢*na*⸣ *ku-nu-uš la ma-gi-ri-im /* ⸢*ú-ša*⸣*-at-mi-iḫ*[112] *qá-tu-ú-a*
>
> When the great gods, for the rulership of the land, called (my) lofty name, they entrusted to me a long (enduring?) scepter always to govern my people; a lofty staff to subdue rebels they(?) caused my hands to grasp.[113]

The *ḫaṭṭu ariktu*, "long (enduring?) scepter" is not granted to the king for rule over all humanity, as the rhetoric of Nabopolassar's successors will later affirm. There may be one important exception to this pattern, if the text describing a Babylonian king's declaration of war against Assyria should be ascribed to Nabopolassar. In that text we read: [*a*]-⸢*na*⸣ ⸢*be*⸣*-lu-tu* KUR.KUR *il-qa-an-ni-ma* UN.MEŠ KUR.KUR.MEŠ *kul-lat-ši-na ú-šat*-⸢*mi*⸣-[*iḫ*] *qa-tu-ú-*[*a*], "for the rulership of the lands he

---

not a royal one, but refers to Marduk-zākir-šumi in his capacity as overseer of corvée or the like, undoubtedly within Babylonia and not from the Persian Gulf to the Mediterranean Sea (even if there is uncertainty about his role; see Brinkman, *PKB*, 303-4, and n. 1996). The phrase may be an uncommon term referring to all of Babylonia, rather than the entire region from the Mediterranean Sea to the Persian Gulf, although the precise meaning of "upper" and "lower" remains uncertain.

[109] Note, incidentally, the archaizing writing of the temple name as É.PA.GÌN.TI.LA; on which, see A. R. George, *Babylonian Topographical Texts*, OLA 40 (Leuven: Peeters, 1992), 314 (hereafter George, *BTT*).

[110] Eḫursagtila: VAB 4 66 (Npl 4=Zyl I,2) 11-12; Imgur-Enlil (with orthographic variants): A Babylon 11 i 19-21 (Al-Rawi, "Imgur-Enlil," 3).

[111] For other references to the *ušparu*, see VAB 4 280 (Nbn 8=Stl. Frgm. XI) viii 27; CT 51: 75, 18; VAB 4 216 (Ner 2=Zyl II,1) i 33.

[112] Possibly an error for *ušatmiḫ*<*ū*>. The loss of final long vowels (as opposed to short ones) is unusual in NB orthography, making the possibility of an apocopated writing of the plural unlikely.

[113] BRM 4 51 i 7-13 (=YOS 9 84=Zyl II,3).

[Marduk] selected me and entrusted into my hands the peoples of all the lands."[114] It is impossible, however, to be sure that this text belongs to Nabopolassar, since the Babylonian king is not named. The building inscriptions, in any case, do not insist that Nabopolassar is the king of the universe, as the Assyrians had insisted even in their Babylonian inscriptions; nor do they say that the gods called him to rule "the widespread peoples" or the whole universe, as Nebuchadnezzar's inscriptions later do. Rather, in Nabopolassar's royal building inscriptions, the focus is on his rule over Babylonia.[115]

The importance of this discussion of Nabopolassar's call narratives for illuminating Babylonian imperial ideas is mainly negative. The king's building inscriptions make no self-conscious claims that the Babylonians saw themselves either as imperial rulers or as heirs of Assyria's empire. The war against Assyria was important for defining the king's reign, but after the messy business of first ousting the Assyrians from Babylonia and then destroying them, documented in other sources, the Babylonians remained focused on consolidating local rule. Even if the "declaration of war" text, where the king is called to rule all lands, should be ascribed to the latter part of Nabopolassar's reign, it is clear that its main purpose is to explain why Babylon and Akkad must be avenged against Assyria. There is no sense that Babylon claims Assyria's imperial heritage. Furthermore, Nabopolassar's inscriptions do not boast that the king brought exotic foreign goods into Babylonia for beautifying its temples, not even cedars of Lebanon;[116] and he never declares that he used foreign workmen in his construction programs. Babylonia was prosperous and secure by the last years of

[114] Gerardi, "Declaring War," 35 obv. 14-15.

[115] We might compare a cylinder inscription of Merodach-baladan II, in which the king's call is similarly parochial: [*ana*] SIPA-*ut* KUR *šu-me-*⌈*rim*⌉ *u* URI.KI MU-*šú ki-niš it-ta-*⌈*bi* LUGAL⌉ DINGIR.MEŠ ^{d}asar-ri, "the king of the gods, Asarri (=Marduk) truly called his name for the shepherdship of the land of Sumer and Akkad" (Gadd, "Cylinder of Marduk-apla-iddina II," 133 pl. 9 14).

[116] There is one exception in the Etemenanki cylinder. For the foundation purification ceremony the text mentions NA$_4$.NA$_4$ SA.DU-*i ù ti-à-am-tim*, "stones from mountain and sea" (VAB 4 62 [Npl 1=Zyl III,1] ii 47-48). This is a nod to the ancient tradition of the use of exotic material in the foundation ritual more than it is a claim about Babylonian imperial reach bringing such things into Babylon. Contrast Nebuchadnezzar's Etemenanki inscription, a large part of which delineates the Babylonian and foreign peoples who bring building goods to Babylon. The absence of evidence is not evidence of absence, but it may be significant that while the chronicle mentions booty being transferred to Babylon under Nabopolassar, the royal inscriptions still do not specify use of such materials in temple building.

Nabopolassar's reign. The Babylonians were the leaders of all southern Mesopotamia, much of former Assyria, and the Middle Euphrates region. They enjoyed military successes as far west as Syria and as far north as Urartu, according to the chronicle. Yet Nabopolassar's building inscriptions never allude to these facts. One might object that the pious language and dedicatory function of the royal inscriptions together with the relative paucity of inscriptions from Nabopolassar's reign skew our perception of the martial and even imperial aspects of Nabopolassar's reign. This could be partly true. However, the significant contrasts between Nabopolassar's inscriptions and those of the Neo-Assyrian kings composed in the Babylonian style for Babylonian projects,[117] as well as between inscriptions of Nabopolassar and his Neo-Babylonian successors, indicate that the same types of inscriptions before and after his reign conveyed considerable information about precisely these topics. The absence of such indications in Nabopolassar's texts is therefore significant.

The Babylonians under Nabopolassar struggled to free themselves from Assyrian domination, but that king's royal inscriptions do not project an image of the Babylonians as Assyria's imperial legatees. All of this, however, changes dramatically under Nebuchadnezzar II, who began to promulgate a different imperial worldview.

1.5 The Evolution of Babylonian Imperial Ideas: Nebuchadnezzar

The report sections of Nebuchadnezzar's inscriptions are longer than those of Nabopolassar. Nebuchadnezzar's give much more information about building projects and employ a greater variety of language about the king's commission and responsibilities. In addition, although we have only brick inscriptions and clay cylinders from Nabopolassar, Nebuchadnezzar's inscriptions encompass a larger variety of physical forms, including one of only two Neo-Babylonian rock reliefs and a prism.[118] This variety could be the result of chance

---

[117] On the Neo-Assyrian use of epithets in inscriptions intended for Babylonia, see above nn. 30, 32, 37, 44. Esarhaddon also explicitly mentions the use of foreign captives in the building projects at Babylon (e.g., Borger Esarh. 20 Ep. 19, Fass. c 3-5), as well as the use of foreign building materials such as cedars from the Amanus Mountains (ibid., 22 Ep. 28). The same holds for Assurbanipal.

[118] A newly discovered rock-relief of a Mesopotamian king in Jordan has been convincingly attributed to Nabonidus; see S. Dalley and A. Goguel, "The Selaʿ Sculpture: A Neo-Babylonian Rock Relief in Southern Jordan," *ADAJ* 41 (1997): 169-76. The characteristics of the king's crown, stance, and staff together with the

discovery and the extremely long reign of Nebuchadnezzar (605-562). It is more likely, however, that it proves that Nebuchadnezzar paid greater attention to propagandistic communication of Babylon's role as a preeminent power than Nabopolassar did. Unlike the inscriptions of Nabopolassar (and of Nabonidus to some extent), however, there are few explicit or even indirect indications of the chronological order for Nebuchadnezzar's texts.[119] Langdon attempted to arrange them according to the sequence of building projects enumerated in the *inūma* sections, but Berger rightly criticized this effort as being too simplistic.[120] A few suggestions appear below about the relative dates of some of the texts, but for the most part this problem remains unresolved, and a diachronic analysis of the inscriptions is not yet possible.[121]

1.5.1 The King's Call and the Language of Imperial Hegemony

The passages in Nebuchadnezzar's inscriptions describing his call to rulership by the gods—usually following the titulary and introduced by the adverb *īnum* (or *inūma, īnu*)—revolve around two ancient ideas about the role of the king, as do those of Nabopolassar. First, the gods

---

divine symbols on the relief make the ascription virtually certain. The text accompanying the relief is too badly eroded to be read. On the difference between cylinders and prisms, see Ellis, *Foundation Deposits*, 108-9. The prism is much more characteristic of the Assyrian tradition than of the Babylonian in the first millennium.

119 According to Landsberger's reading, the prism-fragment from the reign of Nebuchadnezzar should be assigned to the king's seventh year. The text is published in E. A. Unger, *Babylon: Die Heilige Stadt nach der Beschreibung der Babylonier*, 2. Auflage, ed. R. Borger (Berlin: de Gruyter, 1970), 282-94 (hereafter Unger, *Babylon*). Unger read the following in col. ii 25: *in* 1 SILA ŠE.NUMUN *ina ša-at-ti-ia*. Landsberger corrected the reading in his review of Unger to: *in se-bu-tim ša-at-ti-ia*, "in my seventh year," (Review of Unger, *Babylon*, in *ZA* 41 [1933], 298). This is confirmed by collation of the prism from photographs, which were kindly supplied by Dr. V. Donbaz.

120 Berger, *Königsinschriften*, 99. Berger's criticism is corroborated by the assignment of Nebuchadnezzar's prism fragment to his seventh year (see above n. 119), since the prism already contained an extensive resume of temple building activities. Langdon's hypothesis would have demanded a date for the text much later in the king's reign, and thus is unreliable for dating the texts.

121 If dated notices pertaining to building in the economic and administrative texts from the main temple archives can be correlated with the projects described in the royal inscriptions, the problem might receive clarification, as it has for the reign of Nabonidus (see Beaulieu, *Reign of Nabonidus*). Such a project has not yet been done.

call the king to rule over certain people and territories. Second, they commission him to renew temples or cities. These ideas occur in a variety of expressions, and a brief review focusing especially on the first idea—language about the people or poeples over whom the king rules—can illuminate Babylonian ideas about the extent of imperial hegemony under Nebuchadnezzar.

The following is perhaps the most succinct expression: [d]AMAR.UTU . . . KUR *šu-te-šu-ru ni-šim re-e-a-am / za-na-an ma-ḫa-zi ud-du-šu eš-re-e-tim / ra-bi-iš ú-ma-ʾe-er-an-ni*, "Marduk sublimely commanded me to lead the land aright, to shepherd the people, to provide for cult centers, (and) to renew temples."[122] This passage, however, seems to focus narrowly on Babylonia as the king's arena of action: the land and people are singular. A slight variant widens the scope: [d]AMAR.UTU . . . *ni-ši ra-ap-ša-a-ti a-na re-e-ú-ti i-dì-nam za-na-an ma-ḫa-zi ud-du-šu e-eš-re-e-ti ra-bi-iš ú-ma-ʾe-er-an-ni*, "Marduk gave me the widespread peoples for shepherding, he sublimely commanded me to care for cult centers (and) to renew temples."[123] The phrase "widespread peoples" (*nišī rapšātim*) includes populations beyond Babylonia. Other examples make this explicit. Thus we read in another call passage: [d]AMAR.UTU . . . *be-e-lu-ti ki-iš-ša-at ni-šim i-qí-pa-an-ni* [d]*na-bi-um . . . a-na šu-te-šu-úr ka-al da-ad-mu ù šu-um-mu-ḫu te-né-še-e-tim* GIŠ.GIDRU *i-ša-ar-tim ú-ša-at-mi-ḫu qá-tu-ú-a*, "Marduk . . . entrusted me with the rule of the totality of peoples, Nabû . . . placed in my hands a just scepter to lead all populated regions aright and to make humanity thrive."[124] In addition to *kiššat nišī*, "the totality of peoples," *kal dadmū*, "all inhabited regions," and (*kala*) *tenēšētu*, "(all) humanity," there are other such phrases that refer to the people or regions over whom the gods designated Nebuchadnezzar to rule: *nišī rapšātim*, "the widespread peoples," *nišī kibrāti arbātim*, "the peoples

---

[122] VAB 4 72 (Nbk 1=Zyl III,3) i 11-14. An identical passage occurs in VAB 4 104 (Nbk 13=III,7) i 22-25. Similar language, also with "land" in the singular and mention of shepherding the people, occurs in VAB 4 (Nbk 10=Zyl II,4) i 7-10; without shepherdship in VAB 4 (Nbk 12=Zyl III,1) i 17-24.

[123] YOS 1 44 (=Zyl II,10) i 11-13.

[124] VAB 4 112 (Nbk 14=Zyl III,5) i 13-17. Identical language appears in VAB 4 122 (Nbk 15=Stein-Tafel X) i 40-46 (the so-called "East India House" inscription). In the latter text we also read twice in hymns addressed to Marduk: *šar-ru-ti ki-iš-ša-at ni-ši ta-qí-pa-an-ni*, "the kingship of the totality of peoples you entrusted to me" (124 i 64-65, and 140 ix 50-51).

of the four corners [of the earth],"[125] *šarrāni kibrāti*, "the kings of the four corners [of the earth]," *kiššūt*[126] *matāti*, "the totality(?) of lands," *ištu tâmti elīti adi tâmti šaplīti*, "from the Upper Sea to the Lower Sea," *kullat mātitān*, "all the nations," and *mātāti rūqāti*, "distant lands." These terms are mainly spatial, rather than political or ethnic. They are of course not unique to Nebuchadnezzar's inscriptions,[127] but they demonstrate how the royal rhetoric was modified compared to that of his predecessors to express the idea of the king's universal rule.

Did the Neo-Babylonian scribes assume that there was a concrete geographical reality behind such rhetorical language? Nebuchadnezzar's Etemenanki inscription offers a clue. The Etemenanki cylinder is unique because it gives concrete expression to the rhetoric about the universality of the king's hegemony: it delineates the cities and regions that contributed corvée laborers or raw materials for work on Marduk's ziggurat in Babylon.[128] First, however, the text intones the rhetorical language:

> *ni-ši ra-ap-ša-a-tim ša* ᵈAMAR.UTU *be-li ia-ti i-qí-pa-an-ni re-é-ú-si-na id-di-nam qú-ra-dam* ᵈUTU-*šum ku-ul-la-at ma-ti-ta-an gi-mi-ir ka-la da-ad-mi ul-tu ti-a-am-tim e-li-tim a-di ti-a-am-tim ša-ap-li-tim* MA.DA MA.DA *ru-qá-a-tim ni-ši da-ad-mi ra-ap-ša-a-tim* LUGAL.MEŠ *ša-di-i ne-su-tim ù na-gi-i bé-e-ru-tim ša qé-re-eb ti-a-am-tim e-li-tim ù ša-ap-li-tim ša* ᵈAMAR.UTU *be-li a-na ša-da-ad si-ir-di-šu ṣé-ra-at-si-na ú-ma-al-lu-ù qá-tu-ú-a ad-ka-am-ma . . . i-na e-pé-šu é-temen-an-ki e-me-ed-su-nu-ti tu-up-ši-ik-ku*
>
> The widespread peoples whom Marduk, my lord, entrusted to me, whose shepherdship the hero Šamaš gave me, the totality of countries, the whole of all inhabited regions, from the Upper Sea to the Lower Sea, remote countries, the peoples of the widespread inhabited regions, kings of distant mountain regions and faraway

---

[125] This phrase occurs among Neo-Babylonian royal inscriptions in one of Nebuchadnezzar's brick inscriptions from the Ebabbar temple of Šamaš in Sippar, VAB 4 150 (Nbk 18=Backst. B III,1) 21-22; and Walker, *Brick Inscriptions*, 73-74, no. 91:20-21.

[126] For the use of this term with the meaning "totality," perhaps in confusion with *kiššatu*, see *CAD* K 463, s.v. *kiššūtu* 2.

[127] An inscription of Samsu-iluna, of the first dynasty of Babylon, e.g., asserts that ᵈAMAR.UTU . . . *a-na sa-am-su-i-lu-na* . . . [Š]U.NÍGIN *ma-ta-tim* [*a*]-*na re-ie-em i-din-nam*, "Marduk . . . granted to Samsu-iluna . . . the totality of lands to shepherd" (*LIH* no. 97 13-19).

[128] It is very probable that the list of officials and foreign kings that concludes Nebuchadnezzar's Prism Fragment (Unger, *Babylon* Nr. 26) was also related to corvée. This is discussed below, in chapter two.

> islands in the Upper and Lower Sea—whose lead ropes Marduk, my lord, placed into my hands[129] in order to pull his chariot pole—I conscripted . . . for the building of Etemenanki I imposed the work-basket on them.[130]

The text then explicitly delineates cities and regions to which this rhetoric refers.[131] It first mentions *ummānāt Šamaš u Marduk*, "the troops/workmen of Šamaš and Marduk." Weissbach argued that this could be a reference to workmen from the principal cult centers of Šamaš and Marduk, namely, Sippar and Babylon.[132] Next the text enumerates cities in southern Babylonia: Ur, Uruk, Larsa, Eridu, Kullab, probably Nēmed-Laguda,[133] and "the land of Ugar-[x]," which is unidentified.[134] After a break of several lines, the list continues with Larak, the land of Puqūdu, the land of Bīt-Dakkūri, the land of Bīt-

---

[129] The idea of the god granting the king the *ṣerretu*, "lead rope," of the people goes back as far as Narām-Sîn, and is common also in the inscriptions of Hammurapi (for references, see *CAD* Ṣ 136, s.v. *ṣerretu* A 4 c). The extension of this concept to include "the widespread peoples," as opposed to the population of "Sumer and Akkad," (i.e., Babylonia) may be an innovation of Nebuchadnezzar. It appears also in another recently published inscription of his (*ṣe-er-re-et ni*$^{!}$*-šì ra-bí-a-tim ú-ma-al-lu-ù qá-tu-ú-a*, "[Marduk and Nabû] placed the lead rope of the numerous peoples into my hands"; see P.-A. Beaulieu, "A New Inscription of Nebuchadnezzar II Commemorating the Restoration of Emaḫ in Babylon," *Iraq* 59 [1997]: 96 col. ii 51-54). Nabopolassar still uses it only of the people of Babylonia (see above n. 108).

[130] BE 1,I 85 (=WVDOG 59 46=Zyl IV,1) 13-30. Langdon's edition of the Etemenanki cylinder, VAB 4 (Nbk 17), was superseded by that of Weissbach's in WVDOG 59 44-48. Additional exemplars have since emerged, including one in the Harvard Semitic Museum (reg. no. 890.3.1) and another fragment in the British Museum (BM 41649) and I hope to prepare a transliteration and translation of the text. Lineation of the text remains a problem. Until a new score is prepared, I will refer to the edition of Weissbach.

[131] WVDOG 59 46 4.11-25. Nebuchadnezzar's prism fragment proceeds in the same way; see below, chapter 2.

[132] See WVDOG 59 47, note d, and above n. 94.

[133] The text, restored by Weissbach, reads *kul-*⸢*la*⸣-[*ab*^{ki}] ^{uru}*ni-mi-it-*^{d}[*la-gu-da*]. (WVDOG 59 46 3.55-56). The restoration seems secure in view of Nebuchadnezzar's prism fragment, where É.MAŠ-officials from these two cities are listed together (Unger, *Babylon* 286 v 7-8). On the location of Nēmed-Laguda "im Süden von Babylonien," see further ibid., 292 nn. 4-5; and Zadok, Rép. géogr. 8, 237.

[134] Perhaps Ugar-Sallu, which also begins KUR.*Ugar-*^{d}-. There is also an ^{uru}A.GÀR-*ka*$_{4}$*-ṣir* (Zadok, Rép. géogr. 8, 318), but this presumably would not require the divine determinative. The context in which the toponym appears suggests that the site is probably to be located in southern Babylonia.

Amūkānim, the land of Bīt-[x], and the land of Birā[ti?], all of which are cities or tribal regions in central Babylonia, with the possible exception of the last, which is obscure.[135] Dēr,[136] Agade[137] (with a short gap at the end of the line), the land of Arrapḫa, and the land of Laḫīru complete the list of specific locations. Dēr, Arrapḫa, and Laḫīru are all east of the Tigris and south of the Lower Zab, in territory controlled by the Assyrians during the Sargonid era. The list concludes with a summary that widens the scope beyond Mesopotamia and the language becomes more general: *napḫar māt Akka*[*dī*] *u māt Aššur*[138] *šarrāni ša Eber-Nā*[*ri*] *pīḫata⌈̄ tim⌉*[139] *ša māt Ḫattim ištu tiāmtim elītim adi tiāmtim šaplītim,*[140] "all of the land of Akkad and the land of Assyria, the kings

---

[135] There are several NB toponyms known as ^{uru}*Bīrāti* (Zadok, Rép. géogr. 8, 75).

[136] Langdon's publication of the Louvre fragment (*ZA* 19 [1905]: 142-46; exemplar B in WVDOG 59 44-48) incorrectly has BÀD^{ki}. This should be corrected to BÀD.DINGIR^{ki}. Collation of the Louvre fragment, accession number Sb 1700, was made from photographs kindly supplied to me by Dr. B. André-Salvini, to whom I am grateful.

[137] Its identification remains uncertain, but for the possibility that it is Tell Muḥammad, see recently C. Wall-Romana, "An Areal Location of Agade," *JNES* 49 (1990): 205-45.

[138] Spelled variously in the different exemplars of this cylinder: ⌈MA.⌉DA AN[+ŠAR] (WVDOG 59 46 4.8 should be restored in the same way), and MA.DA A.ŠUR$_4$ (=A.LÁL+SAR).[^{ki}] (HSM 890.3.1 iii 6, unpublished). I am grateful to Prof. Stephen Cole for pointing out this writing to me. A.ŠUR$_4$, previously unknown from Nebuchadnezzar's inscriptions, is otherwise confined largely to the second millennium, but it is attested three times in NA according to S. Parpola, *Neo-Assyrian Toponymns*, AOAT 6 (Kevelaer: Butzon & Bercker; Neukirchen-Vluyn: Neukirchener, 1970), 50. Interestingly, it appears in the prologue to Hammurapi's Laws as ^{uru}A.ŠUR$_4^{\text{ki}}$ (CH IV 58). Some Neo-Babylonian scribes were familiar with the writing in that source. A badly broken Neo-Babylonian copy of Hammurapi's Laws (BE 35271) preserves their prologue, and contains precisely this spelling, although it is only partly preserved: [*a*-]⌈*na*⌉ ^{uru}A.⌈LÁL+⌉[SAR^{ki}]; see Bergmann, *Codex Ḫammurabi*, 52 Rs. ii 12. This writing of Aššur seems to be another example of the delight which the Neo-Babylonian scribes took in giving learned or archaic orthographies, especially of GNs and temple names.

[139] The spelling, *pi-ḫa-ta-a-⌈tim⌉* (HSM 890.3.1 iii 8, unpublished), is unusual, but confirmed by the available space at the end of the line in three exemplars of the cylinder. It is presumably another example of the sort of hyperarchaizing that the Neo-Babylonian scribes relished, and yields an unprecedented form of the pl. *piḫātu*. Subsequently, in the same text, the rulers of Ḫatti are referred to as *šakkanakkātim*, "viceroys," and perhaps this unusual (but attested) plural influenced the previous term.

[140] WVDOG 59 46 4.7-13, restored from the Harvard exemplar, HSM 890.3.1, which confirms the readings Akkad, Assyria, and Eber-Nāri.

of Eber-Nāri, the governors of Ḫatti, from the Upper Sea to the Lower Sea."[141] In summary, after the reference to the workers of Šamaš and Marduk, perhaps meaning Sippar and Babylon, the list of regions mobilized for corvée moves from cities of southern Babylonia northward (although there is a break in the text between the two), then to former Assyrian regions east of the Tigris, to Eber-Nāri, and finally to Ḫatti; no specific toponyms are given in the last-named regions. The list probably included the regions that Nebuchadnezzar controlled when his scribes composed the inscription. For these scribes, then, the empire stretched from the Upper Sea to the Lower Sea (although the list moves in the opposite direction).[142]

The stock phrases of imperial hegemony imply the fiction of world domination. Nebuchadnezzar's scribes, however, acknowledged that a more limited imperial dominion lay behind the phrases. Thus, the Etemenanki list does not claim territories for Nebuchadnezzar that were, according to other evidence, beyond his control. It mentions no areas in northern Assyria, since these were probably under Median control; no areas in the Zagros mountains or east of Dēr, as these were controlled by the Medes and Persians; no areas in the Taurus mountains or Anatolia,

---

[141] There is, however, no verb following the summary, which moves directly into another apparent summary of different but equivalent terms: *māt Šumeri u Akkadîm māt Subarti kalašu šarrāni nagîm nesûtim ša qereb tiāmtim elītim šarrāni nagîm bērūtim ša qereb tiāmtim šaplītim šakkanakkātim māt Ḫattim neberti Puratti ana erib Šamši*, "the land of Sumer and Akkad, all of the land of Subartu (Assyria), the kings of distant regions within the Upper Sea and kings of faraway places within the Lower Sea, governors of the land of Ḫatti beyond the Euphrates to the west." Perhaps the repetition adds emphasis to the sense of totality of Nebuchadnezzar's hegemony. Another possibility is that the Etemenanki inscription was composed by culling geographical summaries from other texts, and that the conflation resulted in the scribe's failure to preserve the final verb.

[142] The same idea is preserved by Nabonidus's scribes. In an inscription memorializing his mother, Adad-Guppi, the king's commission is described as follows: Sîn called Nabonidus for kingship and entrusted into his hands *šarrūti māt Šumeri u māt Akkadî ultu pāṭu māt Miṣir tâmti elīt adi tâmti šaplīti napḫar mātāti*, "the kingship of the land of Sumer and Akkad, from the border of the land of Egypt, (from) the Upper Sea to the Lower Sea, all the lands" (Gadd, "Harran Inscriptions," H1, B i 41-43). Later, at his mother's death, Nabonidus summons the population of his realm for mourning: *āšib nagî nesūtu* [*šarrāni rubû* ??] *u šakkanakkū ultu* [*pāṭ*] *māt Miṣir tâmti e*[*līti*] *ana tâmti šaplīti*, "[people] who dwell in far off regions, [kings, princes ??] and governors from [the border] of Egypt (from) the U[pper] Sea to the Lower Sea" (ibid., iii 19-23). Nabonidus also calls up (*šutbû*) his "widespread troops" (*ummānīya rapšāti*) from his entire realm, designating the empire's western terminus as "the land of Gaza on the border of Egypt (on) the Upper Sea across the Euphrates" (VAB 4 220 [Nbn 1=Zyl III,2] i 39-41).

where the Lydians, Scythians, and Medians were powerful; nor does it list Egypt. The text does not precisely define the boundaries of Eber-Nāri and Ḫatti. Ḫatti refers to the entire east Mediterranean coastal region, from Cilicia in the north to the border of Egypt in the South.[143] In sum, the rhetoric of universal hegemony in Nebuchadnezzar's texts is meant to point to his newly expanded imperial power, but the scribes appear to have recognized a disjunction between the rhetoric and the reality. We may also reiterate by way of contrast that Nabopolassar's Etemenanki inscription, which clearly was the literary model for Nebuchadnezzar's,[144] shows no traces of this language of imperial hegemony; it indicates that Nabopolassar levied only local workmen for the project, and does not mention that he imported foreign building material. Thus, even if Nebuchadnezzar's rhetoric is characterized by hyperbole, his inscriptions reflect a new understanding of the imperial geography.

This language also differs from that of the Neo-Assyrian kings. In keeping with the apolitical tenor of the Neo-Babylonian royal inscriptions, there are no narratives concerning the conquest of "the widespread people," and no effort to suggest that they represent, as aliens, a destabilizing threat to the Babylonian imperial enterprise. Divine justification for conquest of the widespread people is muted or absent in the call passages: the gods simply "give" (*nadānu*) or "entrust" (*qepû*) the widespread peoples to the king, or they "fill (his) hands" (*qātī mullû*) with the responsibility to rule them. The Babylonian chronicle, of course, illustrates militaristic attitudes and accomplishments, while the archeological record in the Levant, as we will see in chapter two, attests to massive destruction wrought by the Babylonian army. The absence of such a perspective in the royal inscriptions, however, is noteworthy, and contrasts with the language of Neo-Assyrian kings in their Babylonian inscriptions and elsewhere. As Machinist and others have shown, the Neo-Assyrian kings were extremely conscious of the "otherness" of non-Assyrian populations, and consistently invoked divine sanction to justify their conquest; Sargon II speaks of teaching these others how to behave like Assyrians so that they may be assimilated into the empire.[145]

143 See below, chapter two.

144 WVDOG 59 46 3.9-13; Nebuchadnezzar refers explicitly to the achievements of his father in the same terms used by Nabopolassar in his Etemenanki inscription; see VAB 4 (Npl 1=Zyl III,1).

145 Machinist, "Assyrians on Assyria," 95-96; Tadmor, "Propaganda, Literature, Historiography," 327.

While the Babylonian inscriptions do appeal to the gods to eradicate the king's foes (see 1.5.4), the Babylonian expressions are entirely unlike those of the Assyrians.

In the Neo-Babylonian inscriptions, the language about the extent of imperial hegemony and the divine commission to expand the realm is muted at best and subordinate to the traditional requirement that the king rebuild or refurbish the temples or cities of the gods. Frequent reference to such building responsibilities is not new to the Neo-Babylonian era, but the emphasis on it almost to the exclusion of other concerns of state may be. Thus, the extension of imperial hegemony is presented simply as the means for Nebuchadnezzar to fulfill his divine obligation "to provide for cult centers and renew shrines." To take the Etemenanki cylinder as an example again, it enumerates regions within the empire by name precisely because they provide personnel for corvée or raw materials (here lumber) for the construction of Marduk's ziggurat. Nabopolassar's inscriptions intone the same royal obligation to build cities and renew temples, but they do not provide the same means to fulfill it. For the Assyrians, on the other hand, imperial expansion was a fundamental component of the imperial creed demanded by Aššur and directed at transforming the non-Assyrian world into the likeness of Assyria. This sentiment is absent from the Neo-Babylonian royal inscriptions.

1.5.2 Nebuchadnezzar as Protector of Humanity

Nebuchadnezzar's inscriptions contain other comments that clarify Neo-Babylonian ideas about empire, ideas that seem to reflect an official propagandistic position. The following passage expands the idea of universal rule discussed above:

> 6. *ni-šim* [*ra*]*-ap-ša-a-ti ša* ᵈAMAR.UTU *bé-e-la* 7. *u-ma-*[*a*]*l-lu-ú qá-tu-ú-a* . . . 9. *in* [*d*]*a-am-qá-a-ti* 10. *aš-te-ne-ʾe-e-ši-na-a-ti*[146] 11. *ús-su ki-i-na ri-id-dam da-am-qu* 12. *ú-ša-aš-bi-iṭ-sì-na-a-ti* . . . 15. *in ša-ri-im ú-ri-im in mi-ḫe-e ṣu-lu-lu* 16. *el-li-ši-na at-ru-uṣ-ma*[147]

---

[146] A closely parallel passage in the Wadi Brisa inscription has a variant: Weissbach's copy of that text suggests ⌈*er-te-ʾe*⌉*-ši-na-a-ti*, "I constantly shepherded them" (WVDOG 5 pl. 35 29; see *AHw* 977a, s.v. *rēʾû* Gtn 2); cf. VAB 4 216 (Ner 2=Zyl II,1) ii 3.

[147] This reading of line 15 was suggested by Landsberger (*ZA* 41 [1933]: 298, n. 1; adopted also in *CAD* Š/2 135 s.v. *šāru* 1 a) 3') and is confirmed by new photos kindly supplied by Dr. V. Donbaz of the Istanbul Archeological Museum.

17. *a-na ba-bi-⌈lam*^{ki} *kà-la-ši-na*[148] *ú-ka⌉-an-ni-iš* 18. *bi-la-at* MA.DA MA.DA *ḫi-ṣi-ib* SA.DU-*um* 19. *bi-ši-it ma-ti-ta-an qi-er*$_4$-*ba-šu am-ḫu-úr* 20. *a-na ṣi-il-li-šu da-ri-i ku-ul-la-at ni-šim* 21. *ṭa-bi-iš ú-pa-aḫ-ḫi-ir*[149]

(As for) the widespread peoples whom Marduk, the lord, gave into my hand . . . I continually strove for their welfare. (In) a just path and correct conduct I directed them . . . I stretched a roof over them in the wind, (and) a canopy in the tempest. I brought all of them under the sway of Babylon. The yield of the lands, the abundance of the mountain regions, the produce of the countries, I received within it (Babylon). Into its eternal shadow I assembled all the peoples for good.

This passage and its parallels emphasize the idea that the king is the protector of all humanity. Thus, the gods grant the king rulership over the "widespread peoples," a phrase that refers to all populations under royal control (see above section 1.5.1). The king is thus able to better their circumstances; he is, in short, their divinely appointed protector and benefactor, not their conqueror. The modern historian might argue that this is merely a pious fraud, designed to blunt the crassness of the more important concern, also expressed here: namely, the material exploitation of conquered populations for the benefit of a ruling elite. The notion of the king as protector of humanity, however, deserves attention as an important aspect of the imperial theory.

Besides the ideas expressed in the "eternal shadow of Babylon" passage above, there are a number of other phrases about the king's largesse and ability to make humanity thrive and prosper. We alluded above to an important idea accompanying the king's call: Nabû grants the king a *ḫaṭṭu išartu*, "just scepter," *ana šutēšur kal dadmē u šummuḫu tenēšētim*, "to lead all the inhabited regions aright and to make humanity thrive."[150] On other occasions Nebuchadnezzar's inscriptions

[148] Landsberger added this word in his review of Unger (ibid.; though *kà-la-ši-na* fits the traces better, and is written in col. iii 23); the new photos support Landsberger's reading, but they are not definitive for this badly preserved line.

[149] Unger, *Babylon* 283 ii 6-21; for very similar passages, see VAB 4 172 (Nbk 19=WBr) B viii 26-35; and VAB 4 94 (Nbk 9=Zyl III,4) iii 18-24 (the Grotefend inscription). Note that all three of these texts are very rare forms in the NB corpus of royal inscriptions: a prism (there is only one other), a rock-relief, and a limestone cylinder. Perhaps these texts had special propagandistic value as rare forms for public display, much like Nebuchadnezzar's rock inscription in the Wadi Brisa.

[150] Similar language occurs in VAB 4 112 (Nbk 14=Zyl III,5) i 16-17; the same language also appears with singular references to land and people in VAB 4

call the royal emblem *šibirru mušallim nišī*, "the scepter for keeping the people well."[151] The peaceful use of the emblem in his texts contrasts sharply with the Assyrian royal inscriptions of the first millennium, where the *šibirru* was a weapon of terror granted by Aššur for crushing recalcitrant groups and expanding the realm.[152] The Neo-Babylonian image of the royal scepter is benign, in the royal rhetoric at least. The idea of deportation, for example, which is explicitly referred to in the Assyrian inscriptions in connection with the *šibirru*, is only hinted at in Nebuchadnezzar's inscriptions. This conforms with Nebuchadnezzar's common assertion that he causes people everywhere to thrive (*šummuḫu*). Marduk placed the people of the entire world under his care; Nebuchadnezzar, as the good shepherd, "directs them in the proper path and the correct way of life." Thus, according to the imperial ideology, the conquest (*kanāšu*) of non-Babylonian populations is not to their detriment, since the Babylonian elite views the "eternal shadow of Babylon" as a restorative one. Similarly, there is no reference in Nebuchadnezzar's inscriptions to the king placing his yoke (*nīru*) upon conquered people, as there so often is in Assyrian royal inscriptions. Rather, Nebuchadnezzar asserts that he gathers the people into Babylon's shadow *ṭābiš*, "for good, peacefully."

The notion of royal responsibility for the well-being of all humanity is an assumption of the imperial creed under Nebuchadnezzar. We may highlight another aspect of this theme revealed in an unusual inscription, published by Lambert, that describes, among other things, legal reforms during the reign of Nebuchadnezzar II. The ascription of the text to Nebuchadnezzar's reign is uncertain, but the evidence cited

---

122 (Nbk 15=Stein Tafel X) i 44, ii 27; similarly VAB 4 102 (Nbk 12=Zyl III,1) iii 11 (only here is the scepter granted by Šamaš instead of Nabû, probably because the inscription commemorated the building of Šamaš's temple in Sippar); it occurs without mention of order or prosperity in VAB 4 98 (Nbk 11=Zyl II,12) i 13-14. The explanation for Nabû granting the scepter to the king is given in the ceremonial name of the temple of Nabû-ša-ḫarê at Babylon, which is called É.GIŠ.NÍG.GIDAR.KALAM.MA.SUM.MA, or, in Akkadian, *bīt nādin ḫaṭṭi ana māti*, "House which bestows the Scepter on the Land." George writes: "Nabu's temple played a special role in the theology of kingship, being the place where the legitimacy of the reign was ratified by the bestowal of the royal insignia. . . . The association of Nabû and scepters may also be owed to his original function as Marduk's vizier" (*BTT*, 311).

[151] VAB 4 140 (Nbk 16=Zyl II,11) i 9; 150 (Nbk 19=Wadi Brisa) A ii 1; also 102 (Nbk 12=Zyl III,1) iii 13.

[152] E.g., Sargon II (cited in Machinist, "Assyrians on Assyria," 95); Sennacherib (OIP 2 85: 5); and Esarhaddon (Borger Esarh. 98 32).

by Lambert is compelling.[153] The text states that the king promulgated *riksātu*, "regulations," *ana dummuq <kiš>šat nišī u šūšubu Akkadî*, "for the betterment of all peoples and the settling of Akkad."[154] Lambert emphasized the antiquity of this tradition about the king upholding justice in the land, and argued that "there is nothing distinctive in this theme at all."[155] But both this text and the "eternal shadow of Babylon" passages discussed above assert that Nebuchadnezzar brought this justice not only to Babylonia, but to the "widespread people" whom he ruled, and this is new. Lambert suggests that the unusual text portrays the king as a second Hammurapi.[156] Two things about the "eternal shadow of Babylon" passages suggest a similar portrayal of Nebuchadnezzar: one of the passages introduces Nebuchadnezzar as *šar mīšarim*, "king of justice," a title inaugurated by Hammurapi.[157] Second, the phrase "I directed them in the proper path and the correct way of life," occurs elsewhere only in Hammurapi's Laws, where it applies to the Babylonians proper.[158] The theme of the just king may be old, as Lambert notes, but Nebuchadnezzar's scribes mold him into the image of a second Hammurapi who now brings justice to the entire empire, not only to the people of Babylonia. The scribes promulgate that image as part of the official propaganda. This is different from Neo-Assyrian formulations, such as Sargon II's assertion about deportees brought to Assyria: he conquered them by the power of his *šibbiru*, "scepter," "he caused them to be of one mouth" (*pâ ištēn ušaškinma*), and he

---

[153] W. G. Lambert, "Nebuchadnezzar King of Justice," *Iraq* 27 (1965): 1-11. Lambert notes in particular the parallels with Nebuchadnezzar's texts, especially the Wadi Brisa inscription. We may add one parallel that Lambert did not mention: the idiom *riksāti urakkis*, "he instituted regulations," occurs in obv. ii 25-27. The Wadi Brisa inscription similarly mentions that blessings will accrue to any future ruler who "does not countermand my regulations" (*riksātiya la ipaṭṭar*) (VAB 4 176 [Nbk 19=WBr] B x 16). This statement presumes that these "regulations" had been promulgated during the king's reign. Among the Neo-Babylonian kings, only Nebuchadnezzar uses *riksu/riksātu* with this meaning; it is otherwise used in the royal inscriptions only to refer to architectural "joints."

[154] Lambert, "Nebuchadnezzar King of Justice," 5 obv. ii 24.

[155] Ibid., p. 4.

[156] Ibid., p. 3.

[157] Seux, *Épithètes royales*, 316-17.

[158] CH XXIV rev. 6-8: *ma-tam ú-sa-am ki-nam ù ri-dam dam-qá-am ú-ša-aṣ-bi-tu*, "I directed the country on the proper course and the correct way of life." The parallel was also noted earlier by Berger, *Königsinschriften*, 95.

"instructed them in the proper culture" (*inūšunu ušāḫiz*).[159] The distinction may be subtle and operate only at a rhetorical level—the subjugated populations might not have cared about such niceties—but where Sargon boasts of military might and the command of Aššur as justification for the conquest and Assyrianization of deportees, Nebuchadnezzar's text alludes to his status as "king of justice" and states that he gathers the people into Babylon's shadow without mention of capture or deportation.

1.5.3 Babylon as Center of the World

There is another idea, absent in the texts of Nabopolassar, that is clear in Nebuchadnezzar's texts: the subject lands furnish commodities and personnel so that Babylon can be made the economic and administrative center of the world. Of course, in Babylonian tradition the city was also the cosmological bond between heaven and earth, as the topographical text TIN.TIR=Babylon, for example, clearly states.[160] Further, Babylon's "shade" (*ṣillu*) can be said to be restorative for those fortunate enough to come under it. On a mundane level, the supply of precious and manufactured items, raw materials, and workmen for Babylon and for the other principal cities of Babylonia is often emphasized in Nebuchadnezzar's inscriptions. The inscriptions mention these things in three contexts: lists of precious building materials used in temple construction;[161] lists of goods furnished for the (offering-)tables of the gods;[162] and mention of goods brought as tribute to the king at his palace. Few concrete hints about the economic geography of the empire emerge from these lists, however, because they tend to be stereotyped. The following text is representative:

> KÙ.GI KÙ.BABBAR *ni-si-iq-tim* NA$_4$.NA$_4$ *šu-qu-ru-ù-tim* GIŠ.EREN GIŠ.EREN *pa-ag-lu-tu bi-il-tim ka-bi-it-tim i-gi-se-e šu-um-⌈mu-ḫu bi⌉-ši-im-tim ma-ti-ta-an ⌈ḫi⌉-ṣi-ib ka-al da-ád-mi a-na*

---

[159] For citation and discussion of these passages, see Machinist, "Assyrians on Assyria," 95-96; and Cogan, *Imperialism and Religion*, 49-50.

[160] This text contains a list of ceremonial epithets emphasizing Babylon's centrality in the cosmos; the majority of extant copies of the text, moreover, date from the NB period (George, *BTT*, 30).

[161] A representative example is CT 37 pl. 6 (=Zyl III,6) i 25-29.

[162] VAB 4 90 (Nbk 9=Zyl III,4) i 13-28; VAB 4 154 (Nbk 19=WBr) A iv 23-57; Unger, *Babylon* 282 i 1-13 (fragmentary); probably include also the very close parallel in Lambert, "King of Justice," rev. v 4-16 (=CT 46 45).

> *ma-ḫa-ar* [d]AMAR.UTU *be-lam ra-bi-ù i-li ba-nu-ú-a ù* [d]*na-bi-um* IBILA-*šu ṣi-i-ri na-ra-am šar-ru-ú-ti-ia ú-bi-lam-ma a-na É-sag-il ù É-zi-da ú-še-ri-ba-am*
>
> Gold, silver, exceedingly valuable gemstones, thick cedars, heavy tribute, expensive presents, the produce of all countries, goods from all inhabited regions, before Marduk the great lord, the god who created me, and Nabû his lofty heir who loves my kingship, I transported and brought into Esagil and Ezida.[163]

Such lists are augmented by the concluding hymns of the royal inscriptions, which also reinforce this idea about the funneling of resources into the heartland. The hymns often note the king's expectation that foreign rulers will present tribute to him at his palace. For example, in several of Nebuchadnezzar's hymns to Marduk we read: *ša* LUGAL.MEŠ *ki-ib-ra-a-tim ša ka-la te-ne-še-e-ti bi-la-su-nu ka-bi-it-ti lu-um-ḫu-ur qé-re-eb-ša*, "from the kings of the four corners, from all the peoples, let me receive their heavy tribute within it (the palace)."[164] Thus, according to the imperial theory as expressed and reinforced in these contexts, the one-way movement of goods was proper and resulted from the recognition of Babylon's preeminence by subject peoples.

---

[163] CT 37 pl. 6-7 (=Zyl III,6) i 25-29; cf. PBS 15 79 (=Zyl III,8) i 22-28. It is useful to compare here the kind of economic geography that Liverani reconstructed from the royal annals of Assurnasirpal II; see M. Liverani, *Studies on the Annals of Ashurnasirpal II, 2: Topographical Analysis*, Quaderni di Geografia Storica 4 (Rome: Università di Roma "La Sapienza," 1992), 155-62. In the case of Assurnasirpal, specific data are provided about what regions furnished tribute or booty. In Nebuchadnezzar's inscriptions, on the other hand, only a few items can be linked with specific regions or ecological niches.

[164] VAB 4 94 (Nbk 9=Zyl III,4) iii 51-55. The identical phrase (with orthographic variants) occurs in VAB 4 120 (Nbk 14=Zyl III,5) iii 50-51; in the so-called East India House stone tablet, VAB 4 140 (Nbk 15=Steintafel X) x 9-12; and in the Prism Fragment of Nebuchadnezzar, Unger, *Babylon* 284 iii 16-18. The same phrase is also used later by Neriglissar's scribes in a hymn to Marduk (VAB 4 214 [Ner 1=Zyl II,3] 38-40). As an aside, we may note that this sort of imperial language may well be behind the idea expressed in Isaiah 60:5-13 that all the nations will stream to Zion and present their tribute. Note in particular the delivery of prized woods, including cedar, for the construction of Yahweh's sanctuary (Isa 60:13); this point was convincingly argued by S. Paul, "Deutero-Isaiah and Cuneiform Royal Inscriptions," *JAOS* 88 (1968): 182-83, upon whose study I depend heavily. I would go further and suggest that Zion is understood by the prophet as the new imperial city of Yahweh, perhaps modeled on the example of Babylon.

I will discuss the different interpretations of the economic realities behind this language about tribute in chapter two. For now, it is sufficient to note again that there was apparently a disjunction between imperial theory and practice. Bilateral trade in fact existed alongside forced delivery of goods to Babylonia, which indicates that the royal inscriptions reflect a carefully crafted but partial picture. As Oppenheim showed in his essay on overland trade, by the time of Nabonidus, but possibly earlier, many commodities did not reach the heartland as a result of the "forcible exchange of goods" (Diakonoff's term).[165] Oppenheim argued on the basis of three economic texts, YOS 6 168, an unpublished duplicate thereof, and TCS 12 84, that commercial trade existed alongside forcible movement of goods into the heartland.[166] Of course, the Babylonians were not unaware of this disjunction between theory and practice. Rather, the accumulation of the wealth that poured in from the periphery was emphasized precisely as an important part of Nebuchadnezzar's newly forged imperial creed. The pattern, admittedly, was an old one in the Near East, and contributed to what Mario Liverani, in his discussion of the Late Bronze Age, has called the "prestige" of the ruling elite: "the afflux of goods from periphery to the center is viewed as a positive fact: as a symptom of power and a prerequisite for the exemplary functioning of the state."[167]

Of course, the Assyrians also emphasized the flow of booty into the heartland in their inscriptions. There is, however, a difference between the descriptions in the two traditions. The Assyrian royal inscriptions frequently indicate where and from what campaign the

---

[165] A. L. Oppenheim, "Essay on Overland Trade in the First Millennium B.C.," *JCS* 21 (1967): 246.

[166] He then suggested that such trade occurred even in the Neo-Assyrian empire, and in the early stages of the Neo-Babylonian. This has now been substantiated for the Neo-Babylonian era before the empire by Cole's publication of the *Early Neo-Babylonian Governor's Archive from Nippur*; see also Cole, *Nippur in Late Assyrian Times*, chapter 4. A different view is expressed by M. Elat, "Phoenician Overland Trade Within the Mesopotamian Empires," in *Ah, Assyria . . .: Studies in Assyrian History and Ancient Near Eastern Historiography Presented to Hayim Tadmor*, ScrHier 33, ed. M. Cogan and I. Eph'al (Jerusalem: Magnes, 1991), 21-35. This debate is discussed below, in chapter two.

[167] *Prestige and Interest: International Relations in the Near East ca. 1600-1100 B.C.* (Padova: Sargon, 1990), 219 and Part III generally. One notes too that the periphery, at least in the Late Bronze Age Egyptian formulation, in turn receives "life"—a multifaceted benefit—from the center. When Nebuchadnezzar says that he gathers people into Babylon's "eternal shadow," it is clear that the benefit which accrues to them is similarly restorative.

booty or tribute comes, and they also frequently list specific commodities and precise amounts. This information may have come from regularly compiled booty or tribute lists.[168] Moreover, Assyrian inscriptions give this information even where beautification of *Babylonian* temples is the subject of the inscription.[169] Such lists are rare or unknown in the Neo-Babylonian tradition,[170] and in the royal inscriptions the Babylonian scribes simply repeat stock phrases about precious commodities and tribute that reached Babylonia.

This emphasis on goods flowing into Babylon converges with Nebuchadnezzar's repeated claims that he made the capital into the most splendid city and the cultic center of the world. Thus he builds the royal palaces, temples, and gates and fills them with *lulû*, "splendor," *ana tabrâti kiššat nišī*, "for the astonishment of all peoples,"[171] and *ana dagālu(m) kiššat nišī*, "for the totality of peoples to gaze at."[172] The emphasis on Babylon's cultic centrality perhaps reaches its height in the following phrase addressed to Marduk: *eli māḫāzika Bābili ina kala dadmī ul ušāpâ māḫāza*, "More than your cult center Babylon I did not glorify any cult center in the entire inhabited world."[173] The city is, then, in some measure the physical demonstration of the divine imprimatur for his imperial rule. When all of the king's achievements concerning the beautification of Babylonia are duly recorded, the king says: *ka-la e-ep-še-ti-ia ša i-na* NA_4.NA.RÚ.A *aš-tu-ru mu-da-a li-ta-am-ma-ar-ma ta-nit-ti* DINGIR.DINGIR *li-iḫ-ta-as-sa-as*, "all of my deeds [i.e. building

[168] See Cogan, *Imperialism and Religion*, 118; and Grayson, "Assyria and Babylonia," 164, and n. 120.

[169] Esarhaddon, for example, delivered booty to Babylonia that had been acquired on campaign; thus, items from Egypt and Kush, including precious metals, are brought into Sumer and Akkad for the beautification of Babylonian temples (Borger, Esarh., 94 Smlt vs. 23-29).

[170] D. J. Wiseman assigned a fragmentary list to the Neo-Babylonian period ("A Late Babylonian Tribute List?" *BSOAS* 30 [1967]: 495-504). But other copies of this text have appeared in the British Museum and the composition is now known to come from the time of one of the Kassite kings called Kurigalzu (W. G. Lambert, "Literary Royal Cassite Correspondence," paper presented at the 45th *Rencontre Assyriologique International*, Cambridge, MA, July 7, 1998).

[171] VAB 4 132 (Nbk 15=St. Tfl. X) vi 19-21; and VAB 4 192 (Nbk 26=Zyl. Frgm. III,1) 13.

[172] VAB 4 118 (Nbk 14=Zyl III,5) ii 52-53; and VAB 4 138 (Nbk 15=St. Tfl. X) ix 29-32.

[173] VAB 4 140 (Nbk 15=St. Tfl. X) ix 54-56; cf. 114 (Nbk 14=Zyl. III,5) i 53, where both Babylon and Borsippa (the location of Nabû's principal temple) are accorded this praise.

works] which I have inscribed in this document, let the learned read, and let him understand the excellence of the gods."[174]

1.5.4 The King's Enemies

The NB royal inscriptions usually end with a hymn or prayer directed to the patron god. The king makes several requests in the hymns, as a survey of Nebuchadnezzar's inscriptions shows: that the new building intercede before the gods for his welfare; that the king be granted a long reign and progeny; and that the gods either place powerful weapons for battle at his disposal or smash the weapons of all his enemies.[175] While there are occasional references to enemies in the titulary, and Nabopolassar uniquely refers to his defeat of the Assyrians in his call narratives, it is principally in the hymns that the king's enemies are mentioned. These passages are formulaic, not surprisingly, and yield little concrete data about particular foes of the state, only that they existed. This is probably because the legitimate king who fulfills the tasks of the gods and is granted rule over all humanity (as enumerated in the *inūma* sections of the royal inscriptions) cannot have rivals or enemies. The inscriptions assert that all humanity recognizes the preeminence of Babylon and its king, because he has been granted rule over humanity. The gods themselves, therefore, are invoked to eradicate the king's foes (called appropriately, *lā māgirī*, "those ill-disposed," *kidrūtū*, "proud ones," etc.), because of their failure to recognize the divine imprimatur for empire. This was sometimes true in the Neo-Assyrian tradition too, but in the Neo-Babylonian inscriptions, Marduk does not command the king to seek out and conquer rebels, as Aššur commands the Assyrian kings. Such subtleties would no doubt have been lost on Babylon's military victims, but the theory, at least, differs

[174] VAB 4 184 (Nbk 20=Zyl III,8) iii 61-64.

[175] A list of the lines in the hymns pertaining to enemies follows: VAB 4 78 (Nbk 1=Zyl III,3) iii 48-49; VAB 4 78 (Nbk 2=Zyl III,2) iii 37-44; YOS 1 44 (=Zyl II,10) ii 27-29; VAB 4 82 (Nbk 4=Zyl II,8) ii 28-32; VAB 4 84 (Nbk 5=Zyl II,5) ii 23-29; VAB 4 88 (Nbk 7=Zyl II,7) ii 31; VAB 4 100 (Nbk 11=Zyl II,12) ii 21-22; VAB 4 102 (Nbk 12=Zyl III,1) iii 17; VAB 4 120 (Nbk 14=Zyl III,5) iii 52-53; VAB 4 140 (Nbk 15=St. Tfl X) x 13-16 (idem); VAB 4 186 (Nbk 20=Zyl III,8) iii 90; VAB 4 188 (Nbk 21=Zyl Frgm. II,4) ii 46; VAB 4 190 (Nbk 23=Zyl II,3) ii 8-15; VAB 4 202 (Nbk 42=Backst. B I,7) 7; Walker, *Brick Inscriptions*, 91, no. 109:14-18 (=Backst. B I, 15). The brick inscriptions implore the deities to eradicate enemies less often, except where cylinder inscriptions are identical to those on the bricks (see those listed above).

from that of the Assyrian kings. This difference might also help to explain why Neo-Babylonian art so seldom depicts the king in battle conquering foes.

1.5.5 Precedents and Summary

The ideas of empire expressed in Nebuchadnezzar's inscriptions had precedents. Just as the Neo-Babylonian kings took care to rebuild physical structures according to their ancient plans, so they took up from the past ideas about empire and the language used to express such ideas. The royal titulary and the allusions to Nebuchadnezzar II as a second Hammurapi, mentioned above, show a scribal dependency on the inscriptions of the Old Babylonian period, especially Hammurapi's Laws.[176] There is much evidence that the Neo-Babylonian kings (and their scribes) looked to anitiquity, and specifically to the Old Babylonian era, as a source of inspiration for their royal ideology: the resuscitation of the Old Babylonian lapidary script for use in royal inscriptions; deliberate linguistic archaisms and archaizing orthographies;[177] the use of many Old Babylonian royal epithets; the excavation of foundation inscriptions of third- and second-millennium kings of Babylonia, including Hammurapi;[178] and the frequent copying (and even forging) of Old Babylonian inscriptions—all illustrate the immense influence of the Old Babylonian era on the Neo-Babylonian kings generally, and on Nebuchadnezzar in particular. When circumstances demanded the articulation of an imperial creed under Nebuchadnezzar, the Neo-Babylonians drew heavily on language and ideas from the dynasty of Hammurapi, under whom Babylon had emerged into history as an

[176] Berger has tabulated numerous instances where Nebuchadnezzar's inscriptions show dependency on the Laws; see *Königsinschriften*, 94-95.

[177] For a few examples, see above, nn. 109, 138, and 139.

[178] The pioneering work is that of G. Goossens, "Les recherches historiques à l'époque néo-babylonienne," *RA* 42 (1948): 149-59. I cite here one example as an illustration: before restoring the temple of Lugal-Maradda in Marad, Nebuchadnezzar dug a drainage ditch (*mazzaltu*)—in effect a probe—in order to locate the foundation deposit (*temennu*) of the temple's first builder. When this turned out to come from Naram-Sin (2254-2218 B.C.E.), care was taken to place Nebuchadnezzar's new foundation text next to Naram-Sin's ancient one, and to give report of its discovery pride of place in the new inscription (YOS 1 44 [=Zyl II,10] i 24-ii 8). Such efforts were taken to new heights later by Nabonidus. No doubt a principal motive was to establish a link with the distant past for the purpose of legitimating the present (innovative) rule. See also Reiner, *Your Thwarts in Pieces*, 1-16; and Berger, *Königsinschriften*, 92-93.

important city and kingdom. There were few occasions in history when a unified territorial state centered in Babylonia exerted geopolitical influence beyond its own territory. Hammurapi's kingdom was understood in Babylonian tradition to be a notable, if brief, exception. Nebuchadnezzar clearly viewed that era as a model and applied Old Babylonian concepts and language to the new political reality of Neo-Babylonian imperialism.[179] In reality, the Neo-Babylonian empire could not have existed had the Neo-Assyrian kings not established geopolitical hegemony over a wide territory before leaving a political vacuum (see chapter two below). Neo-Babylonian language about empire in Nebuchadnezzar's reign, however, diverges so substantially from Assyrian patterns where we have compared the two that it is reasonable to conclude that the Babylonians were not indebted to Assyrian ideas of empire. On the contrary, they took pains to avoid such ideas. The degree of continuity between Assyria and Babylonia in military and administrative procedures is quite another issue (chapter two below), but at the conceptual level, the Babylonians under Nebuchadnezzar seem not to have taken up the Assyrian mantle.

1.6 Nabonidus's Reformulation

Nabonidus (555-539 B.C.E.), a usurper from outside the royal family and the last native ruler of a Mesopotamian polity, significantly

[179] For a similar phenomenon in seventh-sixth century Saite Egypt, see the discussion (esp. the introduction) of P. Der Manuelian, *Living in the Past: Studies in the Archaism of the Egyptian Twenty-sixth Dynasty* (New York: Routledge, 1994). In Judah during the seventh and sixth centuries there was also a tendency to legitimate the present through past paradigms and personalities: the Deuteronomic presentation of the Torah as a dictation of Moses is a clear example. W. F. Albright already understood this "revival of interest in the past and . . . pronounced tendency to archaism" as a wider phenomenon of the Near East of the seventh century (*From the Stone Age to Christianity*, 2d ed. [Baltimore: Johns Hopkins University Press, 1946], 240-44). For a recent discussion of the phenomenon, see the essays of B. Halpern, "Jerusalem and the Lineages in the Seventh Century B.C.E.: Kinship and the Rise of Individual Moral Liability," in *Law and Ideology in Monarchic Israel*, JSOTSup 124, ed. B. Halpern and D. W. Hobson (Sheffield: Academic, 1991), 11-107; and especially his "Sybil, or the Two Nations? Archaism, Kinship, Alienation, and the Elite Redefinition of Traditional Culture in Judah in the 8th-7th Centuries B.C.E." in *The Study of the Ancient Near East in the Twenty-First Century*, ed. J. S. Cooper and G. Schwartz (Winona Lake, Ind.: Eisenbrauns, 1996), 291-338.

altered the imperial program shaped by Nebuchadnezzar.[180] Two of Nabonidus's best known alterations loom larger than all others. First, he attempted to elevate Sîn, the moon god, to the premier rank in the cult, thereby demoting Marduk, who had been the patron deity of the state probably since the time of Nebuchadnezzar I.[181] Second, Nabonidus attempted to establish continuity between his reign and those of the Sargonid kings of Assyria, especially Assurbanipal.[182] Nabonidus's royal inscriptions reflect these changes not only in their content, but also in their form; he jettisoned or modified many of the literary patterns established by the earlier Neo-Babylonian kings. His break with his predecessors in these matters no doubt owed much to his personality, the topic of much debate, but it also reflects a different conception of the king's role as head of the state and empire. Thus even if the biographical problems remain unclear, the political changes can be assessed. The present discussion requires analysis of the impact that Nabonidus's two principal innovations had on the expression of Babylonian imperial ideas in his royal inscriptions.

As we noted, Nabonidus signals his nonconformist tendencies in the literary form of his royal inscriptions. Langdon summarized a number of these formal innovations and we may update some of his observations.[183] It remains true that only two of Nabonidus's cylinder inscriptions approximate the "titulary . . . *inūma* . . . *inūmīšu* . . . hymn" type that was so common with his predecessors.[184] On the other hand,

---

[180] Scholars pay more attention to the reign and personality of Nabonidus than most subjects associated with the Neo-Babylonian era. It is unnecessary here to discuss all of the issues, as many superb studies are available: see especially R. P. Dougherty, *Nabonidus and Belshazzar: A Study of the Closing Events of the Neo-Babylonian Empire*, YOR 15 (New Haven: Yale University Press, 1929); Landsberger, "Basaltstele"; J. Lewy, "The Late Assyro-Babylonian Cult of the Moon and its Culmination at the Time of Nabonidus," *HUCA* 19 (1946): 405-89; Gadd, "Harran Inscriptions"; Tadmor, "Inscriptions of Nabunaid"; Reiner, *Your Thwarts in Pieces*, 1-16; Beaulieu, *Reign of Nabonidus*; and Machinist and Tadmor, "Heavenly Wisdom."

[181] W. G. Lambert, "The Reign of Nebuchadnezzar I: A Turning Point in the History of Ancient Mesopotamian Religion," in *The Seed of Wisdom; Essays in Honour of T. J. Meek*, ed. W. S. McCullough (Toronto: University of Toronto Press, 1964), 3-13; and more recently W. Sommerfeld, *Der Aufstieg Marduks: Die Stellung Marduks in der babylonischen Religion des zweiten Jahrtausends v. Chr.*, AOAT 213 (Kevelaer: Butzon & Bercker; Neukirchen-Vluyn: Neukirchener, 1982).

[182] Landsberger, "Basaltstele," 147-49.

[183] See his comments in VAB 4, pp. 12-14.

[184] The texts are VAB 4 (Nbn 3=Zyl III,1); and VAB 4 (Nbn 7=Zyl II,8).

one of these two cylinders is unique because instead of describing a building project, it reports the detailed results of a favorable extispicy and the fashioning of a tiara for the cult statue of Šamaš.[185] Another inscription that differs significantly from those of Nabonidus's predecessors is the so-called Sippar cylinder.[186] Moran noted two literary peculiarities in this text, paralleled among Neo-Babylonian inscriptions only in the Harran stele of Nabonidus's mother, Adad-Guppi. These are: the very rare introductory formula *anāku* royal name . . . *anāku*, and the use of the *mannu atta*, "whoever you are" formula to introduce the concluding hortatory section.[187] Moran argued that the *anāku* royal name . . . *anāku* formula has its closest parallels in Assyrian inscriptions,[188] and we have already alluded above to Nabonidus's unique willingness among Neo-Babylonian kings to emulate Assyrian inscriptions, particularly those of Assurbanipal.[189] Three other inscriptions of Nabonidus break with earlier Neo-Babylonian patterns and begin not with the titulary, but with a temporal clause introduced by the adverb *inum*, "when."[190] Yet another inscription is unique in that four independent texts were edited together into a single whole, each unit of the composite text concluding with a hymn to Sîn.[191] Nabonidus's inscriptions introduce still other elements or *topoi* that are unattested in the earlier Neo-Babylonian royal inscriptions: dream reports, dialogues between the king and his building experts, historical narratives, and narratives (once comprising an entire inscription) describing the installation of En-nigaldi-Nanna, Nabonidus's daughter, as *entu* priestess of Sîn at Ur. Not all of these literary innovations point to changes in the imperial program of the earlier Neo-Babylonian kings. Inasmuch as the royal inscriptions served as a public expression of the royal program, however, Nabonidus clearly was signaling a break with his immediate predecessors.

It is well established that Nabonidus attempted to exalt Sîn to premier status in the state cult. The evidence for this has been compiled

---

[185] VAB 4 (Nbn 7=Zyl II,8).

[186] VAB 4 (Nbn 1=Zyl III,2).

[187] Moran, "Notes," 131, and n. 2.

[188] Ibid.

[189] See above, p. 21, n. 62, and below, n. 206.

[190] YOS 1 45 (=Zyl II,7) and OECT 1 pls. 23-28 (=Zyl III,3) and *RA* 11 110 i 1 (=Zyl II,5; duplicate in CT 36 21).

[191] S. Langdon, "New Inscriptions of Nabuna'id," *AJSL* 32 (1915): 102-17.

elsewhere, and need not be rehearsed here.[192] Interest here focuses on the changes that this theological innovation introduced into the language about the divine justification for empire, which with the other kings had previously issued from Marduk. The divine commission undergoes numerous changes under Nabonidus in comparison with the commissions of Nabopolassar and Nebuchadnezzar, discussed above. Such commissions occur less regularly in the inscriptions of Nabonidus and are confined to the first half of his reign, before he returned from his ten-year residency at Teima, in North Arabia.[193] In a stele from the second year of his reign that programmatically outlines his claim to the throne, we read: *i-na a-mat* dAMAR.UTU EN-*ia a-na be-lu-ti* KUR *an-na-ši-ma*, "at the command of Marduk, my lord, I was elevated to rulership of the land."[194] In a cylinder describing the decision to restore the tiara of the cult statue of Šamaš in Sippar, we read: *e-nu-ma* dAMAR.UTU EN GAL-*ú be-lu-ut* KUR-*šú i-qí-pa-an-ni za-na-nu-ut ma-ḫa-za ud-du-šu eš-re-e-ti ú-mal-lu-ú qa-tu-ú-a*, "when Marduk the great lord entrusted me with the rulership of his land, he commissioned me (lit. filled my hands) to provision cult centers and to renew sanctuaries."[195] The restoration of the Ebabbar temple of Šamaš in Sippar, for which the last quoted cylinder is the culminating statement, probably began in Nabonidus's second year.[196] A similar statement probably occurs in another cylinder that commemorates the rebuilding of the Ebabbar temple in Sippar, but the passage in question is mostly broken.[197] After the titulary, which closes with the expected pronoun

---

192 See for a recent survey, with literature, Beaulieu, *Reign of Nabonidus*, 43-65; also Machinist and Tadmor, "Heavenly Wisdom."

193 On the chronology of his stay in Arabia, lasting from his third to thirteenth regnal years, see Tadmor, "Inscriptions of Nabunaid"; and Beaulieu, *Reign of Nabonidus*, 149-69.

194 VAB 4 276 (Nbn 8=Stl. Frgm. XI) v 8-10.

195 VAB 4 262 (Nbn 7=Zyl II,8) i 17-19.

196 Beaulieu, *Reign of Nabonidus*, 25; 132-37

197 The text probably dates to Nabonidus's second or third year, when the king rebuilt the Ebabbar temple of Sippar; see OECT 1 32-37 (=Zyl III,3); Berger, *Königsinscriften*, 111. Beaulieu prefers a date in the tenth year (*Reign of Nabonidus*, 30-31), but I do not find his argument persuasive. He suggests that this text would not have been commissioned to commemorate the rebuilding of the Ebabbar of Sippar because another text already commemorated that construction (VAB 4 [Nbn 6=Zyl II,9]). Thus, in Beaulieu's view, OECT 1 32-37 (=Zyl III,3) must have commemorated a different construction project, perhaps the reconstruction in Nabonidus's tenth year of the ziggurat of Sippar. But the possibility that there were multiple inscriptions (and not simply multiple copies of

anāku, "I," the next line should probably be restored [*e-nu-ma* ^dAMAR.UTU EN GAL-*ú be-lu-ut*] ⌜KUR⌝-*šú i-qí-pa-an-*⌜*ni*⌝, "[when Marduk the great lord] entrusted me [with the rulership] of his land."[198] In one other example we read: *e-nu-ma* ^dAMAR.UTU . . . *a-na be-lu-tu ma-a-tim im-bu-ù ni-bi-tim*, "when Marduk called my name for rulership of the land."[199] The date of this text is uncertain, but Tadmor and Beaulieu both argue that it comes from early in the reign, perhaps between years three and six.[200] In these instances, all from the first nine years of his reign, Nabonidus acknowledges, in conformity with earlier Neo-Babylonian theory, that Marduk designated the king to rule "the land" or "his [Marduk's] land."

Several further observations are warranted. The call reports of Nabonidus discussed above do not refer to "the widespread peoples" or to the king's rule of "the four corners," unlike so many of Nebuchadnezzar's inscriptions. Admittedly, Nabonidus's inscriptions do refer to his reign over the entire world, but they do so only in the titulary and, less often, in the hymns.[201] Mention of the widespread peoples in the titulary, we noted above, is exceptional in the other Neo-Babylonian inscriptions. It is normal in Assyrian royal inscriptions, however, which suggests the possibility that Nabonidus followed an Assyrian paradigm by indicating his rule over the world in the titulary rather than in the commission passages.

During the latter third of his reign, Nabonidus's inscriptions do not mention that he is called to rule by Marduk. This is probably a

---

the same inscription) pertaining to a single building enterprise cannot be ruled out. See above n. 20 for an argument against Beaulieu's conclusion that the temple of Šamaš at Larsa and the ziggurat of Šamaš at Sippar were rebuilt contemporaneously, a conclusion that he bases on the fact that the present Sippar cylinder was found at Larsa. More likely, the cylinder was simply a duplicate copy of a Sippar inscription that the scribes at Larsa used for reference.

198 OECT 1 pl. 23 i 21.

199 *RA* 11 110 (=Zyl II,5) i 24 (duplicate CT 36 21 i 25).

200 Tadmor, "Inscriptions of Nabunaid," 359; Beaulieu, *Reign of Nabonidus*, 26-27.

201 For epithets in Nabonidus's titulary, note the following: *kāšid šadî elûti*, "conqueror of the lofty mountains" (VAB 4 234 [Nbn 3=Zyl III,1] i 10); *rē'û nišī rapšāti*, "shepherd of the widespread peoples" (VAB 4 252 [Nbn 6=Zyl II,9] i 5); and (*ša*) DINGIR.MEŠ GAL.GAL . . . *i-na ki-ib-ra-a-ta er-bé-et-ti ú-ša-ar-bu-ú be-lu-ut-su ku-ul-la-at da-ad-me a-na qí-bi-ti-šu ú-še-ši-bu*, "(the one) whose lordship the great gods have exalted in the four corners, at whose command they settled all inhabited regions" (H. W. F. Saggs, "A Cylinder from Tell al Lahm," *Sumer* 13 [1957]=Zyl II,6 i 25-31).

consequence of his intention to relegate Marduk to a lesser position in the pantheon. Thus, as his program for elevating Sîn in the cult proceeded, the official acknowledgment of Marduk's role as guarantor of royal and imperial prerogatives declined. Sîn then conspicuously assumes this role in a few of Nabonidus's texts: when a summary of the king's career is placed in the mouth of Adad-Guppi, his mother;[202] and in the programmatic stele describing the king's reign and the plan to restore Eḫulḫul, the temple of Sîn in Ḫarran.[203] Now, one might expect that the king's commission would be said to stem from Sîn rather than Marduk in these two texts, given their close associations with the cult of Sîn in Ḫarran. But the issue is a more general one, for in the second half of Nabonidus's reign, reference to Marduk altogether as the patron of the king and the empire becomes attenuated if it does not disappear.

Nabonidus's plan to exalt Sîn changed more than the call narratives and the references to divine authority for imperial rule. His "Harran-Politik," as Landsberger called it, focused on the reconstruction of the Eḫulḫul temple of Sîn in Harran, to which numerous inscriptions are dedicated.[204] Similarly, his Arabian sojourn in the oasis of Teima, probably influenced in part by the devotion paid to the moon god in that region, required construction of a suitable royal palace there. Regardless of whether Nabonidus's religious devotion was the primary consideration in his thinking, the building projects in Harran and Teima necessarily redirected a significant part of the imperial work force, army, and distribution of material goods away from Babylonia. This diminution of Babylon's role as the imperial center of gravity lasted for more than half of Nabonidus's reign. Even if significant economic advantage accrued to Babylonia as a consequence of the king's control of the trade routes in northern Arabia, this shift of gravity could not have been well received by the central establishment, and the polemics against Nabonidus composed after his reign, most notably the Verse Account, confirm this.[205] More important for present purposes, this geopolitical shift westward also directly influenced the language about the justification for empire. Nebuchadnezzar declared in numerous

---

[202] Gadd, "Harran Inscriptions," H1, B i 41-43.

[203] Ibid., H2, A and B i 10-11: *Sîn ana šarrūti* ⌈*ib*⌉*banni*, "Sîn called me to the kingship."

[204] Landsberger, "Basaltstele," 147; for the Harran inscriptions, see Gadd, "Harran Inscriptions," and for a recent addition to the corpus, see W. L. Moran and G. F. Dole, "A Bowl of *alallu*-stone," *ZA* 81 (1991): 267-73.

[205] See especially the discussion of Smith, *BHT*.

inscriptions that he brought the widespread people into the eternal shadow of Babylon, and that he beautified no other place on earth like it. The city itself was in some measure the physical justification of his imperial creed, its splendor a testament to his role as ruler of the world divinely sanctioned by Marduk. None of these sentiments appears in Nabonidus's texts. The shift of focus to the west during Nabonidus's reign ran counter to the previous sixty-five years of Babylonian history. This is not to say that Nabonidus ignored Babylonia; clearly he did not. Nevertheless, the centrifugal forces set in motion by his activities in the west weakened the strong emphasis on the core of the empire established by his predecessors. He thereby disenfranchised important elements of the Akkadian population of Babylonia and possibly hastened the collapse of the state.

This leads to discussion of Nabonidus's second major innovation vis-à-vis Nebuchadnezzar's imperial program: the effort of Nabonidus to forge a link between his reign and those of the Sargonid kings of Assyria. Several literary devices and *topoi* in his royal inscriptions that demonstrate this intention were alluded to above.[206] On the basis of several stelae and a newly discovered rock relief in Jordan, Dalley has remarked too "that Nabonidus was depicted on his official monuments in a way that distinguishes him from his various predecessors."[207] There can be little doubt about the fact of Nabonidus's intention to forge this

---

[206] A list of some of these, and a few others, follows: the Assyrian building consecration ritual using honey mixed in the brick mortar (above n. 62); the use of the royal epithets *šarru dannu*, *šarru rabû*, *šar kiššati*, and *šar kibrāt erbetti*, otherwise exceedingly rare in the NB titulary (above p. 21 and n. 61); the use of other typically Assyrian epithets, e.g., *šar lā šanān*, "king without rival" (VAB 4 230 [Nbn 2=Zyl II,4] i 4; Seux, *Épithètes royales*, 314); references in the titulary to conquest of foreign lands and to rule over "the widespread peoples," which are absent in the other NB titularies but common in the Assyrian ones (above n. 201); reference to "Assurbanipal, king of Assyria, son of Esarhaddon" as a royal predecessor (VAB 4 220 [Nbn 1=Zyl III,2] i 47-48); the reference to the twenty-one years after Sennacherib's sack of Babylon that Marduk turned back his anger from the city, a date that coincides with the early reign of Assurbanipal (VAB 4 [Nbn 8=Stl. Frg. XI] i 26-34; Berger, *Königsinschriften*, 110); respectful mention of the building projects of Assyrian predecessors, especially Assurbanipal (VAB 4 222 [Nbn 1=Zyl III,2] ii 3-4; idem ii 43-46; VAB 4 286 [Nbn 8=Stl. Frg. XI] x 32-37; and compare Gadd, "Harran Inscriptions," H1, B i 29-30; ii 26); use of the epithet *ilu ellu*, "shining god" for Sin, common in late Assyrian tradition (Beaulieu, *Reign of Nabonidus*, 49); use in the titulary of the formula *anāku PN* . . . *anāku*, attested in NA inscriptions (Moran, "Notes," 131); and reference to the imposition of the *nīru*, "yoke," upon conquered people (above n. 75).

[207] Dalley, "A Neo-Babylonian Rock Relief in Southern Jordan," 174.

link, and in particular to portray himself as a successor of Assurbanipal. The question remains as to why he did it and how it bears on the problem of Neo-Babylonian imperial ideology.

The sympathy for Assyrian idioms of imperial rule, like the devotion to Sîn, may have resulted partly from Nabonidus's origins in the Aramaic West, which in the seventh century was heavily Assyrianized, and the fact that his mother (at least, and perhaps his father too) owed her status to the patronage of Assurbanipal, as several scholars argued long ago.[208] Beaulieu recently suggested another reason. He argued that the central political problem of Nabonidus's early reign was whether the Medes or Babylonians would maintain the geopolitical upper hand in the Near East; resolution of the problem, in Beaulieu's view, would determine the true imperial heir of the Assyrians.[209] No doubt the Median/Persian conflicts were a significant problem for Nabonidus. However, given the arguments above about Nabopolassar's and especially Nebuchadnezzar's efforts to forge a model of Babylonian imperial rule that consciously avoided Assyrian imperial idioms, it would seem that the idea of imperial succession to Assyria was already a moot point. The great imperial successes of the Babylonians under Nebuchadnezzar, grounded in a coherent and specifically Babylonian ideology, weaken Beaulieu's argument. It is necessary to think of a revival of Assyrian concepts more than a continuation of them, and this is what Nabonidus attempted to accomplish. Perhaps a fully satisfactory answer as to why Nabonidus sought to forge a link with the Assyrian tradition may not emerge. Possibly Nabonidus viewed his Neo-Babylonian predecessors' excessive preoccupation with Babylon and the refurbishing of the great cities of Babylonia as a fundamentally unstable political policy, one that left the imperial periphery underdeveloped. Perhaps he thought that the empire could not thrive absent a more rationally developed bureaucracy in the periphery, although it is not clear that he attempted to implement such a bureaucracy. An example of a devolved bureaucratic system was available in the Assyrian tradition. Nabonidus may then have sought to establish regular relations with distant western regions and to justify his notions of imperial rule by frequent references to Assyrian ideas and procedures. This reconstruction is admittedly speculative, and should be understood as

---

[208] Landsberger, "Basaltstele"; Lewy, "Assyro-Babylonian Cult of the Moon," 418 and n. 74.

[209] Beaulieu, *Reign of Nabonidus*, 109-11.

such. The question as to why Nabonidus pursued policies and ideas that deviated so considerably from his predecessors, however, is one that still requires a satisfactory solution.

CHAPTER 2

BABYLONIAN IMPERIAL ADMINISTRATION IN THE LEVANT

2.1 Introduction

The diachronic analysis of Babylonian imperial ideas in chapter one provides a framework within which to investigate Neo-Babylonian military actions and administrative procedures in the western part of the empire. The largely parochial Babylonian interests in the reign of Nabopolassar, the development of a self-conscious imperial worldview under Nebuchadnezzar, and the significant alterations to that worldview in the inscriptions of Nabonidus should find some expression in the military actions and administrative mechanisms that consolidated and sustained the empire in the conquered territories. The first purpose of the present chapter, then, is to outline the military and administrative mechanisms of the Babylonian empire. In conformity with the method pursued in chapter one, the second purpose will be to evaluate whether there was significant continuity between the Babylonian imperial system and that of the Assyrians.[1] In view of the conclusion reached above that

[1] There is a large literature on Assyrian imperialism, including, among others, the pioneering study of E. Forrer, *Die Provinzeinteilung des assyrischen Reiches* (Leipzig: Hinrichs, 1920); for a recent series of essays that reassesses the geography of the empire and its administration, see M. Liverani, ed., *Neo-Assyrian Geography*, Quaderni di Geografia Storica 5 (Rome: Università di Roma "La Sapienza," 1995); also J. N. Postgate, *Taxation and Conscription in the Assyrian Empire* (Rome: Pontifical Biblical Institute, 1974); J. Pečírková, "The Administrative Organization of the Neo-Assyrian Empire," *ArOr* 45 (1977): 211-28; idem, "The Administrative Methods of Assyrian Imperialism," *ArOr* 55 (1987): 162-75; I. Eph'al "Assyrian Dominion in Palestine," WHJP 4/1, *The Age of the Monarchies: Political History*, ed. A. Malamat (Jerusalem: Massada, 1979); P. Machinist, "Palestine, Administration of (Assyro-Babylonian)," *ABD*, ed. D. N. Freedman (Garden City, N.Y.: Doubleday, 1992), 5.69-81; with attention to the possibility of using modern theories of imperialism in analyzing the Neo-Assyrian period, see R. Lamprichs, *Die Westexpansion des neuassyrischen Reiches: Eine Strukturanalyse*, AOAT 239 (Kevelaer: Butzon & Bercker; Neukirchen-Vluyn: Neukirchener, 1995); and S.

there was a disjunction between the imperial ideas of the Assyrians and Babylonians, we should not assume that their administrative procedures were identical, or that the Babylonians, as the putative heirs to empire, simply adopted Assyrian practices.[2]

In chapter one, it was necessary to note that the content of the Neo-Babylonian royal inscriptions placed certain limitations on the specificity possible for describing imperial ideas. Elements of the imperial worldview emerge from the inscriptions, but they must be described at a relatively high level of abstraction; it is not possible to articulate a set of operative imperial principles. Similarly, the sources that bear upon imperial administration are problematic. The subject of the present chapter is specifically the administration of the western territories, rather than the economic or political organization of the heartland as revealed in the many thousands of Neo-Babylonian archival texts. Cuneiform sources concerning the periphery, however, are few; only the Babylonian chronicles and a few administrative tablets are directly relevant for reconstructing aspects of the imperial administration in the periphery. The royal inscriptions yield some data regarding the administrative and economic geography of the empire, and a few lists of Babylonian officials and foreign tributaries in the royal inscriptions together with studies of the foreign onomastica in Babylonian inscriptions offer some details about the territories under Babylonian control. Still, given the many thousands of Neo-Babylonian archival tablets, the evidence for imperial administration beyond the heartland is sparse.[3] Additional evidence comes from non-cuneiform textual sources:

Gitin, "The Neo-Assyrian Empire and its Western Periphery: The Levant, with a Focus on Philistine Ekron," in *Assyria 1995*, ed. S. Parpola and R. M. Whiting (Helsinki: Neo-Assyrian Text Corpus Project, 1996), 77-103; I. J. Winter, "Art *in* Empire: The Royal Image and the Visual Dimensions of Assyrian Ideology," in *Assyria 1995*, ed. S. Parpola and R. M. Whiting (Helsinki: Neo-Assyrian Text Corpus Project, 1996), 359-81 with literature.

[2] For a similar caution about assuming continuity between Assyrian and Babylonian procedures, but in an analysis that focuses on the Achaemenid period, see K. Hoglund, *Achaemenid Imperial Administration in Syria-Palestine and the Missions of Ezra and Nehemiah*, SBLDS 125 (Atlanta: Scholars, 1992), 18-23.

[3] The thesis that much of the documentation may have been written in Phoenician or Aramaic and upon perishable materials is probable, but hard to prove. Oppenheim emphasized that Nebuchadnezzar's "chief merchant" (^{lú}GAL.DAM.GAR) bears the Phoenician name Ḫanunu, and may have composed records in a West Semitic script on perishable materials ("Essay on Overland Trade," 253). Of course the steady increase in the practice of adding Aramaic dockets to cuneiform tablets and the emergence of a class of scribes of alphabetic scripts (called

the HB, the Greek historians, and Egyptian texts. Also important is the increasing volume of archeological data, mainly from Cisjordan and Philistia. The archeological materials provide an important perspective on the problem that the textual sources alone do not illuminate. A selective review of these sources where they bear on Babylonian rule in the Levant should prove helpful.

How, then, did the abstract imperial ideas of the Neo-Babylonian kings, especially Nebuchadnezzar, find expression in the mechanics of imperial administration? It is the task of chapter three to assess the variety of responses to Babylonian imperial ideas and procedures that subjugated groups, particularly Judah, generated. In this chapter it is first necessary to clarify the mechanisms that would have mediated Babylonian actions and ideas to those populations. The analysis focuses on the southern Levant, where the data are most plentiful.[4]

2.2 The Contraction of Assyria and Egypt's Rise in the Southern Levant

The largely parochial focus of Babylonian politics under Nabopolassar dovetails with the absence of that figure from the biblical record and the absence in the Levantine archeological record of clear indications of Neo-Babylonian incursions or influence before the reign of Nebuchadnezzar. To understand the logic of subsequent Neo-Babylonian policy and administration in the west during Nebuchadnezzar's reign, however, it is necessary to review briefly the situation there before his arrival. Two related issues in particular deserve attention: the waning and collapse of Assyrian control in the west during the second half of Assurbanipal's reign (668-627 B.C.E.); and the

---

sepīru, see *CAD* S, 225) demonstrate that there was increased dependence on that language. The other common explanation for the absence of such information is the fact that excavators have uncovered temple archives, but not palace ones.

[4] The surveys of Babylonian rule in the west concentrate largely on Judah. The following are examples of thorough, balanced accounts: H. Tadmor, "The Period of the First Temple, the Babylonian Exile and the Restoration," in *A History of the Jewish People*, ed. H. H. Ben-Sasson (Cambridge: Harvard University Press, 1976), 91-159; A. Malamat, "The Last Years of the Kingdom of Judah," in WHJP, Vol. 4/1, *The Age of the Monarchies: Political History*, ed. A. Malamat (Jerusalem: Massada, 1979), 205-21; J. H. Hayes and J. M. Miller, *A History of Ancient Israel and Judah* (Philadelphia: Westminster, 1986), 377-436; and Machinist, "Palestine, Administration of."

resurgence of Egyptian power during the reign of Psammetichus I (664-610 B.C.E.).

2.2.1 The Contraction of Assyria

Within a span of little more than fifteen years, between about 657 and 639, several important events badly eroded Assyria's expansionist imperial program. The first was Assurbanipal's inability to maintain control of Egypt after his conquests there, followed by the emergence of a reunited Egypt under Psammetichus I. The Assyrian loss of Egypt was not an isolated event, however, but converged with several others. In the northwest, several emerging powers, including the Cimmerians and the Lydians, actively challenged Assyrian hegemony in Asia Minor. Closer to home, between 652 and 648 there was a protracted anti-Assyrian rebellion in Babylonia, led by Šamaš-šuma-ukīn, Assurbanipal's brother.[5] The rebellion had been a long time in the making, and although Assurbanipal did quell it, many populations that had been previously subjugated by Assyria rose up to aid the Babylonians, notably the Arabs and the Elamites.[6] Assurbanipal's victory over Šamaš-šuma-ukīn, therefore, ultimately did not enhance the interests of the empire abroad, since the Assyrians had to launch numerous campaigns of reprisal against Babylon's erstwhile allies. The most costly of these may have been against the Elamites, for although Assurbanipal succeeded in almost completely annihilating the Elamite state, it was a Pyrrhic victory.[7] In sum, the loss of Egypt and the encroachment on Assyrian territory in the northwest, coupled with the debilitating military expenditures in Babylonia, Elam, and against the Arabs, effectively brought an end to the expansionist era of the Assyrian state.

Other indications support this general reconstruction. The decade of the 640s witnessed several important shifts in Assyrian literary and recording procedures connected with the royal administration. First,

---

[5] For analyses of the Babylonian revolt, see, e.g, Frame, *Babylonia, 689-627 B.C.*, 131-87; and Brinkman, *Prelude to Empire*, 93-104.

[6] For discussion of the Elamite wars, see the previous note; on the Assyrian campaigns against the Arabs, see I. Eph'al, *The Ancient Arabs. Nomads on the Borders of the Fertile Crescent, 9th-5th Centuries B.C.* (Leiden: Brill, 1982), 155-69.

[7] So A. K. Grayson, "Assyria 668-635 B.C.: The Reign of Assurbanipal," in *CAH*, 2d ed., vol. 3, part 2, *The Assyrian and Babylonian Empires and Other States of the Near East, from the Eighth to the Sixth Centuries B.C.*, ed. J. A. Boardman, et al. (Cambridge: Cambridge University Press, 1991), 147-54, 160.

towards the end of the decade, or by 638 at the latest, the royal scribes ceased compiling the annals of Assurbanipal, so that no royal inscriptions exist for the last twelve or so years of his reign. Apparently, the Assyrian king no longer engaged in annual campaigns that demanded continued updating of the annals. Second, the canonical eponym lists and eponym chronicles end at the beginning of the decade, in 649. The appointment of eponyms for the purpose of year dating continued after 649, but evidence for the existence of eponyms comes from disparate administrative tablets; compilation of systematic lists apparently ceased. Moreover, there are too many eponyms for the available years between 648 and 612, a fact that demands some hypothesis for its resolution—perhaps there were competing royal centers appointing eponyms during part of the period.[8] It would seem that no recording system replaced either the royal annals or the canonical eponym lists during the last three decades of Assyria's existence. The disappearance of these methods—inferred, admittedly, from the absence of data—is perhaps another indication of disruptions in the Assyrian imperial program and administrative bureaucracy well before the death of Assurbanipal.

Some scholars have suggested that the Assyrian provincial organization of the southwestern part of the empire nevertheless remained intact down to the death of Assurbanipal in about 627.[9] Na'aman in particular has argued that Assyrian control of the region did not diminish before the 620s, although he acknowledges that clear evidence in support of this argument is lacking.[10] While Na'aman argues for continued Assyrian hegemony, Malamat and Eph'al have argued for the opposite view: that Assyrian intervention in the governance of the

---

[8] For the problem and various possible solutions to it, including the idea of competing centers, see, R. Whiting, "The Post-Canonical and Extra-Canonical Eponyms," in *The Eponyms of the Assyrian Empire, 910-612 B.C.*, by A. Millard, SAAS 2 (Helsinki: The Neo-Assyrian Text Corpus Project, 1994), 72-73; and Reade, "Assyrian Eponyms," 255-65.

[9] For the persistence of the province of Samaria, e.g., see A. Alt, "Die Rolle Samarias bei der Entstehung des Judentums," in *Festschrift Otto Proksch zum 60. Geburtstag* (Leipzig: Dekhurt and Hinrich, 1934); reprinted in *Kleine Schriften zur Geschichte des Volkes Israel* (Munich: C. H. Beck, 1959), 2.316-37 (page references are to the reprint edition); and for a more general statement, Y. Aharoni, *The Land of the Bible: A Historical Geography*, 2d ed., trans. and ed. A. Rainey (Philadelphia: Westminster, 1979), 408.

[10] Na'aman states that "it seems that no one managed to oust Assyria from Syria and Palestine before Ashurbanipal's death" ("The Kingdom of Judah under Josiah," *TA* 18 [1991]: 38); and "it seems that no element endangered the Assyrian control of Syria and Palestine prior to the death of Ashurbanipal" (ibid., 40).

southern Levantine provinces and subject states disappears by about the end of the 640s.[11] At Gezer, an Assyrian tablet from Sivan 651 bears a date according to the eponym of the previous year (*ša arki*), even though there had been no delay in determining the eponym for that year in the heartland (attested in Nineveh by the fourth of Nisan).[12] Ephʿal infers that this indicates a breakdown in communication with the west. In addition, the Rassam cylinder of Assurbanipal, written about 643/642, states that the king undertook a punitive action to quell a rebellion in Ušu (mainland Tyre) and Akko in 645/44.[13] Apart from razzias against the Arabs, which Ephʿal argues continued until the late 640s,[14] this is apparently the last punitive action of the Assyrians in the west,[15] and none of Assurbanipal's annals can be dated securely after 639/638; the annals probably did not continue.

All of this indirect evidence for declining Assyrian influence in the western periphery perhaps receives additional support from the geographical distribution of the Assyrian eponym officials. The canonical eponym list ends in 649, as mentioned, and in the years 651-649 the eponym officials come from Harran, Tyre, and Carchemish, all western provinces. The post-canonical eponomy of Nabû-šar-aḫḫēšu, *bēl pāḫiti/šaknu*, "governor," of the province of Samaria, dates to 646/645.[16] After this, however, the only eponym of the post-canonical group chosen from the Levant is Mannu-kī-aḫḫē, *šaknu*, "governor," of Ṣimir in northern Phoenicia, but it is not possible to fix the date of his eponymy, and J. Reade has wondered whether Mannu-kī-aḫḫē is perhaps identical with Iddin-aḫḫē, eponym in 688.[17] Although the

---

[11] A. Malamat, "Josiah's Bid for Armegeddon: The Background of the Judean-Egyptian Encounter in 609 B.C.," *JANES* 5 (1973 [Gaster Festschrift]), 270-71; and Ephʿal, "Assyrian Dominion," 281-82; this view was upheld recently by Cogan and Tadmor, *II Kings*, 291-92; and by Machinist, "Palestine, Administration of," 72-73.

[12] R. A. S. Macalister, *The Excavation at Gezer* (London: Palestine Exploration Fund, 1912), 1.23-29 (and for a photo of the tablet, see the frontispiece); Ephʿal, "Assyrian Dominion," 281; Brinkman, *Prelude*, 94 and n. 463.

[13] Borger, *BIWA* 69 A ix 115-28; Cogan and Tadmor, *II Kings*, 275-76 and n. 2.

[14] Ephʿal, *Ancient Arabs*, 157-59, 164-65 and n. 562.

[15] Ephʿal, "Assyrian Dominion," 282.

[16] Whiting, "The Post-Canonical and Extra-Canonical Eponyms," 75.

[17] Reade, "Assyrian Eponyms," 255. Among other western eponyms—as distinct from those in the southern Levant—from the post-canonical period, we have: Nabû-daʾʾinanni (643?) and Marduk-šarru-uṣur (631?), both of whom were *šākin* [uru]*Qūʾe*, "governor of Cilicia" (Millard, *Eponyms*, 100; and Reade, "Assyrian

eponym officials were not the only representatives of the administration in the provinces—and the lists thus provide only a partial picture—nevertheless in outline the geographical distribution of the canonical and post-canonical eponyms at the end of the 640s down to 609 points to continued Assyrian administration in the upper Euphrates region and Cilicia, but not in points south. Another piece of evidence pointing to continued Assyrian control of the upper Euphrates and Cilicia is the ability of Aššur-uballiṭ II, the last Assyrian king, to retreat to Harran and establish temporary rule there after the destruction of Nineveh in 612. Also, four recently discovered Neo-Assyrian tablets from Tell Šēḫ Ḥamad (Dūr Katlimmu) on the Ḫabur, which date to the first years of the reign of Nebuchadnezzar II, demonstrate that Assyrian scribal and presumably other institutions had persisted in this region too until the collapse of the Assyrian state, and even beyond.[18] Evidence from Tell Aḥmar on the left bank of the Euphrates south of Carchemish likewise indicates a continuous Assyrian presence in the region until the rise of the Babylonian state.[19] The Assyrians, thus, maintained an administrative presence in the upper Euphrates region almost until the collapse of the state. The evidence does not exist, however, to affirm that this was true of the southern Levant too.

It has been argued that Josiah of Judah (640-609) initiated his program of religious reforms just at the moment of Assurbanipal's death, when struggles over accession arose in Assyria, and that Josiah's reform might have been contemporary with the first stages in the dissolution of Assyrian rule in the Levant.[20] The serious problems in correlating the date of Assurbanipal's death and the beginning of Josiah's reform,

---

Eponyms," 256); Aššur-šarru-uṣur was *turtānu* of Marqasu (north of Zinjirli) during Assurbanipal's reign (about 643 B.C.E. according to Whiting, "Post-Canonical Eponyms," 75; 641 B.C.E. according to Reade, "Assyrian Eponyms," 256); while the latest western eponym was apparently Ṣalmu-šarru-iqbi, the *turtānu* of Kummuḫu (north of Carchemish) during the reign of Sin-šar-iškun, who came to the throne after Assurbanipal's death (627) and reigned until 612. Ṣalmu-šarru-iqbi's eponymate might date to about 623 (Whiting, "Post-Canonical Eponyms"; the precise date of Sin-šar-iškun's accession remains uncertain).

[18] See Röllig, "Zur historischen Einordnung der Texte," 129-32.

[19] G. Bunnens, "Til Barsib under Assyrian Domination: A Brief Account of the Melbourne University Excavations at Tell Ahmar," in *Assyria 1995*, ed. S. Parpola and R. M. Whiting (Helsinki: Neo-Assyrian Text Corpus Project, 1997), 17-28.

[20] The hypothesis received influential expression by F.M. Cross, Jr. and D. N. Freedman, "Josiah's Revolt Against Assyria," *JNES* 12 (1953): 56-58.

however, make a direct causal relationship uncertain.[21] According to the account in 2 Kings, the reform began no earlier than Josiah's eighteenth year, 622 (2 Kgs 22:3). The Chronicler, however, antedated the start of the reform to the king's twelfth year, 628 (2 Chr 34:3). The question remains unresolved whether the Chronicler's order of events is a more plausible reconstruction than that of Kings.[22] Even if it is, the emerging consensus that Assurbanipal died in 627 still does not coincide with the beginning of the reform, and J. Reade continues to argue for 631 as the date of Assurbanipal's death.[23] Furthermore, if, as just argued, there had been a decline in Assyrian control over the region before Assurbanipal's death, it would be unnecessary to argue that Josiah's reform must have coincided with the demise of Assurbanipal.[24] Whether, finally, Josiah's reform included the intention to establish a "greater Judah," and whether he did expand the state to include part or all of the province of Samaria, the Shephelah, and perhaps coastal sites such as Meṣad Ḥashavyahu, likewise is uncertain.[25]

All of the above evidence argues for the contraction of Assyrian imperial hegemony already beginning in the 640s, during the second half of the reign of Assurbanipal but before his death. There were disruptions in Assyrian administrative recording procedures during the decade of the 640s; there is a lack of evidence for Assyrian administration or governance of the southern Levant after the 640s; with one possible exception—an eponym of uncertain date from northern Phoenicia—there are no post-canonical Assyrian eponyms in the southern Levant after 646/645; and the Josianic religious reform and associated political expansion cannot be used as evidence to date the beginning of Assyria's contraction. There is no reason to suppose, in other words, that the Assyrians still exerted effective control in the southern Levant after the 640s.

---

[21] For bibliography on the Assyrian chronology, see above chapter 1, n. 84; see also Cogan and Tadmor, *II Kings*, 298-99.

[22] For discussions, with literature, see Cogan and Tadmor, *II Kings*, 298-99; Na'aman, "Judah under Josiah," 38 and n. 45; and S. Japhet, *I & II Chronicles*, OTL (Louisville: Westminster/John Knox, 1993): 1018-20.

[23] For bibliography on the problematic Assyrian chronology in this period, see above, chapter 1, n. 84; for Reade's perspective, see "Assyrian Eponyms," 261-63.

[24] Cogan and Tadmor, *II Kings*, 293.

[25] Na'aman, e.g., has recently argued for a minimal reconstruction of Judean territorial control during Josiah's reign ("Judah under Josiah").

2.2.2 Egypt's Rise in the Southern Levant

With the waning or collapse of Assyrian control in the Levant during the latter half of the reign of Assurbanipal, Egypt moved to reestablish its influence in the region. Pharaoh Psammetichus I (664-610 B.C.E.), founder of the Twenty-Sixth or Saite Dynasty, threw off Nubian and Assyrian domination and reunited Egypt; during his rule the country experienced something of a political and cultural renewal, in part modeled on earlier eras of Egyptian imperial grandeur.[26] Psammetichus may have attempted to revive the New Kingdom policy of expansion into the Levant. Two questions related to the Egyptian presence in Syria-Palestine are important for understanding subsequent Babylonian policy and administration there. First, when did the substantive shift from Assyrian to Egyptian influence in the Levant take place? Second, was the presence of the Egyptians in the region a function of an expansionist foreign policy, or was it a by-product of increased commercial ties with the Levantine coastal region?

Sometime before 653, Psammetichus I withheld tribute from Assurbanipal and expelled the Assyrian garrison stationed at Memphis. After a short time he consolidated his control over the petty rulers of Lower and Middle Egypt and governed without further interference from Assurbanipal.[27] As mentioned above, Assurbanipal could no longer exert effective pressure in the Nile region because of serious disruptions

---

[26] For the early history of the Twenty-Sixth Dynasty, see the study of F. K. Kienitz, *Die politische Geschichte Ägyptens vom 7. bis zum 4. Jahrhundert vor der Zeitwende* (Berlin: Akademie, 1953), 11-47; and idem, "Die Saïtische Renaissance," in *Fischer Weltgeschichte*, vol. 4. *Die altorientalische Reiche, III: Die erste Hälfte des I. Jahrtausends*, ed. E. Cassin et al. (Frankfurt: Fischer Taschenbuch, 1968), 256-82; also A. Spalinger, "Psammetichus, King of Egypt I," *JARCE* 13 (1976): 133-47; idem, "Psammetichus, King of Egypt II," *JARCE* 15 (1978): 49-57; idem, "Egypt, History of (Dyn. 21-26)," *ABD*, ed. D. N. Freedman (Garden City, N.Y.: Doubleday, 1992), 2.360-61; and D. B. Redford, *Egypt, Canaan, and Israel in Ancient Times* (New Jersey: Princeton University Press, 1992), 430-35. For a detailed discussion of certain archaizing tendencies of the Twenty-Sixth Dynasty "renaissance," see Der Manuelian, *Living in the Past*.

[27] On Psammetichus's achievement of independence, see Kienitz, "Die Saïtische Renaissance," 258; also Spalinger, "Psammetichus, King of Egypt I"; T. G. H. James, "Egypt: the Twenty-fifth and Twenty-sixth Dynasties," in *CAH*, 2d ed., vol. 3, part 2, *The Assyrian and Babylonian Empires and Other States of the Near East, from the Eighth to the Sixth Centuries B.C.*, ed. J. A. Boardman, et al. (Cambridge: Cambridge University Press, 1991), 708-14; and Redford, *Egypt, Canaan, and Israel*, 432-33. For the Palestinian perspective, see Eph'al, "Assyrian Dominion," 364-65, n. 12.

closer to home, including the rebellion of Šamaš-šuma-ukīn in Babylonia between 652 and 648, and the Assyrian wars with the Elamites and Arabs that continued to the end of the 640s.[28]

Evidence for Egyptian presence in the Levant increases throughout the second half of the seventh century. Much of this evidence comes from excavations and therefore lacks a precise date, while datable textual sources that clearly point to Egyptian control of the region cluster in the period after 620. Thus, for the period from about 640 to about 620, only indirect evidence exists to illuminate the Egyptian presence in the Levant.

A disputed datum that possibly concerns this poorly documented period is the brief narrative of Herodotus about Psammetichus's twenty-nine year siege and ultimate capture of the city Ἄζωτος (Azōtus), Ashdod (1.2.157).[29] Tadmor suggested the possibility that Herodotus's reference to a twenty-nine year siege might refer to Psammetichus's capture of Ashdod in his twenty-ninth regnal year, thus 635 B.C.E.[30] Herodotus notes, without his customary incredulity, that this is the longest siege of which he had ever heard. If Tadmor's suggestion is correct, this would be important evidence for Egyptian military penetration into Philistia quite soon after the waning of Assyrian influence.

In any event, the Egyptian presence is most clear in the coastal region—from the Philistine plain as far as the cities of Phoenicia—which suggests that Egyptian interest focused on the Via Maris and sea traffic in the eastern Mediterranean. Again, it is necessary to emphasize that extant Egyptian inscriptions that refer to or were discovered in the region have either imprecise dates or date only to the last two decades of the century: the statue inscription of Hor, probably from the reign of Psammetichus I, refers to "cedar of the (royal) domain," and implies some type of Egyptian control over Phoenicia and the Lebanon;[31] there is a statue of Psammetichus I from Arwad, and possibly another

---

[28] See above nn. 5 and 6, and the survey of I. Diakonoff, "Elam," in *The Cambridge History of Iran*, vol. 2, *The Median and Achaemenian Periods*, ed. I. Gershevitch (Cambridge: Cambridge University Press, 1985), 1-24.

[29] Herodotus, *Works*, rev. ed., trans. A. D. Godley, Loeb Classical Library 117 (Cambridge: Havard University Press, 1990), 468-70. All citations and quotations of Herodotus are from the Loeb edition.

[30] Tadmor, "Philistia under Assyrian Rule," 102; Cogan and Tadmor, *II Kings*, 300 and n. 29.

[31] *ARE* §970 and §967 note g.

fragment from Tyre; there is a stele of Necho II at Sidon;[32] and the Walters Art Gallery statuette of Pa-di-ese, the so-called "messenger of Canaan and Philistia," may come from this period.[33] There is only indirect proof that Egypt exerted its influence in the region earlier. When Egyptian presence does become tangible, the question arises whether this points only to commercial contact, or rather to direct political domination. Redford and Spalinger see the Egyptian presence as a reflex of expansionism, while Katzenstein, for example, prefers the commercial interpretation.[34] Whether there was overt political intervention remains unclear; at the least, there seems not to have been any systematic military pressure, if the absence of recorded battles in the Levant during the reign of Psammetichus I is indicative. Furthermore, destruction layers at both coastal and inland sites in the Levant from the late seventh and early sixth centuries are more plausibly linked with Babylonian incursions. An exception may be Ashdod, if, as we discussed, Herodotus's narrative concerns Psammetichus's capture of the city (Azōtus) after a twenty-nine year siege (1.2.157). M. Dothan, the excavator of Ashdod, suggested that the occupational level represented by stratum 7 covered much of the seventh century. He identified two phases within stratum 7, an earlier, 7b, and a later, 7a. Dothan hypothesized, on the basis of Herodotus's narrative, that the transition between the two phases might have been linked to the conquest of the

---

[32] For references to these, see Katzenstein, *Tyre*, 299 n. 24; 313 n. 100; and Malamat, "Twilight," 128 n. 10.

[33] Spalinger, "Egypt and Babylonia," 229. The broader question of Egyptian cultural influence in the Levant and its relationship to the political influence of the Twenty-Sixth Dynasty would repay further study. A broadly Egyptianizing style in the art of the Levant during this era need not be directly correlated to the rise of Saite power, since Egyptian cultural influence was mediated through Phoenician channels throughout the eighth and seventh centuries. One notable example is a recently discovered incised bovine scapula from Tel Dor, which the excavator dates to the second half of the seventh century. It has a Phoenician maritime scene but betrays strong Egyptianizing influences (see E. Stern, "A Phoenician-Cypriote Votive Scapula from Tel Dor: A Maritime Scene," *IEJ* 44 [1994]: 1-12).

[34] On Saite commercial achievements, see Redford, *Egypt, Israel, and Canaan*, 435 and nn. 21-22. Katzenstein writes that "it should be stressed that until that year [610] there was no real Egyptian overlordship over Greater Syria and Phoenicia . . ." but that with Necho II "an active policy of Egyptian expansion was inaugurated" (*Tyre*, 298, 302). Kienitz argues the opposite: "Der Thronwechsel in Ägypten [Psammetichus I to Necho II] bedeutete keinen Wechsel in der Außenpolitik," which had been expansionist since the reign of the former (*Politische Geschichte Ägyptens*, 20).

site by Psammetichus I.[35] There are some Egyptian objects associated with stratum 7a, but too few to argue that it was occupied by Egyptians.[36] Dothan's interpretation of the stratigraphy at Ashdod was so clearly influenced by Herodotus's narrative that one would do well not to invoke Ashdod 7b as corroborating evidence for Egyptian penetration into Philistia. The duration and scope of the Egyptian influence are difficult to assess precisely because most sites in the region were undisturbed through the seventh century until the Babylonian invasions.

Additional data for evaluating the Egyptian presence exists in the form of material culture from late seventh-century destruction layers at other sites. Remains from the 604 B.C.E. destruction of Ashkelon by Nebuchadnezzar, confirmed by the Babylonian chronicle, include numerous Egyptian artifacts.[37] Stager argues that not all of these artifacts derive from purely commercial interaction.[38] In addition to a hoard of bronzes discovered by Iliffe in 1936, but attributed incorrectly by him to the Persian period,[39] recent excavations at Ashkelon have uncovered seven bronze *situlae* depicting Egyptian religious scenes, ceramics composed of Nile clay, a figurine of Osiris, fragments of an Egyptian

---

[35] M. Dothan and Y. Porath, *Ashdod IV. ʿAtiqot* (English Series) 15 (1982): 57-58.

[36] Note the impression on a clay bulla depicting a man (a king?) crouching, facing right, from area M. "On the right side is a cartouche, probably *men-kheper-re*" (*Ashdod IV*, 40-41; fig. 27:7; pl. 24:11). There is also at least one unstratified scarab attributed to the seventh century (ibid., 48).

[37] On the destruction of Ashkelon in 604, reported in the Babylonian chronicle, see TCS 5 chron 5 obv. 18. Dr. Irving Finkel of the British Museum collated the tablet anew on behalf of Prof. Lawrence Stager, and Finkel confirms that the best reading is URU.⌈*iš-qi*⌉-*il-lu-mu*. See L. E. Stager, "Ashkelon and the Archaeology of Destruction: Kislev 604 B.C.E.," *EI* 25 (Joseph Aviram Volume) (1996): 72* n. 1.

[38] See Stager, "Ashkelon and the Archaeology of Destruction," *68-*69. It is probable that the material from the destruction level should not date too long before the moment of destruction in Kislev 604. The large amount of restorable pottery in the destruction layer indicates that most of it was actually in use in late 604. Thus the other material excavated in association with such end-use pottery, including the Egyptian finds, cannot date long before such pottery would have become functional.

[39] Stager redates the hoard on the basis of a related Osiris figurine excavated in the 604 B.C.E. destruction and the discovery of bronze cuboid weights that are found in seventh-century Philistine contexts, but not in the Persian period ("Ashkelon and the Archaeology of Destruction," 69*).

bronze offering table,[40] a figurine of the god Bes, and nine small Egyptian (or Egypto-Phoenician) amulets in an abalone-shell box. These all suggest the presence of an Egyptian enclave at Ashkelon sometime before the city's destruction; Stager suspects that there may have been an Egyptian sanctuary at the site.[41]

The excavations at Tel Miqne-Ekron have also produced a number of Egyptian objects, mainly from stratum IB, the last stratum before the destruction of the site by the Babylonians at the end of the seventh century.[42] The small finds include a fragment of an inscribed sistrum,[43] a Twenty-Sixth Dynasty scarab, an Egyptian (or Egyptianizing) figurine,[44] a remarkable gold uraeus which presumably was part of a diadem,[45] and numerous faience and shell amulets and figurines. Two other Egyptian finds are noteworthy: a 40-centimeter long elephant tusk with an image of an Egyptian goddess and the cartouche of Merneptah (thirteenth century);[46] and an ivory knob with the cartouche of Ramses VIII (twelfth century), both from what the excavators label

---

[40] Compare another fragment of "une table à libation" of Saite style from Tyre, where there was also Egyptian influence in this period (Katzenstein, *Tyre*, 299, n. 24).

[41] Stager, "Ashkelon and the Archaeology of Destruction," 69*; see also, with additional photos, idem, "The Fury of Babylon: The Archaeology of Destruction," *BAR* 22 (1996): 59-66.

[42] The excavators suggest a date around 630 for the transition from stratum IC to IB, which corresponds with their presumed date for the transfer of control in the southern Levant from Assyria to Egypt (S. Gitin, "Tel Miqne-Ekron: A Type-Site for the Inner Coastal Plain in the Iron Age II Period," in *Recent Excavations in Israel: Studies in Iron Age Archaeology*, ed. S. Gitin and W. G. Dever, [AASOR 49; Winona Lake, Ind.: Eisenbrauns, 1989], 45-46). Given the uncertainty about the date for this historical transition, however, the beginning of stratum IB at Ekron cannot be dated with precision.

[43] See the photo in S. Gitin and T. Dothan, "Ekron of the Philistines, Part II: Olive-Oil Suppliers to the World," *BAR* 16 (1990): 41.

[44] S. Gitin, "Tel Miqne-Ekron in the 7th Century B.C.E.: The Impact of Economic Innovation and Foreign Cultural Influences on a Neo-Assyrian Vassal City-State," in *Recent Excavations in Israel: A View to the West*, ed. S. Gitin, Archaeological Institute of America Colloquia and Conference Papers 1 (Dubuque, Iowa: Kendall Hunt, 1995), 72 and fig. 4.17.

[45] See the photo in "Golden Cobra from Ekron's Last Days," *BAR* 22 (1996): 28.

[46] S. Gitin, "The Neo-Assyrian Empire and its Western Periphery: The Levant, with a Focus on Philistine Ekron," in *Assyria 1995*, ed. S. Parpola and R. M. Whiting (Helsinki: Neo-Assyrian Text Corpus Project, 1997), 101 and Fig. 23.

"temple complex 650."[47] These objects with cartouches of pharaohs who ruled six hundred years earlier led Gitin to propose that they were "curated," probably by Egyptians during the stratum IB phase.[48]

The excavators at Ekron associate the transition from stratum IC to IB with the transition from Assyrian to Egyptian domination in the region. Gitin interprets the vast olive oil industry at Ekron, established in stratum IC, as a consequence of Assyrian domination and patronage.[49] He argues too that during the period of stratum IB there was a diminution in oil production, which was "caused by the transition in political authority, resulting in a loss of Assyrian and Assyrian-Phoenician markets and their extensive distribution system."[50] It may be possible to refine these conclusions. The hypothesis that there was a diminution in oil output during the period of stratum IB depends upon the reuse of some discarded oil-pressing vats and weights in building construction. It is difficult to determine from the instances where this happened if this was a general phenomenon in stratum IB; most of the pressing installations have not been excavated, and it is clear from those that have that many continued in use to the end of the seventh century in stratum IB. This has led Stager to argue recently that the Egyptians might have been the main sponsors of the oil industry at Ekron from the beginning, not the Assyrians; Egyptian demand for olive oil was always prodigious.[51] The suggestion merits review, since Assyrian hegemony in the region broke down already in the 640s, while the oil industry at Ekron continued to the last years of the century. Perhaps it is possible that the expanded oil industry arose during the period after the collapse of Assyrian hegemony, beginning about 640, with Egyptian control or sponsorship as its main impetus. Gitin has vigorously rejected this hypothesis, however, and his contention that stratum IC, in which the oil industry was at its peak, should be assigned to the first half of the seventh century receives support from the discovery of a monumental inscription, probably from stratum IC, which mentions Achish ben Padi (flourished ca. 680s to 650s) as the builder of "temple complex 650."[52]

---

[47] S. Gitin, T. Dothan, and J. Naveh, "A Royal Dedicatory Inscription from Ekron," *IEJ* 47 (1997): 7.

[48] Ibid., 8.

[49] Gitin, "Miqne-Ekron in the 7th Century"; idem, "The Neo-Assyrian Empire and its Western Periphery," 77-103.

[50] Gitin, *NEAEHL*, s.v. "Miqne, Tel," 3.1057.

[51] Stager, "Ashkelon and the Archaeology of Destruction," 70*-71*; idem, "The Fury of Babylon," 66.

[52] Gitin, Dothan and Naveh, "A Royal Dedicatory Inscription," 1-16.

Tel Batash-Timnah stratum II, where there was also a significant olive-oil industry in the mid-seventh century, suffered destruction at the end of the century in a massive conflagration, likely perpetrated by the Babylonians.[53] Evidence for Egyptian presence at Batash, however, is not so rich as at Ashkelon and Ekron.

Ashdod, as noted above, possibly came under the direct control of Psammetichus I. The excavators suggest, as we have seen, that Psammetichus I might have destroyed the city of stratum 7b in the mid-seventh century, while the existence of Egyptian objects in level 7a at least suggests an Egyptian presence at the site in the second half of the seventh century. The Babylonians were likely responsible for the ultimate destruction of stratum 7, while the meager remains of stratum 6 point to a severe decline during the Babylonian period.[54]

This brief survey of the archeological data from several cities in Philistia and adjacent territories points to increased contact between Egypt and the southern Levant during the second half of the seventh century. These data are finally indecisive, however, for determining precisely when such Egyptian material arrived in Philistia or whether it was because of trade or direct political intervention. Herodotus's narrative about Psammetichus capturing Ashdod, if that happened in 635, indicates that more than commercial activity was at stake in that instance. The Egyptian cultic objects from Ashkelon might suggest that a permanent Egyptian enclave existed at that site. It is also possible that Egypt may have been the driving force behind the oil industry at Ekron in stratum IB and at Timnah in the second half of the seventh century. By the end of the seventh century, the Saqqara papyrus, or Adon letter, points to political rather than commercial intervention by the Egyptians in Philistia. The papyrus, written during the period of the Babylonian campaigns to Philistia at the end of the seventh century, perhaps comes from Ekron.[55] It is an appeal in Aramaic from Adon, perhaps the ruler of Ekron, to Pharaoh, which requests that the latter supply military aid in the face of a Babylonian attack. The language of the plea indicates that a treaty relationship existed between the parties and demonstrates Adon's

---

[53] See the summary discussion in G. L. Kelm and A. Mazar, *Timnah: A Biblical City in the Sorek Valley* (Winona Lake, Ind.: Eisenbrauns, 1995), 150-51, 155-62.

[54] Dothan and Porath, *Ashdod IV*, 58.

[55] This was argued by B. Porten, "The Identity of King Adon," *BA* 44 (1981): 43-45.

status as a client of Egypt at the end of the seventh century.[56] There is not enough evidence to determine, however, whether the Egyptian presence and the client status of such cities in the coastal region and Shephelah date all the way back to the 640s, although several scholars assume this.[57]

It is worth asking, too, whether the increased Greek presence in the Eastern Mediterranean in the second half of the seventh century might also be a consequence of Egyptian influence in the region before the Babylonian incursions under Nebuchadnezzar. The increased Greek presence is especially notable in the southern Levant, where there is an expanded volume of East Greek and some Corinthian ceramics from the period.[58] East Greek ceramics had been reaching the Levantine coast already in the eighth and early seventh centuries, especially at such northern sites as Al Mina and Tell Sūkās. At these sites and in the southern Levant, however, the Greek wares from the second half of the seventh century are more numerous, are distributed more widely, and include more forms than those of the earlier period.[59] In addition, the appearance at several sites of utilitarian wares that would presumably not have been objects of trade, such as the typical one-handle cooking

---

[56] Ibid., 39.

[57] E.g., Kienitz, "Saïtische Renaissance," 264-65; Malamat, "Josiah's Bid for Armegeddon"; Hayes and Miller, *History of Ancient Israel and Judah*, 383.

[58] For recent analyses of the East Greek and Corinthian ceramics in the southern Levant, often including unpublished material, see the study of J. Waldbaum, "Early Greek Contacts with the Southern Levant, ca. 1000-600 B.C.: The Eastern Perspective," *BASOR* 293 (1994): 53-66; and Waldbaum and J. Magness, "The Chronology of Early Greek Pottery: New Evidence from Seventh-Century B.C. Destruction Levels in Israel," *AJA* 101 (1997): 23-40; for the East Greek ceramics from the 604 B.C.E. destruction layer at Ashkelon, including considerable amounts of Wild Goat pottery, see Stager, "Ashkelon and the Archaeology of Destruction," 67* and figs. 10-12. For developments in the northern Levant, including Greek imports, see G. Lehmann, "Trends in the Local Pottery Development of the Late Iron Age and Persian Period in Syria and Lebanon, ca. 700 to 300 B.C.," *BASOR* 311 (1998): 7-37. The destruction of many coastal sites by the Babylonians in their campaigns in the region at the end of the seventh and early sixth centuries provides much evidence for this period. The destroyed or abandoned sites include: Kabri Area E (*IEJ* 43 [1993]: 183-84); Meṣad Hashavyahu; Tel Keisan IV; Megiddo II; Ashkelon; Tel Miqne-Ekron; Tel Batash-Timnah II; Dor; Akko; Tel ʾErani; Tel el-Hesi; Tell Jemmeh; Tell Malhata; Tell er-Ruqeish.

[59] Waldbaum, "Early Greek Contacts," 59-61; Lehmann, "Local Pottery Development in Syria and Lebanon," 19.

jug,[60] suggests that the East Greek pottery was arriving along with Greeks who took up residence in the Levant, perhaps as merchants or mercenaries. Although the increase in East Greek ceramics is measurable and probably reflects the presence of some Greeks in the Levant, Waldbaum has rightly cautioned that such pottery is still vastly outnumbered by local pottery types and that quantity alone is a poor indicator of Greek presence.[61] Still, the fact is that East Greek ceramics do begin to show up in greater quantity in the seventh century, and it is worth asking whether the decline of Assyrian control and the emergent Egyptian influence in the Levant played a role in this.

It was precisely during the reign of Psammetichus I that the Egyptians began to strengthen their army by employing Carian and Ionian mercenaries, according to Herodotus (1.2.154).[62] The establishment of Greek trading colonies in the Delta followed this, most notably at Naucratis in the west and Daphnae in the east.[63] Such colonies were a catalyst for Greek penetration into the eastern Mediterranean. The exact date of Naucratis's foundation remains uncertain, but 620 seems the latest possible date according to Boardman's analysis of the typology of Corinthian ceramics excavated there; it may have been several decades earlier.[64] This dovetails too with the narrative of Diodorus of Sicily that Psammetichus I went to great lengths to encourage the Greeks in their trade with Egypt (1.67).[65] Egyptian goods flowed back into Greece from Naucratis as well, and

---

[60] E.g., J. Naveh, "The Excavations at Meṣad Ḥashavyahu–Preliminary Report," *IEJ* 12 (1962): fig. 6:7-8; there are some sherds from Ashkelon as well (Stager, private conversation); this point was emphasized by Waldbaum, "Early Greek Contacts," 60 and fig. 10; although she has also urged caution in evaluating the strength of this argument, since the number of cooking pots remains quite small; see her study "Greeks *in* the East or Greeks *and* the East? Problems in the Definition and Recognition of Presence," *BASOR* 305 (1997): 8 and fig. 6.

[61] Waldbaum, "Greeks *in* the East or Greeks *and* the East?," 1-17. Waldbaum also offers a useful critique of earlier analyses of purported Greek influence at northern Levantine sites such as Al Mina (2-4).

[62] See also the summary discussion of Redford, *Egypt, Canaan, and Israel*, 433 and n. 12.

[63] The latter is Jeremiah's תחפנחס, Taḥpanḥēs (Jer 2:16; 43:7-9; 44:1; 46:14).

[64] J. A. Boardman, *The Greeks Overseas: Their Early Colonies and Trade*, new and enl. ed. (London: Thames and Hudson, 1980), 121.

[65] Diodorus of Sicily, *Bibliotheca Historica*, trans. C. H. Oldfather, Loeb Classical Library (Cambridge: Harvard University Press, 1933-1967). All citations and quotations are of the Loeb edition.

there is further evidence, as Boardman has shown, that the Greeks adopted numerous specifically Egyptian architectural and artistic styles beginning in the seventh century.[66] Perhaps, then, the close relationship between Egypt and the Greeks helps to explain the appearance of increasing volumes of East Greek ceramics in the southern Levant through the second half of the seventh century. The Egyptians may have employed Greek mercenaries to administer or protect the coastal route and sea traffic, abetting the influx of East Greek wares and merchants into the region. This fits with what Diodorus says: "since Psammetichus had established his rule with the aid of the mercenaries, he henceforth entrusted these before others with the administration of his empire and regularly maintained large mercenary forces" (1.67).

The clearest evidence for Greek presence in the southern Levant in our period comes from the coastal fortress of Meṣad Ḥashavyahu, where excavations revealed a considerable amount of East Greek pottery, both fine ware such as the so-called Wild Goat pottery and utilitarian items such as the one-handle cooking jugs mentioned above, which presumably indicate that Greeks were residing at the site. Additional East Greek pottery continues to emerge from excavations at Ashkelon too, including numerous sherds of the Wild Goat style.[67] Naveh, who excavated Meṣad Ḥashavyahu, suggested that there might have been a Greek settlement at the site.[68] He argued that the Greeks may have arrived as mercenaries in the service of Psammetichus I, or, less likely in his opinion, as merchants.[69] Waldbaum and Magness have recently suggested again that Meṣad Ḥashavyahu may indeed have been a Greek merchant colony, or at least that it may have housed Greek merchants. They note close parallels between the East Greek pottery at Meṣad Ḥashavyahu and the pottery excavated inland at Tel Miqne-Ekron and Tel Batash-Timnah. The inland sites lay on routes connected to the Sorek Valley, with Meṣad Ḥashavyahu situated at the coastal end of that valley.[70] Such ceramic parallels make it likely that there was a Greek merchant contingent at Meṣad Ḥashavyahu.

---

[66] Boardman, *Greeks Overseas*, 142-53; also T. F. R. G. Braun, "The Greeks in Egypt," in *CAH*, 2d ed., vol. 3, pt. 3, *The Expansion of the Greek World, Eighth to Sixth Centuries B.C.*, ed. J. A. Boardman et al. (Cambridge: Cambridge University Press, 1982), 37-43.

[67] See, e.g., Stager, "The Fury of Babylon," 60.

[68] J. Naveh, "Excavations at Meṣad Ḥashavyahu," 97.

[69] Ibid., 98-99.

[70] Waldbaum and Magness, "The Chronology of Early Greek Pottery."

Naveh, Cross and others, however, argue on the basis of the Hebrew ostraca discovered at Meṣad Ḥashavyahu that Josiah controlled it.[71] Naveh recently suggested that any Greeks at the site may have been employed by Josiah as mercenaries.[72] It is certain that Judeans were present, since the famous Hebrew ostracon detailing the complaint of a harvester about the wrongful seizure of his garment clearly indicates that legal procedures recognized in Judah could be appealed to at the site (cf. Exod 22:25-26; Deut 24:10-13). On the other hand, Na'aman's recent lengthy study, building on the work of others, throws the issue of Judean domination of the site into question.[73] He argues that the site was more likely an Egyptian garrison, stocked with East Greek, Judean, and other mercenaries or clients of Egypt. There was a Judean presence at the site, but it does not necessarily follow that Josiah controlled the site. Indeed, it seems equally plausible that the Egyptians controlled it (as they probably controlled nearby Ashdod) and sponsored the mercenaries, although there is no clear evidence for Egyptian presence. We referred above to the well-known Egyptian reliance on Greek mercenary forces beginning under Psammetichus I. In Judah, too, the references to the *ktym* in the Arad ostraca point to the presence of Greeks, probably mercenaries, at about the same time.[74] Their status vis-à-vis Egypt remains uncertain; Aharoni proposed that they were in the employ of Josiah.[75] If, as Na'aman argues, Judah was under Egyptian control in the second half of Josiah's reign (which fits with Josiah's resistance against Necho and apparent alliance with Babylon in 609), then even the presence of Greeks in Judah does not contradict the hypothesis that they were there as a consequence of Egyptian initiatives.

It is important not to present a reductionist view of the matter, however. While Egyptian influence in the Levant and friendly relations between the Egyptians and Greeks possibly hastened Greek penetration of the southern Levant, demographic pressures in the East Greek states

---

[71] J. Naveh, "A Hebrew Letter from the Seventh Century B.C.," *IEJ* 10 (1960): 135-36; F. M. Cross, "Epigraphic Notes on Hebrew Documents of the Eighth-Sixth Centuries B.C.: 2. The Murabba'ât Papyrus and the Letter Found Near Yabneh-Yam," *BASOR* 165 (1962): 42-45.

[72] See his recent summary, *NEAEHL*, 2.586, s.v. "Ḥashavyahu, Meẓad."

[73] "Judah under Josiah," 3-71.

[74] Y. Aharoni, *Arad Inscriptions* (Jerusalem: Israel Expolration Society, 1981), 12-13; 144-45. Biblical texts make it clear that the *ktym* are Greeks: in Genesis 10, the *ktym* are sons of *yāwān*, a term connected with "Ionia" (Gen 10:4). For the maritime origin of the *ktym*, see Jer 2:10 and Ezek 27:6.

[75] Ibid., 13.

also encouraged the process. These states were growing in the seventh century, and eastward expansion of trade and settlement was a natural option given constraints in the west and north.[76] As Braun states, "the last third of the seventh century brought about a prodigious acceleration of Greek trade."[77] Nevertheless, we may hypothesize that the presence of a contingent of East Greeks in the Egyptian military, the foundation of the Greek trading colonies at Naucratis and Daphnae, and the expanded Greek presence in the southern Levant (especially at Meṣad Ḥashavyahu, but also, e.g., Ashkelon) point to Egyptian sponsorship of Greek mercenaries *and* merchants in the eastern Mediterranean. This reconstruction is tentative, but the possibility that Egyptian and Greek interaction, abetted by the Phoenicians in the north, propelled more rapid Greek penetration into the Levant in the period immediately after the Assyrian withdrawal deserves consideration.

In any event, even if we cannot speak of a "Saite empire in the Levant," as Redford has,[78] there was definitely a strong Egyptian presence in the southern Levant, which may have been enhanced by the expanding penetration into the region by their Greek allies and trading partners. Thus, as Malamat argued, by the time Nabopolassar had consolidated his rule in Babylonia during the late 620s, the Egyptians were already ensconced along the Via Maris and in Syria as far as the region of Hamath and probably Carchemish.[79] The Egyptians decided, by 616 at the latest, to support the declining Assyrians in their wars against the Babylonians;[80] the decision must have depended upon established Egyptian interests and logistical bases in Syria-Palestine. Psammetichus I had probably founded such bases and interests well before the 616 entente with Assyria. This was Malamat's reason for arguing that the public building at Megiddo (stratum II) was probably an Egyptian administrative center, although there is nothing in the material

---

[76] Boardman, *Greeks Overseas*, 129.

[77] Braun, "Greeks in Egypt," 39.

[78] *Egypt, Canaan, and Israel*, 441.

[79] Waldbaum notes that relatively few East Greek sherds from before about 630 have turned up in excavations in the Levant, so if the East Greek presence is a function of Egyptian dominance, then perhaps it does not date as far back as the 640s. The sites where E. Greek sherds predating the 630s have been found, moreover, are all coastal (except for Dan) as one might expect: Kabri, Tell Keisan, Acco, Dor, and Ashkelon (Waldbaum, "Early Greek Contacts," 59).

[80] TCS 5 chron 3:10.

record that points unequivocally to this conclusion.[81] The discovery of a bronze ring bearing the cartouche of Psammetichus I at Carchemish might also suggest Egyptian interests in the Upper Euphrates region, although such items of jewelry could travel long distances as trophies or heirlooms.[82] The Deuteronomistic historian states that Necho II, successor of Psammetichus I, had a foothold at "Riblah in the land of Hamath" (2 Kgs 23:33). When Nebuchadnezzar pushed the Egyptians out of Syria in 605, after the battle of Carchemish, the Deuteronomistic historian summarized the geopolitical status quo ante as follows: "The king of Egypt did not leave his country any more, for the king of Babylon captured all that had belonged to the king of Egypt, from the brook of Egypt to the Euphrates River" (2 Kgs 24:7).

It is possible that Egypt only began to reassert its influence in Syria-Palestine in the period after the death of Assurbanipal (627), twenty years before Babylonian incursions into the area. More likely, however, the Egyptian influence dated back to the late 640s and 630s. Assyrian rule in the region, therefore, had been defunct for more than three decades before Nebuchadnezzar's arrival. This evidence, coupled with the clear and self-conscious attempt of the Babylonians under Nebuchadnezzar to avoid Assyrian imperial ideas (see chapter one), renders the idea of direct continuity between Assyrian and Babylonian administrative procedures in the west problematic. On the other hand, if there was an entrenched Egyptian presence dating all the way back to the time of the departure of the Assyrians from the region, then this would better explain the logic, methods, and consequences of Babylonian rule in the Levant under Nebuchadnezzar, to which we now turn.

2.3 Nebuchadnezzar's Arrival in the Levant

Egyptian penetration into the Levant shaped the military policy of Nebuchadnezzar in the west. In his accession year (605), and after more than a decade of Egyptian hostilities against the Babylonians in the

---

[81] Malamat, "Josiah's Bid for Armegeddon"; and idem, "Twilight of Judah," 125. Malamat's chief argument for Egyptian domination of the site comes from the dimensions of this one monumental building: he suggests it was laid out on the basis of the Egyptian cubit. Beyond that, he can point only to a few faience figurines ("Josiah's Bid for Armegeddon," 269-70 and n. 11).

[82] C. L. Woolley, *Carchemish* (London: British Museum, 1929), 2.123-29 and pl. 26:1-4, cited in Malamat, "Josiah's Bid for Armegeddon," 273, n. 22.

Middle and Upper Euphrates regions, Nebuchadnezzar routed the Egyptians at Carchemish and Hamath and pushed them out of Syria (TCS 5 chron 5:1-8; Jer 46:1-12). In the following year he turned his attention to the Philistine cities, where Egyptian influence in the southern Levant, as we have seen, had been strongest. Ashkelon fell in 604 in a massive conflagration, Ekron similarly in a subsequent campaign (603 or 601[83]), Ashdod VI and Tel Batash-Timnah (stratum II) undoubtedly in the same period, and perhaps Tel Seraʿ V[84] and other sites as well. As Stager has rightly argued, Nebuchadnezzar's "scorched earth" policy in the Philistine plain, abundantly evident at Ashkelon, shows how important eradication of Egyptian influence along the coast was to the Babylonian king.[85]

Nebuchadnezzar's actions represent a different policy toward Philistia that of the Assyrians.[86] The Assyrians placed greater emphasis on the strategic and economic importance of Philistia, and when cities there rebelled the Neo-Assyrian kings were reluctant to subject the region to the usual treatment meted out to rebel states, namely, provincialization.[87] If possible, the Assyrians reinstated subject status under a new king. Their intent may have been to create an intermediate administrative organization in Philistia, something of a compromise between subservient status and provincialization.[88] Nebuchadnezzar's systematic destruction of Ashkelon, Ekron, Ashdod, Tel Batash-Timnah,

---

[83] 603 is ruled out if one accepts Na'aman's argument that Nebuchadnezzar's campaign in that year was to Cilicia rather than Palestine ("Nebuchadrezzar's Campaign in Year 603 B.C.E.," *Biblische Notizen* 62 [1992]: 41-44).

[84] Although the excavator suggests that the late seventh century destruction could have been perpetrated by a Saite pharaoh (E. Oren, *NEAEHL*, 4.1333-34, s.v. "Seraʿ, Tel").

[85] Stager, "Ashkelon and the Archaeology of Destruction," 67*-68*.

[86] For an incisive survey of Assyrian procedures, see H. Tadmor, "Philistia under Assyrian Rule," *BA* 29 (1966): 86-102.

[87] Tadmor, "Philistia under Assyrian Rule," 91; also Ephʿal, "Assyrian Dominion," 287-88. Under Sargon II, however, the Assyrians did import foreign population groups into Philistia, which shows that in some instances they transferred populations not just into provincialized territories, but also into independent subject (city-)states; see N. Na'aman and R. Zadok, "Sargon II's Deportations to Israel and Philistia (716-708 B.C.)," *JCS* 40 (1988): 36-46. Ephʿal suggests that this was a short-lived policy in the region ("Assyrian Dominion," 367, n. 51).

[88] Cogan has recently acknowledged that the dual categories of "vassal" and "province" do not cover all of the known examples of Assyrian subjugation; exceptions occur especially in the region of Philistia ("Judah under Assyrian Hegemony: A Re-examination of Imperialism and Religion," *JBL* 112 [1993]: 406-8).

and other cities in Philistia and adjacent regions, seems to indicate a different attitude: he considered the economic viability of the region secondary to the imperative of pushing the Egyptians out by razing their client cities. Such a policy had another benefit for the Babylonians: it eliminated the necessary expense of installing garrisons in this distant region to patrol the southern border. This, again, is different from the Assyrian policy in Philistia and adjacent subject territories. At Tel Jemmeh, and (farther north) Gezer, where excavators discovered Neo-Assyrian tablets dated to 651 and 649, the Assyrians constructed and staffed administrative buildings. Such buildings and Neo-Assyrian cuneiform inscriptions attest to an interventionist policy perhaps just short of full provincialization.[89] In addition to the architectural and textual evidence for Assyrian presence, Assyrian ceramics such as the so-called palace ware and its local imitations are also common. The Babylonians seem to have had no such interventionist intentions in the region. Concomitantly, as Stager has argued, we find nothing comparable, even in Judah, to the material evidence for Assyrian presence in Philistia, the Shephelah, and Judah.[90] Biblical texts do refer to the presence of Babylonians at Mizpah (Tell en-Naṣbeh) during Gedaliah's tenure after the fall of Jerusalem,[91] and there are a few objects that may reflect Babylonian presence at that site.[92] In any event, the key factor in defining Nebuchadnezzar's policy in the southern Levant was the entrenched Egyptian presence there established under Psammetichus I and Necho II. Babylonian policy sought the eradication of Egyptian clients, and not the economic exploitation of the region.

This may also help to explain a well-known phenomenon in the Levantine archeological record for the first half of the sixth century: with the notable exception of phases II and III of stratum G at Tell Sūkās on the Syrian coast, the importation of Greek pottery, which had risen in the last third of the seventh century, declined in the Levant during the first

---

[89] For the Assyrian architecture and ceramics at Jemmeh, see G. van Beek, "The Arch and the Vault in Ancient Near Eastern Architecture," *Scientific American* 257 (1987): 96-103; and idem, *NEAEHL*, 2.670-72, s.v. "Jemmeh, Tell." Similar arrangements may have existed farther inland at Tel Seraʿ.

[90] Stager, "Fury of Babylon," 69 and verbal communication.

[91] E.g., 2 Kgs 25:25; Jer 41:3. For discussion of the Babylonian presence in Judah, see below.

[92] C. C. McCown, *Tell en-Naṣbeh, I: Archaeological and Historical Results* (New Haven: ASOR, 1947), pl. 55:80; for discussion of the evidence of Babylonian presence at Tell en-Naṣbeh, see below p. 108.

half of the sixth.[93] As S. Weinberg showed, this occurs uniformly throughout the Levant early in the reign of Nebuchadnezzar, with Greek pottery appearing again in quantity only at the end of the sixth century (and then almost exclusively Attic wares).[94] In the south, the fortress of Meṣad Ḥashavyahu, which, as discussed earlier, may have housed a Greek mercenary contingent and (or?) a merchant group under Psammetichus I and perhaps Necho II, ends with Nebuchadnezzar's penetration into Philistia. Waldbaum and Magness suggest that if Meṣad Ḥashavyahu was primarily a trading post, then the destruction of the cities that represented its inland markets erased its raison d'être.[95] On the Syrian coast, the Greek entrepôt of Al Mina also stopped receiving Greek wares very early in the sixth century, and there is a gap there between strata V and IV until trade resumes in the Persian period.[96] At Tell Sūkās, as noted, Greek imports continue through the sixth century, although the excavators detected two destruction levels in the first half of the sixth century, which may well have resulted from conflict with the Babylonians.[97] Several scholars have linked this almost complete cessation of Greek imports in the Levant with the shift to Babylonian hegemony.[98]

---

[93] P. J. Riis, *Sūkās I. The North-East Sanctuary and the First Settling of Greeks in Syria and Palestine*. Det Kongelige Danske Videnskabernes Selskab Historisk-Filosofiske Skrifter 5,1 (Copenhagen: Publications of the Carlsberg Expedition to Phoenicia 1, 1970), 40-91; Boardman, *Greeks Overseas*, 49-50; and especially S. S. Weinberg, "Post-Exilic Palestine," *Proceedings of the Israel Academy of Sciences and Humanities* 4/5 (1971): 91-92.

[94] Weinberg, "Post-Exilic Palestine," 89.

[95] Waldbaum and Magness, "Chronology of Early Greek Pottery."

[96] S. Smith, "Greek Trade at Al Mina," *The Antiquaries Journal* 22 (1942): 105; Weinberg, "Post-Exilic Palestine," 91; Boardman, *Greeks Overseas*, 49-50; Braun, "Greeks in the Near East," 10; and Stern, *Material Culture*, 140. For the decisive architectural break at the site between levels V and IV, see L. Woolley, "Excavations at Al Mina, Sueidia," *JHS* 58 (1938): 21.

[97] Riis suggested possible events with which these may have been associated, but cautiously refrained from a definitive statement (*Sūkās*, 58-59; and 86-87). Explanations for the persistence of Greek imports into Sukas are few. Boardman suggests simply "that the new overlords found it expedient that the Greeks should continue their trading activities at Tell Sukas rather than Al Mina" (*Greeks Overseas*, 52). Perhaps the Babylonians simply brought the trade under tight enough control to ensure that western goods would flow toward the heartland, but quashed distribution along the Mediterranean coast. See also S. Smith, "The Greek Trade at Al Mina," 87-112.

[98] This was already Sidney Smith's hypothesis about of the phenomenon at Al Mina, "Greek Trade at Al Mina," 105-8.

But why should Nebuchadnezzar have taken any steps to inhibit the lucrative western trade? That the southern Levant was significantly depopulated in the wake of Nebuchadnezzar's conquests provides a partial but not complete explanation for the decline in trade there, and perhaps the same was true in the north. Life did go on, however, both on the coast and in the hinterland.[99] If it is correct that the expanded East Greek penetration particularly into the southern Levant derives from Psammetichus's encouragement of Greek trade—not only with Egypt (as Diodorus states), but also with Egyptian client cities and allies in the Levant (including Phoenicia)—then Nebuchadnezzar's aim of eradicating Egyptian presence had the concomitant effect of disrupting the western trade, whether the effect was intended or not. Perhaps the Babylonians tolerated such trade at Tell Sūkās to ensure transportation of goods imported from the Aegean into the Babylonian heartland, unless Nebuchadnezzar was responsible for one or both of the destructions of Sūkās.

After the Babylonian penetration into the Levant, Greek trade in the eastern Mediterranean seems to have shifted toward Egypt proper, where instead of falling off in the first half of the sixth century it obviously increased, especially at Naucratis but also at Daphnae. At the latter site the majority of Greek pottery dates from about 570-525.[100] Indeed, Herodotus (1.2.178) places the foundation of the trading colony at Naucratis under Amasis, i.e, after 570. The archeological finds from Naucratis clearly point to an earlier foundation, but, as Boardman suggests, Herodotus's narrative may have to do with reorganization of the status of Naucratis under Amasis, perhaps in the wake of the southward shift in Greek commercial activities.[101] A fortress excavated by E. Oren in the northern Sinai along the "Ways-of-Horus," about 25 km northeast of Daphnae, also produced substantial evidence of East

---

[99] For a discussion, e.g., of the continuation of occupation in the traditional territory of Benjamin, see S. Weinberg, "Post-Exilic Palestine"; also see the recently published surface survey by Y. Magen and I. Finkelstein, *Archaeological Survey of the Hill Country of Benjamin* (Jerusalem: Israel Antiquities Authority, 1993; Hebrew with English summary); note too the arguments for the persistence of settlement in the Jerusalem region by G. Barkay, "Excavations at Ketef Hinnom in Jerusalem," in *Ancient Jerusalem Revealed*, ed. H. Geva (Jerusalem: Israel Exploration Society, 1994): 86-106; and also the comments of A. Ofer, *NEAEHL*, 3.814-15, s.v. "Judean Hills Survey."

[100] Braun, "Greeks in Egypt," 43-52.

[101] Boardman, *Greeks Overseas*, 117; 120-21; also Braun, "Greeks in Egypt," 38.

Greek pottery from this period.[102] Considerable amounts of East Greek pottery mainly from the very end of the seventh and first half of the sixth centuries were excavated at the site, with the closest parallels coming from Naucratis and Daphnae.[103] Local imitations of the Greek wares and evidence for the potters' workshops in which they were produced also suggest that numerous Greeks were actually settling in the region.[104]

This shift of Greek interest from the eastern Mediterranean littoral to the Nile Delta must have been a result of Babylonian imperial policy in the Levant.[105] It is possible that Babylonian actions against coastal sites resulted in the deportation of Greeks (probably from such places as Al Mina): increasing numbers of "Ionians" begin to appear in Babylon as craftsmen and mercenaries in the early sixth century.[106] Just as the Babylonians deported West Semites and others from the Levant into Babylon, they may have deported the Greeks who had settled in Asia Minor, Cilicia, and the north Levant, in part because they were skilled merchants and mercenaries.[107] In addition to the larger policy of ousting the Egyptians—who were the Greeks' main clients and partners—the deportation of Greeks from the Levant would have put a brake on the Aegean trade, and may be a further indication of the Babylonian lack of interest in encouraging such commerce.

Apparently, then, Nebuchadnezzar did little to foster trade between the Levant and the Greek world, although he apparently tolerated such trade at Tell Sūkās, for whatever reason. The Babylonians, it seems, lacked the interest to organize or bolster the economies of the western territories so long as Nebuchadnezzar's almost

---

[102] E. D. Oren, "Migdol: A New Fortress on the Edge of the Eastern Nile Delta," *BASOR* 256 (1984): 7-44.

[103] Ibid., 24-30.

[104] Ibid., 27-28.

[105] Weinberg thought that with time and further excavation, Greek pottery of the early sixth century ultimately would turn up in Palestine. So far this has not been the case, and its absence is probably not an accident of discovery.

[106] See the evidence in E. F. Weidner, "Jojachin, König von Juda, in Babylonischen Keilschrifttexten," in *Mélanges Syriens offerts à Monsieur René Dussaud*, Academie des inscriptions et belles-lettres (Paris: Geuthner, 1939), 2.923-35; a more recent and comprehensive survey of Greeks who are mentioned in Neo-Babylonian texts in available in J. A. Brinkman, "The Akkadian Words for 'Ionia' and 'Ionian,'" in *Daidalikon: Studies in Memory of Raymond V. Schoder, S.J.*, ed. R. F. Sutton (Wauconda, Ill.: Bolchazy-Carducci, 1989), 57-61.

[107] That some of the Greeks who came to Babylon were from Asia Minor is suggested by the Anatolian characteristics of their names; see Weidner, "Jojachin," 932-33.

annual campaigns quelled residual restiveness and filled the coffers. Numerous factors—elimination of the Egyptian presence in the region, deportations, lack of local political stability, failure or unwillingness of the Babylonians to stimulate local economic productivity, constant campaigning, and the wholesale destruction of many cities (especially in the southern Levant)—so disrupted the potential eastern markets for Aegean goods that the Greek traders shifted their attention almost exclusively to trade with Egypt proper, where they had earlier founded trading colonies and now, it appears, received special trading concessions.

As it turned out, Nebuchadnezzar was correct in his assessment of Egyptian interests in the Levant. Continual strife with the pharaohs of the Twenty-Sixth Dynasty punctuated the course of his rule there. Anticipating from the outset Egyptian reluctance to let the coastal regions go, Nebuchadnezzar quickly determined to destroy Egypt's clients in the Levant, which he did with alacrity in Philistia, as we have seen. He then attacked Egypt itself in 601, although he did not achieve victory, as we learn from the Babylonian chronicle and Herodotus.[108] The Wadi Brisa inscription alludes to a campaign against "enemies" who were occupying and despoiling the Lebanon mountains, and some have surmised that the enemies might have been the Egyptians.[109] In 588, when the Babylonians put Jerusalem under siege after the rebellion of their refractory appointee, Zedekiah, the Egyptians mounted an ultimately ineffective campaign to interrupt the siege (Jer 37:5-11). Another cuneiform source reports the following concerning a Babylonian king, almost certainly Nebuchadnezzar: [*ina*] *kašādu ištu* ^{kur}*mi*[*ṣ*]*ir a*[*di/na*] [^{uru}*ḫ*]*u-me-e* ^{uru}*pi-rid-du* ^{uru}*lu-*⸢*ú*⸣*-du*, "[upon] conquering from Egypt as far as Ḫumê, Piriddu, and Lydia."[110] The phrase is incomplete but suggests that Nebuchadnezzar understood the border of Egypt to be the southern terminus of the empire. All of this suggests that the Egyptians did not readily relinquish their earlier

[108] TCS 5 chron 5, rev. 6-7; and Herodotus 1.2.159; see Malamat, "Josiah's Bid for Armegeddon," 275-76; and Redford, *Egypt, Canaan, and Israel*, 458.

[109] For the text, VAB 4 174 (Nbk 19=WBr=WVDOG 5 pl. 39 23-24) ix 23-24; cf. Oppenheim, *ANET*, 307; for the identification of the enemy with the Egyptians, see already Weissbach, WVDOG 5 (1906): 43. For the possibility of Egyptian control over Phoenicia in this period, see above, n. 31.

[110] Lambert, "King of Justice," 7 v 20. Lambert is no doubt correct that such conquests could not be assigned to another Babylonian monarch of the era. It is probable, however, that the prepositions *ištu* . . . *a*[*di/na*] mean that the king's conquests were not inclusive of Egypt, but extended from its border.

influence in the Levant, despite Nebuchadnezzar's concerted efforts to dislodge them.

Whether Nebuchadnezzar later invaded Egypt successfully remains uncertain. A fragmentary tablet from his thirty-seventh year (568-67) raises that possibility: it refers to a campaign of Nebuchadnezzar against Egypt. The name of pharaoh Amasis is probably to be restored: [*a-ma*]-⌈*a*⌉-*su* LUGAL *mi-ṣir*, "[Ama]sis, king of Egypt."[111] Edel suggested that this tablet demonstrates that the Babylonians penetrated into Egypt, a conclusion dependent on the identification of URU *pu-ṭu-ia-a-man*, mentioned in the text, as the name of a single city, Pūṭu-Yāman, perhaps Cyrene.[112] Berger has argued, however, that this reading is probably incorrect, and that the text more likely preserves a series of three toponyms: [. . . URU/KUR?] *ku-ú-šá* uru*pu-ṭu* <uru>*ia-a-man* [. . .], "Kūšu (Cush), Pūṭu (Libya), and Yāman (Ionia)."[113] In offering this proposal, Berger suggests that the scribe omitted the URU (or KUR) sign before Yāman, just as he apparently omitted the KUR sign before the toponym in the title LUGAL *miṣir*, "king of Egypt," in the preceding line. Further, the toponym Pūṭu-Yāman is unattested, whereas Kūšu, Pūṭu, and Yāman are all well known. These were likely the regions from which Amasis "called up [troops] to assist him" ([*ana r*]*e-ṣu-ti-šú id-kám-ma*) during the battle, according to the Egyptian policy of hiring mercenaries at this time.[114] Finally, as Berger points out, precisely these three toponyms occur together in an inscription of Darius I.[115] This tablet from Nebuchadnezzar's thirty-seventh year, therefore, does not prove that he penetrated into Egypt during a campaign at that time, although it does show that some military action was taken against Egypt as late as 568-567.[116]

---

[111] VAB 4 206 (Nbk 48); for a copy, Wiseman, *CCK*, pl. xxi (BM 33041) rev. 1.

[112] E. Edel, "Amasis und Nebukadrezar II," *GM* 29 (1978): 15-16.

[113] Berger, *Königsinschriften*, 6; and for the text, Wiseman, *CCK*, pl. xxi (BM 33041), rev. 2.

[114] Ibid., rev. 6, and also Jer 46:9, which mentions Kush, Put, and the Lydians.

[115] Berger, *Königsinschriften*, 6; the text is the Naqš-i-Rustam inscription, published by Weissbach, VAB 3 89 18-19.

[116] V. Donbaz will publish a Neo-Babylonian tablet from the Assur collection of the Istanbul Museum (A 628, Ass. 17676) which mentions the campaign of a Neo-Babylonian king against Egypt and its pharaoh. Neither king's name is preserved, and the presence of the text among tablets from the Assur archive is problematic. It may well relate to the reign of Nebuchadrezzar, like another tablet

Katzenstein and Edel, apparently independently, suggested that the invasion of Egypt in the fourth year of Amasis, recounted in Amasis's victory stele, by a joint force of "Asiatics" (a reference to Semitic people) and the deposed pharaoh Apries, who is perhaps referred to by the circumlocution "the arrogant one,"[117] is in fact identical with the campaign of the Babylonians described in the fragmentary cuneiform tablet of Nebuchadnezzar's thirty-seventh year.[118] The thesis is speculative, and depends in part upon the problematic identification of URU *pu-ṭu-ia-a-man* with Cyrene, but one recalls that during the era after the fall of Jerusalem in 586, Jeremiah (e.g., 43:10-13) and Ezekiel (e.g., 32:11-12) both expected that Nebuchadnezzar would attack Egypt. In any event, Egyptian presence in the Levant before the Babylonian arrival and ongoing conflicts during the reign of Nebuchadnezzar shaped the king's policies toward the southern Levant. This of course had a decisive impact on such inland kingdoms as Judah, which, like that of the Philistine Adon, repeatedly allied itself to Egypt, with similarly disastrous effects.

2.4 Nebuchadnezzar's Empire

How did the Babylonians rule the west after Nebuchadnezzar's conquests? Examination of their rule can be outlined under several rubrics. The first may be labeled the "administrative geography" of the region. This includes the related problems of territorial divisions imposed upon (or recognized in) the region by the Babylonian empire, whether imperial officials were assigned to the region, and the deportation of local population groups to the heartland. The second rubric may be labeled the "economic geography" of the region. This includes a brief assessment of Neo-Babylonian economic activity in the west.

(A 643 Ass. 37714) from the same archive dated to Nebuchadrezzar's 36th regnal year (V. Donbaz, "A Group of Neo-Babylonian Tablets in the Assur Collection," paper presented at the 45th *Rencontre Assyriologique International*, Cambridge, MA, July 7, 1998).

117 Egyptian *mḥ-jbf*, see Edel, "Amasis und Nebukadrezzar II," 16.

118 Katzenstein, *Tyre*, 338; Edel, "Amasis und Nebukadrezzar II," 15.

2.4.1 Administrative Geography

2.4.1.1 Territorial Divisions in the Empire

An important component of Neo-Assyrian imperial rule was the maintenance of a web of subservient states and kingdoms in the periphery of the empire and the reorganization of any conquered subject states into discrete provinces; the provinces were often named after important cities in the conquered region, as in the cases of Samerīna and Magiddû, but they were administered by Assyrian officials appointed by the crown.[119] Some scholars assert that the Babylonians not only inherited the territory that the Assyrian empire had controlled, but also perpetuated a provincial administrative system like the Assyrian one. Mitchell, for example, writes that "the Babylonians had taken over the Assyrian provincial administrative system largely as they had found it."[120] Grayson, in discussing the fall of Assyria, argues that "the event was . . . a transfer of power from Nineveh to Babylon. The geography of the empire and its administration remained basically the same and there was no prolonged period without a central authority."[121] Eph'al makes a similar claim about imperial administration in the Levant but from the vantage of the Achaemenid era: "It is a logical assumption that, by the Babylonian period, the entire region (including Judah) had already been organized along the well-defined administrative lines that Cyrus and his successors were to inherit."[122] The question is, can such assertions be sustained? The answer, for the moment, is no. A few scholars have

---

[119] The classic study is Forrer, *Provinzeinteilung des assyrischen Reiches*. For a survey of Assyrian provincialization in Palestine, see Eph'al, "Assyrian Dominion," 282-86. For situations that could be conceived as intermediate between or overlapping subject states and provinces, see above, n. 88. For the administrative documentation, see now F. M. Fales and J. N. Postgate, *Imperial Administrative Records, Part II*, SAA 11 (Helsinki: Helsinki University Press, 1995).

[120] T. C. Mitchell, "The Babylonian Exile and the Restoration of the Jews in Palestine (586-c.500 B.C.)," in *CAH*, 2d ed., vol. 3, part 2, *The Assyrian and Babylonian Empires and Other States of the Near East, from the Eighth to the Sixth Centuries B.C.*, ed. J. A. Boardman et al. (Cambridge: Cambridge University Press, 1991), 415; similarly Saggs, *Greatness*, 261; Machinist also expressed this view, "Palestine, Administration of," 76-77.

[121] Grayson, "Assyria 668-635 B.C." 161.

[122] I. Eph'al, "Syria-Palestine under Achaemenid Rule," in *CAH*, vol 4. *Persia, Greece and the Western Mediterranean c. 525 to 479 B.C.*, ed. J. A. Boardman et al. (Cambridge: Cambridge University Press, 1988), 161; similarly Hoglund, *Imperial Administration*, 21.

likewise argued that the continuity between Assyrian rule and Babylonian is not patent, including Stager on the basis of the material culture,[123] and Hoglund on the basis of Achaemenid rule.[124] The problem merits further review.

The following inscriptions of Nebuchadnezzar preserve some information about the geographical subdivisions of the empire: the Etemenanki cylinder; the Istanbul prism fragment; and the text edited by Lambert under the title "Nebuchadnezzar king of justice" (CT 46 45). The chronicles also yield some information. A survey of the relevant portions of each of these sources provides some evidence about Babylonian imperial geography, evidence that is more concrete than the rhetorical statements concerning the universal hegemony of the Babylonian king discussed above in chapter one.

Nebuchadnezzar's Etemenanki cylinder lists the territories within the empire that contributed corvée workers or lumber for the construction of Marduk's ziggurat in Babylon.[125] After a list of localities within Babylonia and mention of "the land of Assyria," the list briefly refers to the regions of Eber Nāri ("Transeuphrates") and Ḫatti. While the list gives only GNs for Babylonia and Assyria, for Eber Nāri and Ḫatti the titles of three classes of officials are named: *šarrāni ša Eber Nā*[*ri*], "the kings of Eber Nāri, *pīḫatā*⌈*tim*⌉ *ša māt Ḫattim*, "the governors of the land of Ḫatti," and *šakkanakkātim māt Ḫattim nēberti Puratti ana erib šamši*, "viceroys of the land of Ḫatti, across the Euphrates toward the west." Eber Nāri refers to northern Syria west of the Euphrates and the adjacent areas in southeastern Turkey,[126] so the implication of the inscription is that there were native kings in this region. This might be evidence that the provincial system that the Assyrians had established earlier, and which seems to have remained intact in the Upper Euphrates region and Cilicia from the period of the last canonical eponym (649) right down to the last stand of Aššur-uballiṭ II at Harran (609), had now lapsed. Admittedly, however, we have little evidence about whether or not imperial officials might have functioned

---

[123] Stager, "Fury of Babylon," 69; "Ashkelon and the Archaeology of Destruction," 61*-72*; and private communication.

[124] Hoglund, *Achaemenid Imperial Administration*, 18-21, but his interpretation of the Neo-Babylonian sources is very problematic.

[125] For a discussion of this list as it relates to the formulaic language about the king's universal imperial hegemony, see above chapter 1, section 1.5.1.

[126] For references, see *CAD* E 8, s.v. *eber nāri* 2; and *AHw* 181b, s.v. *Eber nāri*.

side by side with local kings (see below 2.4.1.2, "Imperial Officials"). Examples from the Assyrian period, noted by Tadmor, suggest that in the Assyrian province Qū'e (Cilicia), which, under the name Ḫumê, later became part of the Babylonian Eber Nāri, there were both Assyrian officials and local rulers.[127] In independent subject states there were frequently Assyrian officials.[128] Even if we assume that the Babylonians followed procedures similar to those of the Assyrians, there is thus uncertainty about whether the existence of local kings precluded the presence of Babylonian officials, or vice-versa. Moreover, the terms *piḫātu* and *šakkanakkū* have a complex origin and use.[129] It may be that the references in the Etemenanki inscription point to officials placed in Ḫatti by the Babylonian king. Alternatively, it may be that they represent imperial officials appointed by the Assyrians in the Upper Euphrates region and Cilicia who continued to exercise power as semiautonomous rulers into the early years of the Babylonian imperial era.[130] It is also possible, though less likely, that the Babylonian scribes subsumed all classes of local officials in Eber Nāri and Ḫatti under these three rubrics. On the other hand, the Babylonians appointed both *pīḫatu* and *šakanakku* officials in Babylonia proper, so the conservative course is to see those in the west as royal appointees. In summary, then, it is difficult to assess this remark in the Etemenanki inscription about the officials in Eber Nāri and Ḫatti; the remark seems to show that these officials, like the local kings, had responsibilities connected to building projects in Babylon.

Another widely discussed text relating to the imperial geography is the Istanbul prism fragment of Nebuchadnezzar, which Landsberger correctly assigned to Nebuchadnezzar's seventh year.[131] It is a building inscription that commemorates the construction of one of

[127] Tadmor, "Philistia under Assyrian Rule," 95.

[128] Eph'al, "Assyrian Dominion," 286-88.

[129] See the discussion in Frame, *Babylonia 689-627*, 225-27.

[130] Something similar may have happened in the early part of the eighth century, when Assyrian control over the western territories weakened and the officials previously appointed there arrogated almost royal prerogatives. Šamši-ilu, the *turtānu* of Shalmaneser IV, for example, claims in an inscription from Til Barsip to have defeated Urartu without even mentioning the Assyrian king (F. Thureau-Dangin, "L'inscription des lions de Tel-Barsib," *RA* 27 [1930]: 57-64); see also the comments of P. Garelli, "The Achievement of Tiglath-pileser III: Novelty or Continuity?" in *Ah, Assyria . . .: Studies in Assyrian History and Ancient Near Eastern Historiography Presented to Hayim Tadmor*, ScrHier 33, ed. M. Cogan and I. Eph'al (Jerusalem: Magnes, 1992), 47.

[131] See above, chapter 1, n. 119.

Nebuchadnezzar's palaces in Babylon. The inscription is unusual because it contains a list of Babylonian and other officials, apparently arranged according to a hierarchy of offices. Within the list, officials are grouped together by geographical regions. A key problem that is too often ignored, however, is that the relationship of these officials to the court in Babylon is not specified. Unger's thesis was that the text represents a "Hof- und Staatskalender" containing a list of court and state officials appointed by Nebuchadnezzar.[132] But this is misleading. As Weissbach argued, apart from the list of officials the text is a regular building inscription; in his view, Unger's designation was completely off the mark.[133] It should be added that although the list of officials is atypical for a building inscription, it parallels rather closely the structure and purpose of Nebuchadnezzar's Etemenanki cylinder, in which there is also a list, but of toponyms (and a few officials). This parallel offers an opportunity for assessing the prism list anew, without assuming that the list functioned simply to name Nebuchadnezzar's appointees.

Unger published portions of only five columns of the prism fragment (another partial column exists in the Istanbul museum[134]); the end of column iii and the preserved portions of columns iv and v contain the names of Babylonian and other officials. The following sentence precedes this list:

> 23. MA.DA MA.DA *kà-la-ši-na* . . . 28. *a-na e-pé-šum e-ka-al-lam* . . . 31. [giš]*al-lam ad-di-in-šu-nu-ši-im-ma* 32. *ú-ša-aš-bi-it-su-nu-ti du-up-šik-ka-a-ti* 33. MUR.MEŠ *? bi? lat? ṣi-bi-it-ti du-ul-lu* 34. *ma-an-za-zu ša re-e-ši-ia ú-ša-aš-bi-it*

> all those lands . . . in order to build the palace . . . I gave to them the hoe and made them take up work baskets, tribute . . .(?) the implementation of the corvée (*ṣibitti dullu*) I assigned my officials.[135]

The last two lines are difficult and have created some problems for understanding the list that follows them. Unger, the editor of the text, translated: "Zur Dienstleistung in Stellung bei meiner Person

---

[132] Unger, *Babylon*, 35-37.

[133] Weissbach, Review of Unger, *Babylon*, *ZA* 41 (1933), 258-59.

[134] Berger knew of it, see *Königsinschriften*, 59; new photographs also confirm this, and I am grateful to Dr. V. Donbaz for supplying the photographs.

[135] Unger, *Babylon* 284 iii 23-34. Line 33 is a crux, but it is difficult to make a reading from the photo, and I am unaware of proposals other than those given here.

verpflichtete ich."[136] Oppenheim rendered: "I ordered the (following) court officials in exercise of (their) duties to take up position in my (official) suite."[137] Both scholars concluded their translations of line 34 with a colon to create a link with the following list of names; Oppenheim makes this even more explicit with the addition of the word "(following)." Landsberger's translation, however, is preferable: "Ich ließ meine Hofbeamten die Ausführung der (Bau)arbeit übernommen."[138] As his translation suggests, he takes *ṣibitti dullu* to refer to implementation of the corvée work ("Ausführung der [Bau]arbeit") on the palace. This last clause, therefore, continues the idea of the preceding lines, which concern the assignment of building tools for corvée.[139] The translations of Unger and Oppenheim break the sense of the text. Moreover, the idiom *dullu . . . ušaṣbit* has a relatively close parallel in the Etemenanki cylinder, and in a passage that is similar to the one in question in that it introduces a list of local and distant regions involved with construction: *napḫar nišī dadmī rapšātim . . . ina epēšu Etemenanki dullum ušaṣbissunūtima emissunūti tupšikku*, "the totality of the people of the widespread inhabited regions . . . in order to build Etemenanki, I made them undertake the work and imposed upon them the work basket."[140] Admittedly, in the prism fragment Nebuchadnezzar assigns implementation of the corvée (*ṣibitti dullu*) to "my officials" (*manzāzu ša rēšiya*), while in the Etemenanki cylinder he assigns the widespread people to the corvée. Nevertheless, the assignment of the work or its implementation occurs in both texts. Furthermore, a list of names that is connected to the building project follows in each, but without an obvious syntactic relationship to the

---

136 *Babylon*, 289 iii 34.

137 *ANET*, 307.

138 *ZA* 41 (1933), 298. He does not defend the translation of *ṣibittu* with "Ausführung," but the meaning is accepted in *AHw* 1097b, s.v. *ṣibittu* 2, "Arbeitsaufnahme."

139 This is how Berger understands the text too: "Der [letzte] Abschnitt der Inschrift, der sich auch auf die beiden anschließenden Kolumnen erstreckt, bringt nach kurzem Einleitungssatz eine Liste der 'Honoratioren', denen zum Palastbau Arbeitsgerät 'in die Hand gedrückt' wurde" (*Königsinschriften*, 59).

140 WVDOG 59 46 3.39-53. Similar language occurs in Nabopolassar's Nēmetti-Enlil cylinder, but without any list of places or persons; indeed, the focus is on Babylonia, in conformity with the restricted perspective in Nabopolassar's texts: "I placed the work-basket on all of my workmen, the hoe and the spade I made the people of the upper and lower land . . . carry" (BRM 4 51 14-19=YOS 9 84=Zyl II,3). For the phrase "upper and lower land" as a reference only to Babylonia, see above, chapter 1, n. 108.

introductory sentence. The lists, therefore, seem to be independent pericopes that delineate those persons or places involved in or that had oversight of the corvée.

There are other close connections between the prism list and the list of toponyms in the Etemenanki cylinder. The sequence of GNs in the Etemenanki list apparently follows a geographical progression from south to north, although there are several gaps in the text that make this uncertain. The prism fragment groups the various classes of officials according to geographical regions. What scholars have not recognized is that the subsections of the prism fragment list correspond quite closely in their geographical extent to the discernible subsections of the Etemenanki list, although not in the same order.

The prism fragment groups the officials under rubrics which enumerate their titles, if the preserved parts of the prism reliably indicate the structure of the whole.[141] The list is partial, since the prism is broken on the top, but the preserved subsections proceed as follows: first come *mašennū*-officials (iii 35-iv 19), persons in high offices not associated with any particular locale, but who probably functioned in Babylon. Second is a list of "nobles of the land of Akkad" (*rabûti ša māt Akkadîm*, iv 20-33), each of whom is identified by name, title and region. In third place is one or more lists of ^{lú}É.MAŠ-officials (v 1-12); the second group of these officials, if col. v 3 represents a heading, comes from southern Babylonia.[142] Fourth is a list of *qēpī alāni* ("city officers"), whose associated GNs are all broken away. Finally, there are "kings" (LUGAL.MEŠ) of Levantine coastal cities.

A comparison with the Etemenanki list of GNs yields interesting results. The Etemenanki list is as follows:

> Ur, Uruk, Larsa, Eridu, Kullab, Nēmed-[Laguda],[143] Ugar-^{d}[?], the totality of [?] . . . Larak . . . the land of Puqudu, the land of Bīt-[Dakkuri], the land of Bīt-Amukānim, the land of Bīt-[?], the land of Birā[ti?], Dēr, Agade . . . the land of Arrapḫa, the land of Laḫīru,

[141] Oppenheim is probably incorrect to assume that the list represents the officials that Nebuchadnezzar appointed to his court, but he is right that iii 35, iv 20, v 3 and 13 are "headings of the following enumerations" of officials (*ANET*, 307b, n. 1, and 308, n. 7).

[142] The nature of this office is uncertain, and Oppenheim argued that it does not refer to *šangu*-priests. The first two lines of col. v list two É.MAŠ officials; col. v 3 then begins another section (if the lacuna at the beginning of the line is indicative of a new section) covering a portion of Babylonia with the heading: ^{lú}É.MAŠ.MEŠ.

[143] For another text that names these six cities, see George, *BTT*, 250; they were all exempted from taxes and corvée by Sargon II.

> and the totality of the land of Akkad and the land of Assyria (*napḫar mât Akkadî u mât Aššur*).

Then comes the mention of officials in Eber Nāri and Ḫatti. The region encompassed by the cities named in the first part of the Etemenanki list, from Ur to "the totality of . . ." (*napḫar* . . .), corresponds to the geographical range of the list of É.MAŠ-officials in the prism fragment (v 3-12): they are all from southern Babylonia. In fact, the names of three cities occur in both lists: Kullab, Nēmed-Laguda, and Larsa. The second part of the Etemenanki list, from Larak to *māt Laḫīru*, corresponds to the geographical range of the list of "nobles of the land of Akkad" in the prism fragment (iv 20-33): namely, central Babylonia and the East Tigris region south of the Lower Zab. Puqūdu, Amukānu, and Dēr occur in both lists, and so too, no doubt, did Dakkuri (broken in Etemenanki); only Dēr is common to both in the East Tigris region.[144] Furthermore, where the prism list introduces this section with the designation "nobles of the land of Akkad," the Etemenanki cylinder concludes the corresponding section with a similar statement: "all of the land of Akkad and Assyria" (where the scribe presumably considered Laḫīru and Arrapḫa part of Assyria). The Etemenanki list finally moves to Eber Nāri and Ḫatti, while the final preserved part of the prism fragment concludes with kings from cities of the Levantine coast, i.e., kings resident in Ḫatti. This is another parallel between the lists. There may have been additional equivalencies, but the breaks in both texts do not allow certainty.

Both lists, then, explicitly concern Nebuchadnezzar's building projects in Babylon. The correspondence between them suggests that their observable geographical divisions were important for the prosecution of the imperial building projects. One could infer too that records would have been kept of the regions that were responsible for contributing to the building projects. An allusion to this practice comes from another of Nebuchadnezzar's cylinder inscriptions which notes that the peoples of "all lands" were conscripted for construction of the royal palace, and that: *ša re-di-i* MA.DA MA.[DA *ra-ap-ša-a-t*]*i? šu-ma-an-šu-un aš-ṭú-úr-ma*, "I recorded the names of the officials of the

---

[144] Sumandar, listed in the prism fragment, may also be in the East Tigris region; see Frame, *Babylonia 689-627 B.C.*, 291; but there is also a toponym of this name near Uruk; cf. Zadok, Rép. géogr. 8, 275, s.v. Sumundar.

[widespread] countries."[145] Thus, the empire was very likely divided into broad geographical divisions which were levied for corvée or taxed for tribute.

As mentioned, each of the last seven lines preserved in the prism fragment begins with LUGAL *ša* KUR X, "king of the land of X." All of the toponyms are partly broken, but Unger convincingly restored them: kur*Ṣú-[ur-ru]* (Ty[re]), kur*Ḫa-az-[za-ti]* (Gaz[a]), kur*Ṣa-ʾ-d[u-ni]* (Sid[on]), kur*Ar-ma-[da]* (Arwa[d]),[146] kur*Áš-d[u-du]* (Ashd[od]), kur*Mir-*[x] (?),[147] and kur[x]. There is no compelling reason to think that the kings of these city-states were "among the captives in Babylon."[148] The Etemenanki list again provides a close parallel to the prism list. There is no suggestion in the Etemenanki list that the "kings of Eber Nāri and governors of Ḫatti" were present in Babylon, only that they had to contribute to building projects through delivery of raw materials. From the evidence of both lists, then, we may conclude that these western kings participated in the building of Nebuchadnezzar's palace, because they contributed either raw materials or workmen. From a geographical point of view, in any case, it appears that the coastal cities were not subsumed within provinces, even though they were under obligation to Nebuchadnezzar. All of these cities, some of which had been subject kingdoms and some provinces under the Assyrian kings, had reverted to

---

[145] P.-R. Berger and J. Zablocka, "Ein vollständigeres Duplikat zur Nebukadnezar II-Inschrift VAB 4 Nr. 46," *Or* n.s. 38 (1969): 123 (=Zyl II,9) ii 8-9. The meaning of *rēdû* here is not entirely clear, see *AHw* 968, s.v., 3a, which suggests "Verwalter, Vertreter eines Amtes." For other NB examples, outside of royal inscriptions, that use similar language to describe the enumeration of personnel for administrative purposes, see *CAD* Š/1 235, s.v. *šaṭāru* 3.4'. I am unaware of such language in other Neo-Babylonian royal inscriptions.

[146] The shift of medial *w* > *m* is ubiquitous in Neo-Babylonian orthography (and Middle Babylonian); see *GAG* §21d. Arwad had been subsumed within the Neo-Assyrian province of Ṣimirra; the mention of its king here is therefore noteworthy: it had possibly reverted to a native kingship after the dissolution of the Assyrian provincial system.

[147] Candidates for a GN beginning with *mir-* are not obvious, and new photographs of the prism seem to confirm the reading.

[148] So Katzenstein, *Tyre*, 319; see too Briquel-Chatonnet, *Relations*, 222. We know of kings who were deported to Babylon, including Aga of Ashkelon and Jehoiachin of Judah (Weidner tablets). But this does not prove that the present list, in a royal inscription, has anything to do with captive kings. It is clear in any case that not all of the officials mentioned in the list were present in Babylon; most were office-holders elsewhere in Mesopotamia. Wiseman makes the same point, although his assertion that the list was "drawn up to record a procession to commemorate a special occasion" (*Nebuchadrezzar*, 74-75) is purely speculative.

kingships by the time of Nebuchadnezzar. The Babylonians exercised political authority in the region, but relied directly on compliant kings in their dealings with these cities. The Assyrian provincial system, we should conclude, had collapsed earlier, even if the existence of subject kingdoms persisted.

The text edited by Lambert under the title "Nebuchadnezzar King of Justice" also gives some information about imperial geography in the west. The last lines preserved on the tablet seem to be part of a summary of the king's conquests: [*ina*] *ka-šá-a-du iš-tu* ^{kur}*mi-ṣi*[*r*] *a*-[*na/di*] [^{uru}*ḫ*]*u-me-e* ^{uru}*pi-rid-du* ^{uru}*lu-*⌈*ú*⌉*-du*, "[upon] conquering from Egypt as far as Ḫumê, Piriddu, Lydia."[149] The text then breaks. If it is correct to assume that the text refers to Nebuchadnezzar, it confirms that the empire in the west reached at least from the border of Egypt to Asia Minor, encompassing the entire region adjacent to the eastern Mediterranean. This is roughly equivalent to the Deuteronomistic Historian's summation: "the king of Babylon [Nebuchadnezzar] captured all that had belonged to the king of Egypt from the brook of Egypt to the Euphrates River" (2 Kgs 24:7). The King of Justice text gives no indication, however, about how the subject regions were organized administratively.

A few further details about the geographical divisions in the empire also emerge from the Babylonian chronicles. The chronicles seem to use the term *piḫātu*, "district, province," without reference to explicitly defined provincial regions: thus Nabopolassar captures Tarbiṣu, *ālu ša piḫat Ninua*^{ki}, "a city of the district of Nineveh"; he marches once *adi piḫat* ^{uru}*Urašṭu*, "as far as the district of (the city of) Urartu," and once *ana GN piḫat* ^{kur}*Urašṭu*, "to GN in the district of (the land of) Urartu"; Nebuchadnezzar routs the Egyptians *ina piḫat* ^{kur}*ḫa-ma-a-t*[*ú*], "in the district of Hamath."[150] Interestingly, neither Urartu nor Hamath was apparently ever an Assyrian province, and there is no evidence that shows they were provinces under the Babylonians either. The occurrences of *pīḫatu* in the chronicles, therefore, provide insufficient evidence to prove that such regions were coherent administrative or political units.

---

[149] Lambert, "King of Justice," v 20-21 (CT 46 45). For the location of these territories in Asia Minor, see the Neriglissar chronicle (TCS 5 chron 6) and the comments of Wiseman, *CCK*, 86-87.

[150] Respectively, TCS 5 chron 3:25; 3:72; 4:3 (also 4:11); and 5 obv. 6. Earlier references in the chronicles include: a battle *ina pīḫat Dēr* (1 i 34); and a battle *ina pīḫat Nippur* (1 iii 3);

The disparate notices concerning imperial geography that we have discussed do not suffice to show, then, that the Babylonian empire divided into provincial units, as had the Assyrian empire. The textual references preserve nothing like the detail and ordered arrangement evident in the Assyrian sources. Wherever the Babylonian data refer to regions beyond the heartland, especially in Eber Nāri and Ḫatti (where local kings ruled in territories that were once Assyrian provinces), it is difficult to specify the larger geopolitical organization of such regions. Thus, the evidence so far does not clearly show that the Babylonians created imperially administered, bureaucratic provincial units in the western reaches of the empire. Further evidence could disprove this conclusion, but what we do know argues against the existence of a structured provincial system.

2.4.1.2 Imperial Officials

What officials had oversight of the imperial administration in the west, such as it was? The Etemenanki inscription, we have noted repeatedly, refers to both kings and governors in Eber Nāri and Ḫatti, but it gives little precise information about them. In this connection, a few administrative tablets from Babylonia, the Babylonian chronicles, the geographical lists discussed above, the Saqqara papyrus, and biblical narratives provide some evidence. The main question is whether imperial officials were appointed in the west, and if so, whether they functioned side by side with local kings.

The most direct evidence for the existence of Babylonian district governors in the west, besides the Etemenanki inscription, comes from a pair of administrative tablets from the Ebabbar temple in Sippar. Joannès recently reanalyzed the two tablets and noted that a beef cow belonging to the governor (LÚ.NAM, *pīḫatu*) of Arpad was stabled at the Ebabbar in Nebuchadnezzar II's nineteenth year (586).[151] As Joannès emphasized, the mention of a western governor in a tablet from Babylonia is exceedingly rare.[152] To account for this he hypothesized that the governor of Arpad may have been obligated to facilitate the deportation of Judean exiles to Babylonia. Jerusalem had fallen to Nebuchadnezzar in the same year and, Joannès noted, Arpad lay on the

[151] "Une visite du gouverneur d'Arpad," *NABU* (March, no. 1, 1994): 21-22; the texts are *Nbk* 74 r. 3-4 and CT 56 439:13.

[152] I am unaware of any other archival texts that mention governors from the west.

route that the Babylonian army might have taken from Riblah—where they are said to have executed members of the Judean royal family (2 Kgs 25:6-7)—to the Euphrates.[153] While Joannès's hypothesis is obviously speculative, he is correct about the rarity of such notices concerning western governors. That a cow offered by the governor of Arpad (*ša irbi ša pīḫati ša Arpadu*, "an offering of the governor of Arpad")[154] rated mention in the temple records, demonstrates an established link between a distant official and the Babylonian temple establishment. Thus there is evidence for a district governor in the Aleppo region during the reign of Nebuchadnezzar II.

Several scholars have argued that there was a Babylonian official stationed farther south, in Tyre, as well. At least eleven cuneiform tablets are known that were written at a city called *Ṣurru* between the thirty-first and forty-second regnal years of Nebuchadnezzar II.[155] Unger argued long ago that Ṣurru should be identified with Phoenician Tyre. He also argued that the presence there of a *šandabakku*-official, Enlil-šāpik-zēri, who is the first witness to a transaction described in one of the tablets, indicates that Nebuchadnezzar installed high officers in Tyre after his long siege and conquest of the city.[156] Katzenstein, and, more recently, Wiseman and Elat, followed Unger.[157] Landsberger, however, already doubted whether the Phoenician city of Tyre was meant in the texts available to Unger, and suggested that there was probably a small site of the same name near Uruk.[158] Joannès has now conclusively proved that the toponym Ṣurru/Ṣūru should be located between Nippur and Uruk, and that the *šandabakku*, Enlil-šāpik-zēri, was resident in Nippur, the usual seat of the *šandabakku*.[159] Settlements near Nippur

---

[153] "Une visite du gouverneur d'Arpad," 21-22.

[154] *CT* 56 439:13.

[155] For a list of the texts composed at Ṣurru, see F. Joannès, "Trois textes de Ṣurru a l'époque néo-babylonienne," *RA* 81 (1987): 147-48.

[156] The text refers to ^{md}*en-lil*-DUB.NUMUN ^{lú}GÚ.EN.NA, "Enlil-šāpik-zēri, the *šandabakku*" (GCCI 94:11-12). See E. Unger, "Nebukadnezar II. und sein Šandabakku (Oberkommissar) in Tyrus," *ZAW* 44 (1926): 315-16. On the siege of Tyre, see Katzenstein, *Tyre*, 330-32.

[157] Katzenstein, *Tyre*, 332-33; Wiseman, *Nebuchadrezzar and Babylon*, 28; idem., "Babylonia 605-539 B.C.," in *CAH*, 2d ed., vol. 3, part 2, *The Assyrian and Babylonian Empires and Other States of the Near East, from the Eighth to the Sixth Centuries B.C.*, ed. J. A. Boardman et al. (Cambridge: Cambridge University Press, 1991), 235; and Elat, "Phoenician Overland Trade," 32-33.

[158] Landsberger, review of Unger, *Babylon*, *ZA* 41 (1933): 298.

[159] F. Joannès, "La localisation de Ṣurru à l'époque néo-babylonienne," *Semitica* 32 (1982): 35-42; and idem, "Trois textes de Ṣurru." The arguments

were sometimes named after the ethnicon or place of origin of the deportees who populated them, which would explain the appearance of the toponym Ṣurru in Babylonia. Later, the toponym ^{uru}*Bīt Ṣurāja*, "settlement of the Tyrians," occurs in texts of the Achaemenid era, although the settlement of Tyrian deportees goes back to the reign of Nebuchadnezzar, since the ration tablets published by Weidner mention 126 Tyrians (^{lú}*ṣur-ra-a-a*) in Babylonia in that period.[160]

Another text written at Ṣurru and dated to 22 Du'uzu in the fortieth year of Nebuchadnezzar (564 B.C.E.) mentions a certain ^{m}*mil-ki-i-ṭi-ri* ^{lú}EN.NAM (*bēl pīḫati*) *šá* ^{uru}*ki-di-iš*, "Milki-eṭēri, governor of the city of Kidiš."[161] Numerous scholars have understood this as a reference to Qadesh on the Orontes River in Syria, which would place a

---

adduced by Joannès in favor of locating Ṣurru in southern Babylonia are conclusive: the office of *šandabakku* is almost always associated with Nippur (see also *CAD* Š/1, 372-73, s.v. *šandabakku*); Enlil-šāpik-zēri is mentioned again three years later as *šandabbakku* in a text that actually comes from Nippur (BE 8/1 no. 31:9); not only the *šandabakku* but also other officials from the Eanna temple of Uruk, the Ebabbar temple of Sippar, and the Eigikalamma temple of Marad are referred to in the tablets; the tablets were discovered in Uruk, Sippar, and Nippur; one of the unpublished tablets written at Ṣurru was composed while the Phoenician city of Tyre was still under siege (Joannès, "La localisation de Ṣurru," 39-40; and "Trois textes de Ṣurru," 149). Elat acknowledges Joannès's argument regarding one of the texts, GCCI I 94, but still thinks that some of the administrative tablets cited by Joannès might come from Phoenician Tyre ("Phoenician Overland Trade," 32-33 and n. 76). In this Elat follows Zadok (Rép. Géog. 8, 281) who equivocates with respect to a few of the tablets (GCCI I 151:6 and 169:3). It is highly unlikely, however, that any of the tablets refers to the Phoenician Tyre. The only probable reference to the city of Tyre from the reign of Nebuchadnezzar (as opposed to Tyrians in Babylonia, see Weidner, "Jojachin," 929), is the reconstructed reading in the Istanbul prism fragment which mentions kings in the eastern Mediterranean region (Unger, *Babylon* 286 v 23).

[160] Weidner, "Jojachin," 929; for the phenomenon of naming settlements after the ethnic groups settled in them, see especially I. Eph'al, "The Western Minorities in Babylonia in the 6th-5th Centuries B.C.: Maintenance and Cohesion," *Or* n.s. 47 (1978): 80-81; also R. Zadok, "Phoenicians, Philistines and Moabites in Mesopotamia in the First Millennium B.C.E. Chiefly According to Akkadian Sources," *BASOR* 230 (1978): 60; and idem, "The Nippur Region During the Late Assyrian, Chaldean and Achaemenian Periods Chiefly According to Written Sources," *IOS* 8 (1978): 297, 300.

[161] The text (BM 81-4-28, 88) was first published by Pinches, *JTVI* 49 and later discussed by Unger, "Nebukadnezar und sein Šandabakku," 316-17. It was reedited by Joannès, "La localisation de Ṣurru," 37, from which source it is cited here. Another text mentioning Kidiš is published by McEwan, ROM 2, no. 2:17.

Babylonian administrator in the region south of Arpad.[162] Again, however, it is very likely that Kidiš was a settlement near Nippur, just like Ṣurru; in fact, Ṣurru is where the scribe wrote the tablet.[163] There is additional evidence in favor of this conclusion. Another tablet that was written at Kidiš, dated one year and two days later than the above mentioned tablet, describes the sale of a female slave. The seller of the slave, Aḫšunu, is to deliver her to Šamaš-iqīša, the father of the slave's buyer, Zērija.[164] Šamaš-iqīša, the person to whom the slave is delivered, lives in Nippur. This shows that Kidiš was near Nippur, not in northwestern Syria.[165] Thus, it is necessary also to dismiss the mention of "Milki-eṭeri governor of Kidiš" as evidence for the appointment of imperial officials in the Levant; he was a local Babylonian official.

The Babylonian chronicles occasionally refer to persons during the Neo-Babylonian era who bore official titles and offices, such as *šakin māti ina Uruk*^{ki} (7 ii 22) and ^{lú}NAM (*pīḫati*) ^{kur}*Guti* (7 iii 15, 20).[166] According to the chronicles, however, none of these offices or officials is attested for the southwestern reaches of the Neo-Babylonian empire.

Much more oblique is a reference in the Saqqara papyrus: in his plea to Pharaoh, Adon refers to *pḥh bmtʾ*, "a governor in the land." The line is not fully preserved, however, and it is not certain what the text means. From the substance of the letter, it appears that Adon's concern is either that a local Babylonian official, a *pḥh*, will attack him, or perhaps that the Babylonian king might install such an official in Adon's city should it fall. Aramaic *pḥh* is the cognate of Akkadian (*bēl*)

---

[162] Unger, "Nebukadnezar und sein Šandabakku," 316-17; McEwan, ROM 2, p. 5, n. 5; Wiseman, *Nebuchadrezzar and Babylon*, 28; idem, "Babylonia 605-539 B.C." 235; Zadok, Rép. géogr. 8, 255, s.v. *Qidiš*; and Elat, "Phoenician Overland Trade," 33.

[163] Joannès also argued for this location of Kidiš, "La localisation de Ṣurru," 42, n. 1.

[164] ROM 2, no. 2 obv. 8-9.

[165] Whether the toponym was named for deportees from Syrian Qadesh who dwelled in Babylonia is uncertain. Qadesh seems to disappear from cuneiform records after the Late Bronze age. There is mention in NA texts of *ki-di-si*, but whether this is the same locale must be left open. There was no NA province called Qadesh, and although none of these observations is decisive, it would appear that the homophony is coincidental.

[166] Officials from earlier in the Neo-Babylonian period include: Nabû-šuma-ukīn, a *bēl pīḫati* (chron 1 i 16), Nabu-zēr-kitti-līšir, *šakin māt tâmtim* (chron 1 iii 30); as well as the *šandabakku* of Nippur (chron 1 iii 43; iv 1).

pīḫatu,[167] but since the term *pḥh* in the Northwest Semitic languages refers to numerous classes of officials, its presence in the papyrus is too uncertain to prove that specifically Babylonian administrators were present or known in the southern Levant.[168]

A seal impression on a stamped jar handle excavated in the seventh-sixth century destruction debris at the site of Ein Gedi, on the west shore of the Dead Sea, was taken by some scholars as evidence that a Babylonian official might have been appointed in Judah. The handle is stamped with a winged sun-disk, and above the wings are four Hebrew letters. Following a suggestion of S. Yeivin, the excavators suggested the possibility that the reading might be *lmrʾ*, "belonging to the lord," where *mrʾ* is an Aramaic title.[169] They thought that this might then be a reference to an imperial official, perhaps even Nebuchadnezzar himself, if he adopted or was ascribed this Aramaic title.[170] On paleographic grounds alone this interpretation is unlikely. Although the use of Hebrew characters for Aramaic words is not unprecedented, the fourth letter of the stamp, partly effaced, is much more likely a *taw* than an *ʾalep*, as Avigad already suggested,[171] since the stance and form are not in keeping with those of an *ʾalep*.[172] The second letter is also

---

[167] See S. A. Kaufman, *Akkadian Influences on Aramaic*, AS 19 (Chicago: University of Chicago Press, 1974), 82 and n. 263.

[168] For the use of *pḥh* in Northwest Semitic, see J. Hoftijzer and K. Jongeling, *Dictionary of the North-West Semitic Inscriptions* (Leiden: E. J. Brill, 1995), 904.

[169] Another undecorated stamp from the Damascus region clearly bearing the inscription *lmrʾ* in Aramaic lapidary characters of the eighth-seventh centuries was published by M. Heltzer ("An Old-Aramean Seal-Impression and Some Problems of the History of the Kingdom of Damascus," in *Arameans, Aramaic and the Aramaic Literary Tradition*, ed. M. Sokoloff [Ramat-Gan: Bar-Ilan University Press, 1983], 9-13). The *mem* with two checks forming the head, the *reš* with a closed triangular head, and the archaic *ʾalep* with two oblique cross-bars meeting at a point to the left of the vertical downstroke give a date much earlier than the Hebrew stamp from Ein-Gedi. The large separation in time and space between the two stamps, not to mention the decoration and uncertain reading of the Hebrew one, makes direct comparison between the two impossible. On the paleography, see J. Naveh, *The Development of the Aramaic Script* (Jerusalem: Israel Academy of Sciences and Humanities, 1970), 15-20; 51-54.

[170] B. Mazar, et al., "En-Gedi: The First and Second Seasons of Excavations 1961-62," *ʿAtiqot* (English Series) 5 (1966): 34-35 and pl. 26:1.

[171] Ibid., 34.

[172] The vertical is slanted much too sharply to the upper left. Moreover, in Hebrew *ʾaleps* of the late eighth-sixth centuries the lower stroke on the right of the vertical does not normally cross it; when it does cross the vertical, it does not come

unclear; the excavators suggested *mem* or *nun*, the latter being the preferable option between these two, but it could well be *kap*.[173] This would yield *lnrt* or *lkrt*.[174] Barkay has also challenged the excavators' view that the stamp has some relationship to a Babylonian official, adding the argument that ceramic parallels for the handle would place it in the late eighth century.[175]

As with the imperial geographical divisions in the west, therefore, there are comparatively few data relating to the various officials who might have been imperial officers. The best evidence that such offices existed in the periphery remains Nebuchadnezzar's Etemenanki inscription, with its *piḫātu* and *šakkanakkū* officials in Eber Nāri and Ḫatti, and the two administrative tablets from the Ebabbar temple in Sippar that mention the *piḫātu* of Arpad, near Carchemish. These few references, however, scarcely point to a well-defined provincial system beyond Babylonia, and cannot easily support the reconstruction of such a system in the southern Levant. Absence of evidence, admittedly, is not a sufficient argument for drawing such general conclusions, so it would be well to test this hypothesis more closely in a specific instance.

2.4.1.3 The Case of Judah

The situation in Judah after Nebuchadnezzar's sack of Jerusalem is discussed in 2 Kings and Jeremiah, and offers a test case. What is the evidence that the Babylonians made Judah into a province after their invasions?

---

so near the baseline as it does in the present example. The fourth letter is more characteristic of the squat, "x"-shaped *taw* of the period.

173 Mazar, *En-Gedi*, 35. The letter has only one horizontal stroke joining the downstroke; if it is *kap* this would mean that the horizontal diverges into two strokes where the letter is effaced. More often, the two strokes comprising the head of the *kap* converge at the downstroke. Parallels to the type with only one horizontal joining the downstroke are, however, attested in Hebrew bullae and seals of the seventh and sixth centuries; see, e.g., N. Avigad, *Hebrew Bullae From the Time of Jeremiah* (Jerusalem: Israel Exploration Society, 1986), 26 no. 6; and 70 no. 91. *Mem* seems very unlikely given the space limitation.

174 The gentilic *krty*, "Cherethite," relating to a group associated with the Philistines, is known from the HB (1 Sam 30:14; Ezek 25:16; Zeph 2:5), although it is not apparently productive of PNs in the first millennium. Without positing any relationship to the ethnicon or the stamp in question, we may note that *krt* is of course also the name of a heroic king in Ugaritic lore.

175 G. Barkay, "The King of Babylonia or a Judaean Official?" *IEJ* 45 (1995): 41-47.

The most important datum is that Nebuchadnezzar appointed (הפקיד) Gedaliah ben Aḥikam over the people left in the land after Jerusalem's final destruction and the Babylonian deportations (2 Kgs 25:22-23; Jer 40:7). Years earlier, of course, Nebuchadnezzar had also deposed Jehoiachin and appointed Zedekiah (Mattaniah) as king of Judah (2 Kgs 24:12,17). Machinist notes, however, that with Zedekiah the verb used by the biblical historian to describe his appointment is המליך, whereas the historian consistently uses הפקיד in reference to Gedaliah's appointment; the latter was not considered a king, at least by the historian.[176] Moreover, Gedaliah's headquarters moved from Jerusalem, which lay in ruins, to Mizpah (presumably Tell en-Naṣbeh), in the traditional territory of Benjamin. At Mizpah, there were כשדים, "Chaldeans," alongside Gedaliah (2 Kgs 25:25; Jer 41:3); and apparently they exercised some authority (2 Kgs 25:24), although what this was and whether it outlasted the brief tenure of Gedaliah is not clear. The question, as Cogan and Tadmor note, is whether the language and circumstances describing Gedaliah's tenure prove that the Babylonians transformed the conquered kingdom, or a part of it, into a province.[177]

The answer is probably no. The Levantine coastal cities mentioned in Nebuchadnezzar's Istanbul prism, for example, were ruled by kings, not governors. The only Babylonian governor of the period singled out in cuneiform sources held office in Arpad, north of Aleppo in the Upper Euphrates region. And Gedaliah was not a Babylonian imperial officer, but rather a local noble appointed by the Babylonians. Even in the Neo-Assyrian provincial system there are few precedents for a local nobleman such as Gedaliah serving as a district governor.[178] What is more, after Gedaliah's assassination, the biblical traditions give no indication that the Babylonians moved to install a replacement or reorganize the territory. If the Babylonian imperial program involved the transformation of Judah into a province, then this left little impression on

---

[176] Machinist, "Palestine, Administration of," 79; *contra* Hayes and Miller, *History of Israel and Judah*, 421-23.

[177] *II Kings*, 327.

[178] So also Cogan and Tadmor, *II Kings*, 327. An exception may be Hadad-yisʿī (Aram. *hdysʿy*), governor of Guzanu, mentioned in the Fakhiriyeh inscription, although this text dates at the latest to the ninth century. The name is Aramaic, although the patronym is Assyrian, so even here the question of the office holder's origin is open. The *editio princeps* is A. Abu Assaf, P. Bordreuil and A. Millard, *La première bilingue assyro-araméenne: la statue de Tell Fekherye* (Paris: Editions Recherche sur les civilizations, 1982).

biblical historiographers. In fairness, however, one could say the same thing about the first half of the fifth century B.C.E., during the Persian imperial era, a period about which the biblical sources are silent even though the existence of provincial Yehud cannot be doubted. Here again, however, the point is precisely that the imperial structure of the Persian provinces existed earlier and is well-attested from other sources and from a vast array of material culture, while for the Babylonian period there are no comparative data to illuminate the dark age.

In addition to these arguments from textual sources, the material culture of Judah and adjacent regions in the first half of the sixth century points to a sharp contraction in demographic terms and to reduced economic activity, signaled, for instance, by the virtual disappearance of Greek ceramics. This evidence for a massive disjunction can hardly sustain the argument that the Babylonians under Nebuchadnezzar implemented a rational economic policy for exploiting a provincialized Judah.[179] Some people remained in Judah after 582, and there are consequently some archeological materials from this period, as Barstad has reiterated. There is, however, a significant occupational gap at many sites that the Babylonians had destroyed, as even a cursory survey of those sites indicates. The evidence for Babylonian destructions of cities and towns in Judah and adjacent regions is overwhelming: Jerusalem, Ramat Raḥel, Lachish, Gezer, Beth-shemesh, Ein Gedi, Arad, Kadesh Barnea, Meṣad Hashavyahu, Tell Keisan (IV), Megiddo (II), Dor, Akko, Tell ʿErani, Tell el-Hesi, Tell Jemmeh, Tell Malhata, and Tell er-Ruqeish, in addition to Ashkelon, Ekron, Timnah, Ashdod, and Tel Seraʿ (discussed above), are among the cities destroyed in the early sixth century.[180]

The picture of destruction is not complete. In the region north of Jerusalem, in the traditional tribal territory of Benjamin, some continuity

---

[179] Contra J. N. Graham, who argues that there was "a deliberate Babylonian economic and agricultural policy towards Judah" ("'Vinedressers and Plowmen': 2 Kings 25:12 and Jeremiah 52:16," *BA* 47 [1984]: 56); and the more systematic, but still deeply flawed, effort of H. M. Barstad, *The Myth of the Empty Land*, Symbolae Osloenses Fasc. Suppl., 28 (Oslo: Scandanavian University Press, 1996) who grossly overestimates the degree of material continuity in Judah through the mid-sixth century.

[180] For a survey of sites, see A. Mazar, *Archaeology of the Land of the Bible, 1000-586 B.C.E.* (Garden City, N.Y.: Doubleday, 1990), 458-60; also (though now dated) E. Stern, "Israel at the Close of the Period of the Monarchy," *BA* 38 (1975): 26-54.

can be detected between the late Iron II period and the Persian era.[181] Tell en-Naṣbeh,[182] Gibeah (Tell el-Fûl),[183] Bethel, and a few other sites have yielded some material from the period, although the stratigraphy at these sites is not clear. And this is the great problem. There may possibly be more pottery that should be assigned to the middle of the sixth century, but in the absence of well-stratified sites by which to establish a ceramic typology, it is hazardous to assign material to the period, since the basis for doing so can only be a hypothetical development of ceramic forms divorced from secure stratigraphic contexts.[184] Even the sparse data for material continuity in the region north of Jerusalem in the mid-sixth century, however, do not conform with the concept of a developed Babylonian administration in Judah.

There are also epigraphic materials that should be dated in the middle of the sixth century, perhaps in the period after the fall of Jerusalem. The more noteworthy among these include the Gibeon jar handles,[185] the so-called *m(w)ṣh* stamps (in Aramaic script),[186] the Khirbet Beit-Lei cave inscriptions,[187] and perhaps the silver amulet

---

[181] See especially S. Weinberg, "Post-Exilic Palestine"; also A. Mazar, *Archaeology*, 548-49.

[182] McCown, *Tell en-Naṣbeh, I*; see recently J. R. Zorn, "Mizpah: Newly Discovered Stratum Reveals Judah's Other Capital," *BAR* 23/5 (1997): 28-38; 66; and idem, "Tell En Naṣbeh: A Re-evaluation of the Architecture and Stratigraphy of the Early Bronze Age, Iron Age and Later Periods" (Ph.D. diss., University of California at Berkeley, 1993).

[183] See N. Lapp, *The Third Campaign at Tel el-Fûl: The Excavations of 1964*, AASOR 45 (Cambridge, MA: ASOR, 1981).

[184] To "triangulate" on an unknown era on the basis of better known earlier and later periods is of course a venerable archeological method, but it can lead to erroneous reconstructions where there are no data to illuminate the independent variables that influence the intermediate period (in our case, the Neo-Babylonian). In the same way, it is dangerous to reconstruct Babylonian imperial bureaucratic methods on the basis of what is found in the Assyrian and Persian eras.

[185] J. B. Pritchard, *Hebrew Inscriptions from Gibeon* (Philadelphia: University Museum, 1959); for a paleographical analysis confirming their sixth century date and significance, see F. M. Cross, "Epigraphic Notes on Hebrew Documents of the Eighth-Sixth Centuries B.C.: 3. The Inscribed Jar Handles from Gibeon," *BASOR* 168 (1962): 18-23.

[186] For an updated catalogue of the extant *m(w)ṣh* stamps, see J. R. Zorn, J. Yellin, and J. Hayes, "The *m(w)ṣh* Stamp Impressions and the Neo-Babylonian Period," *IEJ* 44 (1994): 161-83; the best discussion of their paleography remains Naveh, *The Development of the Aramaic Script*, 61-62.

[187] F. M. Cross, "The Cave Inscriptions from Khirbet Beit Lei," in *Near Eastern Archaeology in the Twentieth Century: Essays in Honor of Nelson Glueck*, ed. J. A. Sanders (Garden City, N.Y.: Doubleday, 1970), 299-306.

bearing the Priestly benediction from Ketef Hinnom.[188] All of these are dated on the basis of script typology, and thus cannot definitely be assigned to a particular decade. The *m(w)ṣh* impressions are potentially of interest for assessing the problem of Judah's status in the mid-sixth century. Thirty of the forty-two exemplars of this stamp type come from Tell en-Naṣbeh, which is likely biblical Mizpah, the seat of Gedaliah's tenure after 586. If these stamps reflect economic activity in the region during the Babylonian period, it is noteworthy that their distribution is confined to a very limited radius, which largely conforms to the borders of the tribal territory of Benjamin, a region that may have escaped extensive Babylonian destruction.[189] Unfortunately, these stamps cannot definitely be assigned to the Neo-Babylonian period; neither provenance nor paleography rules out a date in the Achaemenid era. The fact that they were written in Aramaic script may even support their ascription to the Achaemenid era, when Aramaic became even more widely used in administration than in earlier periods.

There is, all told, very little material that can definitely be labeled "Babylonian" in the Cisjordanian archeological record of the first half of the sixth century. What little there is comes from Tell en-Naṣbeh. Zorn has argued that fragments of several ceramic "bathtub" coffins from Naṣbeh might be of Mesopotamian origin, or at least reflect Mesopotamian burial practices.[190] The pieces come from uncertain stratigraphic contexts, however, and both their presence earlier throughout the Assyrian empire and their distribution in the Levant in the late Iron II period make their ascription specifically to the Babylonian period tentative. There is also one Neo-Babylonian inscription from Tell en-Naṣbeh. It is an inscribed bronze ring (?), from an uncertain stratigraphic context, which reads as follows: [. . .]⌈*a*⌉*-ia-da-a-ra* MAN-*šú ana* TIN ŠI-*šú* x [. . .].[191] The fragmentary text is difficult to reconstruct. In the published report, W. F. Albright, G. Cameron, and A. Sachs all ventured tentative readings, and agreed that the text most likely represents a dedicatory formula. The most plausible reading is that of

188 G. Barkay, "The Priestly Benediction on Silver Plaques from Ketef Hinnom in Jerusalem," *TA* 19 (1992): 139-92. Barkay suggests a seventh-century date, but Prof. F. M. Cross prefers a date in the sixth century on paleographical grounds (private communication).

189 Zorn, Yellin, and Hayes, "*m(w)ṣh* Stamp Impressions," 183; see also above n. 181.

190 J. R. Zorn, "Mesopotamian-style Ceramic 'Bathtub' Coffins from Tell en-Nasbeh," *TA* 20 (1993): 216-24.

191 McCown, *Tell en-Naṣbeh I*, pl. 55:80, and pp. 150-53.

Sachs: . . .]*a-ia-da-a-ra šarrišu ana balāṭ napištišu*, [. . .], "To . . .-]aiadāra?, his king, for his life, [So-and-so has dedicated this object]."[192] If this is correct, we know nothing more about the individual named. The script is definitely Neo-Babylonian, and Sachs, who analyzed the paleography most closely, suggested an eighth- to seventh-century range, although he did not rule out a date in the sixth century.[193] It seems reasonable to assume that the text comes from the era of the Neo-Babylonian empire, but its meaning and significance remain elusive.

The meager material evidence for Babylonian presence in Judah is telling. Given that Babylonian hegemony over the region lasted for a period of about sixty years—forty-five years in the era after Jerusalem's destruction—the imperial administration in the periphery was poorly developed. This is in sharp contrast, as Stager has also argued,[194] to the wealth of material from the southern Levant that dates to the first fifty years of the seventh century and that obviously derives from the Assyrian imperial administration: the existence of Assyrian governors, the presence Neo-Assyrian tablets, architecture, and ceramics. Apart from the Neo-Babylonian inscription from Naṣbeh, which cannot be dated precisely, there are few obvious Babylonian materials from the southern Levant. The remains from the first half of the sixth century are admittedly meager for the entire region, but this is part of the point; there is simply too little material to argue for widespread or durative Babylonian intervention or presence. Babylonian involvement, we should conclude, was not aimed at colonization or systematic economic exploitation, but was rather focused on control of the region through periodic military appearances that insured delivery of tribute.

This conclusion is supported too by a glimpse at the wider Levantine picture. Lehmann has shown, on the basis of an analysis of pottery from sites in Lebanon and Syria dating between 700 and 300 B.C.E., "that there was a major break within the pottery tradition" at roughly 580 B.C.E. There is a "clear separation" in the pottery traditions in the period after 580 (Lehmann's "Assemblage 5," dating c. 580-540)

---

[192] Ibid., 152; see there for other similar reconstructions. MAN ŠÚ should probably not be read *šar kiššati*, "king of the universe," as Albright argued, but rather as MAN-*šú*=*šarrišu*, "his king," as Sachs suggested, since the former title is exceedingly rare in the Neo-Babylonian period; on this, see above chapter one, section 1.3.

[193] Ibid., 152.

[194] "The Fury of Babylon," 69; "Ashkelon and the Archaeology of Destruction," 71*.

from the preceding Iron Age pottery traditions (his "Assemblage 4," dating c. 650-580). More signficantly, Lehmann concluded that "most pottery types from Assemblage 4 go out of use" in Assemblage 5, while there is a sharp reduction in the overall number of pottery types in Assemblage 5. Distribution patterns also change dramatically around 600-580.[195] All of this evidence from the northern Levant reinforces the conclusion reached on the basis of material from the southern Levant: the Babylonian imperial state brought about a massive reduction of economic activity throughout the Levant during the first half of the sixth century.

Although more information is slowly emerging from excavations and surveys to illuminate this period, such evidence, contrary to the arguments of Graham and Barstad, for example, does not point to direct Babylonian administration of the southern Levant, nor to a systematic economic plan for exploiting its resources. On the contrary, the archeological data point to a minimalist reconstruction of the Babylonian imperial bureaucracy.

2.4.1.4 Deportation

If the conclusions drawn above about the underdeveloped Babylonian administration and the lack of a well organized provincial system in the west are correct, then this might help to explain the logic of Babylonian procedures for the deportation of conquered foreign populations.

The Babylonians, it seems, did not practice the sort of cross-deportation that characterized Assyrian rule.[196] Rather they deported populations into the Babylonian heartland and settled them in discrete enclaves. This explains the phenomenon whereby settlements, especially in the vicinity of Nippur, were named after the ethnicon or place of origin of the exiles settled in them.[197] The prophet Ezekiel, of course, mentions the settlement of Judeans in Tel Abib (3:15), near the *nĕhar*

---

[195] Lehmann, , "Local Pottery Development in Syria and Lebanon," 21, 29-32 and figs. 8 and 13.

[196] For the most thorough analysis of the Assyrian procedures for deportation, see B. Oded, *Mass Deportations in the Assyrian Empire* (Wiesbaden: Reichert, 1979).

[197] Above p. 101 and n. 160.

kěbār (1:1), one of three canals in Babylonia with this name.[198] Just as important as the preservation of ethnic appellations in Babylonian geographical names is the formation of such names compounded with Akkadian *galūtu*, and *galû*, "exile."[199] Eph'al refers to ^{uru}*galūtu* and ^{uru}*galīya* as examples of settlements where foreign exiles were settled.[200] In contrast to this evidence for the settlement of foreign exiles in Babylonia, there is no evidence that the Babylonian kings transferred populations into the now depopulated territories from which the exiles came. Together with the evidence adduced above, this suggests that the Babylonians lacked the will to propagate a provincial system in the periphery of the empire.[201]

If the Babylonians did not perpetuate the Assyrian provincial system or generate any obvious system of their own, then deportation of foreign populations was necessarily one way. Unlike the Assyrians, the Babylonians had no reason to shift populations into the imperial periphery, because a centrally administered provincial system designed to achieve maximum political stability and economic prosperity did not exist. This would dovetail with the lack of Babylonian interest in the economic vitality of the west, as well as with the virtual cessation of East Greek trade in the Levant in the first half of the sixth century. As Stager suggested, it also helps to explain Nebuchadnezzar's scorched earth policy in Philistia and later Judah: the Babylonians had no interest in supervising the local economies, or in potential benefits to be derived from direct management of them. They were interested in receiving tribute, but apparently periodic (initially annual) campaigning ensured this, not a systemic bureaucratic presence.

Furthermore, the immense building projects that Nebuchadnezzar initiated in the heartland no doubt required infusions of labor, as several of his building inscriptions emphasize. Nebuchadnezzar's fixation with

---

[198] It was earlier thought that the canal was in the vicinity of Nippur (Zadok, "Nippur Region," 287), but additional evidence has proved the existence of two more canals of this name, so a decision about the location of the site is impossible (R. Zadok, "Notes on Syro-Palestinian History, Toponomy and Anthroponomy," *UF* 28 [1996]: 727).

[199] The words are loans in Assyrian and Babylonian from West Semitic; see Eph'al, "Western Minorities," 81, n. 20.

[200] Ibid., 81 for references.

[201] Stager has suggested that they may have lacked the means ("Ashkelon and the Archaeology of Destruction," 71*), but given the impressive military accomplishments and vast building efforts of Nebuchadnezzar in particular, this seems unlikely.

transforming Babylon into the center of the world, a tangible representation of divine favor, was intense, as noted in chapter one. Ultimately, however, such a policy may have created a centripetal force that was difficult to arrest, and which contrasts with the centrifugal force that seems to have played a role in pulling apart the Assyrian empire.

2.4.2. Economic Geography

Under Nebuchadnezzar II, as I have suggested, the Babylonians did not pursue a policy of systematic, bureaucratic economic exploitation of conquered territories in the west. Wholesale destruction of the cities of Philistia fits this reconstruction. Archeological evidence from Judah also provides a regional illustration of the minimal imperial economic bureaucracy. Lehmann concluded that there was likewise a sharp decline in the number of pottery types in Lebanon and Syria after about 600 B.C.E. and a complete reorganization of the distribution pattern of that pottery. His conclusions dovetail with those for the southern Levant. A more general phenomenon that illustrates the same point is the decrease in East Greek trade in the Levant in the first half of the sixth century. All of this is not to say, however, that there was no Babylonian involvement in the economies of the west. The delivery of items of tribute, notably cedar, from the Levant to Babylon is attested in the royal inscriptions, while the Babylonian chronicle states that booty and tribute were collected during Nebuchadnezzar's almost yearly campaigns to the west in the first decade or so of his reign. Is it possible to describe more closely Babylonian economic activity in the west?

In an important article dealing with overland trade, Oppenheim argued that the picture of forced delivery of commodities to the heartland presented in the royal inscriptions does not adequately describe the economic realities in the empire.[202] The royal inscriptions offer a picture designed to enhance what Mario Liverani, describing the period of the Late Bronze Age, has called the "prestige" of the royal court in the eyes of its native population.[203] Oppenheim argued, primarily on the basis of several economic texts from early in the reign of Nabonidus, that bilateral trade was also an important component in the exchange of goods. His argument is persuasive for the early part of Nabonidus's reign. The question is whether this reconstruction can be

---

[202] "Essay on Overland Trade"; see above p. 47 and nn. 165 and 166.
[203] *Prestige and Interest*, 205-10.

generalized for the whole of the Neo-Babylonian imperial period and for all regions. Elat, for example, argued that such bilateral trade was a relatively limited phenomenon, characteristic perhaps only of relations between Babylon and the Phoenician cities, and only during the reign of Nabonidus.[204] In Elat's opinion, bilateral trade did not characterize the Neo-Assyrian period or the Neo-Babylonian before the fall of Tyre, when one-way forced exchange was normative.

Oppenheim's reconstruction is strengthened (and Elat's weakened) on the basis of new evidence from the mid-eighth century Governor's Archive from Nippur, published by Cole. Precisely the sort of bilateral trade identified by Oppenheim for the early part of Nabonidus's reign was characteristic of Babylonian commerce two centuries earlier. Cole documents how Babylonian merchants sent traders out along established routes with capital in the form of silver or goods to obtain desired items for import. In the Nippur texts, both the goods acquired through trade and the capital used to obtain them were called *mēreštu*, literally "what is requested."[205] This basic procedure is also characteristic of the sixth-century texts discussed by Oppenheim. The Nippur Governor's archive illuminates trade contacts extending from Elam and the Zagros mountains in the east to the Middle Euphrates region, although networks extending farther afield probably also existed.[206] The continued participation in the Neo-Babylonian imperial era of private and royally sponsored merchants in international trade is not very well documented, but Dandamayev has adduced some additional evidence to this effect in recent years.[207]

It is possible to conclude, therefore, that some Babylonian merchants maintained trading arrangements with the west—those parts that did not come under Nebuchadnezzar's scorched earth policy—throughout the Neo-Babylonian era. From the point of view of the royal inscriptions, however, the mercantile focus is on the delivery of tribute and goods to Babylon from subject kingdoms, an expression of imperial hegemony. Indeed, for the subjugated communities as well, represented,

---

[204] Elat, "Phoenician Overland Trade."

[205] Cole, *Early Neo-Babylonian Governor's Archive*, 6-7; idem, *Nippur in Late Assyrian Times*, 58 and n. 15; Oppenheim, "Essay on Overland Trade," 239.

[206] Cole, *Nippur in Late Assyrian Times*, 56, 62-63.

[207] M. A. Dandamayev, "The Neo-Babylonian *tamkārū*," in *Solving Riddles and Untying Knots, Biblical, Epigraphic, and Semitic Studies in Honor of Jonas C. Greenfield*, ed. Z. Zevit, S. Gitin and M. Sokoloff (Winona Lake, Ind.: Eisenbrauns, 1995), 523-30.

for example, by the Judean prophets (see chapter three), it is this propagandistic interpretation of economic arrangements in the empire that receives attention. In other words, while the economic reality was multifaceted and included some bilateral trade, its interpretation by both the ruling kings and the subject populations focused on its imperial characteristics, the prestige element, to borrow Liverani's term. It is precisely this problem of how the imperial worldview and practices were perceived by the subjugated communities, and how such perceptions enhance the study of the empire, that informs the following discussion of the depiction and significance of Babylon in the Latter Prophets in the HB.

CHAPTER 3

BABYLON IN THE LATTER PROPHETS

3.1 Introduction

In his analysis of the literary form of the Neo-Babylonian royal inscriptions, Berger wondered "what literary influence from the realm of the Babylonian inscriptions could possibly have radiated outward beyond its speech area."[1] This is a useful comparative question to ask, but, in the end, too restrictive for the present study. It is restrictive first of all because not only Babylonian "literary influence" reached outward, but so too did the Babylonian theory and practice of empire as described in chapters one and two. During the reign of Nebuchadnezzar II in particular, imperial ideas and institutions were exported both through overt propaganda (e.g., the Wadi Brisa inscriptions and reliefs) and through various military and administrative mechanisms, even if the latter were minimally developed. Berger's question is restrictive in a second way, for it is necessary to think not only about the influence or impact that imperial ideas and institutions had on subject populations. Empire is fundamentally a dyadic relationship involving a superior and an inferior group. Babylon was politically dominant, and asserted as a corollary of that dominance the supremacy of its imperial ideas (described above in chapter one). Resistance to and acquiescence in these ideas would naturally have developed among conquered people. Examination of the subjugated component of this dyadic imperial relationship contributes to an understanding of the dialectical aspect of imperialism.

---

[1] "Welche literarische Einfluß aus dem Bereich der babylonischen Inschriften über ihr Sprachgebiet hinaus möglicherweise ausgegangen sein könnte" (Berger, *Königsinschriften*, 96).

In the case of the Neo-Babylonian empire, as with the preceding Neo-Assyrian one, the perspective of the subjugated is most fully preserved in the HB, and more particularly in the Latter Prophets. The decision to focus on the Latter Prophets is based on the fact that the prophetic writings more than any others reflect explicitly and self-consciously on the character and the fate of the empire. Through the lens of the prophetic writings it is possible to investigate the ideas and institutions of imperialism from the perspective of a subjugated community. In analyzing the prophetic point(s) of view about the empire, the question is not simply whether the biblical writers protested the imposition on their culture of the imperial ideas and practices, but how they did so. That is, one wants to know the degree to which the language about the empire, reflected in the sources emanating from the subjects, was given its particular character and force by the empire itself, and whether the imperial perspective was transformed by the subjects.

The present chapter, then, tries to accomplish two things in examining one subjugated group's perspective on the empire. First, it provides a survey of contemporary prophetic references to Babylon in the HB, those which can most plausibly be placed in the period of the Neo-Babylonian dynasty, or which otherwise concern Babylon of this dynasty. The main purpose of this survey, which is selective rather than exhaustive, is to describe and categorize the language about empire and to provide a composite portrait of prophetic attitudes toward the imperial overlord during the closing decades of the Judean monarchy and in the exilic era. This contemporary (essentially hostile) Judean portrait of Babylon naturally differs from the Babylonian self-portrait, and therein lies its value: it complements the picture of the empire developed independently above in chapters one and two.[2]

This leads to the second objective of the present chapter: to examine how the biblical writers resisted or acquiesced in the ideas and practices of the empire. Did the biblical writers attempt to subvert or otherwise engage the ideas and practices by which the imperial kings justified and maintained their rule? In this connection, there is also the opportunity to ask whether the prophetic language about Babylon differed in any significant way from prophetic language about Assyria, Babylon's imperial predecessor. This picks up the problem of continuity

---

[2] This method of analyzing the prophetic material is indebted to the work of Peter Machinist ("Assyria and its Image"), as noted in the Introduction above. We might label the present investigation Bible on Babel, to adapt a phrase.

between Assyria and Babylon as discussed in the previous two chapters, but from the point of view of a subjugated community.

The discussion in the present chapter focuses on prophetic texts that explicitly name Babylon (or Chaldea), the Babylonian king, or his representatives, usually as objects of derision, or as agents of Yahweh's wrath against Judah. These texts include Micah 4:10; Isaiah 13:1-22, 14:1-23, and 21:1-10; a variety of texts in Jeremiah 1-49 pertaining to the "foe from the north" and to the Babylonian king and his administration; Habakkuk 1-2; Ezekiel 17 and 21; several of the "idol passages" of the Second Isaiah (40:18-20; 46:1-2); Isaiah 47; and the anti-Babylon oracles of Jeremiah 50-51.

3.2 Micah 4:10

In perhaps the earliest reference to Babylon in the latter prophets, Micah designates Babylon as the place of exile for Judeans and as the place from which Yahweh will redeem a remnant of his people: ובאת עד־בבל שם תנצלי שם יגאלך יהוה מכף איביך, "you shall go to Babylon;[3] there you will be rescued; there Yahweh will redeem you from the hand of your enemies" (4:10). If the context of Micah's prophecy is the late eighth century, as the superscription to the book declares (1:1), then, as Hillers and others note, mention of exile to Babylon is troublesome.[4] Assyria, and not Babylon, was Judah's nemesis in the eighth century. If the reference belongs in the eighth century, then it is not obvious whether it has anything to do with the era of the Neo-Babylonian

---

[3] There is ambiguity in the biblical usage of the proper noun Babylon; it can refer either to the city or to the wider region of which the city was the capital (see below nn. 39 and 40 for the Mesopotamian perspective concerning the nomenclature). Generally, only context can aid in distinguishing between the two. There are some exceptions: ארץ בבל, "the land of Babylon" occurs twice in the anti-Babylon oracles in Jeremiah (50:28; 51:29), although even here the geographical reference is not precise. The use of מדינת בבל, "province of Babylon" is different. This usage derives from the administrative reorganization of Babylon into a province (satrapy) in the Persian period, and appears in biblical texts only beginning in the fifth century (e.g., Ezra 7:16; Dan 2:48,49; 3:1,12,30). On the Achaemenid organization of the empire according to satrapies, see especially O. Leuze, *Die Satrapieneinteilung in Syrien und im Zweistromlande von 520-320* (Halle, 1935; reprinted Hildesheim: Gerstenberg, 1972); and C. Tuplin, "The Administration of the Achaemenid Empire" in *Coinage and Administration in The Athenian and Persian Empires*, British Archaeological Reports International Series 343, ed. I. Carradice (Oxford: British Archaeological Reports, 1987), 109-66.

[4] D. R. Hillers, *Micah*, Hermeneia (Philadelphia: Fortress, 1984), 59.

empire. It is important to consider, therefore, why and by whom the author of the text thought that Judeans would be exiled to Babylon.

The possibility that a prophet of the eighth century would have considered the name Babylon to be interchangeable with Assyria, or as a cipher for Assyria, is an unlikely solution. Assyria and Babylonia were bitterly opposed during the latter part of the eighth century, especially during the reign in Babylon of the Chaldean sheikh Merodach-baladan II (721-710 and 703).[5] Substantial segments of the Babylonian population consistently resisted the imposition of Assyrian hegemony during these decades, and actively sought military assistance against Assyria from foreign groups. Merodach-baladan was a well-known anti-Assyrian coalition builder, and his diplomatic overtures to Hezekiah of Judah could hardly have gone unnoticed by Micah (2 Kgs 20:12-19//Isa 39:1-8). For these reasons, it is improbable that a Judean author of the late eighth century would have confused Assyria and Babylonia, or treated them as interchangeable.

Furthermore, after Assyria transformed Babylon into a province, Sargon II (721-705 B.C.E.) and his successors are said to have deported some Babylonians to Samaria (2 Kgs 17:24,30).[6] There is no clear evidence, however, that Israelites from Samaria or the northern kingdom of Israel were relocated in Babylonia after 722. The Deuteronomistic Historian (2 Kgs 17:6) refers to the exile of Israelites to Assyria, specifically to Ḥalaḥ (northeast of Nineveh[7]), to the region of the Ḫabur, the river of Gozan (Tell Halaf), and to ערי מדי, "the cities of the Medes."[8] Evidence for Israelites in Assyria and in the Ḫabur region comes from specifically Hebrew personal names (i.e., West Semitic

---

[5] J. A. Brinkman, "Babylonia under the Shadow of Assyria (747-626 B.C.)," in *CAH*, 2d ed., vol. 3, pt. 2, *The Assyrian and Babylonian Empires and Other States of the Near East, from the Eighth to the Sixth Centuries B.C.*, ed. J. A. Boardman et al. (Cambridge: Cambridge University Press, 1991), 26-28; see also Brinkman, "Merodach-baladan II," in *Studies Presented to A. Leo Oppenheim* (Chicago: University of Chicago Press, 1964), 6-53; and idem, "Sennacherib's Babylonian Problem," 89-95; and Machinist, "The Assyrians and Their Babylonian Problem."

[6] On the chronology of the deportations, see M. Cogan and H. Tadmor, *II Kings*, AB (Garden City, N.Y.: Doubleday, 1988), 209.

[7] Ḥalaḥ is both a city and a province, see ibid., 197.

[8] See I. Diakonoff, "ערי מדי. The Cities of the Medes," in *Ah, Assyria . . .: Studies in Assyrian History and Ancient Near Eastern Historiography Presented to Hayim Tadmor*, ScrHier 33, ed. M. Cogan and I. Eph'al (Jerusalem: Magnes, 1992), 13-20.

names compounded with the theophoric element **yhw*, **yaw*), which are plentiful in Assyrian administrative texts of the Sargonid period.[9] If Sargon had deported Israelites to Babylon, there might be grounds for Micah's statement that Judeans would also be exiled there, but the available evidence does not support this conclusion.

If Sargon did not deport Israelites to Babylon, did Sennacherib perhaps deport Judeans there after his third campaign of 701? The answer is not clear. There is apparently no direct evidence for the presence of Judeans in Babylonia, as opposed to the evidence for Israelites in the Ḫabur region and in Assyria during the seventh century. The possibility that Judeans might have been deported to Babylon by Sennacherib cannot be ruled out, but it cannot be proved either. It is therefore too speculative to assert on the basis of this possibility that Micah considered Babylon a potential destination for *Judean* deportees. It is worth asking, too, whether the Sargonid kings would transfer into Babylon a population that had presumably colluded with Merodach-baladan II against Assyrian rule, especially since fierce opposition to Assyrian hegemony persisted in Babylonia during the late eighth and first half of the seventh centuries.[10] On the whole, then, it seems unlikely

---

[9] R. Zadok collected the evidence for persons with Hebrew PNs in Assyria during the late eighth and seventh centuries, *The Jews in Babylonia during the Chaldean and Achaemenian Periods According to the Babylonian Sources*, Studies in the History of the Jewish People and the Land of Israel, vol. 3. (Haifa: University of Haifa Press, 1979), 35-38; see also I. Eph'al, "Israel: Fall and Exile," in WHJP, vol. 4/1, *The Age of the Monarchies: Political History*, ed. A. Malamat (Jerusalem: Massada, 1979), 190-91. For persons of Samarian origin in the cavalry of Sargon II whose names were compounded with the theophoric element **yaw* (one of whom was *ia-u-ga-a* < **ywgy̆*), see S. Dalley, "Foreign Chariotry and Cavalry in the Armies of Tiglath-pileser III and Sargon II," *Iraq* 47 (1985): 31-48. Israelites (or, again, individuals bearing West Semitic names compounded with a form of the divine name Yahweh) are also attested at Dūr-Katlimmu (Tell Šeḫ Ḥamad) in the Ḫabur region at the end of the seventh century, in the first three years of Nebuchadnezzar's reign; they may have been descendants of deportees from the Northern Kingdom of Israel. The texts mention *Aḫziyau* (^{m}*aḫ-zi-iá-a-u* 1:32), biblical *ʾăḥazyāhû*, *ʾăḥazyā*, *ʾaḥzay*; *Ḫazaqiyau* (^{m}*ḫa-za-qi-iá-a-u* 1:4), biblical *ḥizqîyāhû*, *ḥizqîyā*, etc.; *Sameʾyau* (^{m}*sa-me-eʾ-iá-a-u*, 1:33), biblical *šĕmaʿyāhû*; and, without any theophoric element, *Menasê* (^{m}*me-na-se-e*, 1:31), biblical *mĕnašše*. For publication of the Neo-Assyrian tablets from Dūr Katlimmu, see J. N. Postgate, "The Four 'Neo-Assyrian' Tablets from Šēḫ Ḥamad," *SAAB* 7 (1993): 109-24. For discussion of these names see F. M. Fales, "West Semitic Names in the Šeḫ Ḥamad Texts," *SAAB* 7 (1993): 142 and n. 27, and 146-48.

[10] See above, n. 5. See also the comments of Diakonoff, who notes that deported populations were typically settled in Assyria proper or in border regions

that Micah would have considered Babylon proper a destination for Israelite or Judean exiles in the late eighth century, and there is no independent evidence for their presence in the region as a consequence of deportations.

If this is correct, then it seems more likely that the reference to exile in Babylon in Mic 4:10, together with the promise of deliverance, is an interpolation that derives from the late seventh or early sixth century, when deportations to Babylon became only too familiar, and when the idea emerged that Yahweh would redeem a remnant of his people from that country. Even Y. Kaufmann, a staunch defender of the integrity of the prophetic books, allows that in this instance the text has been retouched by a later hand.[11]

To identify an interpolation without accounting for the logic of the interpolator, however, is unsatisfactory. What is the logic for the insertion in Mic 4:10b? It can perhaps be found in the sixth-century conflict about the correct Judean policy toward Babylonian political hegemony in Syria-Palestine. In the so-called Temple Sermon in Jeremiah 26, for example, the prophet argues that the temple will be razed and Jerusalem captured, no doubt by the Babylonians, if the Judeans do not observe the Torah of Yahweh. Zion, Jeremiah argues, is not inviolable. The priests, prophets, and people make a legal plea to the "the officials of Judah," and seek a משפט מות, "death sentence," against the prophet, "because he prophesied against this city just as you have heard with your own ears" (26:11). The leaders, however, reject the call for a death sentence, citing the prophecies of Micah the Moreshite against Jerusalem as a precedent for Jeremiah's word. In particular, the elders quote Micah 3:12 in defense of Jeremiah:

ציון שדה תחרש וירושלים עיים[12] תהיה והר הבית לבמות יער

where they could be entrusted with arms for their own defense and yet still be supervised ("The Cities of the Medes," 13).

[11] Y. Kaufmann, *The Religion of Israel: From its Beginnings to the Babylonian Exile*, trans. and abridged by M. Greenberg (Chicago: University of Chicago Press, 1960), 352. Alternatively, an editor might have replaced mention of Aššur with mention of Babylon, but this did not happen elsewhere in the book, and such a hypothesis requires the assumption that a capricious editor left his mark only once.

[12] Mic 3:12 has עיין; on the masculine plural termination in *-în*, a relatively less common biform of *-îm*, see GKC §§ 44k, 87e.

> Zion will be a plowed field, Jerusalem will become rubble, and the temple mount will become a high place[13] of the forest (Jer 26:18bβ = Mic 3:12).

When Assyria was dominant in the west in the late eighth century and threatened Judah's independence, Micah attacked the Judeans' blithe optimism about Zion's and the Temple's inviolability (3:11b). Jeremiah launched a similar attack during the period of Neo-Babylonian domination.[14] As long as the people were perceived to be acting corruptly, both prophets argued, the people should not retain confidence that the symbols of Yahweh's protection against imperial aggression, most obviously the temple, had the capacity to confer automatic safety. In Jeremiah, this assertion is followed in chapter 27 by the prophet's attempt to link the Judeans' moral corruption with the dominant anti-Babylonian political perspective of the "false prophets." Jeremiah states that if the people remain unwilling to capitulate to the Babylonians, against Yahweh's will but in accordance with the arguments of the false prophets, then their confidence in Zion's inviolability will have been badly misplaced (e.g., Jer 27:8-10). The reference to Micah's prophecy by the leaders of Judah in defense of Jeremiah is thus perceptive: in both cases, the question of Jerusalem's inviolability was under scrutiny, and with it the question of national existence in the face of a clear imperial threat.

Perhaps the secondary reference to the Babylonian exile at Micah 4:10 was inserted by a later author who wished to refer to Jeremiah's argument, which established the equation between moral behavior acceptable to Yahweh and political capitulation to Babylon. Failure to submit, Jeremiah perceived, was a recipe for disaster. The succession of Mesopotamian imperial powers in the Levant insured that the issue of whether Yahweh would permit Jerusalem to be conquered remained central in the thinking of the prophets, even after Hezekiah's deliverance from the armies of Sennacherib (2 Kgs 19:25). A relapse into the easy

---

[13] Translating a sg לבמת (see *BHS*); alternatively one might propose לבהמות יער, "(the temple mount will belong to) the animals of the forest," i.e., wild animals (compare Mic 5:7; and see Hillers, *Micah*, 47).

[14] For a discussion of the relationship between Jeremiah 26 and Micah, see Hillers, *Micah*, 8-9. On the broader intellectual background of Jeremiah's attack, see B. Halpern, "'Brisker Pipes than Poetry': The Development of Israelite Monotheism," in *Judaic Perspectives on Ancient Israel*, ed. J. Neusner, B. A. Levine and E. S. Frerichs (Philadelphia: Fortress, 1987), 77-115.

assurance that the city could not fall, Jeremiah argued, was a deadly error. The "officials of Judah" recognized a precedent for his words in Micah 3:12. The reference to Babylonian exile in Micah 4:10 might then have been inserted to point to the correctness of Jeremiah's stance vis-à-vis Babylon and to the reality of the Babylonian exile. At the same time, Micah 4:10 deflects the apparent finality of the Babylonian conquest by simultaneously announcing the hope of restoration, not unlike the Second Isaiah and other texts of the exilic era.

Micah 4:10, then, probably alludes to the sixth-century exile, and Jeremiah 26 appeals to the precedent of Micah (3:12) in speaking candidly about the possible destruction of Jerusalem. This reciprocity would seem to be an inner Judean dialogue, but it illuminates well how the phenomenon of imperialism, whether Assyrian or Babylonian, raised political and religious problems that transcended the moment. The biblical writers came to see a close connection between the Assyrian and Babylonian regimes. Elsewhere, in fact, particular language and intellectual responses to Assyrian domination were appropriated and applied to the later situation under Babylon.[15] A sixth century comment from the oracles against Babylon in Jeremiah gives a later biblical writer's perception of this trajectory:

שה פזורה ישראל אריות הדיחו[16] הראשון אכלו מלך אשור וזה
האחרון עצמו נבוכדראצר מלך בבל (Jer 50:17)

> Israel is a scattered ewe, (which) lions deported; the first to devour it was the king of Assyria, and now this is the last to crush its bones, Nebuchadrezzar, king of Babylon.

The addition of a reference to Babylonian exile at Micah 4:10 demonstrates how the earlier problem of the Assyrian menace was later interpreted as a typological precursor for understanding the Babylonian

---

[15] See the remarks of M. Weinfeld, "The Protest against Imperialism in Ancient Israelite Prophecy," in *The Origins and Diversity of Axial Age Civilizations*, ed. S. N. Eisenstadt (Albany, N.Y.: State University of New York Press, 1986), 169-82.

[16] The absence of a suffix on the pl verb presents a minor difficulty. It is possible that the 3 f sg suffix ה- was lost through haplography and the antecedent was שה construed as a feminine noun. Alternatively, הו- may have been lost, as LXX ἔξῶσαν αὐτόν, "they expelled him" (= 27:17) suggests. LXX may have construed either שה or, more likely, ישראל, as the antecedent. The verb נדח, הדיח is common in Jeremiah and elsewhere with the specific meaning "deport," or "exile," usually with Yahweh as subject. For references, see BDB 623a.

menace. It illuminates as well the ongoing struggle of the biblical writers to comprehend the role of imperial power, and Babylonian power in particular, in Judean affairs.

3.3 The Foreign Nation Oracles in the First Isaiah

The First Isaiah's foreign nation oracles refer explicitly to both Babylon and the Chaldeans[17] (Isa 13:1,19; 14:4,22; 21:9). Two issues require attention in the present discussion. First, the context in which these oracles were composed should be assessed. The issue here is like that for Micah 4:10: the Isaianic references to Babylon ostensibly have

---

[17] On the Chaldeans, see Brinkman, *PKB*, 260-67; Frame, *Babylonia 689-627 B.C.*, 36-43; and D. O. Edzard, "Kaldu," *RLA* 5 (1977): 291-97. Although scholars frequently call the Neo-Babylonian dynasty, which was inaugurated by Nabopolassar, Chaldean, its Chaldean origin has yet to be proved from Akkadian sources. One Seleucid era colophon describes Nabopolassar as *šar māt tâmtim*, "king of the Sealand" (RAcc 65 49), the traditional homeland of the Chaldeans, but the reference need not refer to the king's place of origin, let alone his ethnicity. In the text about a declaration of war published by Gerardi, a king of Babylon, perhaps Nabopolassar, says: [*ul*]-*tu qé-reb* KUR *ti-amat šap-li-tum* ^{d}AMAR.UTU EN GAL-*ú ina ni-ši* ⌈IGI⌉-[*šú*] *ip-pal-sa-ni-*⌈*ma*⌉, "fr[om] the midst of land of the lower sea, Marduk, the great lord, looked favorably upon me" (Gerardi, "Declaring War," 35 obv. 10-11). As Gerardi notes, however, it is not certain whether this is a reference to the Sealand (ibid., 37; see also above, chapter 1, n. 108). See for evaluations of the Akkadian evidence about the origin of the Neo-Babylonian dynasty, Brinkman, *Prelude to Empire*, 110, n. 551; idem, "Meerland" *RLA* 8 (1993): 10; R. H. Sack, *Images of Nebuchadnezzar: The Emergence of a Legend* (Selinsgrove: Susquehanna University Press, 1991), 110, n.3; and Frame, *Babylonia 689-627 B.C.*, 211-12 and n. 102.

In biblical usage, absent a gentilic formed from בבל (as opposed to such phrases as "inhabitants of Babylon," and "men of Babylon"), the inhabitants of Babylonia are identified by the ethnicon כשדים, "Chaldeans," which in itself does not prove the Chaldean origin of the Neo-Babylonian dynasty, only that the ethnicon came to stand for the inhabitants of Babylonia, *pars pro toto*. The clearest case in the HB of the use of the ethnicon for all Babylonians comes from Ezekiel. In his derisive allegory about Oholibah (Judah), he says she saw carved reliefs depicting אנשי מחקה על־הקיר צלמי כשדיים חקקים בששר, "men engraved upon the wall, images of Chaldeans engraved with vermillion" (23:14). They are called בני בבל כשדים ארץ מולדתם, "sons of Babylon, Chaldea is the land of their birth" (23:15). These בני בבל come to Oholibah's land to defile her. There may be a biblical parallel to this use of Chaldea as a GN in the less common term Shinʿar (Gen 10:10; 11:2; 14:2,9; Isa 11:11; Zech 5:11; Dan 1:2). This term refers to southern Babylonia (traditional Sumer), and may derive from the name of a Kassite tribal group resident there in the second millennium, if Zadok's argument on this point is correct ("The Origin of the Name Shinar," *ZA* 74 [1984]: 240-44).

nothing to do with the Neo-Babylonian empire if they derive from the eighth century and the time of Isaiah of Jerusalem, unlike the other prophetic materials discussed below which more clearly originate in the period of the empire. It is possible, however, that the oracles were revised or composed after the time of the First Isaiah, or that they derive from the sixth century and thus from the era of the empire.[18] Once the context of the oracles is discussed, the second issue is to assess how these oracles are related to Babylonian imperialism.

3.3.1 Isaiah 13

Do the references to Babylon in Isaiah's foreign nation oracles prove that the oracles were either composed or revised after the time of Isaiah of Jerusalem? We begin with Isaiah 13.

After the Day of Yahweh poem in Isa 13:2-16 there follows the announcement that Babylon, צבי ממלכות תפארת גאון כשדים, "the glory of kingdoms, the splendor of the pride of the Chaldeans" (v. 19), will be made into a ruinous, uninhabited heap. Its women will be violated (v. 16b) and wild animals will occupy its ruins (vv. 21-22). Yahweh's agents for destroying Babylon are the Medes (v. 17, also in Isa 21:2). The reference to the Medes is significant, since they did not emerge as enemies of Babylon before the sixth century. Moreover, Babylon posed no threat to Judah in the time of the First Isaiah. Would an eighth-century prophet have headed his foreign nation oracle collection with the announcement of Babylon's fall to the Medes? In all likelihood, this and the other references to Babylon in First Isaiah do not derive from the eighth century, but rather from the sixth.

The superscription of Isaiah 13 labels what follows a משא בבל, "oracle of Babylon." What is the context of the oracle and how does the prophet depict Babylon in it? The lack of specific references makes the

---

[18] There are, of course, numerous perspectives on this problem. S. Erlandsson, for example, argues that Isaiah 13-14 may be attributed to the eighth century prophet (*The Burden of Babylon: A Study of Isaiah 13:2-14:23*, Coniectanea Biblica Old Testament Series 4 [Lund: Gleerup, 1970]). B. Gosse argues that these same chapters should be dated to the time of Darius I (*Isaïe 13,1-14,23 dans la Tradition littéraire du livre d'Isaïe et dans la tradition des oracles contre les nations*, OBO 78 [Freiburg: Universitätsverlag; Göttingen: Vandenhoeck and Ruprecht, 1988]). A. Macintosh argues that Isaiah 21 is a "palimpsest" oracle which originated in the eighth century but was updated in the sixth (*Isaiah XXI: A Palimpsest* [Cambridge: Cambridge University Press, 1980]).

dating of Isaiah 13 difficult. If the mention of the Medes as attackers of Babylon is both historically accurate and part of the original oracle, or even if it is dependent upon Isaiah 21, then the text should not date before the early sixth century, when the Median-Babylonian coalition that had brought down the Assyrian state in 612-609 began to crumble and Media became a threat to Babylon.[19] One might also infer that the placement of this oracle against Babylon at the beginning of Isaiah's collection of foreign nation oracles derives from a time when Babylon was politically ascendant, likely in the early sixth century.[20]

How does the writer describe Babylon? On the basis of its content, the oracle in Isaiah 13 may be divided into two parts, vv. 2-16 and vv. 17-22, with a superscription in v. 1. Before v. 17, there is no obvious reference to Babylon, or Assyria for that matter, apart from the superscription. Rather, vv. 2-16 use cosmic terms to relate Yahweh's intention "to destroy [the earth's] sinners" (חטאיה ישמיד 9b). Yahweh says through the prophet: ופקדתי על־תבל רעה ועל־רשעים עונם והשבתי גאון זדים וגאות עריצים אשפיל, "I will punish the world for [its] evil,[21] and the wicked for their iniquity; I will make an end of the pride of the arrogant, and will lay low the insolence of tyrants"[22] (13:11). The several

[19] See S. Zawadski, *The Fall of Assyria and Median-Babylonian Relations*, Adam Mickiewicz University, Poznán, Historical Series, 149 (Poznán: Adam Mickiewicz University Press, 1988).

[20] So also C. T. Begg, "Babylon in the Book of Isaiah," in *The Book of Isaiah–Le Livre d'Isaïe: Les oracles et leur relectures. Unité et complexité de l'ouvrage*, BETL 81, ed. J. Vermeylen (Leuven: Leuven University Press/Peeters, 1989), 122.

[21] Read perhaps רעהּ for the MT's רעה. The literal reading would be "I will visit evil upon the world." LXX adopts this reading, though renders a plural, ἐντελοῦμαι . . . κακά.

[22] The verb ערץ, "to make tremble, to terrorize," and the substantive עריץ, "tyrant," are used elsewhere specifically of Babylon or the Chaldeans in Ezek 28:7 (an oracle against Tyre); of Nebuchadnezzar's army against Egypt in Ezek 30:11 and 32:12 and presumably also in 31:12 (Tyre). In discussing the deliverance of the Judeans from captivity, the Second Isaiah refers to the Judeans as מלקוח עריץ, "the prey of the tyrant" (49:25). Similarly, when the Second Isaiah taunts Babylon in 47:12, he derides its knowledge and suggests that it blithely carries on magical and divinatory arts in order to ערץ foes. If the context of the so-called little apocalypse of Isaiah 24-27 is the mid-sixth century, then it is also possible that several references to the עריצים in 25:3-5 allude to Babylon(ians). The preponderance of usages where the referent is clear or likely pertain to Babylon. Nowhere, it would seem, is the term used expressly of Assyria, although it would be reckless to say that it could not have been so used in Isa 13:11. If Isaiah 13 did not originally refer to Babylon, this term may have been one element that encouraged such a reapplication.

references to יום יהוה, "the Day of Yahweh" (vv. 6, 9), and the destruction of כל־הארץ, "the entire earth" (v. 5) also suggest a cosmic struggle. On the other hand, there are intimations already in vv. 2-16 that suggest the enemy came to be understood as Babylon. For example, Yahweh summons his "host" מארץ מרחק מקצה השמים, "from a distant land, from the ends of the heavens" (13:5). This language is similar to the summons of the foe from the north against Judah in Jeremiah, where the foe is probably to be understood as Babylon (e.g. Jer 6:22-26).[23] The response of the wicked enemy to this assault of Yahweh's forces is also noteworthy: על־כן כל־ידים תרפינה וכל־לבב אנוש ימס, "therefore, all hands are paralyzed, and the heart of every man melts" (Isa 13:7).[24] We can compare this with the Assyrian portrayal of enemy responses to the approach of the king: *ana zikir šumīya libbūšun itruku irmâ idāšun*, "at the (mere) mention of my name their heart trembled, their arms became limp."[25] While Isa 13:2-16 does not speak of particular Babylonian crimes, the language of the attack and the response of those assaulted made this hymn amenable to interpretation in light of the tradition of Assyro-Babylonian assault against Israel and Judah. The fact that the imagery is not specifically tied to either Assyria or Babylon, however, seems to show that there could be a free interchange of imagery in connection with the Mesopotamian empires.

The second section of the poem begins with v. 17. References to the cosmic battle of Yahweh of Hosts disappear, the terrestrial combatants come into focus, and the typical consequences of military battle are emphasized.[26] Yahweh states: הנני מעיר עליהם את־מדי, "I am

---

[23] Hezekiah also describes Babylon to the prophet Isaiah as ארץ רחוקה, "a distant land" (2 Kgs 20:14//Isa 39:3); of course this language is rather generic.

[24] See the incisive discussion of Hillers on the language of paralysis as a response to the receipt of "bad news" in the HB ("A Convention in Hebrew Literature: The Reaction to Bad News," *ZAW* 77 [1965]: 86-90).

[25] Sargon II, cited in *CAD* I/J 12, s.v. *idu* A.

[26] Dobbs-Allsopp draws attention to the elements of Isaiah 13, especially in vv. 14-22, that conform to his putative "city-lament genre" (*Weep, O Daughter of Zion: A Study of the City-Lament Genre in the Hebrew Bible*, BibOr 44 [Rome: Pontifical Biblical Institute, 1993], 123). His suggestions merit consideration. Note, for example, how many images of Babylon in these verses are applied to Jerusalem in Lamentations, where Dobbs-Allsopp discerns the genre in its purest manifestation: fallen Jerusalem is described there as formerly תפארת ישראל, "the splendor of Israel" (Lam 2:1a); wild animals appear in Lam 5:8; women are violated in Lam 5:11; Jerusalem is compared with Sodom and Gomorrah (Lam 4:6, Isa 13:19). While it is therefore possible that the description of Babylon's fall is influenced by the Israelite incarnation of the city-lament genre, a number of unique

now awakening the Medes against them." We then finally learn that the object of punishment is Babylon. But no reason is given in vv. 17-22 for the destruction of Babylon. Its fall, however, is compared with that of Sodom and Gomorrah, which implies that Babylon's crime is archetypal: it is destroyed not because of a specific crime against Judah, but because its very existence is somehow an affront to the moral order of Yahweh's creation. No more specific reasons are given for Yahweh's wrath in this second section of the poem; such reasons must be sought in the foregoing cosmic hymn, but even there the reasons are not well developed. The two sections of the poem thus cannot easily be separated.

The consequence of the assault on Babylon orchestrated by Yahweh is complete devastation, the overthrow of the city. The results are predictable: Babylon will be uninhabitable forever and a lair for wild animals. Not even Arab merchants will bother to stop there. The motif of wild animals haunting the ruined city (vv. 21-22) is a common one in the HB,[27] and is also used frequently in the curse formulae of Near Eastern treaties. Weinfeld, for example, cites parallels with the Aramaic treaty texts from Sefire, as well as inscriptions of Esarhaddon and Assurbanipal.[28] In Isaiah 13, then, the prophet interprets the crimes of Babylon in cosmic terms, and describes its fall in stereotyped language: like Sodom and Gomorrah, it will become an uninhabited desolation.

---

aspects should be noted. Most important is that while the genre may be Mesopotamian in origin (whatever the mechanics of its transmission to Israel, and Dobbs-Allsopp is vague on this), in Mesopotamia it is not applied to foreign cities. The fact, therefore, that Israelites use the genre (assuming that Dobbs-Allsopp's argument is accepted) in reference to Babylon (and Nineveh in Nahum) is inadequately stressed by Dobbs-Allsopp, and would provide important evidence for the ways in which Mesopotamian literary forms are taken over and pointed back at the source.

[27] E.g., Jer 9:10; 10:22. See the previous note for connection of this motif to the "city-lament genre."

[28] Specifically, Sefire I A: 32-33 (J. A. Fitzmyer, *The Aramaic Inscriptions of Sefire*, BibOr 19 [Rome: Pontifical Biblical Institute, 1967], 14; see M. Weinfeld, *Deuteronomy and the Deuteronomic School* [Oxford: Oxford University Press, 1972; reprint, Winona Lake, Ind.: Eisenbrauns, 1992], 142, nn. 7,8; 143 [page references are to the reprint edition]). See for a fuller discussion D. R. Hillers, *Treaty Curses and the Old Testament Prophets*, BibOr 16 (Rome: Pontifical Biblical Institute, 1964), 44-54.

3.3.2 Isaiah 14:1-23

Several scholars have argued that Isa 14:1-23 was not originally a משל uttered against the king of Babylon, as stated in 14:4a, but rather that it was directed against a king of Assyria, perhaps Sargon II.[29] Analysis of the chapter suggests that vv. 1-4a form an editorial link between the foregoing chapter and the poem preserved in 14:4b-21; vv. 1-2 provide a coda for Isaiah 13 and vv. 3-4a introduce the subsequent poem.[30] Isa 14:1-2 apparently presume the exile of Israel; this is shown by the assertion that Yahweh will "again choose Israel," and will settle them upon their land (v. 1), whereupon Israel's captors will become its captives (v. 2). But which exile is meant? Does it refer to a time after the conquest of the northern kingdom of Israel in 722, or possibly to the deportation of Judeans after the 701 campaign of Sennacherib, or even to the Babylonian exile of the sixth century? The last possibility seems most likely. Judean writers explicitly asserted that Yahweh had rejected Israel and caused its fall in 722 (2 Kings 17), which makes the assertion of v. 1 that he would again choose Israel unexpected. Meanwhile, after 701 both Isaiah and 2 Kings maintain that Yahweh had not rejected his people, even if he had punished them in Isaiah's view, and certainly they had not all been removed from their land. After the opening rubric, vv. 3-4a begin a new section, as the formula והיה ביום, "on that day," suggests.[31] These two verses then explicitly relate the משל that follows in vv. 4b-21 to "the king of Babylon"; vv. 3-4a thus represent an introduction to the משל, which preserves no reference to the king of Babylon. Similarly, vv. 22-23 provide the poem with a concluding comment, and connect it with the fall of Babylon.[32]

There is considerable debate about which king was initially the subject of the poem in Isa 14:4b-21. The internal evidence is ambiguous, and perhaps not finally decisive. That the poem is a unified composition, however, is suggested by its formal and thematic consistency: it is a

---

[29] H. L. Ginsberg, "Reflexes of Sargon in Isaiah after 715 B.C.E.," *JAOS* 88 (1968): 49-53; O. Kaiser, *Isaiah 13-39*, OTL (London: SCM, 1974), 24; for a discussion of the complexities of this chapter, see H. Wildberger, *Jesaja 13-27*, BKAT 10/2 (Neukirchen-Vluyn: Neukirchener, 1978), 531-64.

[30] See Wildberger, *Jesaja*, 536-37; and more recently, Gosse, *Isaïe 13,1-14,23 dans la Tradition littéraire du livre d'Isaïe*, 201.

[31] The formula serves in this introductory capacity elsewhere in the First Isaiah, as Wildberger shows (*Jesaja*, 112-14; 536).

[32] Kaiser, *Isaiah 13-39*, 43; Wildberger, *Jesaja*, 560-61.

taunt song that deals with the fall and debasement of a tyrant and the ignominious treatment of his corpse.[33] Our focus is less with the poem itself than with the identification of its subject as the king of Babylon. In the introduction to the poem, it is referred to as a משל against or over מלך בבל, "the king of Babylon" (14:4a). It is worth noting that the title, "king of Babylon," occurs 132 times in the HB, and of these 118 refer to Nebuchadnezzar.[34] Thus the title "king of Babylon," when it is not further qualified, usually refers to Nebuchadnezzar, who was the "king of Babylon" par excellence in biblical tradition. The title is not used in the HB of any Assyrian king, even one who did rule over Babylon. This is tentative evidence for a date during the time of the Neo-Babylonian empire. If it is also correct that Isaiah 13, the משא בבל, was a composition of the sixth century, as I have argued, then this might also have been the period when the poem of Isa 14:4b-21 was interpreted in reference to *the* king of Babylon, Nebuchadnezzar. This does not tell us to whom the poem originally referred, but as Machinist among others has noted, such a typological association illuminates how the biblical writers of the sixth century could interpret ideas and, as here, entire compositions that had referred to Assyria in view of experiences under Babylon.[35] Regardless of whether there was obvious continuity between Assyria and Babylonia in historical terms, the biblical prophets perceived such continuity in the imperial worldviews and institutions.

3.3.3 Isaiah 21:1-10

The climax of Isaiah 21, if it is taken as a unit, is the announcement of v. 9: "Fallen, fallen is Babylon, and all the statues of

---

[33] Wildberger, *Jesaja*, 537.

[34] Fifty-one occurrences are by name, and 67 by title only but in contexts which leave no room for doubt about the identification. Of the remaining 14 occurrences, 7 name other kings of Babylon (Merodach-baladan, Evil-Merodach [Amel-Marduk], Cyrus, and Artaxerxes). The other 7 occurrences are indeterminate. They include a statement from the prophet Isaiah that the sons of Hezekiah will be eunuchs in the palace of "the king of Babylon" (Amel-Marduk?, Isa 39:7//2Kgs 20:18). Also, twice in Jer 25:11-12 the prophet states that Judah will serve "the king of Babylon" for 70 years. This prophecy probably stems from the days of Nebuchadnezzar, but multiple kings could have been anticipated. Finally, three more times in texts from Jeremiah 50-51, the "king of Babylon" is mentioned but not named, and his identity remains uncertain (Nabonidus?).

[35] See the comments of Machinist, "Assyria and its Image," 736-37; and, among others, Wildberger, *Jesaja*.

her gods are smashed[36] to the ground." Much like Isaiah 13, however, this oracle lacks an explicit statement of why Babylon has fallen. It does not cite hubris, Hebrew גאוה, גאון, which is used elsewhere in Isaiah (and cf. Isa 14:11). Nor does it cite Babylonian military crimes against Judah or other nations. Such crimes, however, may be implicit in v. 2, where presumably it is the Babylonian king that is referred to as הבוגד, "the betrayer," and השודד, "the despoiler."[37] Nevertheless, the oracle does not delineate the specific depredations that have elicited Yahweh's vengeance against Babylon, so investigators continue to debate the question of the oracle's date.

The best evidence for dating the oracle is the geographical terminology in the text. This includes the cryptic מדבר־ים in the superscription (v. 1), the invocation in v. 2 for Elam and Media to rise up at God's behest, and the reference to Babylon itself in v. 9. If the passage is a unity, and if it refers to a single historical moment, then it is difficult to reconcile mention of these different terms.

The reference to מדבר־ים, "wilderness of the sea," was taken by Schrader in 1883 as the Hebrew equivalent of Akkadian *māt tâmtim*, "the Sealand," that is, the region adjacent to the Persian Gulf in which the Chaldean tribes resided.[38] It is true that "Babylon" was not typically used in Akkadian as an equivalent to our modern "Babylonia"; instead such sobriquets as "Sumer and Akkad" or "Karduniash" were normally used. Lambert argued, in fact, that Babylon was always used specifically with reference to the city, not the wider region.[39] Machinist argued differently, principally on the basis of the Assyrian kings' use of the title "king of Babylon" to signal control over the whole of southern Mesopotamia, that "the city title was simply expanded to become one designation of the enlarged territorial state."[40] This is, however, not so clear.[41] In any case, the idea that a biblical writer might use a

---

36 Reading שֻׁבְּרוּ with 1QIsa[a].

37 On several occasions Babylon is referred to as בוגד (Hab 1:5 [with 1QpHab], 13; and 2:5), while שדד characterizes Babylon in Jer 6:26b; 12:12; 48:8, 15, and 18.

38 E. Schrader, *Die Keilschriften und das Alten Testament*, 2d ed. (Giessen: J. Ricker, 1883), 353; see the discussion of Macintosh, *Isaiah xxi*, 4-7.

39 W. G. Lambert, "The Babylonians and Chaldaeans," in *Peoples of Old Testament Times*, ed. D. J. Wiseman (Oxford: Clarendon, 1973), 179.

40 Machinist, "On Self-Consciousness in Mesopotamia," 187 and n. 16.

41 There is room for doubt, since *šar Bābili*, "king of Babylon," is not the only title used by the Assyrian kings to signal their rule over the south. All of the Assyrian kings who use *šar Bābili* also use (though not necessarily in the same

designation other than Babylon to refer to the entire region is not beyond question, but there is no indication that "Sealand" was ever used in the Neo-Babylonian era to refer to all of "Sumer and Akkad," still less that a Judean writer would have known it. Moreover, Hebrew מדבר־ים is not an exact equivalent of *māt tâmtim*, which would have to be ארץ ים. This cryptic reference, then, does not obviously help to clarify the historical context of Isaiah 21.

The mention in Isa 21:2 that Yahweh summons Elam and Media to attack Babylon is more solid evidence.[42] Elam was a bitter enemy of Assyria, not Babylonia, in the late eighth and seventh centuries, until Assurbanipal finally defeated the Elamites and sacked Susa in 646. In fact, during the late eighth and early seventh centuries, Merodach-baladan II and his successors in Babylonia were frequently allied with the Elamites against the Assyrians.[43] As for the Medes, the Assyrians created several provinces in their territories in the eighth century (and exiled Israelites there, 2 Kgs 17:6), but the Medes themselves do not seem to have posed a military threat to the Assyrians until the time of the collapse of the Assyrian empire in the last quarter of the seventh century.[44] Both Elam and Media, therefore, might have been identified as enemies of Assyria in the late eighth century and through much of the seventh, but they were not enemies of Babylon during that period. In the late seventh century, the Medes and Babylonians were actually allied

---

texts) the title *šar māt Šumeri u Akkadî*, "the king of Sumer and Akkad," which is the title that more explicitly points to rule over the entire south (Seux, *Épithetes royales*, 301-303). What is more, many such usages occur in inscriptions that were composed in the Babylonian style and intended for Babylonian use (see above, chapter one, section 1.3), where one might not expect the scribal circles responsible for the texts to introduce innovations.

[42] On the "divine agent of destruction" in the Sumerian city-lament genre, represented frequently by a storm or enemy invasion, and the possible influence of the genre on this passage, see Dobbs-Allsopp, *Weep, O Daughter of Zion*, 57, and 103, n. 28. Dobbs-Allsopp never really engages the question of what historical circumstances elicited use of the city-lament genre in Israel. While his study clarifies the conventional elements of the genre, this does not preclude the possibility that historical data have been employed in the individual poems.

[43] For a detailed discussion of the period, with literature, see Brinkman, "Babylonia under the Shadow of Assyria," 26-38.

[44] See Diakonoff, "Cities of the Medes," 15-18; and for a general survey of Median history, idem, "Media," in *The Cambridge History of Iran*. Vol. 2, *The Median and Achaemenian Periods*, ed. I. Gershevitch (Cambridge: Cambridge University Press, 1985), 36-148.

and participated jointly in the sack of Nineveh in 612.[45] Only in the early sixth century, if Zawadski's hypothesis is correct,[46] did Median-Babylonian relations cool to the point that the alliance broke down. Xenophon later identified Nebuchadnezzar's defensive wall north of Sippar between the Tigris and Euphrates, now identified with Ḥabl-aṣ-Ṣaḫr, as the "wall of Media," which reflects the tradition about Babylonian-Median animosity.[47] While Elam probably posed no real threat to Babylonia in the early sixth century, the Babylonian Chronicle for 596/5 (two years after the initial assault of Nebuchadnezzar on Jerusalem) may indicate that a king of Elam sought to engage Nebuchadnezzar II in battle, although the unnamed king then took flight.[48] The oracle on the destruction of Elam in Jeremiah 49, dated to the beginning of Zedekiah's reign in about 597/6,[49] may provide further evidence for a punitive Babylonian action against the rump state of Elam about this time.[50] All this is to say that a Judean author in the mid-590s might reasonably have hoped, whether with justification or not is another matter, for an alliance of Medes and Elamites to attack Babylon. Such a reconstruction would ill suit the late eighth or seventh century. If this is correct, then the prophecy of Isaiah 21 would not date before the sixth century.

The announcement of the fall of Babylon in Isa 21:9 also presents interpretive problems. Babylon was ravaged by Sennacherib in 689, and suffered some kind of destruction again in 648 after the revolt against Assyria led by Šamaš-šuma-ukīn;[51] but in those instances Assyria was responsible for the destruction, and received no aid from either Elam or

---

[45] TCS 5 chron 3:38-45.

[46] *The Fall of Assyria and Median-Babylonian Relations*.

[47] See R. D. Barnett, "Xenophon and the Wall of Media," *JHS* 83 (1963): 1-26; also J. A. Black, "Babylonian Textual Evidence," in *Ḥabl aṣ-Ṣaḫr 1983-85: Nebuchadnezzar II's Cross-country Wall North of Sippar*, *NAPR*, vol. 1, ed. J. A. Black, H. Gasche, et al. (Ghent: University of Ghent Press, 1987), 15-25.

[48] The name of the country is broken on the tablet; Grayson reads: *[š]àr* [kur]*E[lamt]i(?)*[ki] *ip-làḫ-ma ḫat-tú* ŠUB-*su-ma ana* KUR-*šú i-t*[*ur (?)*], "[The k]ing of E[lam] took fright and fear overcame him so he *we*[*nt*] home" (TCS 5 chron 5 rev. 20).

[49] For an interpretation of ראשית מלכות as an imprecise term meaning "beginning of the reign," similar to the sometimes imprecise use of the Akkadian *rēš šarrūti* in some royal inscriptions, see Tadmor, "Inscriptions of Nabunaid," 353, n. 13.

[50] So Malamat, "Twilight," 136.

[51] Brinkman, *Prelude to Empire*, 64-68, and 93-104.

Media. On the contrary, Elam was an ally of Babylon at least in the first instance, and a source of continual problems for the Assyrians, who were forced to undertake large-scale military operations against the Elamites after crushing the revolt. It is unlikely that Isaiah 21 refers to either of these instances. Of course, Babylon fell to Cryus of Persia in 539 B.C.E., but it may be objected that the image of Babylon's smashed religious statues in Isa 21:9 can hardly be a *vaticinium ex eventu* describing that event. According to the Cyrus cylinder (admittedly a pro-Persian text) and the Nabonidus chronicle, but against the sense of the Isaianic verse, the takeover of Babylon was without a battle (*ba-la ṣal-tum*), and Cyrus is credited with respecting the Babylonian cults.[52] This objection to Isa 21:9 as a prophecy from after the fall of Babylon in 539 may not be insurmountable, however, since there is at least circumstantial evidence (discussed below in connection with Jeremiah 50-51) suggesting that Babylon's fall in 539 may not have been peaceful. More troublesome for interpreting Isaiah 21 as a prophecy reflecting on Babylon's fall to Cyrus is that such a reading would require the assumption that the writer subsumed the Elamites and Medes within the conquering Persian empire. This is possible, but such imprecision should not be assumed, and one wonders whether a Judean writer of the sixth century would have been unaware that the Medes and Persians were actually enemies.[53]

A possible context for Isaiah 21 might be the years after Nebuchadnezzar's first assault on Jerusalem in 598/7. We noted above the possibility of an abortive Elamite raid on Babylonia at this time. Isaiah's statement (21:2) that Yahweh would raise up Elam, then, becomes a reasonable reflection of political antagonisms in that period. The prophet's assumption that the Medes could attack Babylon might also fit this period if the Babylonian-Median coalition had crumbled. If the context of the oracle is the mid-590s, this could also clarify why the prophet addresses God's people as the "threshed and winnowed one" (v.

---

[52] For the text of the Cyrus cylinder, see P. R. Berger, "Der Kyros-Zylinder mit dem Zusatzfragment BIN II Nr. 32 und die akkadischen Personennamen im Danielbuch," *ZA* 64 (1974): 196; for the Nabonidus chronicle, TCS 5 chron 7 iii 15-16.

[53] See, however, the so-called Dynastic Prophecy, a Seleucid text, (Grayson, *BHLT* 25 ii 17) where LUGAL ^{kur}NUM.MA, "king of Elam," does apparently refer to Cyrus; perhaps this is a late effort at archaizing. Compare the identification of Darius as a Mede in Daniel (9:1; 11:1); a misidentification on the basis of incomplete knowledge?

10). The image suggests that they had undergone some trauma, such as Nebuchadnezzar's assault on Jerusalem in 597. The focus on the destruction of the Babylonian cult images in v. 9 might express a longing for revenge after Nebuchadnezzar's removal to Babylon in 597 of some cult paraphernalia from the Solomonic Temple (see 2 Kgs 24:13). Perhaps, then, Isaiah 21 could be seen to express the hope of a Judean prophet that Babylon will not be permitted to prosper, and that its eastern enemies will rise up to overthrow it.

We may now summarize our discussion of the references to Babylon and Chaldea in the foreign nation oracles of the First Isaiah. On the basis of internal evidence and historical inferences, the conclusion was reached that each of these oracles derives in its present form from the early sixth century. There is, however, no unitary perspective in them on the importance of Babylon in relation to Judah, neither is there clear reference to specific military depredations against Judah. We may hypothesize that such depredations lie behind the texts, especially Isaiah 21 with its reference to Judah as "the threshed and winnowed one." Nevertheless, none of the oracles explicitly concerns what is known about the interaction between Babylon and Judah. They show instead that Babylon is identified as the archetypal wicked city, comparable to Sodom and Gomorrah (so Isa 13:19). Babylon and its deities are deserving of destruction, and in Isaiah 13 and 21 Yahweh's agents for accomplishing this are known historical entities, the Elamites and Medes. Nevertheless, even Babylon's destruction is described in conventional terms, an observation that is supported too by Dobbs-Alsopp's arguments about the relationship of these oracles to the "city-lament genre." Despite this lack of specificity and the use of conventional language, the impression is gained that the Isaianic references already demonstrate an established tradition of thought about the role of Babylon as an imperial power. This is most clearly true of the poem in Isaiah 14:4b-21 about the fall of an Assyrian(?) imperial tyrant, where the verses that introduce (1-4a) and conclude (22-23) the poem bring it into connection with Babylon and probably Nebuchadnezzar, if he is the referent of the title "king of Babylon." We have in the First Isaiah, then, a series of texts revised or composed in the Babylonian imperial era that concern Babylon and its ultimate demise, but which do not refer specifically to imperial ideas or practices. Perhaps this shows that the responsible writers viewed Babylon in strictly typological terms, as the successor to Assyria, not according to the terms of the intellectual and practical framework that the Babylonians themselves were attempting to promulgate.

In any event, the images of Babylon in the First Isaiah and the laconic mention of Babylonian exile in Micah contrast sharply with the images of Babylon in Jeremiah, Habakkuk, Ezekiel, the Second Isaiah, and the anti-Babylonian oracles of Jeremiah 50-51. Within these prophetic texts, more consistent images emerge that correlate well with the vicissitudes of Judean-Babylonian interaction, and that furnish more specific information about the perspective of subject populations on the empire.

3.4 Jeremiah

The largest collection of materials pertaining to the problem of Babylon's imperial domination of Judah comes from Jeremiah. Jeremiah's career began in the last quarter of the seventh century and partly overlapped the reigns of Nabopolassar (626-606) and Nebuchadnezzar II (605-562). The momentous changes in Near Eastern geopolitics during this era, coupled with Nebuchadnezzar's efforts to transform Babylon into the most splendid city in the world, permeate Jeremiah's prophecy. The wrenching debates in Judah concerning political alignment and religious practice (the two were inseparable in Jeremiah's thought, as they were for his contemporaries and forebears) are often phrased with the awareness of Babylonian imperial policies and procedures firmly in view. Jeremiah was an advocate of capitulation to Babylonian hegemony, and sharply criticized both other prophets and members of the Judean royal court who were not. The thrust of Jeremiah's program was to insure continued existence of the kingdom of Judah, subservient to Babylon if necessary, in order to preserve cultural and religious autonomy.

It is not possible to examine each text in Jeremiah that refers to Babylon with equal thoroughness. It will be productive to group the references studied under two subheadings: 1) the foe from the north; and 2) descriptions of Nebuchadnezzar and his administration. The anti-Babylon oracles of Jeremiah 50-51 are treated separately (below section 3.8).

3.4.1 The Foe From the North

From the time that Assyria's empire in the west gradually began to dissolve in the second half of the reign of Assurbanipal (640s, see above chapter 2), the kings of Judah began to struggle with the problem of Judah's political alignment in an emerging bipolar world.[54] A correct assessment of Assyrian, Egyptian, and then Babylonian ambitions was crucial for Judah's fortunes (see Jer 2:18,36; Ezekiel 23). That such assessments could not be made easily or dispassionately is clear. By the end of the seventh century, in any case, the balance of power, uncertain since the waning of Assyria in the 640s and 630s, clearly had shifted back to Mesopotamia, and Jeremiah recognized this. The motif of the attacker from the north in Jeremiah should be understood in terms of this geopolitical trajectory.

Scholars have long debated the identity of the so-called "foe from the north."[55] Debate has turned on the question of whether the texts pertaining to the foe, or at least some of them, refer to a discernible historical enemy, such as Babylonia or the Scythians.[56] If so, is this a preexistent, perhaps mythological motif that was adapted to the reality of a particular historical foe, or was it generated in response to one of these powers? Or is it necessary to pose the question as a stark choice?

The foe is most readily identified with Babylon, even though the Neo-Babylonian dynasty began to exert decisive influence in the Levant only during the early reign of Nebuchadnezzar, well after the beginning

---

[54] For the application of the concept of bipolar politics to the latter part of the seventh century and the beginning of the sixth, see Malamat, "Judah Between Egypt and Babylon."

[55] The following texts in Jeremiah refer to the foe: 1:13-15; 4:5-8, 13-21, 29-31; 5:15-17; 6:1-5, 22-26; 8:14-16; and 10:22; in the foreign nation oracles the motif occurs in 25:9 (almost a duplicate of 1:15); 46:24; and 47:2. Several references in chapters 50-51 (50:3, 9, 41; and 51:48) also bear on the problem, and will be taken up here rather than in the discussion below of Jeremiah 50-51.

[56] B. S. Childs surveyed the problem in, "The Enemy From the North and the Chaos Tradition," *JBL* 78 (1959): 185-98 (for earlier bibliography, see there n. 3); see also J. Bright, *Jeremiah*, AB (Garden City, N.Y.: Doubleday, 1965), lxxxi-ii; also H. Cazelles, "Sophonie, Jérémie, et les Scythes en Palestine," *RB* 74 (1967): 24-44; R. P. Vaggione also provides a survey of the views expressed in the many commentaries on Jeremiah published up to the time of his study, "All Over Asia? The Extent of the Scythian Domination in Herodotus," *JBL* 92 (1973): 523-30; see also W. L. Holladay, *Jeremiah 1*, Hermeneia (Philadelphia: Fortress, 1986), 42-43.

of Jeremiah's career in the 620s.[57] Precisely because the foe is mentioned in texts from the first part of the book, texts that are thought to come from Jeremiah's early career, the search for a historical referent is complicated. Several scholars, beginning with J. G. Eichhorn, suggested that the texts refer to the Scythians.[58] The argument is made on the basis of a reference in Herodotus (1.1.105) to Scythian penetration as far as the border of Egypt in the last quarter of the seventh century.[59] Some still accept a modified form of the Scythian hypothesis, such as Hayes and Miller in reference to Jer 1:13-16 and 4:5-6:30.[60] It has largely fallen into disfavor, however, especially because of Vaggione's analysis of the meaning of Herodotus's account of Scythian expansion "all over Asia."[61] Vaggione argued that Herodotus's reference to Scythian rule all over Asia (ὁι δὲ Σκύθαι τὴν 'Ασίην πᾶσαν ἐπέσχον, 1.1.104) should be understood, on the basis of Herodotus's geographical usage elsewhere, to refer to "an undefined but extensive area running along an east-west axis from Asia Minor to Persia."[62] It does not mean, on this view, that the Scythians ruled the whole of the Near East. Na'aman also recently reviewed the evidence for a Scythian invasion and concluded that Herodotus reconstructed it typologically, and that such an invasion never occurred.[63]

Other scholars, however, take a different approach and emphasize that the conventional, even mythological, descriptions of the foe in Jeremiah suggest that the prophet did not construe the historical referent narrowly.[64] No doubt there are mythological allusions in the use of this

---

[57] Holladay's "downdating" of the beginning of Jeremiah's career to just before 609 partly obviates the problem (*Jeremiah 1*, 42-43). Even if that hypothesis is not accepted, it seems likely that although Nabopolassar does not figure overtly in any biblical text, in strictly political terms the Judean elite must have been aware of the emerging Babylonian might at least by 616, when Egypt allied with Assyria against Babylon.

[58] See the summary of opinions in Vaggione, "All Over Asia?" 523-24.

[59] For a thorough discussion of Herodotus's account, see Cazelles, "Sophonie," 24-28.

[60] *History of Ancient Israel and Judah*, 390; see also Redford, *Egypt, Canaan, and Israel*, 438-41.

[61] Vaggione, "All Over Asia?" 523-30; see also Bright, *Jeremiah*, lxxxi and n. 25.

[62] Vaggione, "All Over Asia?" 528-30.

[63] Na'aman, "Judah under Josiah," 36-37; see also Cogan and Tadmor, *II Kings*, 301, n. 35.

[64] E.g., W. Staerk, cited in Childs, "Enemy from the North," 191.

motif.[65] Nevertheless, as the following discussion will show, neither the Scythian identification nor the mythological approach is adequate: the motif is best understood in its prophetic usage as referring to the Assyrian and Babylonian imperial powers, which, beginning in the ninth century, threatened Israel and Judah in turn. In Jeremiah specifically, the tradition of the foe should be linked to the emergence of Babylon as an imperial power under Nebuchadnezzar, even if Babylon is not mentioned by name except in the oracles against Egypt and Philistia (chapters 46 and 47).

The first reference in Jeremiah to danger from the north occurs in 1:13-15. In a vision, Jeremiah sees a סיר נפוח, "boiling pot" threatening from the north (ופניו מפני צפונה[66], "its rim [lit. face] is from the north," 1:13). Yahweh affirms that רעה, "evil," will come out of the north against the inhabitants of Judah, for he is calling "to all the *mišpĕḥôt*[67] of

[65] In particular scholars point to the use of צפון in describing the origin of the foe; see Childs, "Enemy from the North." Ṣapōn is linked already in Ugaritic lore with the abode of the gods, especially Baʿl, and this tradition still echoes in biblical materials (e.g., Isa 14:13b). Baʿl reveals himself from his temple on Mount Ṣapōn in the storm theophany, and causes the earth to quake (KTU 1.101 1-4; see Cross, *CMHE*, 147-50; 185). Yahweh the Divine Warrior likewise makes the earth quake (רעש) in his theophany (e.g., Judg 5:4; Nah 1:5; Ps 18:18), which reflects the tradition of the Storm God's defeat of chaos. Childs linked the shaking (רעש) of the earth that frequently occurs in conjunction with the onslaught of the foe from the north with the "chaos tradition" ("Enemy from the North," 189). This is true in Jer 4:23, where the land is described as תהו ובהו in the wake of the enemy onslaught (see also Isa 14:16b). There is undoubtedly a reference to Gen 1:2 here, or at least to the same tradition of primordial chaos that underlies the Priestly text. In fact, Jer 4:23-26 portrays the undoing of creation and a reversion to chaos. Another point of contact with the "chaos" motif is found in Jer 6:23, where the sound of the invading army from the north is likened to ים יהמה, "the roaring sea."

[66] The seemingly redundant locative on צפונה is otiose following another preposition (GKC §90e). For discussion of the phrase, see Holladay, *Jeremiah 1*, 39.

[67] Here the meaning "clans," "tribes," or the like should be rejected. משפחה is used in the HB most frequently to refer to an extensive patrilateral association of kin sharing common title to a particular plot or region. The fact that the group so labelled is characterized by geographical propinquity allows for extension of the term as a synonym for גוי, a political entity with a specific territory. This use is particularly common in prophetic texts pertaining to international relations (see Jer 10:25; Nah 3:4; Ezek 20:32; Zech 14:17-18). Whether משפחות is to be retained in the present text, however, is an open question; it is lacking in LXX and is taken by many as an expansion (W. Rudolph, *Jeremia*, 3e Auflage, Handbuch zum Alten Testament 12 [Tübingen: Mohr, 1958], 8; Bright, *Jeremiah*, 6; Holladay, *Jeremiah I*, 40-41). The prophetic use of משפחה as a synonym of גוי and the collocation משפחות

the kingdoms of the north" (1:15, so also 25:9, which is identical but lacks ממלכות); "they will come and each will place his throne at the opening of the gates of Jerusalem." This last image may indicate a specific military procedure. An analogous act may be depicted in a scene from Sennacherib's palace at Nineveh which shows the fall of Lachish in 701. In the relief, Sennacherib, who is seated just beyond the walls of Lachish, receives information from his officers concerning the city's fall; a caption above the king reads, *Sîn-aḫḫê-eriba šarru ašarēdu šar māt Aššur ina kussi nēmedi ūšibma šallat Lakisu maḫaršu ētiq*, "Sennacherib, supreme king, king of Assyria, sat upon a *nēmedu* -throne while the booty of Lachish passed before him."[68] It is not clear whether the Neo-Babylonian kings adopted comparable procedures at conquered cities. This and another text in Jeremiah, however, might suggest that they did. After the army of Nebuchadnezzar conquered Jerusalem in 586, a passage unique to Jeremiah notes that: ויבאו כל שרי מלך־בבל וישבו בשער התוך, "all of the officials of the king of Babylon came and sat within the Middle Gate"[69] (Jer 39:3a). The Babylonian officials no doubt took up their positions within the gate, a legal forum, in order to coordinate procedures such as spoliation and deportation of the population after the city's conquest.[70] This notice differs slightly from the image in Jer 1:13-15, where rulers do not sit within the gates but set their thrones "at the opening of the gates of Jerusalem." Still the legal and administrative connotations of the act depicted in Jer 39:3 approximate those of Jer 1:15, as well as Sennacherib's act at Lachish. The image in Jer 1:15 of thrones placed at the opening of Jerusalem's

---

ארץ perhaps suggest that משפחות here may be original; it is the more difficult reading.

[68] OIP 2 156 no. 25; Barnett, *Assyrian Sculpture*, pl. 76; *ANEP* 129: fig. 371. This approach to the image of Jer 1:15, including the parallel with Sennacherib's relief, was already elaborated by M. Cogan, "Sentencing at the Gate in Jeremiah 1:15-16," *Gratz College Annual of Jewish Studies* 1 (1972): 3-6. Cogan sees a "judicial tableau" in the positioning of the thrones at the gates, the traditional locus for dispensing justice. Holladay follows him: "One must conclude that we have a description of the defeat of the city and its submission to the judicial acts of the victor" (*Jeremiah I*, 40-41).

[69] The location of this gate, mentioned only here in the HB, is uncertain. See, for one suggestion, N. Avigad, *Discovering Jerusalem* (Oxford: Basil Blackwell, 1984), 50-59. Although there is apparently no evidence in the versions, one could speculate that the final elements of the phrase have been inverted, which would suggest the reconstruction בתוך השער, "in the midst of the gate," although this would leave the gate unspecified.

[70] Bright, *Jeremiah*, 243.

gates is therefore best understood as an allusion to the conqueror's future review of booty and captives after the city's fall. This interpretation would support the identification of the foe from the north with a Mesopotamian power.

Most of the references to the foe from the north are in Jeremiah 4-6. The first portrays an impending invasion and siege (4:5-8). The שׁופר, "trumpet," is blown to announce an imminent battle and to warn the people of Judah to flee to the fortified cities (vv. 5b-6a). Yahweh is bringing evil מצפון, "from the north." The foe is described as a "lion" (אריה), and a "destroyer of nations" (משחית גוים), whose intent is to lay waste the land and to annihilate its population (v. 7). The description of the invader from the north as a lion is common in Jeremiah. The lion simile also appears in 5:6, where the אריה, זאב (wolf) and נמר (leopard) besiege the cities of Judah and "tear" anyone who comes forth from them, probably a metaphor for siege conditions.[71] כפירים, "lions," also appear as the ravagers of Israel in Jer 2:15, although there the north is not specified as their origin.[72] The ferocity of the lion is of course proverbial, and the image therefore could easily apply to any invading enemy (e.g. Ps 7:3; 17:12).[73] On the other hand, there is precedent in the HB for portraying an imperial king or army as an attacking lion. Among

---

[71] For this image and specifically the inclusion of the זאב it may be instructive to compare several inscriptions of Assurbanipal and Esarhaddon. A text of Assurbanipal states: *šīrēšunu nukkusūti ušākil kalbī šaḫî zībī erî* MUŠEN.MEŠ *šamê nūnī apsî*, "I had dogs, swine, jackals/vultures, eagles, all kinds of birds, and fish of the ocean feed on their [slain enemy warriors'] torn flesh" (*BIWA* 44 A IV 74-76); and in Esarhaddon: *pagar qurādīšunu ina la qebēri ušākil zībû*, "I let jackals/vultures feed on the unburied corpses of their warriors" (Borger Esarh. 58 v 6; *CAD* Z 106, s.v. *zību* B; see also *AHw* 1525a, s.v. *zību* II). The Akkadian word for "wolf" is *barbaru*, which, however, is apparently not used in such contexts, while *zību*, "jackal/vulture," is. Perhaps Hebrew זאב, "wolf," the etymological cognate of Akkadian *zību*, was chosen here by Jeremiah under the influence of such Akkadian usages as those just quoted, although it would of course be hazardous to suggest that Jeremiah knew Assyrian inscriptions in all their details. The influence of Assyrian political propaganda and treaty curse formulae, however, was presumably quite widespread during the seventh century, even to the point where Deuteronomic curse formulae, as Weinfeld has shown, adapted Assyrian treaty curses (*Deuteronomy and the Deuteronomic School*).

[72] In Jer 51:38 the image is inverted and the כפירים roar against Babylon. Such inversion of imagery that is applied to Judah elsewhere in Jeremiah is typical of chapters 50-51 (see below).

[73] In Ezek 32:2, Pharaoh is mocked for considering himself a lion among the nations.

other images, the First Isaiah likens the Assyrian invader to roaring lions (לביא and כפירים, 5:29) that carry off prey unhindered. Nahum reflects on this image in the wake of Nineveh's fall and Assyria's collapse; he asks sarcastically what became of the ferocious lions (2:12-14). Machinist suggested the possibility that the lion imagery used by Isaiah and Nahum in reference to Assyria was influenced by Assyrian portrayals of the king as a raging lion.[74] The popular motif of the heroic defeat of the hunted lion, common in Mesopotamian art from early on, could have given rise to the metaphor of the king as more powerful than a lion.[75] The Neo-Assyrian kings, particularly Assurbanipal, relished the lion hunt.[76] Perhaps the Neo-Babylonian kings did too: it is noteworthy that the bas-relief in the western niche of Nebuchadnezzar's Wadi Brisa inscription in the Lebanon depicts the king battling a lion.[77] This image of Nebuchadnezzar is one of only two extant depictions of the king; the other comes from the eastern niche in the Wadi Brisa and depicts him felling a tree.

Jeremiah's application of the lion simile to the foe from the north may be an adaptation of an image that in the biblical prophetic tradition was originally used of Assyria. The sixth-century writer of Jeremiah 50

---

[74] See Machinist, "Assyria and Its Image in the First Isaiah," 728 and 735-36.

[75] For a very early example of a Mesopotamian king subduing a lion, possibly from the Jemdet Nasr period, see *ANEP* 56: fig. 182.

[76] For depictions in the reign of Assurnasirpal II (883-859 B.C.E.), see Barnett, *Assyrian Sculpture*, pl. 32; in the reign of Assurbanipal, see ibid., pls. 103 and 110-25; and for a detailed study of the textual evidence, see E. Weissert, "Royal Hunt and Royal Triumph in a Prism Fragment of Ashurbanipal (82-5-22,2)," in *Assyria 1995*, ed. S. Parpola and R. M. Whiting (Helsinki: Neo-Assyrian Text Corpus Project, 1997), 339-58.

[77] Erosion had effaced the relief by the time of its modern publication. Only the general outlines of the image appear in the published photos (WVDOG 5 Abbildung 2, and Tafel 1), but they confirm that this is the correct interpretation. The king faces to his left, grasping the struggling lion with his left arm, and wields an implement in his lowered right hand (for a description, see Weissbach, WVDOG 5, p. 8). The badly preserved end of col. B ix of the inscription includes mention of the king's construction of *ṣa-lam šar-ru-ti-ia da-ri-[a-tim]* "a perma[nent] image of my kingly self" (VAB 4 174 [Nbk 19=WBr] B ix 51), no doubt a reference to the reliefs accompanying the inscription. A few parallels to this scene from Wadi Brisa may be cited: an approximate parallel from the reign of Assurbanipal is given in Barnett, *Assyrian Sculpture*, pl. 122; and a cylinder seal naming the Chaldean Merodach-baladan II bears a similar scene (see D. Collon, *First Impressions: Cylinder Seals in the Ancient Near East* [Chicago: University of Chicago Press, 1987], 81, no. 369).

recapitulates this development of the motif, as noted above in the interpretation of Micah's reference to Babylonian exile: "Israel is a scattered ewe, (which) lions deported; the first to devour it was the king of Assyria, and now this is the last to crush its bones, Nebuchadrezzar, king of Babylon" (Jer 50:17). That the lion image had a long life in prophetic usage[78] does not negate the fact that in reference to foreign enemies it applies most often to Mesopotamian foes. Babylon, therefore, is likely also Jeremiah's intended foe from the north.

Jeremiah's depiction of the foe from the north as a lion, therefore, could well reflect Assyrian and Babylonian royal traditions, and this may also be true of his description of the invading Chaldean army: וכסופה מרכבותיו קלו מנשרים סוסיו, "his chariots are like a whirlwind, his horses are swifter than vultures" (4:13). The description of the army as invincible is not unique to this passage in the HB, but other comparable images also concern Assyria and Babylon.[79] In particular, this passage calls to mind Hab 1:8, which refers to the Chaldeans: וקלו מנמרים סוסיו וחדו מזאבי ערב, "its horses are swifter than leopards, fleeter than wolves of the steppe."[80]

In Jer 5:15 Yahweh states that he is bringing a nation ממרחק, "from afar," to consume (אכל) Judah. The nation is described as follows: גוי איתן הוא גוי מעולם הוא גוי לא־תדע לשנו ולא תשמע מה־ידבר, "It is an enduring nation, it is a nation from of old;[81] it is a nation whose language you do not know, nor do you understand what they say" (v. 15). Elsewhere in Jeremiah, when the prophet describes the land to which Yahweh will exile the Judeans, he uses similar language. In Jer 16:13, Yahweh says, "I will hurl you out from this land, to the land which neither you nor your fathers knew." Similarly, Jer 17:4 reads: "I will make you serve your enemies in a land which you do not know."[82] Jeremiah specifically describes the land to which Coniah (Jehoiachin)

---

[78] In addition to referring to foreign enemies, lion imagery can of course also be used of Yahweh, of Israel, and of individual humans; for a survey, see *TDOT* 1.374-88, s.v. *ʾarî*.

[79] Machinist, "Assyria and its Image," 722.

[80] Taking ערב either as an error for ערבה (cf. זאב ערבה in Jer 5:6) or as a masculine biform; see Roberts, *Nahum, Habakkuk, Zephaniah*, 92.

[81] עולם here may have the connotation "primeval."

[82] MT at Jer 15:14, העברתי את־איביך בארץ לא ידעת, "I will make your enemies pass over to a land you do not know," should probably be emended along the lines of 17:4 (cf. T), העבדתיך את־איביך, "I will make you serve your enemies"; this is against Holladay, *Jeremiah 1*, 455, who thinks the deviation is deliberate.

and his kin shall be exiled by Nebuchadnezzar as הארץ אחרת אשר לא־ילדתם שם, "another land in which you were not born," (22:26) and הארץ אשר לא־ידעו, "the land which they do not know" (22:28). Jeremiah obviously refers to Babylon as the unknown, strange land. Conversely, the prophet announces that Yahweh will one day redeem Jacob (i.e. Israel), that he will bring his people back to Zion מארץ צפון, "from the land of the north" (31:8), that is, from their exile in Babylon.

This language about the strangeness of the land of exile, the land of the north, has close similarities to several covenant curses in Deteronomy 28. There the description in the MT is slightly different from Jeremiah's: Yahweh, according to the text in Deuteronomy, will bring against Israel גוי מרחוק מקצה הארץ כאשר ידאה הנשר גוי אשר לא־תשמע לשנו, "a nation from far off, from the end of the earth, which will swoop down like the vulture, a nation whose language you do not understand" (Deut 28:49). Just as in Jeremiah, this nation will consume (אכל) Israel's produce.[83] Deut 28:33a also reads: פרי אדמתך וכל־יגיעך יאכל עם אשר לא־ידעת, "the fruit of your arable land and all your labor a people will consume whom you do not know." The covenant curses in Deuteronomy, which are indebted to the language of the eighth-seventh century Neo-Assyrian *adê*-treaties, as Weinfeld, McCarthy, and others have shown, suggest that this language in Deuteronomy about deportation to a strange land may be dependent on the language of the Assyrian treaty oaths.[84] That such similar language should be used by Jeremiah to describe Babylon as the nation that will fulfill the covenant curses against Judah, and to which the people will be exiled, is therefore

---

[83] Note that the Greek translators seem to have recognized this close parallel: OG to Jer 5:15 is nearly a verbatim parallel to Deut 28:49b:

ἔθνος, οὗ οὐκ ἀκούσῃ τῆς φωνῆς τῆς γλώσσης αὐτοῦ (Jer 5:15)
ἔθνος, ὃ οὐκ ἀκούσῃ τῆς φωνῆς αὐτοῦ (Deut 28:49b)

Rudolph thinks Jeremiah influenced Deuteronomy (*Jeremia*, 37); Weinfeld takes the opposite view (*Deuteronomy and the Deuteronomic School*, 360), and is probably correct. The shorter text of OG in Jer 5:15 (versus the longer text of MT) was probably influenced by Deut 28:49; in this case MT is not expansionistic, as is the case so often elsewhere in Jeremiah.

[84] Weinfeld, *Deuteronomy and the Deuteronomic School*, 116-29, esp. 117-19; D. J. McCarthy, *Treaty and Covenant*, AnBib 21, 2nd ed. (Rome: Pontifical Biblical Institute, 1978). The language about exile to a strange land is, however, apparently not directly paralleled in the Akkadian treaty curses. Somewhat similar ideas do occur in other Neo-Assyrian texts from the time of Esarhaddon, where the usage is somewhat different: enemy rulers who remain unsubmissive to the Assyrian king are said to have "fled to a land not known" (*ana māt lā idû innabtu*) at the approach of Esarharddon (Borger, Esarh. 45 Ep. 2:84; cf. ibid. 15 Ep. 9).

understandable. We may add that Assyrian procedures recorded for the reign of Sargon II (Babylonian procedures are unclear) add verisimilitude to Jeremiah's usage about the strangeness of the land of exile: deportees of diverse linguistic origins were instructed in proper Assyrian cultural and linguistic deportment after they were uprooted from their native lands and settled elsewhere in the empire.[85] In the end it is the frightful and strange image of the nation from the north that is the central focus in Jer 5:15. Nevertheless, closely related language elsewhere in Jeremiah refers to Babylon, while the covenant curses of Deuteronomy 28 suggest that the foreign land *par excellence* would have been Mesopotamian.[86]

Moreover, Jeremiah's emphasis on the antiquity of the foreign nation, גוי איתן . . . גוי מעולם, while it is literally applicable to Babylon, also conforms with the image of the land that the Neo-Babylonian kings assiduously projected.[87] Such a description would not aptly describe the Scythians, a group of nomadic warriors who were relative newcomers to the international scene in the seventh century. This lends further strength to the conclusion that Jeremiah saw Babylon as the successor of Assyria; his language about Yahweh's punishing agent from the north evokes an image of the Babylonian imperial overlords. As was the case with Micah 4:10, this again shows how the phenomenon of Mesopotamian imperialism was understood typologically: experiences

---

[85] For the texts from Sargon II and a more thorough discussion, see Machinist, "Assyrians on Assyria," 94-96. We do not know the extent to which this was the case under the Babylonian kings.

[86] A somewhat different idea is expressed in Isaiah, in a passage which describes the peace that will prevail in Zion when the imperial oppressor, probably Assyria, is banished. At that time nobody will see עם עמקי שפה משמוע נלעג לשון אין בינה, "a people of unintelligible speech, impossible to understand, stammering a language that is incomprehensible" (Isa 33:19). In a sharply ironic context, Ezekiel is instructed by Yahweh to take his message to the rebellious Israelites, who, although they can understand the prophet's language, will not believe his message. Although Yahweh does not send the prophet אל־עמים רבים עמקי שפה וכבדי לשון אשר לא־תשמע דבריהם, "to many peoples of unintelligible speech and difficult language, whose words you do not understand" (Ezek 3:6), such people would probably heed Ezekiel's message before the Judeans. Since Ezekiel delivers his prophecy in Babylonia, perhaps the עמים רבים were the Babylonians, or perhaps the many exiled populations dwelling in Babylonia.

[87] See the discussion in chapter one of the Neo-Babylonian fascination with perpetuating the legacies of ancient kings such as Sargon of Agade, Naram-Sin, Šulgi and especially Hammurapi and the first dyansty of Babylonia (above ch. 1, n. 178).

under Assyria offered an interpretive framework for analyzing those under Babylon.

Jer 6:1-5 speaks again of רעה נשקפה מצפון, "evil looming from the north" (6:1), and of a terrifying battle which will ensue and culminate in the sack of Zion's ארמנות, "strongholds" (6:5). The quotation of the opposing army's thirst for attack (6:4-5) is particularly dreadful: the Judeans can give no thought to serious opposition. The description of the enemy continues in 6:22-26. Once again it is a people coming from the "land of the north," "from the extremities of the earth" (22). The warriors brandish bow and spear, they come mounted upon horses אכזרי הוא ולא ירחמו, "it is cruel and they will show no mercy" (23).[88] Paralysis of the population sets in when report of the army's approach reaches Jeruslem: רפו ידינו צרה החזיקתנו חיל כיולדה, "our hands were paralyzed, anguish seized us (like) the writhing of a woman birthing" (v. 24). Similar language is used in Isa 13:7, in the משא בבל,[89] while the Akkadian semantic equivalent *aḫu/idu ramû*, "to let the arm fall," is used in military contexts in the same way (see above, p. 126).[90] The connection of such language to Assyro-Babylonian military depredations is plausible.

The foe from the north reappears in Jer 8:14-16 and 10:22. In the former passage, Jeremiah describes again how the Judeans determine to flee to the fortified cities in response to attack (see 4:5-6). In the cities, Yahweh gives them מי ראש "poisoned water," probably a product of siege, perhaps a fouled water supply or a reference to drinking urine in

---

[88] Precisely this language about a cruel foe is used to describe Babylon's attacker in Jer 50:42, another example of how imagery that is used of Judah's assailant earlier in Jeremiah is applied to Babylon in Jeremiah 50-51. W. Brueggemann ("At the Mercy of Babylon: A Subversive Rereading of the Empire," *JBL* 110 [1991]: 7-8) also recognized this inversion, although his larger theological understanding of the significance of the term "mercy" (רחם) in connection with the Babylonian empire and for biblical theology does not persuade this reader.

[89] See, again, Hillers, "Reaction to Bad News."

[90] See *AHw* 953b, s.v. *ramû*. Again, precisely this language is used of the king of Babylon when he learns of the enemy attacking from the north in Jer 50:43:

> שמע מלך־בבל את־שמעם ורפו ידיו צרה החזיקתהו חיל כיולדה
>
> "The king of Babylon heard their report and his hands were paralyzed, anguish seized him (like) the writhing of a woman birthing."

This is another example of language that had referred to Judah earlier in Jeremiah now being applied to Babylon.

conditions of siege.[91] The people hear the terrifying sound of the enemy approaching "from Dan" (8:16). The enemy comes and devours (אכל) the land and its produce, just as in Jer 5:15 and Deut 28:33, 49. The enemy's approach from Dan is noteworthy. A messenger similarly brings word of the enemy's march from Dan and the mountains of Ephraim in Jer 4:15. This undoubtedly refers literally to the invasion route of Mesopotamian or other armies into Palestine via the eastern branch of the Via Maris.[92] A more ominous note is sounded in 8:16 too, for it was one of those armies, that of Tiglath-pileser III, that marched down this route into the northern kingdom and annexed territories in Israel (2 Kgs 15:29).[93] Under Tiglath-pileser's successors, Israel was dismembered and made into several Assyrian provinces, including Du'ru, Samerīna, and Magidû.[94] Jeremiah understands the foe from the north as Assyria's successor.

The foe reappears in Jeremiah's foreign nation oracles. Jeremiah 46 consists of two oracles against Egypt, vv. 1-12 and vv. 13-28. The former presumably dates shortly after the battle at Carchemish in 605, when Nebuchadnezzar decisively defeated the Egyptians and pushed them out of Syria. The second oracle is probably later, as there appears to be a pun in v. 17 on the name of Pharaoh Apries, who came to power in 589 (see also Jer 44:30).[95] In any case, the superscriptions to the two oracles, 46:1-2 and 13-14, tie them to the Babylonian attacks of Nebuchadnezzar against the Egyptians. The prophet writes in 46:20 that

---

[91] Compare the following ceremonial curse in Esarhaddon's Succession Treaty: "May Ea, king of the Abyss, lord of the springs, give you deadly water to drink (A.MEŠ *la* TI.LA *liš-qi-ku-nu*)" (S. Parpola and K. Watanabe, *Neo-Assyrian Treaties and Loyalty Oaths*, SAA 2 [Helsinki: Helsinki University Press, 1988]), 51 §60 521-22.

[92] On the Via Maris, see, e.g., Aharoni, *Land of the Bible*, 45-54.

[93] For a discussion of Tiglath-pileser's campaigns, see now H. Tadmor, *The Inscriptions of Tiglath-pileser III King of Assyria* (Jerusalem: Israel Academy of Sciences and Humanities, 1994), 280-81; for the geography of 2 Kgs 15:29, Aharoni, *Land of the Bible*, 371-74. Isa 10:28-32 apparently describes an Assyrian assault against Judah from the territory of Benjamin, north of Jerusalem, perhaps by Sennacherib. The itinerary mentions Laishah, but this is apparently not Laish=Dan; see ibid., 393.

[94] See recently N. Na'aman, "Province System and Settlement Pattern in Southern Syria and Palestine in the Neo-Assyrian Period," in *Neo-Assyrian Geography*, ed. M. Liverani, Quaderni di Geografia Storica 5 (Rome: Università di Roma "La Sapienza," 1995), 105-7.

[95] On the word-play, see Holladay, *Jeremiah II*, 330; Redford, however, suggests the reference is to Necho II (*Egypt, Canaan, and Israel*, 458, n. 132).

a קרץ, "gadfly,"[96] from the north alights on the heifer Egypt to plague it. This is a reference to real or anticipated incursions of the army of Nebuchadnezzar against Egypt. V. 24 reads: "Daughter Egypt is shamed; she is given into the hand of a people from the north." In both of these cases Babylon is again clearly identified with the people from the north.[97]

In addition to these notices about the northern enemy in the oracles against Egypt, Jeremiah 47 also describes the northern foe as the attacker of Philistia. Once again, the foe is Babylon, and the date of the oracle should not be long after Nebuchadnezzar's invasion of Philistia in 604, at which time he razed Ashkelon (vv. 5, 7), "turning the city into a tell and ruin" according to the Babylonian chronicle.[98] The foe is described as an overwhelming flood מצפון, "from the north," that sweeps over Philistia. The flood image is not unique. It is used earlier of Assyria in the First Isaiah (Isa 8:7-8), and Machinist has convincingly argued that there it has a connection to the larger Mesopotamian tradition.[99] Jer 47:2 (and perhaps also 46:7-8) is presumably dependent on this earlier prophetic use of the flood motif in connection with Assyria, and once more points to Jeremiah's typological interpretation of the northern foe as the incarnation of a military threat from Mesopotamia.

It is unnecessary to describe fully and in detail the frequent Assyrian and Babylonian military incursions into Israel and Judah, but it is reasonable to suppose that such incursions informed Jeremiah's descriptions of the destructive capacities of the foe from the north. In fact, it seems probable that the foe from the north motif developed as a response to such impositions.[100] The ferocity of the foe and the concrete

---

[96] See, e.g., BDB 903a; *HALAT* 1071a suggests simply "ein peinigendes Insekt."

[97] For the problems in delineating Nebuchadnezzar's campaigns against Egypt, see above, chapter two.

[98] TCS 5 chron 5 obv. 18; for the archeological evidence, see Stager, "Ashkelon and the Archaeology of Destruction," *64-*72.

[99] Machinist, "Assyria and its Image," 726-28, and especially n. 49. For *abūbu*, "flood" as a weapon of or description of the Mesopotamian king, see Seux, *Épithètes royales*, 34, n. 5.

[100] Of course, the possibility of a Mesopotamian foe invading from the north existed earlier. In 853 B.C.E., Shalmaneser III's armies met a coalition of western kings at Qarqar. His advance was stopped in part because of the participation of Ahab of Israel. Jehu of Israel subsequently submitted to Shalmaneser, an act vividly depicted on the Black Obelisk (Barnett, *Assyrian Sculpture*, pls. 45-46). Both

references to its military procedures were not simply the reflex of a mythological template. They reflect the literal mayhem caused by an attacking army. Furthermore, the well-established idea that both Assyria and Babylon were "the staff of Yahweh's anger" (Isa 10:5) used to punish recalcitrant Israel and Judah should be remembered. Jeremiah too thought that the foe would come to punish Yahweh's people; the connection to the tradition of the Mesopotamian powers as the instrument of Yahweh's punishment is clear. The failure of Jeremiah to mention the foe by name in chapters 1-10 and his possible use of the foe motif prior to the emergence of a fully formed Neo-Babylonian imperial program under Nebuchadnezzar do not demand the search for an alternate foe, such as the Scythians. The earlier prophetic use of such language in connection with Assyria, and the awareness in Judah, indicated by Josiah's ill-fated meeting with Pharaoh Necho II in 609,[101] that a Mesopotamian imperial successor loomed on the horizon, provided ample reason for Jeremiah to warn of a threat from Mesopotamia, i.e., from the north. Moreover, this language persists, and in Ezekiel's oracle against Tyre, for example, the prophet has Yahweh declare that Nebuchadnezzar and his army will come against Tyre מצפון, "from the north" (Ezek 26:7).

If in Jeremiah the "foe from the north" refers consistently to an actual historical force, which is Babylon, the prophet could still use mythological imagery to emphasize the terror and consequences of the Babylonian attack, which is analyzed as a resurgence of primordial chaos (תהו ובהו, Jer 4:23).[102] Childs was thus correct to link the foe motif with the "chaos" tradition and to see the appearance of the foe as a reversion to chaos. This does not, however, preclude identification of the foe with a historical force. Yahweh's victory over Rahab/Leviathan, with its antecedents in Canaanite and Ugaritic lore, has mythological roots.

---

strategies, opposition and capitulation, demonstrate awareness already in the mid-ninth century of the potential military threat that the Assyrian kings posed in the region.

[101] 2 Kgs 23:29-30; Malamat, "Josiah's Bid for Armegeddon." The alliance of Egypt with Assyria against Babylonia, as mentioned above, dates at the latest to 616 according to the Babylonian chronicle, and it is difficult to suppose that Judah would have been unaware of this alliance until 609.

[102] For a superb discussion of the idea that chaos could erupt without warning, notwithstanding God's defeat of chaos at the creation, see J. Levenson, *Creation and the Persistence of Evil: The Jewish Drama of Divine Omnipotence* (New York: Harper and Row, 1987; reprint, Princeton: Princeton University Press, Mythos Series, 1994).

Yet in Israelite usage tangible foes can be depicted as watery forces of chaos and destruction: Egypt in Jer 46:8; Nebuchadnezzar himself in Jer 51:34 (where he is actually called תנין). The Song at the Sea (Exodus 15) provides a very early example of the recombination involved in this interpretive process, as Cross has demonstrated.[103] The plasticity of the mythological antecedents about chaos bursting forth in the human arena and the specific language describing the Assyrian menace in the earlier prophetic tradition provided Jeremiah with a rich fund of images and language that could be reapplied to the possibility of a new Mesopotamian imperial threat. Jeremiah's use of the motif of the foe from the north was conditioned by the persistent threat of military incursions by Mesopotamian forces. By the last decades of the seventh century an astute observer, like Jeremiah, would have recognized that Babylon represented a threat to the people of the west similar to that of the Assyrians.

3.4.2 The Babylonian King and His Administration

Jeremiah also provides information about Babylonian military procedures. One good example is the preservation, albeit apparently garbled in the MT, of a list of royal officials, כל שרי מלך־בבל, "all of the officers of the king of Babylon," who were responsible for determining the fate of Jerusalem and its population after the final Babylonian conquest of the city in 586 (Jer 39:3, 13). The MT reads as follows:

נרגל שר־אצר סמגר־נבו שר־סכים רב־סריס נרגל שר־אצר רב־מג
(Jer 39:3)

נבחראדן רב־טבחים ונבושזבן רב־סריס ונרגל שר־אצר רב־מג
(Jer 39:13)

Several of these names and titles are attested in the list of officials in Nebuchadnezzar's prism fragment from his seventh year.[104] Commentators often take v. 13 as a gloss on v. 3, following the narrative

---

[103] See Cross, *CMHE*, 121-44.

[104] Unger, *Babylon* 282-94 (=Nbk Prismen-Fragment [VIII]); for cols. iii 33-v 29 see also Oppenheim, *ANET*, 307-8. For the date of the prism fragment, see above ch. 1, n. 119.

unit that intervenes in vv. 4-12, which is lacking in LXX.[105] The two verses are not identical, and it is possible that v. 3 is a corrupt version of v. 13, or that they represent separate conflations of a single list. I tentatively harmonize:

נבוזראדן רב־טבחים נרגל שר־אצר סמגר נבו שר־סכם
רב־סריס נבושזבן רב־מג

> Nabuzaradan the chief cook, Nergalśar'eṣer the *smgr*, Nabuśarsekim the *rab sārîs*, and Nabušazban the *rab māg*.

This tentative reconstruction associates each personal name with a title. The first, "Nabuzaradan, the chief cook," perhaps fell out of v. 3, or perhaps it was absent altogether in v. 3; it is present only in v. 13. In favor of its originality is that the name and title are attested together often in Kings and Jeremiah.[106] They appear first in Nebuchadnezzar's list of *mašennū*-officials[107] in the Istanbul prism fragment: md*Nabû-zēra-iddinam* lú*rab nuḫtimmu*.[108] Here, the Hebrew רב־טבחים, "chief cook," is a loan translation of the Akkadian lú*rab nuḫtimmu*, which literally means "official in charge of the kitchen."[109] Feigin argued that the name and title were originally present in v. 3, because of the inexplicable duplication of the name Nergalśar'eṣer in v. 3, which is perhaps a conflation of the two names, and because of the importance of Nabuzaradan's participation in the events surrounding the fall of Jerusalem.[110]

The second name in the reconstruction is preserved as the first in v. 3: *Nergalśar'eṣer samgar*. While the MT construes *samgar* together with Nebo as another personal name, this is probably incorrect. In fact,

---

105 Rudolph, *Jeremia*, 227; Bright, *Jeremiah*, 245; Holladay, *Jeremiah 2*, 291.

106 2 Kgs 25:8 // Jer 52:12; 2 Kgs 25:11 // Jer 52:15; 2 Kgs // Jer 52:26; Jer 39:9,10,11; 40:1; 41:10; 43:6; Jer 52:30. On the other hand, that could be an indication of its secondary status: a well-known figure intrudes into a list where he was originally absent.

107 The translation of the title is uncertain, but the reference is to a high official; see Oppenheim, *ANET*, 307, n. 1.

108 This is the first name in the list if one accepts Oppenheim's argument that the preceding line, m lú*ma-še-en-nim* (Unger, *Babylon* 284 iii 35), is the heading for the subsequent enumeration of officials (*ANET*, 308, n. 7).

109 *CAD* N/2 316, s.v. *nuḫtimmu*; Cogan and Tadmor, *II Kings*, 319.

110 S.I. Feigin, "The Babylonian Officials in Jeremiah 39:3,13," *JBL* 45 (1926): 149-55; so also Cogan and Tadmor, *II Kings*, 319.

md*Nergal-šarra-uṣur* lú d*Sîn-māgir*, a proper name and title, are also preserved in Nebuchadnezzar's prism fragment.[111] Sin-magir, or Simmagir, was understood by some scholars as a place name,[112] but it is actually the title of a high royal official.[113] Nergalśar'eṣer is undoubtedly Neriglissar, a son-in-law of Nebuchadnezzar who ascended the throne of Babylon in 560 B.C.E. This reconstruction, however, makes the preservation of נרגל שר־אצר רב־מג at the end of both verses problematic. It is unlikely that two officials bearing the name Nergalśar'eṣer, but with different titles, were present at Jerusalem's fall. On the other hand, the preservation of *Nergal-šarra-uṣur* with the title *simmagir* in Nebuchadnezzar's list of officials argues for *simmagir* as his correct title. Yet רב־מג is an accurate reflection of the well-attested first-millennium Akkadian royal official, *rab mugi*.[114] Perhaps Nergalśar'eṣer held both titles and was mistakenly identified as two separate individuals. Or perhaps נבושזבן was identified as the *rab māg*, his name was then incorrectly copied together with the title *rab sārîs* in v. 13, and that of Nergalśar'eṣer was then reduplicated with the title *rab māg*.

The name preceding the title *rab sārîs* is different in the two verses. If we take *samgar* as the correct title of *Nergalśar'eṣer*, then v. 3 would continue with נבו שר־סכם. This could reflect an Akkadian name such as *Nabû-šarrūssu-ukīn*, and the final "*n*" could have been corrupted or perhaps reanalyzed as the Hebrew masculine plural termination "-*îm*" once שר was understood as a noun ("leader") in construct with the final element. A certain *Nabû-šarrūssu-ukīn* held the office of *rēš šarri* under Amel-Marduk in 561 B.C.E., although it is impossible to prove that this is the same individual as the one named in Jeremiah.[115] Jer 39:13 has נבושזבן instead of נבו שר־סכם. The former is another good Akkadian name, *Nabû-šezibanni*. It can hardly be correct simply to excise it, however, since it is unlikely that an editor would

---

111 Unger, *Babylon* 285 iv 22.

112 Unger, *Babylon*; Rudolph, *Jeremia*, 224; Bright, *Jeremiah*, 243; Holladay, *Jeremiah 2*, 291.

113 W. von Soden, "Der neubabylonische Funktionär *simmagir* und der Feuertod des Šamaš-šum-ukīn," *ZA* 62 (1972): 84-90; *AHw* 1045; *CAD* S 272; Cogan and Tadmor, *II Kings*, 319.

114 *CAD* M/2 171, s.v. *mugu*; *mugu* is not understood.

115 The Akkadian source has mdAG.LUGAL-*ut-su*-DU LÚ.SAG.LUGAL, md*Nabû-šarrussu-ukīn* lú*rēš šarri* (R. H. Sack, *Awel-Marduk 562-560 B.C.*, AOAT, Sonderreihe 4 [Neukirchen-Vluyn: Neukirchener, 1972], 68-69, no. 23:4).

produce it from thin air; it is more likely to have been present in the original list. Perhaps the original list preserved both names but with different titles. These suggestions, however, are speculative and it may be impossible to decide the matter.

In any event, the passages in Jeremiah prove that Nebuchadnezzar's highest officials, already in office by the king's seventh year (598), were military commanders responsible for overseeing the conquest of the western kingdoms. These officers were not, however, permanently installed to rule over the conquered territories. Indeed, Nergal-šarra-uṣur clearly held office in southern Babylonia, as Nebuchadnezzar's prism list indicates. As we have argued above, it was not Babylonian policy to install imperial officials in the southern Levant. Jeremiah's presentation of these officials, arriving at Jerusalem after its destruction to oversee its spoliation and the deportation of its population, fits this reconstruction.

3.5 Habakkuk 1-2

Habakkuk 1-2 contains a sustained reflection on the problem of Babylonian imperialism and its influences on Judah. Although Habakkuk was evidently a contemporary of Jeremiah, active perhaps in the early years of the reign of Nebuchadnezzar,[116] there are numerous differences in perspective between the two prophets. Habakkuk 1-2 lack the presentation of geopolitical depth provided in Jeremiah, and unlike Jeremiah, Habakkuk does not advocate Judean capitulation to Babylonian might. Furthermore, whereas Jeremiah focuses on Judean religious practice and the related issue of political alignment as these bear on the people's relationship to Yahweh, Habakkuk reverses the focus and concentrates on the question of Yahweh's justice toward his people. Habakkuk 1 is a complex consideration of imperial power. Habakkuk 2 resolves the tensions inherent in chapter one in favor of Yahweh's supremacy over the empire, but only after acknowledging that Yahweh permits such power to flourish as part of his design. The third chapter is an archaic hymn celebrating the inevitable victory of Yahweh

---

[116] On the setting and date of the Habakkuk 1-2, see the balanced discussion of J. J. M. Roberts, *Nahum, Habakkuk, and Zepheniah: A Commentary* (Louisville, Ky.: Westminster John Knox, 1991), 82-84 with literature.

over enemies, but will be left out of consideration here since it predates the activity of the prophet.[117]

The book opens with Habakkuk's plea to Yahweh: "How long, Yahweh, will I call for help but you will not listen, will I cry out to you 'violence' (חמס), but you will not save? Why do you cause me to see iniquity and trouble; why do you look on while there are plunder (שׁד) and violence (חמס) before me?" (1:2-3a). Although the language of this plea conforms with well-attested patterns of lament that are common, for example, in the Psalms, the issue of Chaldean crimes is foreshadowed. The term חמס in the prophet's cry is particularly important; it is used in Habakkuk after this plea only to characterize the crimes of the Chaldeans.[118] Thus the prophet says of the invading Chaldean cavalry: "all of it enters for violence" (כלה לחמס יבוא, 1:9). The prophet provides a litany of crimes for which the nations will ultimately repay the Chaldeans, these crimes include "(shedding of) human blood, and violence to the earth" (מדמי אדם וחמס־ארץ, 2:8b, repeated in 2:17b). Finally, the conquerors are accused of "violence against Lebanon" (חמס לבנון, 2:17a).

The last accusation, the heroic conquest of the Lebanon and acquisition of its prized cedars, is a well-known topos in Akkadian royal inscriptions beginning in the Old Babylonian period, and it receives special attention in Assyrian and Neo-Babylonian texts.[119] The emphasis in this tradition about the conquest of the Lebanon is precisely that such conquest demonstrates the king's imperial achievement. Nebuchadnezzar recounts the achievements of his reign in his Wadi Brisa inscription in the Lebanon, where he boasts of securing peace for the inhabitants of the region from a marauding enemy. In addition to the

---

[117] See the discussion of T. Hiebert, *God of My Victory: The Ancient Hymn in Habakkuk 3*, HSM 38 (Atlanta: Scholars, 1986).

[118] The Chaldeans are identified in 1:6. Several Greek witnesses, AQW, have τους μαχητας "the warriors" after the ethnicon, while BS*LC* lack it. The Göttingen LXX suggests "Chaldeans" is secondary, but this seems unlikely, as Roberts argues (*Nahum, Habakkuk, and Zephaniah*, 92, following Rudolph), given that V, S, and T all have "Chaldeans" and lack "the warriors." A text-critical judgment in favor of the MT's כשדים is warranted. While there is no solid evidence that the Neo-Babylonian dynasty was Chaldean in origin (see above, n. 17), biblical writers identified the "Babylonians" by one of the principal ethnic groups that resided in the region.

[119] Machinist, "Assyria and its Image," 723-24; for the Neo-Babylonian kings see Langdon, VAB 4, p. 304, s.v. *Libanon*; and J. Elayi, "L'exploitation des cèdres du mont Liban par les rois Assyriens et Néo-Babyloniens," *JESHO* 31 (1988): 14-41.

symbolic affirmation of the king's might, an important motive for Nebuchadnezzar's Lebanon campaign was to maintain the supply of cedar for Babylonian building projects. The use of cedar is often emphasized in Nebuchadnezzar's inscriptions. Weissbach also noted that in the east niche of the inscription at Wadi Brisa there is an eroded relief of the king felling a tree, possibly a cedar.[120] Habakkuk could have been aware of this topos directly through such Babylonian propaganda. On the other hand, Habakkuk is not the first biblical prophet to condemn Mesopotamian imperial aggrandizement as reflected in the conquest of the Lebanon and acquisition of its cedars. The First Isaiah mocks the Assyrian (Babylonian?) king who boasted of conquering the Lebanon (Isa 14:8; 37:24//2 Kgs 19:23).[121] Still, Habakkuk seems to go beyond the First Isaiah's statement inasmuch as the violence against the Lebanon is now to be repaid. The prophet, thus, may have known the image from earlier Israelite usage, but he seems to extend it as a result of Israel's fresh encounter with the Babylonians. Such violence, in any case, clearly has associations with the Mesopotamian imperial tradition. Thus the "violence" Habakkuk condemns is not abstract or unrelated to the specific goals of the empire under Nebuchadnezzar; it reflects precisely the imperial activity of the Babylonians.

Habakkuk's concern is to understand how Yahweh could permit the Chaldeans to prosper in their criminal behavior. The problem must have been particularly poignant in view of the reasoning represented, for example, by Nahum and Zephaniah 2:4-15: namely, that Yahweh had finally destroyed the might of Assyria. Yahweh's response to Habakkuk is that the Chaldeans are the instrument of punishment against Judah, a notion which is very similar to Isaiah's view of the Assyrian king as the rod of Yahweh's anger (Isa 10:5-6). Habakkuk then delineates the military ferocity of the king and his army: the king gathers captives like

---

[120] Weissbach, WVDOG 5, p. 8. The image visible in the published plates is from the west niche and depicts the king's battle with a lion (see above n. 77). Only a small fragment of the relief from the east niche appears, in Tafel 5: the upper left portion of the tree. Weissbach notes that the Wadi Brisa text mentions that the king himself felled cedars in the Lebanon (A iv 7-8; and A vi 18). To this reference we may add, e.g., PBS 15 (=Zyl III,8) pl. 25 i 43-44; and CT 37 (=Zyl III,6) i 42-43.

[121] The political allegory of Ezekiel 17 also depicts the great eagle (Nebuchadnezzar) plucking a prime shoot (Jehoiachin) from the top of a cedar of Lebanon (Jerusalem). Here too it seems possible that Neo-Babylonian exploitation of the Lebanon inspired the prophet, but he might also have been influenced by earlier biblical imagery.

sand, mocks lesser kings and rulers, laughs at fortified cities and captures them through siege (1:8-10).

Habakkuk remains indignant even after Yahweh's response, and in his second plea (1:14-17) accuses Yahweh of treating humans as fish or creeping animals. The rationale for this accusation also comes from the prophet's observation of Babylonian imperial practices. The Babylonian king, with Yahweh's consent, treats people like fish: "Every one he draws up with a hook (חכה), snares him in his net (חרם), gathers him into his trap (מכמרת). Therefore he rejoices and exults. Therefore he sacrifices to his net, burns incense to his trap. For by them his portion is fat, his food abundant" (1:15-16). There are two other places in the HB where rulers are said to fish for enemies,[122] while in Ezekiel Yahweh captures Pharaoh, depicted as a sea monster (תנין), in his net (חרם, רשת, 32:3). The metaphor of snaring the foe in nets has to do with fishing in each of these contexts, but it is noteworthy that Habakkuk's charge of cultic aberration against the imperial king has no precedent in the HB. Given the prophet's preoccupation with Babylonian crimes, it might be productive to investigate whether the satirical reference to the king sacrificing to his net and burning incense to his trap receives clarification from the Mesopotamian world.

In Mesopotamia, and especially Babylonia, fish was a staple in the diet from early times.[123] In royal inscriptions and art, the idea of the king or god snaring his foes like fish in a net, an apt metaphorical extension of the economic reality, goes back to the third millennium B.C.E., as the famous "stele of the vultures" of Eannatum indicates.[124]

---

[122] The image is used of the Assyrians, presumably, in Amos 4:2 (see the excellent discussion of S. Paul, "Fishing Imagery in Amos 4:2," *JBL* 97 [1978]: 183-90; and idem, *Amos*, Hermeneia [Minneapolis: Augsburg Fortress, 1991], 130-35), and of another national foe, likely the Babylonians, in Jer 16:16, where it is coupled with language of the hunt. Holladay has suggested that דיגים (Qr), "fishermen," and צידים, "hunters," in Jeremiah 16 are representative of successive powers, respectively Egypt and Babylon (*Jeremiah I*, 478-79). The only pre-Jeremianic usage of the term דיגים is in Isa 19:8, where the reference is presumably to Egypt. But Holladay fails to consider the comparable imagery of Amos 4:2 or Habakkuk, which shows that such language is particularly applicable to Mesopotamian imperial predators, who seem clearly to be in Jeremiah's view.

[123] E. Ebeling, "Fisch" *RLA* 3 (1957-1971): 66-67; also Oppenheim, *Ancient Mesopotamia*, 46; and M. A. Dandamayev, "Die Fischerei in neubabylonischen Texten des 6. und 5. Jahrhunderts v. u. Zeit," *Jahrbuch für Wirtschaftsgeschichte* IV (1981): 67-82.

[124] *ANEP* 94: fig. 298.

The military metaphor subsequently had a long history. It is found, interestingly, in an Old Babylonian "prophetic" letter from Mari where a visionary warns that Babylon will be gathered into a net.[125] In the cultic sphere, fish offerings already played an important role in the veneration of several deities as early as the late fourth millennium.[126] This continued down to the Neo-Babylonian era. Numerous administrative texts in the late period refer to furnishing the temples with fish for offerings. In royal inscriptions, Nebuchadnezzar II indicates that among the offerings brought to the tables of the gods were regular allotments of fish.[127] He particularly emphasizes in the Wadi Brisa inscription that he revived the practice of providing fish offerings for Marduk because these had fallen into desuetude.[128] Does this help clarify the cultic imagery in Habakkuk?[129]

Several commentators understand the language as a metaphor for the Babylonian king's worship of his military might, and this may be one aspect of the meaning (see also Hab 1:11).[130] But it does not account for the specific selection of imagery, which is explicitly associated with fishing, or its satirical cultic application. Is it possible that the prophet had a more literal referent in mind? This remains speculative, but perhaps the use of the image in Habakkuk represents the same sort of polemic against Babylonian cultic practices as the prophet's derisive comments about religious statues: "Woe, to one who says to wood, 'Wake up,' 'Arise'; to mute stone, 'It instructs.' Look, it is sheathed in gold and silver, and there is no breath at all inside it" (2:18-19). This polemic relies on a caricature of the use of religious images in the

---

[125] ARM XIII 23:6-15; for discussion, see A. Malamat, "A Forerunner of Biblical Prophecy: The Mari Documents," in *Ancient Israelite Religion. Essays in Honor of Frank Moore Cross*, ed. P. D. Miller, P. D. Hanson, and S. D. McBride (Philadelphia: Fortress, 1987), 41 and n. 23.

[126] Ebeling, "Fisch"; Dandamayev, "Fischerei," 78.

[127] VAB 4 90 (Nbk 9=Zyl III,4) i 19; ii 29; iii 13; 154 (Nbk 19=WBr) A iv 38; A iv 58-v 18; A vii 10, B vii 19; and we should probably restore a reference to fish also in Unger, *Babylon* 282 i 8-9. Note also the close relationship of these lists of offerings to that in the "Nebuchadnezzar King of Justice" text published by Lambert, where a reference to fish should probably also be restored (CT 46 45, pl. 44 v 7).

[128] VAB 4 154-56 (Nbk 19=WBr) A iv 38-v 18: He commissioned 20 Babylonian fishermen to bring a daily allotment of fish.

[129] Roberts, *Nahum, Habakkuk, and Zephaniah*, 104 also discusses the possible Mesopotamian background for the image, but more briefly and without attention to the cultic aspect.

[130] E.g., Roberts, *Nahum, Habakkuk, and Zephaniah*, 104.

Babylonian cult.[131] Could there be a similar caricature of the royal provision of fish offerings in the cult? Habakkuk goes one step further; he plays on the image of the king as one who snares his foes in a net, an image common in Mesopotamia and known within the prophetic tradition (Amos 4:2; Jer 16:16), and implies that the king not only supplies fish for the cult, he actually is foolish enough to sacrifice to his fishing implements. Whether this exegesis clarifies the meaning of the text, the image of the king sacrificing to his "hooks" and "net" is unique in the HB, and since it does have strong Mesopotamian echoes, it may reflect Habakkuk's manipulation and reversal of Mesopotamian ideas.

At the end of chapter 1, Habakkuk's accusation that Yahweh is complicit in permitting Chaldean depredations is unresolved. The tone shifts in chapter 2. Whether appeased by Yahweh's discourse or not, now the prophet is depicted as a lookout, stationed at his post, awaiting Yahweh's response to his "reproach" (תוכחת, 2:1). The motif and the specific language of the prophet as lookout in 2:1 are probably indebted to Isa 21:6-8, where, as we saw, the prophet related the fall of Babylon and its gods. Here Habakkuk describes the wicked behavior of the imperial power and mediates four הוי oracles that further delineate the crimes of the conquerors and guarantee retribution against them: כי אתה שלות גוים רבים ישלוך כל־יתר עמים, "Because you have plundered many nations, the whole remnant of the peoples will plunder you" (2:8a).

Yahweh commands the prophet that he should write down the vision that he will receive in response to his "reproach." This command is interesting in its own right: כתוב חזון וּבָאֵר על־הלחות למען ירוץ קורא בו[132], "transcribe the vision and document (it) upon the tablets, so that the one who proclaims it[133] may run [as a prophetic messenger]"

---

[131] For a reconstruction of the Babylonian perspective, see T. Jacobsen, "The Graven Image," in *Ancient Israelite Religion. Essays in Honor of Frank Moore Cross*, ed. P. D. Miller, P. D. Hanson, and S. D. McBride (Philadelphia: Fortress, 1987), 15-32.

[132] A syntactic problem complicates interpretation of this sentence: it would seem that the object of באר must be inferred; alternately, it may have been "ellipsized" (so D. T. Tsumura, "Hab 2:2 in the Light of Akkadian Legal Practice," *ZAW* 94 [1982]: 295). Roberts argues that the verbs are a hendiadys for "write the vision clearly" (*Nahum, Habakkuk, and Zephaniah*, 105).

[133] Roberts has difficulty accepting חזון as the antecedent of בו, arguing that the collocation "to read in/from" (קרא ב-) is always construed as reading from documents, and not their contents. If the documents were meant here, in his view, the suffix would have to be masc pl. to agree with לחות (*Nahum, Habakkuk, and Zephaniah*, 109). This may be overzealous; cf. Deut 27:8 and the discussion above.

(2:2).[134] A crux here is the word באר. In the Pi'el it is used only three times, all in regard to written words (Deut 1:5; 27:8). Deut 27:8 is analogous to the passage in Habakkuk. There Yahweh instructs Moses: וכתבת על־האבנים את־כל־דברי התורה הזאת באר היטב[135], "you will transcribe upon the stones all the words of this Torah, clarifying well." It is possible that here the verb refers to the legibility of the written word, but it more likely refers to the clarity of sense. This is clearer in Deut 1:5, where באר refers to clarification or promulgation of the content of the torah, not to its legibility. Von Soden notes that Hebrew באר is cognate with Akkadian *bâru(m)* III D, "deutlich machen, überführen."[136] In Old Babylonian legal contexts the verb is often used transitively with the meaning "to establish the true legal situation (ownership, amounts, liability, etc.) by a legal procedure involving an oath."[137] The Akkadian usage, as Tsumura also suggested, may clarify the biblical passages. Tsumura argued that Hab 2:2 might have a "legal connotation," inasmuch as it may reflect "'writing down' a contract, testimony, etc., and 'confirming' it by witnesses."[138] This suggestion of a legal connotation is insightful, and can be further corroborated. In Old Babylonian legal usage, once the testimony of a witness under oath was "established" (*ubīr*, D *bâru*) it could be "transcribed" (*šaṭāru*). Such a deposition, a *ṭuppi būrti*, "a tablet with a sworn deposition,"[139] could

---

[134] On the use of רוץ in the sense "run as messenger/prophesy," compare Jer 23:21, "I did not send the prophets, but they ran (רוץ); I did not speak to them, but they prophesied"; and Jer 51:31, where the "runner" (רוץ) and "messenger" (מגיד) bring word to the king of Babylon that his city has fallen. Perhaps "the runner" in Hab 2:2 is also supposed to transmit the vision to the oppressor, in this case, therefore, the Babylonian king.

[135] Numerous mss read the first verb as an imperative, just as Hab 2:2. It is possible that this is the correct reading. Even the infinitive absolute, however, could be used as a replacement for a finite form, such as the imv. As vocalized, however, the final verbs in Deut 27:8 are infinitive absolutes: the second, היטב, is used adverbially and in this instance may be "added epexegetically to another adverbial infinitive absolute" (GKC § 113k). The absence of the copula could support this interpretation, since the adverbial infinitive is asyndetic (see also Deut 9:21; *IBHS* 35.3.2.a)—on the other hand, so is use of the infinitive absolute as a word of command. What is more, the volitional usage of the infinitive absolute is extremely old (*IBHS* 35.5.1a and n. 49). It could, then, be volitional rather than adverbial, but in either case it qualifies the finite verb כתב.

[136] *AHw* 108b, s.v. *bâru* III; and 1547a; see also *CAD* B 127, s.v. *bâru* A.

[137] *CAD* B 127, s.v. *bâru* A 3.

[138] Tsumura, "Hab 2:2," 295.

[139] *CAD* B 339, s.v. *būrtu*.

then be considered independently valid in a court. Admittedly, this usage is attested only in the Old Babylonian period, so a genetic relationship with the Hebrew concept is unlikely. Nevertheless, the sense of the Hebrew usage of the verb in question is congruent with the Akkadian. The meaning of the Hebrew is not "write down legibly," but rather, "write down and document (for promulgation)."

That this legal explanation fits the context is proved by Yahweh's subsequent statement to Habakkuk:

כי עד[140] חזון למועד ויפח לקץ ולא יכזב
אם־יתמהמה חכה־לו כי־בא יבא לא יאחר (2:3a)

> For the vision is a witness to the appointed time, a testifier to the end, and will not deceive. If it delays, wait for it; it will surely come and will not tarry.

The sense of Habakkuk 2:2-3 is not simply that the content of the revelation by Yahweh to the prophet is legally confirmed through transcription, as Tsumura suggests, but also that the vision should be documented for authoritative promulgation to a wider audience (perhaps including the Babylonian king). Precisely because the veracity of the prophetic vision will have to be confirmed in the future, when the oppressor will meet his demise, appeal to a binding written record, called an *ʿd/ypḥ*, will be necessary to confirm that the vision the prophet uttered was accurate (a sensible concern too for torah, as in Deut 27:8).[141] Here comparative West Semitic and Akkadian legal concepts

---

[140] I follow S. Loewenstamm, who emends עוד to עד, "witness," the complement of יפח, another noun, which was misconstrued as a verb after the corruption of עד to עוד (see his "*Yāpēaḥ, yāpiaḥ, yāpîaḥ*," *Leš* 26 [1962]: 205-8, 280 [Hebrew]; reprinted in S. E. Loewenstamm, *Comparative Studies in Biblical and Ancient Oriental Literatures*, AOAT 204 [Neukirchen-Vluyn: Neukirchener, 1980, English]: 140-41). The "word pair" *ʿd/ypḥ* is common with such connotations, and *ypḫ* is attested already in Ugaritic with the meaning "witness" (*UT* 412, 1129; see also Roberts, *Nahum, Habakkuk, and Zephaniah*, 106).

[141] Note that the same idea is probably behind the command to Isaiah that his prophecies be written down for future reference (Isa 30:8; cf. 5:19). Loewenstamm also clarifies Isa 30:8 by ingeniously emending the problematic prepositional phrase לָעַד עד־עולם, "forever to eternity," to לְעֵד עד־עולם, "for a witness forever" (*Yāpēaḥ*, 143). The problem of deferred prophecies was of course real: if, as here in Habakkuk, an utterance was to be realized in the future, how could one establish the speaker's present credibility? Precisely this problem is at issue in Ezekiel's quotation (and repudiation) of popular proverbs about prophetic utterances which concern the future. The repudiated proverbs run: "the days draw on and every vision perishes";

clarify biblical usage. Habakkuk uses concrete legal language, familiar in both the Mesopotamian and the West Semitic spheres, for recording his prophecy against the Chaldeans.

The remainder of Habakkuk 2 describes the wicked actions of the גבר יהיר, "arrogant man" (2:5), for which he will ultimately be repaid. The identity of the man is unstated, but in view of the crimes subsequently attributed to him, and the connections between these crimes and those of the Chaldeans in chapter 1, the Babylonian king, Nebuchadnezzar, is the best suggestion.[142] The "arrogant man" has a rapacious appetite: "he has widened his gullet like Sheol,[143] but like Death he is not[144] sated. He gathered (ויאסף) for himself all the nations, collected (ויקבץ) for himself all the peoples" (v. 5b). The dominant image of the Babylonian king in Habakkuk, reflected not only here but also in 1:9b and in the "fishing" image discussed above, is of the conqueror who displaces populations by "collecting" them. Interestingly, Babylonian procedures for deportation, poorly understood in their particulars, are similarly, if indirectly, described in Nebuchadnezzar's imperial propaganda: he says of "all humanity" that he "gathered them for good" into Babylon.[145] The Akkadian verb *upaḫḫir*, "collect, assemble," is semantically close to אסף and קבץ. As noted in chapter one, Nebuchadnezzar sought to project an image of himself as the protector of the populations under his sway, and to portray Babylon's "eternal shadow" as a restorative one, wherein the peoples were gathered for their own well-being. The contrast between the propaganda of the subjugator and the perception of the subjugated could not be more stark. The exilic author of the anti-Babylon oracles in Jeremiah 50-51 goes one step farther and expressly undermines the Babylonian idea about gathering the people peacefully into Babylon: once Babylon is finally destroyed, he writes, "the nations will no longer stream" to "Bel in Babylon" (Jer 51:44).

Even according to Habakkuk, however, it is the conquered peoples who will have the last laugh. They will raise up a משל, "taunt,"

---

and "the vision that he sees is many days off, he prophesies for distant times" (Ezek 12:21,26). In Habakkuk's case, Yahweh initiates the solution to the problem by ordering the prophet to record the vision.

[142] Roberts, *Nahum, Habakkuk, and Zephaniah*, 117.

[143] Note the very similar description of Nebuchadnezzar in Jer 51:34, who is compared to the primordial serpent (תנין) who swallows (בלע) his enemy.

[144] Omit the copula before לא with 1QpHab.

[145] For the texts, see above, chapter 1.

against the Babylonian, and will speak a מליצה, "satire," and חדות, "riddles" (v. 6). Four הוי oracles follow which elaborate the conqueror's insatiable appetite and assure the prophet's audience that the Babylonian will receive retribution for his crimes. Economic spoliation in connection with imperial conquest is highlighted in 2:6b-7. The Babylonian is described as מרבה לא־לו, "one who increases what is not his," and מכביד עליו עבטיט, "one who makes heavier for himself heavy pledges."[146] Such accusations probably echo the typical response of subjugated communities to imperial exactions. The procedure of funneling resources from the subject populations of the empire to the heartland through seizure and exaction was no less important to the Babylonians than it had been to the Assyrians, and the massive building projects of the Neo-Babylonians, and those of Nebuchadnezzar II in particular, indicate how well these practices were refined in the sixth century. Nebuchadnezzar campaigned almost yearly in the west, in part to insure order, but also to fill the royal coffers.[147] Habakkuk's excoriation of the Babylonians for such procedures rates second only to his fear and condemnation of deportation and exile. We saw that the image of the king as a conqueror who deports people had its reflex in imperial propaganda too, where the formulation, however, naturally was benign. Similarly, the image of the king as recipient of foreign tribute is highlighted in Nebuchadnezzar's imperial propaganda. The assumption of the imperial creed, however, is that the populations of the empire benefit from the king's divine commission to rule them: he is their shepherd, leads them justly, gathers them peacefully into the shadow of Babylon, and causes them to prosper. Their recognition of Babylon's preeminence therefore justified the one-way flow of goods into the heartland. This was not, however, the perception of the subjugated communities.

The themes of Babylonian depredations and rapacity are elaborated in the following three הוי oracles (2:9-11, 12-14, 15-17) with an addendum concerning the futility of idol worship (vv. 18-19). The second הוי oracle condemns three related actions: acquisition of unjust gain; "cutting off" of many peoples to obtain it; and the corruption of the

[146] The form is a *hapax legomenon*, but is related to the noun עבוט, "pledge," and the denominative verb, "to take or give a pledge." Nouns of the form *qatlīl* seem to have an intensive meaning (*GKC* §84^{b}m; Joüon 88J). Could this be a reference to the payment of tribute?

[147] 2 Kgs 24:1-17; TCS 5 chron 5 obv. 11-13.

king's בית, "house," through ill-gotten gain. The issues of imperial exactions and the "cutting off" of peoples have already been discussed. We should probably understand the corrupt בית here as the royal "palace," and there may be a reference specifically to Nebuchadnezzar's palatial building projects.[148] He rebuilt two palaces in Babylon proper as well as the extramural Summer Palace north of the city. It is well known from his building inscriptions that materials from the west, especially cedar, were used extensively in these constructions.[149] Therefore, the prophet's image of the stones (אבן מקיר) and beams (כפיס מעץ) crying out further implicates the king in his abuse of the nations (v. 11). This image of the stones and beams crying out also contrasts sharply with the Neo-Babylonian royal inscriptions. These conclude, as we have seen, with a hymn of praise to the patron deity or deities. On occasion, a request is made in the hymns that the newly built structure intercede before the god(s) on behalf of the king. For example: *si-ip-pi ši-ga-ri mi-di-lu* ^giš^IG.MEŠ *ša* É.BABBAR.RA *dam-qa-tu-ú-a la na-pa-ar-ka-a li-iz-ku-ru ma-ḫa-ar-ka*, "May the thresholds, locks, and bar of the doorwings of Ebabbar unceasingly recall before you (Marduk) my good works."[150] In Habakkuk, the building materials are witnesses against the king, and the prophet thus neatly inverts the Babylonian conception.

The next הוי oracle continues the attack on the immorality of the king's building programs: הוי בנה עיר בדמים וכונן קריה בעולה[151], "Woe, builder of a city through blood, founder of a settlement through iniquity" (2:12) This perspective contrasts sharply with the ubiquitous notion in Mesopotamian building inscriptions that such construction is a divinely ordained royal obligation, and a method of achieving notoriety or immortality.[152] There follows a reference to the forced labor of the

---

[148] Roberts, *Nahum, Habakkuk, and Zephaniah*, 120.

[149] For evidence of the use of cedar from the royal inscriptions, see above, n. 119.

[150] VAB 4 96 (Nbk 10=Zyl II,4) ii 22-26.

[151] Roberts draws attention (*Nahum, Zephaniah and Habakkuk*, 122) to a very close parallel in Micah which refers to Judeans: בנה ציון בדמים וירושלם בעולה, "builder of Zion through blood, Jerusalem through iniquity" (Mic 3:10). The application of the phrase to Babylon as opposed to Jerusalem perhaps was influenced by Nahum's address to the Assyrian imperial capital, Nineveh: הוי עיר דמים "Woe, city of blood" (3:1). Ezekiel, in turn, applies it again to Jerusalem; see, e.g., Ezek 24:6: אוי עיר הדמים, "Woe, city of blood."

[152] For a recent comparative discussion, see A. Hurowitz, *I Have Built You an Exalted House: Temple Building in the Bible in Light of Mesopotamian and Northwest Semitic Writings*, JSOTSup 115 (Sheffield: Academic, 1992).

deported "peoples" in 2:13b.[153] Unlike other texts about the metropolis of Babylon, Habakkuk does not even allude to its grandeur (contrast Isa 13:19; 47:1). Rather, he condemns both the means and the ends of the building projects.

Throughout Habakkuk 1-2, therefore, there are allusions to Neo-Babylonian imperial ideas and practices from the perspective of a subject population. At least three central ideas of the Babylonian imperial creed are expressly condemned: the idea that the king rules by divine fiat; that the one-way flow of material wealth and captives into Babylonia results from the recognition of Babylon's greatness by subject peoples; and that the king honors his deities through building programs. The Babylonian ideas are undermined in Habakkuk's assessment: the king is actually a blasphemous fool; he is a looter who violently dislocates populations without regard for their well-being; and he is the author of building projects that he thinks please his gods but which only emphasize his corruption. Habakkuk accepts the notion that Yahweh has designated the Chaldeans as agents of punishment against Judah, but in the human sphere the prophet judges their ideology and actions as reprehensible. At the end of the day, he asserts, they will receive their just desserts.[154] The topics that were identified above as central to the Babylonian empire are precisely those that the prophet attempts to undermine. In other words, Nebuchadnezzar's propaganda determined the topics of debate.

3.6 Ezekiel

The Babylonian imperial context clearly and dramatically influenced Ezekiel's perspective on the crisis of the Judean exile and his perception of its cause, namely Judah's apostasy. Like another prophet of the exile, the Second Isaiah, Ezekiel was also present in Babylon(ia) during the exile, probably from its very beginning with the first

---

[153] This is later quoted in Jer 51:58.

[154] This acceptance of punishment from God conjoined with the conviction that God will finally demonstrate his faithfulness by destroying the enemy, is articulated well by Weber: "It is a stupendous paradox that a god does not only fail to protect his chosen people against its enemies but allows them to fall, or pushes them himself, into ignominy and enslavement, yet is worshipped only the more ardently" (*Ancient Judaism* [New York: The Free Press, 1967], 364).

deportations of 597.[155] However, unlike the Second Isaiah, whose prophecies will be treated below, Ezekiel was less concerned with the realia of daily life in exile or with the assumptions of the Babylonian ruling elite.[156] His prophecy clearly is infused with the atmosphere of the diaspora, but it is not formulated so directly as a polemic against the imperial ideology or the physical environment in Babylon as is that of the Second Isaiah.

It is not feasible here, just as it was not feasible with Jeremiah, to analyze every text that refers to Babylon directly or indirectly. The focus instead will be on passages in Ezekiel that provide insight into Babylonian imperial ideas and administration during the reign of Nebuchadnezzar.[157] How does the prophet typically speak about Babylon, and do his oracles provide data that improve understanding of the empire?

3.6.1 Ezekiel 17

Perhaps the most noteworthy datum in Ezekiel referring to the Babylonian imperial administration in the west is the description of a covenant or treaty between Nebuchadnezzar and his appointee, Zedekiah, the last king of Judah. In Ezek 17:1-10 there is a complex allegory (called both a חידה, "riddle,"[158] and a משל, "fable") in which a "great eagle" plucks off a shoot from the crown of a cedar of Lebanon, transplants it in his merchant city, and then plants a new seed which is meant to prosper in place of the shoot that was removed. The new seed grows into a vine, but turns for sustenance to a second eagle and thereby spurns the first. The first eagle deals harshly with the vine, tearing out its roots so that it withers. The prophet then provides clarification of the figures of the allegory with reference to contemporary events: the first

---

155 For a discussion of the prophet's career and the veracity of his comments about being present in Babylon (e.g., 1:1,3; 3:15, etc.) see W. Zimmerli, *Ezekiel 1*, Hermeneia (Philadelphia: Fortress, 1979), 16; and M. Greenberg, *Ezekiel 1-20*, AB (Garden City, N.Y.: Doubleday, 1983), 15-17.

156 Zimmerli, *Ezekiel 1*, 16.

157 On the chronological notices in the book and the duration of Ezekiel's prophetic career, which apparently did not extend beyond the reign of Nebuchadnezzar, see K.S. Freedy and D. B. Redford, "The Dates in Ezekiel in Relation to Biblical, Babylonian and Egyptian Sources," *JAOS* 90 (1970): 462-85; and Malamat, "Twilight of Judah," 144-45.

158 Note that the same term is used in Hab 2:6 of the taunts uttered against Babylon.

eagle is the king of Babylon, the topmost shoot of the cedar is Jehoiachin, the vine is Zedekiah, and the second eagle is the Pharaoh (17:12-16). Both the explicit commentary provided in the clarification and the images chosen for the allegory deserve comment.

M. Tsevat argued that the prophet's clarification of the allegory provides unique information about imperial procedures in the west, because it plainly states that a treaty existed between Nebuchadnezzar and his appointee, Zedekiah.[159] The language is explicit: ויכרת אתו ברית ויבא אתו באלה, "he [the king of Babylon] made a covenant with him [the appointed ruler] and imposed a curse-oath on him" (17:13). The terms ברית and אלה refer in this context to a binding treaty between political entities, and it appears that the king of Babylon initiates the treaty. Parallels to this phenomenon are abundant from the Neo-Assyrian period, where the terms *adê u māmītu* are used to refer to such treaties and oaths.[160] However, from the entire Neo-Babylonian period, including the period of the Neo-Babylonian dynasty, there are very few data relating to such treaties between Babylon and other polities.[161] There are several references to Nebuchadnezzar promulgating *riksātu*, "official pronouncements," but it is not clear that these were political agreements.[162] If one assumes that Ezekiel's political allegory reflects

[159] M. Tsevat, "The Neo-Assyrian and Neo-Babylonian Vassal Oaths and the Prophet Ezekiel," *JBL* 78 (1959): 201; recently also Machinist, "Palestine, Administration of," 77.

[160] There is a large literature on the subject; see the introductory summary and edition of the Neo-Assyrian texts in Parpola and Watanabe, *Neo-Assyrian Treaties and Loyalty Oaths*.

[161] See the discussion of J. A. Brinkman, "Political Covenants, Treaties, and Loyalty Oaths in Babylonia and Between Assyria and Babylonia," in *I Trattati nel mondo antico. Forma Ideologia Funzione*, ed. L Canfora, M. Liverani, and C. Zaccagnini (Rome: Istituto Gramsci, 1990), 81-112. Brinkman notes that there is only one certain surviving Assyro-Babylonian treaty, which dates to about 821 B.C.E. (ibid. 96, 107-12); otherwise there are only scattered references (100-2).

[162] In his Wadi Brisa inscription, there is reference to the blessings that will accrue to any king who "does not countermand my regulations (?)" (*riksātiya la ipaṭṭar*) (VAB 4 176 [Nbk 19=WBr] B x 16). In the "Nebuchadnezzar king of Justice" text, the king "drew up regulations" (*riksātu urakkis*) for a city as part of his legal reforms (Lambert, "Nebuchadnezzar King of Justice," 5 ii 25-27). The term *riksu*, pl. *riksātu*, is itself problematic. Brinkman notes that in the Old Babylonian period, *riksu* designated a "contract" or "solemn agreement." He writes that "in Middle Babylonian, a singular *rikištu/rikiltu* was introduced; but in Babylonian the new term had the distinctive sense of 'decree' or 'official pronouncement.'" In the late second millennium, according to Brinkman, there is no indication that *rikiltu* meant "political covenant/treaty" (Brinkman, "Political Covenants," 90-93). It is

actual treaty relations, it is of considerable independent value for clarifying Nebuchadnezzar's method of rule over one subject kingdom—not province—in the Levant.

Not only did Nebuchadnezzar appoint a compliant king from among the Judean "royal seed" (מזרע המלוכה, 17:13), he initiated a treaty with him, and in this respect the Babylonian practice appears not unlike the Assyrian. If this instance is representative of Babylonian procedures, then it seems that Nebuchadnezzar attempted to insure the loyalty of subject kings through imposition of treaties. Tsevat has also argued that the phrase ממלכה שפלה, literally "a low kingdom" (v. 14) is a technical reference to a "vassal kingdom," but this is much less likely.[163] There may be a further parallel between the Assyrian and Babylonian practices if the text of Ezekiel implies that Nebuchadnezzar invoked Yahweh as a witness to the treaty. The prophet has Yahweh refer to Zedekiah's breech of אלתי, "my oath," and בריתי, "my covenant" (v. 19), which could suggest that Nebuchadnezzar invoked Yahweh as a witness to the treaty.[164] This is exactly the interpretation of the Chronicler, who states that Nebuchadnezzar "made him [Zedekiah] swear an oath by God" (השביעו באלהים, 2 Chr 36:13). For Ezekiel, in any case, the treaty made between the kings of Babylon and Judah was binding, so that flouting it would bring retribution.[165]

Furthermore, the terms of Ezekiel's allegory are not chosen randomly, but reflect concrete Babylonian imperial administrative ideas and procedures. The image of the great eagle removing the shoot from the cedar of Lebanon to Babylon, the "merchant city," reflects at one level the archaic tradition of Mesopotamian acquisition of this prized

---

therefore uncertain whether Nebuchadnezzar used the term *riksātu* specifically in reference to political agreements.

[163] Tsevat, "Neo-Assyrian and Neo-Babylonian Vassal Oaths," 201.

[164] Greenberg doubts this interpretation, and seeks to discredit it by suggesting that even Assyrian practice did not depend on committing local rulers to a treaty by invoking their own deities (*Ezekiel*, 315, 320-22). This is disproved, however, by the treaty between Esarhaddon and Ba'al of Tyre, where the text plainly states that the curses invoked for transgressing the treaty will be administered not only by the Assyrian deities, but also by "the gods of Eber Nāri," including Ba'al-Shamem, Ba'al-Malage, Ba'al-Ṣaphon, Melqart, Eshmun and Astarte (Borger Asarh. 109 iv 3-19). The case of the treaty (*'dy*) between Bir-ga'yah of KTK and Matī'el of Arpad, recorded in the Sefire inscriptions, similarly suggests that the gods of both parties were invoked as witnesses to a treaty in the Aramaic sphere (Fitzmyer, *Sefîre* A II 7-13).

[165] E.g., Zimmerli, *Ezekiel 1*, 366.

wood for building purposes.[166] The idea that the eagle takes the shoot of the cedar (צמרת הארז, v. 3), and that he clips off its topmost twig (את ראש יניקותיו קטף, v. 4), suggests that the purpose was transplantation. There is precedent for such a notion in the native Israelite tradition, where, for example, cedars of Lebanon were transplanted "in the house of Yahweh" in Jerusalem (Ps 92:13-14), probably a reference to Temple gardens. Zion, in fact, could be referred to as Lebanon (Jer 22:6; Isa 18:7), which seems to be true also of Ezekiel.[167] The image of the imperial Mesopotamian king cutting down cedars or transplanting them (and other exotic flora) into the Mesopotamian royal gardens, however, was also important in the Mesopotamian imperial tradition, as Greenberg notes.[168] Nebuchadnezzar exhibited a particular preoccupation with the Lebanon, concretized in the Wadi Brisa rock relief, in Lebanon, which apparently depicts him felling a cedar.[169] While there may be an allusion to Zion as Lebanon in Ezekiel's allegory, the terms chosen nevertheless suggest that the prophet alludes to the literal imperial acquisition of cedars, the transplantation of exotic flora into Mesopotamia, and the initiation of treaties with independent subject kings.

3.6.2 Ezekiel 21:23-29

Ezekiel also provides an outsider's perspective on Babylonian procedures for sanctioning military operations. In a passage that shows how the Babylonian decision to besiege Jerusalem was really reflective of Yahweh's decision to punish the city, the prophet describes the king of Babylon's solicitation of oracular confirmation for a military operation (Ezek 21:26-28). The "king of Babylon," Nebuchadnezzar, stands at a fork in a road, the two branches of which lead to Rabbah of the Ammonites and to Jerusalem. According to the prophet, the king seeks an oracle (לקסם קסם) to ascertain what road he should take: קלקל

[166] See above, n. 119.

[167] Greenberg, *Ezekiel 1-20*, 310.

[168] *Ezekiel 1-20*, 310, where he cites Neo-Assyrian examples pointed out by A. L. Oppenheim, "On Royal Gardens in Mesopotamia," *JNES* 24 (1965): 328-33. The Neo-Babylonian texts do not specifically refer to this practice, but if there is credence to the legends about the Hanging Gardens (for a list of relevant classical texts, see Koldewey, *Wieder erstehende Babylon*, 104-6; also Wiseman, *Nebuchadrezzar and Babylon*, 56-60) then similar practices occurred in Babylon.

[169] See above, p. 153.

בחצים שאל בתרפים ראה בכבד, "he shook arrows, he inquired of teraphim, he inspected the liver (of a sacrificial animal)" (21:26). The first method has only an imprecise parallel in the biblical corpus,[170] and none apparently in the Mesopotamian sphere. The second method seems likewise to refer to procedures familiar in Israel but not Babylon.[171] The third method, extispicy, otherwise unattested in the HB, was perhaps the most highly regarded method of divination during the second and first millennia in the Mesopotamian sphere.[172] In the second millennium, Mesopotamian extispicy practices were known as far west as the Levant, as the discovery of liver models at Middle Bronze Age Hazor proves.[173] Mesopotamian procedures associated with extispicy perhaps illuminate another phrase in Ezekiel's description: בימינו היה הקסם ירושלם (21:27). Greenberg suggests that the antecedent of the third masculine singular suffix of בימינו is the liver, and he translates: "In its right part is the divination-omen 'Jerusalem.'"[174] Greenberg argues that this passage reflects the knowledge that extispicy was an important Babylonian method of divination, and the assumption that the right side of the liver was somehow auspicious for determining divine purposes.[175] There is no independent evidence from the era of the Neo-Babylonian dynasty for the use of such procedures in association with military planning, but there is considerable evidence for the use of extispicy in conjunction with Assyrian campaigns under Esarhaddon and Assurbanipal.[176] Thus, it is possible that Ezekiel furnishes information about Babylonian military practices unavailable from native cuneiform

---

[170] Michael Coogan called my attention to 2 Kgs 13:14-19, where Elisha instructs king Joash of Israel to shoot an arrow out of a window and then to strike the ground with additional arrows to signify Israel's future conquest of Aram.

[171] Greenberg, *Ezekiel 1-20*, 443-44.

[172] See, e.g., Oppenheim, *Ancient Mesopotamia*, 212-17.

[173] H. Tadmor and B. Landsberger, "Fragments of Clay Liver-Models from Hazor," *IEJ* 14 (1964): 201-17.

[174] M. Greenberg, "Nebuchadnezzar and the Parting of the Ways: Ezek. 21:26-27," in *Ah, Assyria . . .: Studies in Assyrian History and Ancient Near Eastern Historiography Presented to Hayim Tadmor*, ScrHier 33, ed. M. Cogan and I. Eph'al (Jerusalem: Magnes, 1991), 270-71.

[175] A. Guinan, "Left/Right Symbolism in Mesopotamian Divination," *SAAB* 10 (1996): 5-10.

[176] See especially the collection of texts edited by I. Starr, *Queries to the Sungod: Divination and Politics in Sargonid Assyria*, SAA 4 (Helsinki: The Neo-Assyrian Text Corpus Project, 1990), and pp. xxxvi-xlvi for a technical discussion of extispicy and the parts of the liver. Starr observes, however, that "fortuitous markings . . . could be found anywhere on the exta" (xxxix).

sources. The irony, of course, lies in Ezekiel's suggestion that it is the Mesopotamian method of divination that determines Nebuchadnezzar's military course of action, but that this is in accord with Yahweh's intent for Jerusalem. Here again is the idea that the imperial conqueror is the agent of Yahweh's punishment—this time of Jerusalem—but the text also expresses the view that Yahweh uses Babylonian mantic arts to accomplish his purpose. The idea is similar to Habakkuk's preoccupation with imperial Babylon, in which imperial procedures and ideas determine the framework for the prophet's presentation of Yahweh's purpose. In Ezekiel 21, Babylonian divination in the service of an imperial agenda becomes an opportunity for Yahweh to punish Jerusalem for cultic infractions.[177]

3.7 Second Isaiah

Babylonian imperial depredations and the development of an imperial program under Nebuchadnezzar serve as the catalyst for a dialogue between Habakkuk and Yahweh about divine election and protection, and as the catalyst for Jeremiah's prophecies of doom against Judah. Ezekiel is less directly concerned with the imperial worldview and its associated practices, but the exile clearly furnishes the background for the prophet's message, and occasionally that message is built around the imperial agenda of the Babylonian king. A very different perspective regarding Babylon emerges in the writings of the so-called Second Isaiah; for this anonymous prophet of the exile, the Babylonian milieu is important for his theological reflections on the uniqueness of Yahweh.

It is commonly argued that the prophet known as the Second Isaiah (Isaiah 40-55) spent part or all of his prophetic career in Babylon(ia). Evidence for this view comes mainly from his descriptions of Babylonian realia, from the expressed hope that the Judeans will return to their land from Babylon, and from the similarities between the

---

[177] It may be added that Ezekiel uses a phrase to describe Yahweh's wrath against his people that is a loan or calque from Akkadian. The phrase אמלה לבתך (Ezek 16:30) should be translated "I am angry against you" on the basis of the Akkadian idiom *libbāti malû*, "to become angry with" (see the discussion of P. V. Mankowski, "Akkadian and Trans-Akkadian Loanwords in Biblical Hebrew" [Ph.D. diss., Harvard University, 1997], 103-6). Not only does God effectively accomplish his purpose through Akkadian divinatory practices, according to Ezekiel, he apparently articulates his emotions with idioms loaned from Akkadian.

language of Second Isaiah and cuneiform inscriptions, which S. Paul, among others, identified.[178] There are opponents of this view, of course. H. Barstad, for example, argues that the geopolitical shifts that rocked the Near East toward the end of Nabonidus's reign would have been sufficiently well known in Syria-Palestine to allow for the Second Isaiah's identification of Cyrus as a liberator.[179] Barstad has written two short books on the problem: one attacks what he calls "the myth of the empty land"—the idea that Palestine was significantly depopulated and underdeveloped between about 580 and 535;[180] the other calls into question the consensus about the Babylonian context of the Second Isaiah.[181] Nevertheless, the evidence for the prophet's presence in Babylon is more nuanced than Barstad's critique suggests, and he fails to grapple with the philological and comparative evidence which supports the view that the prophet knew native Babylonian traditions and probably Babylonian royal inscriptions.[182] The Babylonian milieu did shape the prophet's thinking and language. For example, verisimilitude in the prophet's various portraits of an artisan fashioning an idol and worship of cult statues demonstrates, as we will see, his firsthand knowledge of Mesopotamian realia. Numerous scholars have argued that the prophet's language was directly influenced by Mesopotamian royal inscriptions, and this too seems likely.[183] More

---

[178] "Deutero-Isaiah and Cuneifrom Royal Inscriptions," 180-86.

[179] "On the So-called Babylonian Literary Influence in Second Isaiah." *Scandinavian Journal of the Old Testament* 2 (1987): 90-110.

[180] *The Myth of the Empty Land*; for a critique of his views, see above, chapter two.

[181] *The Babylonian Captivity of the Book of Isaiah* (Oslo: Novus, 1997).

[182] On the other hand, such knowledge does not prove the prophet was present in Babylon. Habakkuk occasionally shows a similar awareness, but there is no reason to assume that his familiarity derives from time spent in Babylonia. Still, in conjunction with the other evidence concerning the Second Isaiah, this remains the most compelling hypothesis.

[183] R. Kittel, "Cyrus und Deuterojesaja," *ZAW* 18 (1898): 149-62; J. W. Behr, *The Writings of Deutero-Isaiah and the Neo-Babylonian Royal Inscriptions*, Publications of the University of Pretoria, Series III: Arts, no. 3 (Pretoria: University of Pretoria, 1937); S. Paul, "Deutero-Isaiah and Cuneiform Royal Inscriptions," 180-86; N. M. Waldman, "A Biblical Echo of Mesopotamian Royal Rhetoric," in *Essays on the Occasion of the Seventieth Anniversary of the Dropsie University*, ed. A. I. Katsh and L. Nemoy (Philadelphia: The Dropsie University Press, 1979), 449-55; I. Eph'al, "Isa 40:19-20: On the Cultural and Linguistic Background of Deutero-Isaiah," *Shnaton* 10 (1986): 31-35 (Hebrew); and idem, "'You Are Defecting to the Chaldeans' (Jer 37:13)," *EI* 24 (Avraham Malamat

important, however, is the fact that the concentration throughout the Second Isaiah is on the Babylonian milieu, ideas, and practices. There is an immediacy to the prophet's polemic and his longing for liberation that is much easier to understand as emerging from the Babylonian context than from that of exilic Palestine. The hypothesis that the prophet was present in Babylonia should, therefore, be sustained. The images in Isaiah 40-55 of Babylonian realia and intellectual structures during the late imperial period consequently deserve close attention.

One contrast that the prophet elaborates in these chapters is between Yahweh's sole claim to knowledge and control of human destiny, on the one hand, and the impotence of Mesopotamian deities and religious experts, on the other. Of course, the prophet's descriptions of Babylonian practices are polemical; he does not strive for objectivity.[184] Whether or not the prophet is strictly accurate in his portrayals, however, the polemics show how an exilic Judean thinker responded to the political and cultural hegemony of Babylon: he sought to undermine the intellectual foundations of Babylonian power and rule by arguing for the preeminence of the God of Israel and the impotence of the Mesopotamian gods. The prophet's conscious effort to assert that only Yahweh has knowledge of humanity's destiny from time immemorial to the end of days is particularly interesting. It is conceded elsewhere in the HB that the land of the Chaldeans was of much greater antiquity than that of Israel; the predatory "nation from afar," very likely Babylon, is described by Jeremiah, as we have seen, as . . . גוי איתן גוי מעולם (5:15). While this may be literally true, the Second Isaiah painstakingly lays out his case that in fact Yahweh has all along been the only true, eternal God. The particular focus of the present discussion is on the ways in which Babylonian concepts and practices create the framework within which the prophet must articulate his argument.

Numerous passages in these chapters give satirical descriptions of the Babylonians' construction and worship of divine images; among them are Isa 40:18-20; 41:5-7, 21-29; 42:8, 17b; 44:9-20; 45:16, 20-21; 46:1-2, 5-7; and 48:5.[185] There are earlier texts in the HB that show a

---

Volume) (1993): 18-22 (Hebrew), are among those who have argued for direct influence in several instances. S. Paul's work, in particular, marked a significant advance in the discussion.

[184] For an excellent attempt to reconstruct Babylonian sensibilities as they relate to cult images, see, e.g., Jacobsen, "Graven Image."

[185] The authenticity of the idol passages has sometimes been contested in modern research. A persuasive case for their integrity is offered by R. Clifford, "The

concern with construction and worship of images, of course, including Jeremiah 10:1-16,[186] Hab 2:18-19, and Deuteronomy. Nevertheless, several of the passages in Second Isaiah are directly dependent on the prophet's knowledge of actual Babylonian practices and language, in a manner that is not evident in Jeremiah, Habakkuk, and Deuteronomy, and these illustrate his contrast between the living Yahweh and the impotent Mesopotamian deities. These passages also show how Babylonian practices and ideas furnish the framework for the debate.

3.7.1 Isaiah 40:18-20

Eph'al recently argued for the prophet's direct dependence upon the language of Babylonian royal inscriptions on the basis of one of the Second Isaiah's polemical idol passages, Isa 40:18-20.[187] In it the prophet asks rhetorically ואל-מי תדמיון אל ומה־דמות תערכו־לו, "to whom will you liken God ('El), or what likeness will you compare to him?" (v. 18). Obviously, the reply comes, God cannot be compared to an impotent פסל, "idol," the mundane manufacture of which proves its powerlessness. Such a comparison, according to the prophet, is absurd. This assertion, and others like it, that the idols are lifeless and powerless precisely because they are fashioned by human hands may be a response to Babylonian assertions to the contrary. In the so-called *mīs pî*, "mouth washing" rituals, the involvement of human artisans in fashioning the images is repudiated through ritual, and the image itself is "wakened" to life.[188] After the rhetorical question, the prophet describes the artisan's

---

Function of the Idol Passages in Second Isaiah," *CBQ* 42 (1980): 450-64; see also C. A. Franke, *Isaiah 46, 47, and 48: A New Literary-Critical Reading*, Biblical and Judaic Studies, vol. 3 (Winona Lake, Ind.: Eisenbrauns, 1994), 6 and nn. 15-16.

[186] On this passage, see P. J. King, "Jeremiah and Idolatry," *EI* 25 (Joseph Aviram Volume) (1996), 31*-36*.

[187] Eph'al, "Isa 40:19-20."

[188] For an interpretive discussion of the Neo-Babylonian *mīs pî* ritual, see Jacobsen, "Graven Image," 23-28, and n. 26 there for a provisional edition of the cuneiform texts which preserve the ritual. Further discussion can be had in C. B. F. Walker and M. B. Dick, "The Induction of the Cult Image in Ancient Mesopotamia," in *Born in Heaven, Made on Earth: The Creation of the Cult Image*, ed. M. B. Dick (Winona Lake, Ind.: Eisenbrauns, forthcoming). Another work came to my attention too late to make use of it in the present study: A. Berlejung, *Die Theologie der Bilder: Herstellung und Einweihung von Kultbildern in Mesopotamien und die alttestamentliche Bilderpolemik*, OBO 162 (Freiburg, Schweiz: Universitätsverlag; Göttingen: Vandenhoeck & Ruprecht, 1998).

manufacture of the idol. The artisan "overlays it with gold" (בזהב ירקענו, v. 19). The final two verses of the description are difficult and contain two *hapax legomena*: רתקות and המסכן. The first term refers to objects manufactured of silver for the image, perhaps chains.[189] The second term, taken by the Masoretes as a Puʿal participle, is more plausibly understood as a reference to the type of wood chosen by the artisan for constructing the statue. It has long been identified with Akkadian *musukkannu* (GIŠ.MES.MÁ.GAN.NA), which is *Dalbergia sissoo* Roxburgh, often used in Mesopotamia for ornamental construction and furniture manufacture.[190] The wood is native to regions east and southeast of Mesopotamia, although it is possible that it was planted locally in Babylonia. It was commonly available, and one archival text from the fourth year of Nabonidus (Nbn 171) mentions that *musukkannu*-wood was given to a craftsman for construction of a bed.[191] The wood did not, however, grow in the Levant. There is evidence that exotic woods, such as boxwood (genus *buxus*), perhaps from Anatolia, were imported and even transplanted near Jerusalem.[192] *Sissoo*-wood, however, has not yet been discovered in the southern Levant.[193] It is much more likely that the prophet learned of the wood's existence and uses in Babylonia. This is supported not only by the Akkadian derivation

---

[189] BDB 958b, s.v. רתקה.

[190] For the identification of the wood and its distribution, see I. Gershevitch, "Sissoo at Susa (OPers. *Yakā-* = *Dalbergia Sissoo* Roxb.)," *BSOAS* 19 (1957): 317-20; for the connection to Hebrew מסכן, see already H. Zimmern, *Akkadische Fremdwörter als Beweis für babylonischen Kultureinfluss*, 2e Auflage (Leipzig: Hinrichs, 1917), 53; more recently C. Cohen, *Biblical Hapax Legomena in the Light of Akkadian and Ugaritic*, SBLDS 37 (Misoula: Scholars, 1978), 133, n. 67; H. G. M. Williamson, "Isaiah 40.20–A Case of Not Seeing the Wood for the Trees," *Biblica* 67 (1986): 1-20; Ephʿal, "Isa 40:19-20," 31-32; and for Akk. usage, *CAD* M/2 238, s.v. *musukkannu* b 1'-3'.

[191] G. van Driel, "Wood, Reeds and Rushes: A Note on Neo-Babylonian Practical Texts," *Bulletin on Sumerian Agriculture* 6 (1992), 174.

[192] The species *buxus* was discovered in excavations at the City of David; see A. de Groot and D. T. Ariel, ed., *Excavations at the City of David 1978-1985, Vol. 3*. Qedem 33 (Jerusalem: Hebrew University Press, 1992), 108, 115.

[193] Gershevitch points out that the Samaritan Pentateuch renders Heb. עצי־גפר, "gopher wood," with which Noah constructed the ark, by "*sysm*, the Aramaic equivalent of Arab. *sāsam*" ("Sissoo at Susa," 319). Arabic *sāsam* is the equivalent of *sissoo*, and hence of Akk. *musukkannu*. While this is noteworthy, it cannot prove that the wood was known in the southern Levant in the sixth century B.C.E. On the relative percentage of imported wood discovered in archeological contexts in Syria-Palestine, see N. Liphschitz and G. Biger, "The Timber Trade in Ancient Palestine," *TA* 22 (1995): 121-27.

of the noun, but also by the prophet's description of *mskn* as עץ לא־ירקב, "wood that will not rot" (v. 20). Precisely this property is emphasized in Akkadian texts, in which *musukkannu* is frequently called *iṣṣu dārû*, "the lasting, durable wood."[194] Furthermore, this is not the only example of a possible Akkadian loanword for the name of a tree in the Second Isaiah's diatribes against idol manufacture. In Isa 44:14, the prophet speaks of the manufacturers who plant ארן, which the context proves is a type of tree.[195] The usual Akkadian term for cedar wood is *erēnu*, whereas the usual Hebrew word is ארז, which makes it possible to argue that ארן is a loanword.[196]

Eph'al compares Isa 40:19-20 with a Neo-Babylonian votive inscription of a late Neo-Assyrian king, Aššur-etel-ilāni (620s B.C.E.), reedited by Leichty.[197] This text describes the king's dedication of a table for the temple of Marduk in Babylon. The table is described as follows:

> GIŠ.BANŠUR (*paššūr*) GIŠ.MÁ.GAN.NA (*musukkanni*) *iṣ-ṣi da-ru-ú šá ṣa-ri-ri* ḪUŠ.A (*ḫušši/rušši*) *uḫ-ḫu-zu* . . . [*i*]-*na ši-pir* DUMU.ME (*mārē*) *im-ma-nu nak-liš šu-pu-šu*
>
> a table of *musukkannu*-wood, the durable wood, which is mounted with glittering gold . . . manufactured with the skill of clever craftsmen.[198]

Eph'al noticed that the table was built of "durable" *musukkannu*-wood and overlaid with gold, like the idol of מסכן "that will not rot" in Isaiah 40, but he also noted that line 13 of the cuneiform text, "manufactured with the skill of clever craftsmen," is similar to the phrase in Isa 40:20:

---

[194] *CAD* D 118, s.v. *dārû* 2b.

[195] The small *nun* was apparently used to prevent confusion with ארז, "cedar"; Cohen, *Biblical Hapax Legomena*, 44-45.

[196] Zimmern, *Akkadische Fremdwörter*, 53; Paul, "Deutero-Isaiah and Cuneifrom Royal Inscriptions," 83, n. 27. Mankowski doubts the correctness of the loan hypothesis in this case and notes that the vocalization in the MT "points to an inherited *qutl* noun . . . *'urn-," and that there is such a noun attested in Ugaritic (*Akkadian and Trans-Akkadian Loanwords*, 51). There is manuscript evidence for the pointing אֶרֶן, however, and while this does not resolve the problem of the Akk. long vowel, the Masoretic vocalization of such a loanword is not sufficient evidence to eliminate the possibility of a loan.

[197] E. Leichty, "An Inscription of Aššur-etel-ilani," *JAOS* 103 (1983): 217-20.

[198] Ibid., 217:10-13.

חרש חכם יבקש־לו להכין פסל לא ימוט, "he seeks out a skilled craftsman for himself to erect an idol that will not topple."[199] Eph'al's comparison is apt. In addition to Aššur-etel-ilāni's votive inscription, we should note that architectural ornamentation using *musukkannu*-wood is often referred to in the inscriptions of the Neo-Babylonian kings.[200] The following example from Nebuchadnezzar's Wadi Brisa inscription is apposite: *ša-mé-e* GIŠ.MES.MÁ.GAN.NA *iṣ-ṣi da-ra-a-am* KÙ.GI ḪUŠ.A *ú-ša-al-bi-iš-ma*, "a canopy of *musukkannu*-wood, the durable wood, I had covered with red gold" (for the goddess Gula).[201] Admittedly, the Neo-Babylonian texts do not show that the Babylonians used *musukkannu*-wood specifically in the construction of divine statues. They did, however, import it (or receive it as tribute) and use it frequently in the construction of votive objects as well as sacred and profane architecture. Its novelty for a Judean exile no doubt contributed to the prophet's description of the idol of מסכן. Given the other examples of Akkadian linguistic influence on Second Isaiah (to be discussed below), it seems plausible that the prophet's description of a votive object of מסכן overlaid with gold and constructed by a skilled artisan derives from his knowledge of such Neo-Babylonian practices or texts.

3.7.2 Isaiah 46:1-2

In another "idol" passage (Isa 46:1-2), the prophet parodies a procession of the statues of Bel(=Marduk) and Nebo(=Nabû), the chief deities of the Neo-Babylonian empire. He depicts them departing into exile, which they are powerless to prevent. The MT reads:

1. כרע בל קרס נבו היו עצביהם לחיה ולבהמה
נשאתיכם עמוסות משא לעיפה[202]

[199] Eph'al, "Isa 40:19-20," 32.

[200] For references, see *CAD* M/2 237-39, s.v. *musukkannu*.

[201] VAB 4 164 (Nbk 19=WBr) B vi 12-13; see also CT 37 pl. 8 (=Nbk Zyl III,6) 38.

[202] The text of v. 1aβ-b is apparently disturbed. The versions are of little help, and attempts to emend the text have not won consensus (for a survey, see H.-J. Hermisson, *Deuterojesaja*, BKAT 11/2 [Neukirchen-Vluyn: Neukirchener, 1987], 85-88). 1QIsa[a] follows the MT except that in place of משא לעיפה it reads משמיעיהמה, "their proclaimers," which it then takes as the subject of v. 2. LXX diverges considerably, as does T. Both of the latter take the idiom -ל . . . היו in its common meaning "to become," and thus they view the statues as identical with the

2. קרסו כרעו יחדו לא יכלו מלט משא ונפשם בשבי הלכה

The text presents difficulties, but may be tentatively translated:

> 1. Bel bows down, Nebo bends over;[203] their images are for animals and cattle.
> Your burdens are borne (as) a weight for the weary.
> 2. They[204] bend over, they bow down together; they are unable to

---

animals. Modern attempts to reorganize the text all assume that some words must be dropped, but text-critical grounds for such excisions are elusive at best. C. Westermann (*Isaiah 40-66*, OTL [London: SCM, 1969], 177 note a) suggests the following:

היו עצביהם משא לחיה
נשאתיכם לבהמה עמוסות לעיפה

"Their idols have become a burden for cattle
Burdens for cattle burdens for the weary."

This translation does not take account of the 2 m pl suffix on נשאתיכם. Clifford ("Idol Passages," 455, n. 19), following C. C. Torrey, deletes היו עצביהם as a gloss which was taken into the body of the text (the cause of the interpretation of LXX and T discussed above). Clifford reads instead:

לחיה ולבהמה נשאת
עמוסות משא לעיפה

"On beasts and cattle are they borne
Carried as a load on weary animals."

Like Westermann, Clifford is forced to delete the 2 m pl suf. Furthermore, this reconstruction does not answer why the passive participles are feminine: עצביהם is masculine, a grammatical problem few commentators seem to notice in identifying the antecedent. Duhm eventually emended to עצבותם, but עצבת never has the sense "images," as Hermisson notes (*Deuterojesaja*, 87). In addition, one doubts that "their images" can be secondary, since that would eliminate the important association of the gods with their images. It is best to maintain the MT and acknowledge that emendations will be speculative.

[203] Perhaps read as Qal pf (performative?) with LXX, T, and Syriac. *qrs* occurs only here and in v. 2. It is interpreted principally from context. The only etymological comparison is to the noun קֶרֶס "hook" (or the like; see BDB, *HALAT*, s.v.), perhaps with the extended meaning, "bend." T translates אתקטיף, "is hewn down"; LXX has συνετρίβη, "is shattered" (which more usually reflects Heb. שבר). These are presumably efforts to interpret the term from context, and probably neither reflects a different Hebrew Vorlage.

[204] The gods or the beasts? It is difficult to rule out either option. I assume, in view of the usage in v. 1, that the gods are still meant, although the text may be

deliver the burden;[205] rather they themselves go into captivity.

If the translation of the MT is defensible here, then the writer implies that the Babylonian gods could go into exile, and that Bel and Nabû would do so in procession together.[206] The symbolic defeat and removal of divine images in times of crisis is of course common in both the HB and Mesopotamia.[207] This provides background for the image. The specific description of Bel and Nabû in procession together, however, probably derives from familiarity with the first-millennium Babylonian *akītu* festival, as several scholars have suggested.[208] The *akītu*-festival was the most important religious festival in the Babylonian year, held during the first twelve days of Nisan, at the new year.[209]

---

deliberately ambiguous to allow for either reading, thus blurring the distinction between the gods and the beasts as a part of the polemic.

205 The text may contain a double entendre: מלט Pi also means "to escape," and משא is frequently used in Isaiah 13-23 (and elsewhere) to designate an "oracle (of doom)." Isaiah 13, for example, is titled משא בבל, while Isa 21:9, also an oracle against Babylon, speaks of the smashing of Babylon's gods. In other words, the text may mean that "the gods are unable to deliver the burden," but also that "they are unable to escape the oracle (of doom against Babylon)" and thus will go into exile.

206 Nabû is not mentioned elsewhere in the HB, although the name does appear as the theophoric element in PNs of Mesopotamian origin. Indeed, LXX^{AS} have here Dagon instead of Nebo (perhaps under the influence of the smashing of Dagon's statue in 1 Sam 5:3-4); this could represent the substitution of a more familiar name for a less familiar one, as Hermisson suggests (*Deuterojesaja*, 85).

207 On the importance of the mobility of the gods and their representations in Mesopotamian cult procedures, see B. Pongratz-Leisten, *Ina Šulmi Īrub: Die kulttopographische und ideologische Programmatik der akītu-Prozession in Babylonien und Assyrien im 1. Jahrtausend v. Chr.* Baghdader Forschungen 16 (Mainz am Rhein: Philipp von Zabern, 1994), 3-4. On the deportation of captured images in the Mesopotamian world, see Cogan, *Imperialism and Religion*, 22-41. For the peregrinations of Marduk's statue in the second millennium, see Sommerfeld, *Der Aufstieg Marduks*, 172; 186-89; 193. For a discussion of the phenomenon as it relates to the Israelite context, see J. M. Miller and J. J. M. Roberts, *The Hand of the Lord: A Reassessment of the "Ark Narrative" of I Samuel*, Johns Hopkins Near Eastern Studies (Baltimore: Johns Hopkins University Press, 1977).

208 E.g., W. W. Hallo, "Cult Statue and Divine Image: A Preliminary Study," in *Scripture in Context II: More Essays on the Comparative Method*, ed. W. W. Hallo, J. C. Moyer and L. G. Perdue (Winona Lake, Ind.: Eisenbrauns, 1983), 14-15; and H. D. Preuss, *Verspottung fremder Religionen im Alten Testament*, BWANT 12 (Stuttgart: Kohlhammer, 1971), 218.

209 J. A. Black, "The New Year Ceremonies in Ancient Babylon: 'Taking Bel By the Hand' and a Cultic Picnic," *Religion* 11 (1981): 39-59; and Pongratz-

During this festival, the statue of Nabû would travel up the Euphrates by boat from the Ezida temple in Borsippa, enter its designated shrine in Marduk's temple complex, Esagil,[210] and later join the statue of Marduk along Babylon's processional street, the Ay-ibūr-šāpû.[211] The cult statues of the deities proceeded together, drawn in chariots by ceremonial animals,[212] along a fixed route to the extramural *bīt akīti*, or "*akītu* temple," and back after seven days. The extramural position of the temple reinforced the underlying mythos of the festival. While there is no scholarly consensus on the festival's essence, and even less concerning all of its specific constituent events, it seems that affirmation of the role of Marduk as the chief divinity and arbiter of human destiny was prominent. Pongratz-Leisten has argued that the liminal status of the *akītu* temple—it is always described as *ina ṣēri*, "in the steppe"—served to dramatize (in the Babylonian version of the festival, at least) Marduk's power over the entire world.[213] Cohen has argued for a more straightforward explanation: the return procession from the steppe celebrated the gods' triumphal entry into the city and Marduk's subsequent reign.[214] Nabû's role in the festival, although not completely clear, was second only to Marduk's.[215] Given the prominence of this festival in the Babylonian world, it is plausible that the Second Isaiah makes allusion to the *akītu* procession when he specifically links the transportation of these two gods. His depiction would then be a parody

---

Leisten, *Ina Šulmi Īrub*. M. Cohen has argued that there were two *akītu*-festivals, one in the first month and one in the seventh, in conjunction with the equinoxes (*The Cultic Calendars of the Ancient Near East* [Bethesda, Md.: CDL, 1993], 400-403. In first-millennium Babylon, clearly its celebration in the first month was preeminent, as the Babylonian chronicle attests.

210 On the route of Nabû through the Uraš Gate and along the street Nabû-dayyān-nišīšu to the Esagil, see the commentary of George to Tintir V 67 (*BTT*, 361-62). For the phenomenon of Nabû's procession as described in Nebuchadnezzar's royal inscriptions, see, e.g., VAB 4 160 (Nbk 19=WBr) 29-34; PBS 15 79 (=Zyl III,8) i 75-76.

211 "May the Obdurate Foe Not Flourish." See Tintir V 64 (*BTT*, 66:64, 359-61; *CAD* Š/1 492, s.v. *šāpû*); on the archeology of the processional street, see Koldewey, *Wieder erstehende Babylon*, chapter 8. The processional street is also described as *uruḫ akīti*, "road of the Akītu (Temple)" (*BTT*, 359).

212 This is inferred from the Assyrian *akītu* festival, in which Aššur's chariot was pulled by ceremonial white horses; on the gods' modes of locomotion during the festival see further Pongratz-Leisten, *Ina Šulmi Īrub*, 193-202.

213 Ibid., 83-84.

214 *Cultic Calendars*, 404-405.

215 Black, "Cultic Picnic," 55-56.

of the gods' ritual procession from Babylon to the *akītu* temple during the festival: he describes the procession as their departure into exile. They go out of the city but do not return after the allotted seven-day stay. The prophet asserts, then, that despite the claim of the *akītu* festival that Marduk held universal power, ultimately both he and his son, Nabû, were powerless to prevent their own exile. They could not find their way back home after proceeding to the *akītu*-temple. The prophet goes on to explain that true power belongs only to Yahweh (46:2-7).

The irony of the prophet's image in 46:1-2 is heightened, and the correctness of the interpretation offered above confirmed, in view of the events of 540-539 B.C.E. The Babylonian chronicle reports that Nabonidus was unable to celebrate the *akītu* festival while he resided in Teima between his third and thirteenth regnal years,[216] and it was not performed in his absence by Belshazzar, his son and vice-regent. The *akītu* festival was celebrated again, however, at least by Nabonidus's seventeenth and final regnal year, the entry for which is preserved in the chronicle.[217] Interestingly, during the summer of Nabonidus's seventeenth year, 539, thus after the Nisan *akītu* festival, the king began to gather the statues and the retinues of many Babylonian gods into the capital to prevent their capture by the Persians, whom Nabonidus knew to be hostile to the kingdom.[218] The chronicle explicitly notes, however, that the gods of Borsippa, of whom Nabû was one (he resided there in the Ezida temple, leaving only for his annual trip to Babylon), did not enter Babylon in the summer of 539. Marduk's statue, already in the highly fortified capital, would not have been moved at all in this instance, or in any other emergency. The allusion in Isa 46:1 to the transportation or deportation of Bel and Nebo, therefore, cannot be a description of Nabonidus's collection of cult statues into Babylon during the summer of his seventeenth year, as some scholars suggest.[219] Furthermore, not only did Nabû remain in Borsippa in the summer of

---

[216] The Nabonidus chronicle for the king's seventh, ninth, tenth, and eleventh years reads: "the king did not come to Babylon in the month Nisan. Nabû did not come to Babylon. Bel did not come out. The Akitu festival did not take place" (TCS 5 chron 7 ii 10-12).

[217] TCS 5 chron 7 iii 5.

[218] TCS 5 chron 7 iii 9-12; Smith, *Babylonian Historical Texts*, 104; Cogan, *Imperialism and Religion*, 32; P. A. Beaulieu, "An Episode in the Fall of Babylon to the Persians," *JNES* 52 (1993): 241-261.

[219] E.g., Westermann: "At the eleventh hour an attempt is made to remove the gods' images from their temples, where they are in danger" (*Isaiah 40-66*, 178).

539, but later, after the Persian takeover of Babylon in the fall of that year, Cyrus treated the cult sites of Babylonia with respect, and divine statues were repatriated to their appropriate cities and temples, not carried into exile.[220] In other words, Nabû's cult statue did not come to Babylon in the summer of 539, and even those deities that did come were apparently returned to their shrines after the Persian takeover.

A hypothesis suggests itself: namely, that the prophet delivered this oracle about the procession of Marduk and Nabû sometime after the new year festival in Nabonidus's seventeenth year, probably once the danger to the outlying cities and their cult statues had become intolerable and Nabonidus ordered the collection of cult statues into Babylon. The prophet delivered the oracle, however, before the Persian conquest, which did not apparently result in the deportation of divine statues. Nabonidus's collection of the gods of Babylonia into the capital, although the prophecy should not be taken as a description of that event, might have contributed to the prophet's reinterpretation of the significance of the *akītu* procession: he reinterpreted it now not as a ritual procession emphasizing the universal might of the chief deities of the empire, but rather as emblematic of their eventual departure into exile.

This reconstruction is tentative, but it seems to explain the background of the text well. It rests on the assumption that the prophet was present in Babylon during the end of Nabonidus's reign. Although, as mentioned, some have contested this assumption, the great hope that he places in Cyrus as a deliverer of the Judean exiles could not have been formulated before the final years of Nabonidus's reign. Given too the prophet's hope for a future repatriation of the Judeans to their homeland, and his assumption that Cyrus had begun but not yet finished his conquests, the long held view that the text comes from the end of the reign of Nabonidus should be upheld. The polemic of Isa 46:1-2 fits this context well.

---

[220] The Persian largesse is recorded in the Babylonian chronicle (TCS 5 chron 7 iii 17-22) and the Cyrus Cylinder (Berger, "Kyros-Zylinder," 198:24-25).

3.7.3 Isaiah 47

Biblical scholars do not much emphasize the importance of Isaiah 47 for the overall message of the Second Isaiah.[221] This text, like those described above, is polemical: it is an oracle against Babylon, personified as a captive woman, that describes the city's fall and debasement. Franke notes that some scholars have considered this text unworthy of the poet known as the Second Isaiah; they emphasize that it is the only foreign-nation oracle in chapters 40-55, and argue that it is uncharacteristically vindictive in tone, and perhaps therefore secondary.[222] Franke has argued persuasively for its literary centrality within Isaiah 40-55. It would seem that the subject matter is also appropriate to the prophet's central concern in the diaspora: to glorify Yahweh as the omniscient creator, and to debase the impotent Mesopotamian gods and their functionaries.

The central argument of the chapter is that Babylon will fall despite its prodigious intellectual achievements, for these are a delusion and Babylon's self-confidence is in fact *hubris*. Throughout the chapter, Babylon is addressed as a shamed woman who will no longer be called רכה וענגה, "tender and delicate" (v. 1) or גברת ממלכות, "mistress of kingdoms" (v. 5).[223] She will fall from her preeminent status and depart from her land.[224] She will be exposed and defiled, images that very likely involve application to Babylon of practices directed toward captives in Mesopotamian military expeditions. This is suggested in particular by the language of v. 2, where Lady Babylon is commanded: "strip off your veil, bare your calf, cross over rivers." The depiction of captive females in the Assyrian artistic tradition may clarify this language: the bronze gates of Shalmaneser III (858-824 B.C.E.) from

---

[221] C. Franke, "The Function of the Satiric Lament over Babylon in Second Isaiah (47)," *VT* 41 (1991): 409; idem, *Isaiah 46, 47, and 48*, 146.

[222] Ibid., 409.

[223] Note that the prophet does not deny the fact of Babylon's preeminent status. On the feminine imagery, perhaps related to the "weeping goddess" motif in the city-lament genre, see Dobbs-Allsopp, *Weep, O Daughter Zion*, 110-11.

[224] This is most clear in the imperative command: עברי נהרות, "cross over rivers" (v. 2), which, although not necessarily meant in reference to specific rivers, seems to imply the removal of lady Babylon from her home, beyond the familiar waterways which bisected and surrounded the Neo-Babylonian city.

Balawat clearly depict Assyrian soldiers leading away captive women who are raising the fronts of their skirts.[225]

There is no direct mention of gods in Isaiah 47. Rather, the author derides Babylon's boastful claims to knowledge. The pinnacle of insolent pride is reached in Babylon's assertion, repeated twice, that אני ואפסי עוד, "I am, and there is no other" (vv. 8, 10). The phrase occurs also in Zeph 2:15, where it is uttered by Nineveh; this is another example of the typological interpretation of Mesopotamian imperial traditions in the prophetic corpus. Babylon's statement contrasts with the statements of Yahweh, כי־אפס בלעדי אני יהוה ואין עוד, "For there is none besides me; I am Yahweh and there is no other" (45:6; see also 45:5), and כי אנכי אל ואין עוד אלהים ואפס כמוני, "For I am El, and there is no other; God, and there is none like me" (46:9). All human efforts to acquire knowledge that do not begin with this assumption, according to the prophet, are fruitless, even blasphemous.[226]

The prophet therefore levels his critique at a series of Babylonian procedures and experts. These include mention of the following: רב כשפיך, "your many sorceries"[227] (vv. 9, 12); עצמת חבריך, "the power of

---

[225] L. W. King, *Bronze reliefs from the gates of Shalmaneser, King of Assyria, B.C. 860-825* (London: British Museum, 1915), pls. 23, 75. Compare Nah 2:15-16, where Assyria first exposes its enemies and then is itself exposed; also Nah 2:8 and 3:5, where Nineveh, addressed in the second person as a woman, is shamed and exposed; see also Deut 28:30a, Amos 7:17, and Jer 6:11-12 where women are violated or captured by enemies; see Jer 50:12 for the shaming of Babylon. In the Mesopotamian sphere, artistic representations of captives (occasionally naked males) being led away after defeat go back to the time of Sargon of Akkad in the third millennium, but are found much later as well, especially in the Neo-Assyrian reliefs (see, e.g., J. Oates, *Babylon*, 2d ed. [London: Thames and Hudson, 1986], 28, fig. 12 [Old Akkadian]; and 31, fig. 14 [Middle Babylonian?]; also Barnett, *Assyrian Sculpture*, pl. 177; and *ANEP* fig. 509 [Neo-Assyrian]).

[226] Westermann has also emphasized the prophet's critique of Babylonian intellectual presumptions (*Isaiah 40-66*, 192-93).

[227] On Akk. *kišpū*, the etymological cognate, see J. Bottéro, "Magie. A," *RLA* 7 (1987-1990): 200-34. Note the description of Nineveh as בעלת כשפים in Nah 3:4. More generally, compare Exod 22:17; Deut 18:10; Mal 3:5. Dan 2:2 identifies four types of functionaries who might interpret Nebuchadnezzar's dream: חרטמים (an Egyptian loan-word), אשפים, מכשפים, and כשדים. Here *mkšpym* are a class of professional religious experts, as are "Chaldeans"; all four groups (and גזרין in 2:27) are subsumed in the class חכימי בבל "sages of Babylon" (2:12,14,18,24,48). The question of a direct loan from the Akkadian, however, is problematic (see Mankowski, *Akkadian and Trans-Akkadian Loanwords*, 99).

your spells"[228] (vv. 9, 12); חכמתך ודעתך, "your wisdom and knowledge" (v. 10); שמים [229]הברו, "diviners of theheavens" (v. 13); החזים בכוכבים, "stargazers"[230] (v. 13); מודיעם לחדשים מאשר יבאו עליך, "those

[228] J. J. Finkelstein suggested that the root of the second noun should be connected with Akkadian *ḫabārum* (<**ḫbr*), "to be noisy, to make noise" rather than with I.חבר (< **ḥbr*) ("Hebrew חבר and Semitic *ḪBR," *JBL* 75 [1956]: 328-31). Cohen objected to this interpretation, arguing that *ḫabārum* is not used with the sense to charm or to cast spells; see his discussion in *Biblical Hapax Legomena*, 139-40, n. 78a.

[229] With the Qr, הברי. The meaning is obscure. LXX already translated όι ἀστρολόγοι τοῦ οὐρανοῦ , "the astrologers of heaven," likely interpreting from context under the influence of the later Hellenistic development which identified Chaldeans as astrologers; on the latter phenomenon see, e.g., O. Neugebauer, *The Exact Sciences in Antiquity*, 2d ed. (New York: Harper Torchbooks, 1962), 98. J. Blau argues that the comparison of the substantive with Arab. *habra*, "piece of meat," and the supposed denominative verb *habara*, "to cut into pieces" i.e., "partition," (suggested already by D. Qimḥi) is weak (J. Blau, "*Hōberê Šāmayim* [Jes xlvii 13]= Himmelsanbeter?" *VT* 7 [1957]: 183-84, and n. 3). Blau suggests instead a connection to Ugaritic *hbr*, "to bow down," with the extended sense of "supplicant, worshipper" (ibid., 183-84). If the reading of the MT is to be retained, this option seems best. An alternative is to emend the text, taking ברו as a loan from Akk. *barû*, "to observe, investigate," or *bārû*, "diviner." See already for this suggestion Zimmern, *Akkadische Fremdwörter*, 67; and S. Smith, *Isaiah Chapters 40-55: Literary Criticism and History*, Schweich Lectures of the British Academy, 1940 (London: Oxford University Press, 1944), 178, n. 65 (credited to Caspari). The verb *barû* is used in Akk. of examining exta or observing omens, but not of "observing the sky." However, in one case the constellation Lybra is described as *ba-rat šamê*, "which watches over the sky," but this is apparently an extension of the usage that is elsewhere applied to gods who "look after" the earth or humans (RAcc 139, 327; *AHw* 109a; *CAD* B 116b). Such an emendation, however, leaves the initial ה- unexplained. It is unlikely to be the definite article, which occurs only rarely with the *nomen regens* (GKC §127f-g). If the emendation should nevertheless be accepted, and there is reason to posit the reading ברים for בדים elsewhere in Second Isaiah (44:25) as well as in Jeremiah (50:36), then objections from Babylonian usage should not rule out the prophet's use of a common Akk. word for diviner in connection with astronomical observation. Another solution is that of M. Held, who suggests emendation to *ḥbry šmym* on the basis of IQIsa and Ibn Janāḥ; this would link the accusation to those in vv. 9 and 12, where Heb. חבר should be linked to Akk. *ubburu* ("Studies in Biblical Lexicography in the Light of Akkadian" [Hebrew], *EI* 16 [Harry Orlinsky Volume] [1982]: 78-79).

[230] This phrase appears to have no Akkadian etymological equivalent. The prophet is again describing the phenomena he observes in the Babylonian milieu as nearly as possible. He knows of Babylonian mantic and astrological procedures, but may not have precise or sophisticated knowledge of them. Analogous is Jeremiah's excoriation of foreign divinatory procedures; he instructs the Judeans: ומאתות השמים אל־תחתו, "do not be afraid of the heavenly portents" (10:2). The polemic

who make known at the new moons what will befall you"[231] (v. 13); and, finally, סחריך, "your merchants"[232] (v. 15). In an earlier text, the Second Isaiah makes the same argument that knowledge proceeds only from Yahweh, and that Yahweh subverts the putative knowledge of the Babylonian wise men, including אתות בדים, "the omens of diviners,"[233] קסמים "soothsayers," and חכמים . . . ודעתם, "wise men . . . and their knowledge" (44:25).

---

against idol manufacture in Jer 10:1-15 has many points of contact with the ideas of the Second Isaiah, and has led some to claim the Jeremiah passage for the Second Isaiah, (see Carroll, *Jeremiah*, 254; and the review of P. J. King, "Jeremiah and Idolatry").

[231] Compare Nabonidus's supplication to Sîn, the moon god, in the hymn which concludes the text detailing the installation of his daughter, En-nigaldi-Nanna, as high-priestess of Sîn at Ur: *e-ma* ITI *liš-tap-pa i-da-a-ti du-um-qi-ia* . . . *e-ma* ITI *i-na i-te-id-du-ši-ka ṣa-ad-da-ka da-mi-iq-tim gi-na-a lu-ut-tap-la-as*, "at each month (i.e., at the new moon) may propitious signs be manifested for me . . . at each month, when you (Sîn) renew yourself, let me always see your favorable sign" (YOS 1 45 [=Zyl II,7] ii 39); see the excellent discussion of this text in Reiner, *Your Thwarts in Pieces*, 4. Although Nebuchadnezzar had earlier also recognized the moon god Sîn as *na-aš ṣa-ad-du da-mi-iq-ti-ia*, "the bearer of signs favorable to me" (VAB 4 130 [Nbk 15] iv 61-62), it was Nabonidus who raised preoccupation with the worship of Sîn to its highest levels (see above, chapter one). Isaiah's accusation may contain an allusion here to the official preoccupation with the cult of Sîn under Nabonidus. Sîn appeared anew in the heavens each month and his appearance was portentous and required interpretation. Alternatively, or in addition, there could be in the use of this phrase a reference to specific Babylonian calendrical and cultic practices. Determination of the first day of the new month was established in Babylonia through lunar observation. Because the length of the month could vary by up to two days, such determination was important in the Neo-Babylonian sphere in order to allow for regulation of the civic and cultic calendar; see A. Aaboe, "Babylonian Mathematics, Astrology, and Astronomy," in *CAH*, 2d ed., vol. 3, pt. 2, *The Assyrian and Babylonian Empires and Other States of the Near East, from the Eighth to the Sixth Centuries B.C.*, ed. J. A. Boardman et al. (Cambridge: Cambridge University Press, 1991), 280; and P. A. Beaulieu, "The Impact of Month-lengths on the Neo-Babylonian Cultic Calendar," *ZA* 83 (1993): 66-87. In any event, Isaiah has in view here Babylonian lunar observation/worship.

[232] On this term, see B. Landsberger, "Akkadisch-hebräische Wortgleichungen," VTSup 16 (1967): 176-204. The interpretation "merchant" was challenged for this passage by Held, who reads instead "your sorcerers," linking the term to Akk. *sāḫiru/sāḫirtu*, used in the Maqlû series with this meaning (Held, "Studies in Biblical Lexicography," 79).

[233] Probably read here ברים, a textual error, *r* > *d*, for the loaned term *bārû*, which was discussed above in connection with הברו שמים (n. 229).

Some of these ideas and the criticism of such persons or practices are familiar from elsewhere in the HB.[234] Those mentioned in 47:13, however, are not, and it seems that the prophet is not thinking in general terms about methods of acquiring knowledge that were frowned upon in Israelite tradition; he is at pains to identify and ridicule Babylonian ideas and practices. He directs his attack specifically against what we might label diviners and astrologers. And even when doing so the prophet seems to adapt Babylonian ideas. He says, "evil will come upon you, but you will not know its origin(?) (שַׁחְרָהּ)" (Isa 47:11). Commentators have struggled with the last word. Some suggest it should be read as an infinitive of a different root, שחד, meaning "to give a present, bribe," i.e., "you don't know how to bribe it (away)" (for example, BDB, s.v.). Others link the term to the Arabic *saḥara*, "to enchant," i.e. "charm (away)," which could be quite appropriate in the context.[235] A further comparison, but with phonological problems, is with Akkadian *saḫāru*, which has a variety of meanings connected to the semantic field "to turn, turn around."[236] In the D-stem this can mean "to repel an enemy, an attack." If Isa 47:11 preserves the Pi'el infinitive of a root cognate with the Akkadian, the prophet may mean that Babylon does not know how to repel רעה (evil, doom).

Another more speculative possibility is that שַׁחְרָהּ may contain an allusion to the exaltation of the moon god during the reign of Nabonidus. The moon-god was known and worshipped in the Akkadian sphere as Sîn, but in the Aramaic/North-Arabian sphere as *šhr* < **śahr*.[237] When the divine name occurs as the theophoric element in personal names

---

[234] Note the following sample of texts referring to foreign religious experts: Philistine "priests" and "diviners" in 1 Sam 6:2; the representation of Babylonian belomancy in Ezek 21:26-27; Egyptian "magicians" in Exodus, labeled חרטמים, itself an Egyptian loan-word (Exod 8:3,14,15; 9:11; cf. Akk. *ḫarṭibu,* attested only in the first millennium and also derived from Egyptian; *CAD* Ḫ 116b; *AHw* 328b). In Dan 1:20 חרטמים and אשפים are paired. The latter term is a loan of Akk. *āšipu* "exorcist."

[235] See P. Machinist, "The Question of Distinctiveness in Ancient Israel: An Essay," in *Ah, Assyria . . .: Studies in Assyrian History and Ancient Near Eastern Historiography Presented to Hayim Tadmor*, ScrHier 33, ed. M. Cogan and I. Eph'al (Jerusalem: Magnes, 1991), 205 and n. 27 (where the idea is traced to G. R. Driver, *JTS* 36 [1935]: 400).

[236] *AHw* 1005; CAD S 37 b. On the problem of the sibilants, see Landsberger, "Akkadische-Hebräische Wortgleichungen," 185.

[237] See Lewy, "Late Assyro-Babylonian Cult of the Moon," 425-33; and F. M. Cross, "A New Aramaic Stele from Taymā', *CBQ* 48 (1986): 391, n. 6.

transcribed in Akkadian, it was realized variously as *tēri* or *teḫri*, less often *šēri/šeḫri*.[238] Probably the accusation against Nabonidus in the so-called Persian Verse Account that he received illicit revelations from ^d^*Ilteri* is a reference to the name of the lunar deity in the West Semitic sphere, where *il*="god," and *tēri*<*šahr/šaḫr*.[239] Hebrew *šḥr*, therefore, could reflect Akkadian *tēri/teḫri*. Nabonidus spent over half of his reign in northern Arabia, and probably the worship of the moon god in that region influenced his decision to reside there.[240] Is it possible that the Second Isaiah's accusation about the Babylonians' failure to know "the dawn" (*šḥrh*) of the "evil" that will overcome them was meant to allude to the deity *šahr/šaḫr*, or, in Akkadian, *tēri*, *Ilteri*, the West Semitic name of the moon god who monthly provided propitious signs to Nabonidus? This would suit the larger purpose of the polemic in Isaiah 47, which attacks Babylonian intellectual crafts generally, but astronomical and lunar observation and worship specifically.

The sarcastic reference in Isa 47:13 to astronomical observation and forecasting as methods for warding off evil (cf. 44:25) is another example of what one might expect in a hostile foreigner's observation of Babylonian intellectual crafts: it is polemic.[241] On the other hand, it reflects how a foreigner was struck by the ubiquity and gravity of such procedures. The immense learning required by Akkadian scribes to master and interpret astronomical omen texts such as the canonical compendium called *Enūma Anu Enlil*, which consisted of at least seventy tablets, must have been impressive. The crown's dependence on scribes who interpreted celestial portents with reference to such compendia is well known.[242] An excellent example from the period of Nabonidus is a tablet from one Šum-ukīn that describes a vision in which he saw portending celestial phenomena and studied them to determine their relevance for the king's and the crown prince's well-

---

[238] Lewy, "Late Assyro-Babylonian Cult of the Moon," 430, n. 137.

[239] *BHT*, 86 col. v 11; Lewy, "Late Assyro-Babylonian Cult of the Moon," 426-29.

[240] Ibid., 433.

[241] Cf. the comments of Oppenheim, *Ancient Mesopotamia*, 227.

[242] For consultation of *Enūma Anu Enlil* in the reign of Nabonidus, perhaps by the king himself, see Lambert, "A New Source," 2 iii 2; and especially the discussion of Machinist and Tadmor, "Heavenly Wisdom," 150-51. For Nabonidus's attempt to interpret a solar eclipse, see the text describing his installation of En-nigaldi-Nanna (YOS 1 45 [=Zyl II,7] ii 39). As Reiner and others have noted, this inscription quotes the protasis of an omen from the series *Enūma Anu Enlil* (Reiner, *Your Thwarts in Pieces*, 8 and n. 8).

being.[243] The Second Isaiah attempts to deflate the legitimacy of such pervasive Babylonian institutions and procedures through his assertion that in fact Yahweh created the cosmos, and specifically the heavens and celestial bodies (e.g., 40:12,22; 45:12; 48:13; 50:3). The Babylonian astrologers, thus, stare vainly for portents into a heaven ruled by Yahweh.

What is important in this analysis of the Second Isaiah's polemic is that its particularity and the force of the prophet's arguments for Yahweh's unique status as creator and arbiter of human destiny, even the specific language and phraseology, required this confrontation with the Babylonian empire and its intellectual experts. No doubt by the end of the monarchic era Judah's religious experts (represented, for example, by Jeremiah, the Deuteronomistic movement, Ezekiel, and perhaps the Priestly writer) had consolidated their critique of the "local" foreign deities, "the baals and the asherah," as heterodox. In so doing they had moved toward a more radical monotheism than was characteristic of earlier Israel, as Halpern, for example, has brilliantly argued.[244] The Second Isaiah presumably took that critique for granted. The Judean elite's polemic against "foreign" gods, the host of heaven, the baals and the Asherah, however, was in fact meant for local consumption, for differentiation of the cult of Yahweh in Jerusalem from heterodox local manifestations. Such a polemic simply did not work in the context of the Babylonian exile. In Babylon, Yahweh was out of his element, and Marduk was at home. The *golâ* constantly had in their view the impressive monuments built to honor the Babylonian gods and they either inferred or knew directly the skills and successes of the Babylonian religious experts. The Second Isaiah was obliged to elaborate his argument for Yahweh's omnipotence on behalf of a conquered community and in relation to the intellectual parameters laid

---

[243] YOS 1 39; for a translation of this text, see Oppenheim *ANET*, 309-10, n. 5; and for a recent edition, see Beaulieu, *Reign of Nabonidus*, 192.

[244] "As the prophetic critique alienated YHWH from his representations, as it strove to apprehend the reality as directly as Israel had on the day YHWH manifested himself at Sinai (Deut 4:9ff.), it assigned the hypostatized regalia, the cult and the temple, to the category of what was 'foreign'" (Halpern, "Brisker Pipes than Poetry," 102; also idem, "The Baal [and the Asherah] in Seventh-Century Judah: Yhwh's Retainers Retired," in *Konsequente Traditionsgeschichte: Festschrift Klaus Baltzer zum 65. Geburtstag*, ed. R. Bartelmus, T. Kruge, and H. Utzschneider, OBO 126 [Freiburg: Universitätsverlag; Göttingen: Vandenhoeck and Ruprecht, 1993], 115-54).

down by the Babylonian rulers. Observation of the heavens, the prophet asserts almost petulantly, does not yield information about the future of kings or individuals, contrary to what Nabonidus may have hoped; it simply verifies the supremacy of Yahweh, the creator of the heavens and earth.[245]

For the Second Isaiah, specific Babylonian ideas and practices provided the framework and functioned as catalysts for the prophet's articulation of the monotheistic creed. It was not simply that this creed, in denying the reality of the Babylonian deities, was the logical extension of the functional monotheism of Jeremiah and the Deuteronomistic school, with their radical critique of heterodox practices local to Judah. The Second Isaiah's creed was a self-conscious effort to carry the monotheistic idea into the international sphere, an effort necessitated both by the military actions of the empire and by the ubiquitous assertions of the Babylonians that their imperial ideology and success was an outgrowth of divine favor (see above, chapter one).

3.8 Jeremiah 50:1-51:58

The long series of oracles against Babylon in Jeremiah 50-51 contains a profusion of images and ideas relating to the imperial city. Modern exegetes have paid relatively little attention to the oracles, however, apart from acknowledging that their main message is that Babylon will fall (or has fallen) and that the people of Israel will return to their land. Two principal questions have dominated modern investigation of Jeremiah 50-51: first, do these chapters contain authentic oracles of Jeremiah? and second, is there any coherent structure discernible in them?[246] A solution to the second problem is not required in the present discussion. A conclusion about the first question can help to establish a relative date for the oracles, and thereby assist the exegete in explicating the ideas that they express about Babylon.

---

[245] The argument, like many polemics, makes no effort at a sympathetic reading of Babylonian ideas. On the other hand, the Babylonians were equally capable of such solipsism, though it is less often expressed in relational terms precisely because they possessed political hegemony. Still, we may note the following phrase in praise of Marduk from a text of Nebuchadnezzar II: *amatika ṣirti ša lā išū nakri*, "your lofty word which is not possessed by foreigners" (Etemenanki; HSM 890.3.1, unpublished).

[246] See for a recent overview D. J. Reimer, *The Oracles Against Babylon in Jeremiah 50-51* (San Francisco: Mellen Research University Press, 1993), 1-6.

Are these oracles secondary to the work of Jeremiah? Jeremiah 50-51 frequently reuse language found elsewhere in Jeremiah: language directed against Judah and its inhabitants is redirected against Babylon in these chapters.[247] Among recent scholars, Holladay understands this reversal of language to originate with Jeremiah, while Reimer, in conformity with most modern scholars who view the oracles as secondary to the prophecies of Jeremiah, concludes that the oracles derive from an exilic setting and represent a supplement to the Jeremiah tradition.[248] It would be hazardous to make a general assessment about the original context for all of the separate oracles on the basis of a few passages, but the allusions to Yahweh's retribution against Babylon for the destruction of Jerusalem and the Solomonic temple (Jer 50:28; 51:11b,24,35,51) seem to suggest that the oracles were composed or revised after 586.[249] Similarly, it is possible to argue that the language of destruction and decimation with which Jeremiah threatened Judah was applied to Babylon in these chapters by another author. It is difficult to conceive that the prophet who so strongly advocated Judah's capitulation to Babylon (e.g., Jer 27-29; 38), and who was treated deferentially by the imperial conquerors (39:12-14; 40:4-6), should have reversed his stance so dramatically.[250] It is true that Jeremiah did think that Babylon's power ultimately would wane (Jer 27:7; 29:10). And if the narrative of Jer 51:59-64 derives from the time of the prophet, then he also prophesied the destruction of Babylon. Even so, these passages do not offer adequate background for the vituperative yearning for Babylon's utter destruction that is expressed throughout Jer 50:2-51:58. This theme is so strong, as Rudolph has noted, that the idea of Judah's great sin and guilt, so prominent elsewhere in Jeremiah, virtually disappears.[251] Meanwhile, the arguments put forward for the literary dependency of these chapters upon material elsewhere in Jeremiah

---

[247] This was noted in a few instances above (see nn. 72, 88, 90, 153), and numerous scholars highlight the same point: note the comment of Bright, *Jeremiah*, 359-60; recent treatments include Holladay, *Jeremiah 2*, 403-10; and, most thoroughly, Reimer, *Oracles Against Babylon*, 159-243, with literature.

[248] Holladay, *Jeremiah 2*, 414-15; Reimer, *Oracles Against Babylon*, 239-42.

[249] Reimer, *Oracles Against Babylon*, 208-13 (with literature).

[250] Thus Carroll, *Jeremiah*, 816-17. I do not follow Carroll, however, in his effort to sidestep the issue of who was responsible for the reversal by suggesting that Jeremiah, as depicted in the text, is less a historical individual than a composite prophetic persona: in Carroll's view the historical individual could not hold such disparate views, but the persona could be made to express them.

[251] Rudolph, *Jeremia*, 275.

suggest that they are derivative and not composed by Jeremiah.[252] The working assumption here, then, is that the oracles of Jer 50:2-51:58 did not originate with the prophet, but more likely date to the late exilic era. There is also the possibility, discussed below, that some of the material reflects a date immediately after the fall of Babylon to the Persians (539 B.C.E.).

For the purpose of clarifying the late imperial portrait of Babylon in these oracles and the question of how the physical and intellectual environment of the imperial city may have impinged upon their author, I will concentrate on two prominent themes in the oracles: the way in which Babylon is depicted, and the description of its fall.

3.8.1 Descriptions of Babylon

That the author of these oracles knew something about Babylon's specific architecture seems to be proved by Jer 50:15:

הריעו עליה סביב נתנה ידה נפלו אשויתיה נהרסו חומותיה

> Raise a shout over her all around, she has surrendered;[253] her turrets have fallen, her walls are thrown down.

The term of particular interest here is אשיותיה[254] "its (Babylon's) turrets." This is a *hapax legomenon*, but as numerous scholars have argued, it is a loanword, possibly via Aramaic, of the Akkadian cognate *asītu*, a defensive turret or tower attached to a city wall.[255] An inscription of Nebuchadnezzar that recounts at length his building projects in Babylon (in connection with the erection of a temple for Muzibasa [Nabû]), proves that he built *dimātu*, "towers" and *asâtu*, "turrets" in conjunction with the third, outer moat wall (*kāru šelalti*)

---

[252] E.g., Rudolph, *Jeremia*, 274-75 and above n. 247.

[253] Lit. "she has given her hand," a phrase pertaining to submission.

[254] Thus Qr; Kt is אשויתיה, a simple transposition of letters. LXX translates ἐπάλξις, "battlement."

[255] The Akkadian parallel was recognized already by Zimmern, *Akkadische Fremdwörter*, 14; see also *AHw* 74 and *CAD* A/2 332-33, s.v. *asītu*; also Kaufman, *Akkadian Influences*, 37; Cohen, *Biblical Hapax Legomena*, 46-47; and Mankowski, *Akkadian and Trans-Akkadian Loanwords*, 52-53, who notes that the term may have been loaned into Akkadian from Northwest Semitic.

which surrounded the eastern section of Babylon.[256] The Hebrew term אשיות is the etymological and semantic equivalent of *asâtu*. The writer of Jer 50:15, in short, knew of and referred to a particular form of defensive architecture that Nebuchadnezzar had constructed at Babylon. Nebuchadnezzar's inscription also states explicitly that these *asâtu* were part of the outer moat wall surrounding Babylon, and thus they were the city's first line of defense. The prophet's description of archers arrayed against the outer walls and turrets in Jer 50:14 is thus perfectly understandable.

Several other texts in Jeremiah 50-51 seem to show that the author had knowledge of Babylon's unique hydrology. Cuneiform and archeological sources provide much evidence that the Neo-Babylonian kings, especially Nebuchadnezzar, constructed extensive fortifications in and around Babylon that employed the Euphrates river, moats, and natural drainage basins. We read the following in a passage from an inscription of Nebuchadnezzar that describes Babylon's fortifications: *mi-li ka-aš-ša-am me-e ra-bí-ù-tim ki-ma gi-pí-iš ti-a-am-tim ú-ša-al-mi-iš ap-pa-ri-im lu-uš-ta-as-ḫi-ir-šu*, "I surrounded (Babylon) with a huge flood of deep (or navigable[257]) water like the mighty expanse of the sea; I had it encircled by a reed marsh."[258] In addition to the reed marsh and extensive work on the river walls,[259] Nebuchadnezzar also constructed two defensive cross-country walls in Babylonia. One ran from Babylon via Kish to Kar-Nergal, and the other, called the "Median

---

256 CT 37 pl. 12 (=Zyl III,6) ii 27 and pl. 14 ii 51; there spelled *a-sà-a-tim*. The citations under *asītu* in the lexica suggest that it is used only in Neo-Assyrian texts, but Nebuchadnezzar's inscription proves otherwise. On the representation of Akk. /s/ by Heb. /š/, see Kaufman, *Akkadian Influences*, 141; and Cohen, *Biblical Hapax Legomena*, 89, n. 223. For a discussion of Akkadian texts relating to Babylon's city walls, see George, *BTT*, 343-47.

257 On *mê rabûtim* as "navigable water" in Neo-Babylonian, see *CAD* M/2, s.v. *mû* A 1g.

258 VAB 4 92 ii 12-14; for parallels in Nebuchadnezzar's inscriptions, see J. A. Black, et al., "Ḥabl aṣ-Ṣaḫr 1983-85: Nebuchadnezzar II's Cross-country Wall North of Sippar." NAPR 1 (1987): 19-20. See also the discussion of S. W. Cole, "Marsh Formation in the Borsippa Region and the Course of the Lower Euphrates," *JNES* 53 (1994): 93-95. Evidence for Babylon's moat walls, and in a few cases the bed of the moat, has been discovered in the excavations, though the moat itself has not been excavated for any length (Koldewey, *Wieder erstehende Babylon*, 15). Note also how Herodotus describes the outer fortifications of Babylon: "Round it runs first a fosse (τάφρος) deep and wide and full of water, and then a wall" (1.1.178).

259 See for the numerous references, *CAD* K 232, s.v. *kāru* A 1b.

Wall" by Xenophon, ran from Sippar to Opis.[260] The latter has been partly excavated at Ḥabl aṣ-Ṣaḫr, just north of Sippar.[261] This wall extended between the ancient courses of the Euphrates and the Tigris where they came nearest one another south of the ʿAqar Quf depression. The eastern terminus of the wall lay near Opis. This wall was not only a barrier to overland penetration, but, as its construction from baked brick set in bitumen indicates, it could also hold back flood waters to the north.[262] It seems that the area to the north of the wall could be flooded intentionally for defensive purposes. These elaborate water defenses in and around Babylon could scarcely have failed to impress a foreigner residing in the region.

It is perhaps of interest, therefore, that the writer of Jeremiah 50-51 describes Babylon as שכנת על מים רבים, "she who dwells by (over?) many waters" (51:13). Further, the prophet notes on two occasions Yahweh's threat to dry up Babylon's waters: והחרבתי את־ימה והבשתי את־מקורה, "I will dry up her sea and will desiccate her source" (51:36); and חרב[263] אל־מימיה ויבשו, "a drought against its waters that they may be dried up" (50:38). Another text speaks of inundation rather than drought: "The sea (ים) has risen over Babylon, she has been covered by its tumultuous waves (המון גליו)" (51:42). This last image probably was intended to evoke images of the destructive primordial flood.[264] But the references to Babylon's "sea" perhaps deserve more attention at a literal level than they have received.[265] In an inscription already cited, Nebuchadnezzar compares his water defenses around Babylon to *gipiš tiāmtim*, "the mighty expanse of the sea." There is an element of hyperbole here, but the existence of vast marshes has now been confirmed (see above on Ḥabl aṣ-Ṣaḫr). Meanwhile, Cole has demonstrated that the marshy morass to the southwest of Babylon around Borsippa, which was fed by the Pallukatu branch of the

---

[260] The most concise references to these fortifications occur in the cylinders published by S. J. Levy in *Sumer* 3 (1947) 7-8 (=Nbk Zyl II,6).

[261] For the excavation reports, see H. Gasche, et al., "Ḥabl aṣ-Ṣaḫr 1986, nouvelles fouilles. L'ouvrage défensif de Nabuchodonosor II au nord de Sippar," *NAPR* 2 (1989): 23-69; and for the textual evidence relating to this wall, see Black, "Nebuchadnezzar II's Cross-country Wall North of Sippar."

[262] Black, "Nebuchadnezzar II's Cross-country Wall North of Sippar," 28.

[263] Some mss read *ḥereb*, which would continue the foregoing series of imprecations employing the "sword" of Yahweh.

[264] See, e.g., Holladay, *Jeremiah*, 429-30.

[265] Holladay, *Jeremiah 2*, 429 does refer to "artificial lakes constructed for the defense of Babylon."

Euphrates, had expanded to such an extent in the reign of Nebuchadnezzar that it was commonly referred to as a "sea" (*tâmtu*).[266] Cole suggests that the flow of this branch of the Euphrates may also have been regulated upstream to permit defensive flooding of the western perimeter of the capital.[267] The considerable economic significance of the reed-marshes in this period made them doubly important. Nebuchadnezzar's inscriptions emphasize that "the best things from the reed-marsh" were placed on the offering tables of his patron deities.[268] Thus, with the Euphrates bisecting the city, vast marshes surrounding it, defensive flooding capabilities to the north of Sippar and to the west in the Borsippa region, the Akkadian references to various "seas" surrounding the capital reflect a unique hydrology. Admittedly, the references to the "sea" in Jeremiah are more laconic. Nevertheless, they conform in general outline and in the specific use of the term "sea" to the reality of Babylon's physical geography. They also bring to mind the phrase from Ps 137:1: על נהרות בבל שם ישבנו גם־בכינו, "by the rivers of Babylon, there we sat down and we wept." We may recall as well the command of Yahweh, in the Second Isaiah's oracle against Babylon, that lady Babylon should "cross over rivers" (עברו נהרות) and go into exile (Isa 47:2). Jeremiah 50-51, Psalm 137 and Isaiah 47 all date to the exilic era, and they all allude to Babylon's physical geography. The physical environment of the city seems to have worked upon the imagination of the biblical writers. This will become important again in discussing the city's fall as depicted in Jeremiah 50-51.

3.8.2 The Fall of Babylon

Numerous passages in Jeremiah 50-51 describe Babylon's fall. Some clearly contain conventional language and are dependent on earlier prophetic writings, especially other parts of Jeremiah.[269] Other passages have no obvious derivation. These may, therefore, be more directly influenced by the actual fall of Babylon to the Persians in 539

---

[266] Cole, "Marsh Formation," 95 and n. 76.

[267] Ibid., 95.

[268] The texts speak of the king offering *nūnim iṣṣūrū ušummū pīlâ simat appārim*, "fish, birds, reed-mice (?), eggs, the best things from the reed-marsh" (VAB 4 [Nbk 9=Zyl III,4] i 19, ii 29-30, iii 13-14; VAB 4 [Nbk 19=WBr] A iv 37-39).

[269] See the examples cited by Reimer, *Oracles Against Babylon*, 180-85.

B.C.E. The Nabonidus chronicle and the Cyrus cylinder, nearly contemporary cuneiform records, state that the Persians did not conquer Babylon through battle, as we will see. The language in Jeremiah 50-51 that expresses hope for Babylon's desolation, spoliation, and depopulation thus seems ill-suited to a context after the events of 539. However, if it is possible to argue that the fall of Babylon as depicted in the cuneiform records was not intended in the first place as an objective military account, and if it can also be shown what language about the city's fall in Jeremiah 50-51 does not derive from the larger prophetic tradition, then it may be possible to suggest that some of the material in these chapters is reflective of the events surrounding Babylon's fall. The late imperial context and the fall of Babylon, in other words, may have impinged directly on the composition of these oracles, which may in turn provide a perspective on the fall of the imperial city not available from other sources.

We already mentioned one reference to Babylon's fall in these chapters. In Jer 51:42 the author writes: "The sea (ים) has risen over Babylon, she has been covered by its tumultuous waves" (המון גליו). There seems here to be an allusion to the destructive capacity of the primeval waters (cf. מים רבים in Jer 51:13, which may have a similar connotation, as it does in Ps 93:4).[270] Such a reference does not encourage a literal reading, and suggests that the author has inherited a rich fund of traditional imagery about the waters of chaos. Yet it is interesting to compare this language with a phrase from one of Esarhaddon's Babylon inscriptions that alludes to the destruction of the city by Sennacherib in 689 B.C.E. Sennacherib sacked Babylon and then obliterated it through the agency of the Euphrates (i.e., Araḫtu), and Esarhaddon's scribe refers to this obliteration: [id]*Araḫti nār ḫegalli agû ezzi . . . tamšil abūbi ibbablamma ālu šubassu (ešrētišu) mê ušbīma ušēme karmeš*, "The Araḫtu, river of abundance, a furious flood . . . a replica of the deluge, flooded over; the water flooded the city, its residences and its temples, and turned it into ruins."[271] Here the obliteration of Babylon through the agency of the Euphrates is explicitly called a "replica of the (primeval) flood" (*tamšil abūbi*).[272] Esarhaddon's

[270] H. May, "Some Cosmic Connections of *Mayim Rabbîm*," *JBL* 74 (1955): 9-21.

[271] Borger Esarh., 14 Ep. 7:38-42.

[272] Compare too the analogous image applied to Nineveh in Nah 2:7-9 and 3:8, and the discussion of these texts in P. Machinist, "The Fall of Assyria in

scribe sees the historical episode of Sennacherib's destruction as analogous to the destruction wrought by the primeval flood. Without arguing that the biblical writer is directly dependent on this analogy, we may nevertheless suggest that his awareness of Babylon's physical geography and the reference to the tumultuous waves of "the sea" (ים) inundating the great city offer an image of Babylon's fall which is not unlike that of Esarhaddon's text.

What other perspectives on Babylon's fall do these passages contain, and what relationship do they have to the Akkadian accounts? Two Akkadian texts describe the circumstances of the Persian takeover of Babylon in 539 B.C.E.: the so-called Nabonidus chronicle and the Cyrus Cylinder. Both texts state that the city was captured without a battle. The Nabonidus chronicle reads: UD 16 ^{m}⌈*Ug*⌉*-ba-ru* ^{lú}NAM ^{kur}*Gu-ti-um u* ERÍN.MEŠ ^{m}*Ku-raš ba-la ṣal-tum ana* E^{ki} KU$_4$, "On the sixteenth day (of Tašrītu),[273] Ugbaru, governor of Gutium, and the army of Cyrus entered[274] Babylon without a battle."[275] The Cyrus cylinder is even more emphatic: *ba-lu qab-li ù ta-ḫa-zi ú-še-ri-ba-áš qé-reb* ŠU.AN.NA^{ki} URU-*šu* KÁ.DINGIR.MEŠ^{ki} *i-ṭe-er i-na šap-ša-qí*, "Without a battle or attack, he (Marduk) caused him (Cyrus) to enter Šuanna, his city; he saved Babylon from hardship."[276] The anti-Nabonidus sentiment in these texts is well known. Nevertheless, the explicit statements about the Persian entry into Babylon without a battle seemingly discourage alternate military reconstructions, even if the precise reasons for Babylon's implied capitulation remain opaque.[277]

There are, however, other ancient texts about the capture and fall of Babylon; these suggest that the cuneiform sources might reflect a

---

Comparative Ancient Perspective," in *Assyria 1995*, ed. S. Parpola and R. M. Whiting (Helsinki: Neo-Assyrian Text Corpus Project, 1997), 181-85.

[273] October 12, 539 (see R. A. Parker and W. Dubberstein, *Babylonian Chronology, 626 B.C.-A.D. 75*, Brown University Studies, vol. 19 [Providence: Brown University Press, 1956], 29; and Beaulieu, *Reign of Nabonidus*, 230).

[274] Note that the semantic range of *erēbu* includes the notion of "penetration," or "invasion" into a city, foreign country, etc. in military contexts (*CAD* E, s.v. *erēbu* 1 f 1').

[275] TCS 5 chron. 7 iii 15-16. Note the slightly different wording for Sippar, which also "was captured without a battle," (*ba-la ṣal-tum ṣa-bit*, TCS 5 chron 7 14). Did the scribe intend a difference between *ṣabātu* and *erēbu*?

[276] Berger, "Der Kyros-Zylinder," 196:17.

[277] Nabonidus was apparently preparing for a long siege. The Cyrus cylinder and the Verse Account imply however that many Babylonians were in favor of a Persian takeover because of their hatred for Nabonidus.

partial picture.[278] Most clear are the narratives of Herodotus (1.1.188-91) and Xenophon (*Cyr.* 7.5.7-31),[279] who both relate an elaborate stratagem of Cyrus: he captured Babylon by diverting the flow of the Euphrates and infiltrating the city by its channel.[280] The Greek accounts turn on several assumptions. First, both Herodotus (1.1.178-181,190) and Xenophon (*Cyr.* 7.5.7) assume that Babylon's defenses were impregnable by conventional means.[281] Second, they agree that the city had been provisioned to hold out in a protracted siege, so that exceptional measures were required to capture it. Third, the plan to divert the river's flow and infiltrate the city through its empty or lowered channel is credited to Cyrus's military brilliance. Finally, the diversion of the river's flow coincided with a festival in Babylon which diminished its defenders' military readiness.

The two ancient historians agree that Cyrus manipulated the river to conquer Babylon, but they diverge in their understanding of the mechanics. Herodotus is apparently better informed concerning earlier building works at the city and their relationship to Cyrus's strategy. He offers a detailed description of the construction of the river's quay walls in his description of the reign of queen Nitocris, the mother of Labynetus (= Nabonidus).[282] His description suggests that he had precise

---

[278] For discussions of the relationship between the cuneiform and Greek texts concerning the event, see Smith, *BHT*, 102-6; Dougherty, *Nabonidus and Belshazzar*, 167-85; Barnett, "Xenophon and the Wall of Media," 12-13; H. Wohl, "A Note on the Fall of Babylon," *JANES* 2 (1969): 28-38; Black, "Nebuchadnezzar II's Cross-country Wall," 15-25; Beaulieu, *Reign of Nabonidus*, 225-26, and Cole, "Marsh Formation," 95.

[279] Xenophon, *Cyropaedia*, rev. ed., trans. W. Miller, Loeb Classical Library 52 (Cambridge: Harvard University Press, 1989). All citations and quotations are of the Loeb edition.

[280] For the gates opening onto the river, see Herodotus (1.1.180,186). On the use of Araḫtu as the name of the Hillah branch of the Euphrates at Babylon in the Neo-Babylonian period see George, *BTT*, 351. Note also that by the fifth century, the Euphrates had shifted its course eastward and cut through the city. It was no longer confined in the north to the bed established and reinforced by Nabopolassar, Nebuchadnezzar, and Nabonidus (George, *BTT*, 356; and idem, "Babylon Revisited: Archaeology and Philology in Harness," *Antiquity* 67/257 [1993]: 735-46).

[281] Sack has emphasized that the Neo-Babylonian kings' principal claim to fame in Greek historiography was their monumental building achievements, including their defensive works around Babylon (*Images of Nebuchadnezzar*, 115, n. 1).

[282] Several proposals concerning her identity have been made: Dougherty argues that she was the wife of Nabonidus (*Nabonidus and Belshazzar*, 39-44). It is

knowledge about Babylonian building techniques, if not about Babylonian builders.[283] We know from the inscriptions of Nabopolassar, Nebuchadnezzar, Neriglissar, and Nabonidus that the Neo-Babylonian kings exerted massive energies in constructing quay walls of baked bricks set in bitumen, particularly along the east bank of the Euphrates.[284] Herodotus also accurately describes a bridge over the Euphrates, which the German excavations at the city uncovered.[285] Whatever the significance of Herodotus ascribing these activities to Nitocris, it seems reasonable that the builders at Babylon would have had the ability to reduce the water level of the river to construct the quay walls. Herodotus then explicitly states that Cyrus adopted this procedure of lowering the river as a military tactic against Babylon:

> he posted his army at the place where the river enters the city, and another part of it where the stream issues from the city, and bade his men enter the city by the channel of the Euphrates when they should see it to be fordable. . . . He himself marched away . . . and when he came to the lake, Cyrus dealt with it and with the river just as had the Babylonian queen [Nitocris]: drawing off the river by a canal into the lake, which was till now a marsh, he made the stream to sink till its former channel could be forded. . . . the Persians . . . made their way into Babylon by the channel of the Euphrates, which had now sunk about to the height of the middle of a man's thigh (1.1.191).

---

perhaps more likely that Nitocris was the wife of Nebuchadnezzar, as others have argued (Barnett, "Xenophon and the Wall of Media"; more cautiously Sack, *Images of Nebuchadnezzar*, 77, and 114, n. 27).

283 Herodotus writes the following:

> when the digging of the basin of the lake [a defensive structure some distance to the north of the city] was done, she [Nitocris] made another monument of her reign out of this same work. She had very long blocks of stone hewn; and when these were ready and the place was dug, she turned the course of the river wholly into it [the basin], and while it was filling, the former channel being now dry, she bricked with baked bricks, like those of the wall, the borders of the river in the city and the descents from the gates leading down to the river; also about the middle of the city she built a bridge with the stones which had been dug up, binding them together with iron and lead (1.1.186).

284 Herodotus, again, had exact knowledge of the Neo-Babylonians' use of bitumen and reed meshing in the baked brick walls: "using hot bitumen for cement and interposing layers of wattled reeds at every thirtieth course of bricks, they built first the border of the fosse and then the wall itself in the same fashion" (1.1.179).

285 On the construction of the bridge as recovered through excavations, see Koldewey, *Wieder erstehende Babylon*, 155-57.

It should be noted too that the Persian tactic, as described by Herodotus, would have been undertaken in October, according to the dates provided in the Babylonian chronicle (capture of Babylon on the 16th of Tašrītu), and this is precisely the time of year when the Euphrates is normally at its lowest level.[286]

Xenophon narrates a different strategy. In his version, Cyrus tackled the problem of the river as follows:

> He took measurements in a circle round about the city, leaving just enough room by the river for the erection of large towers, and began on either side of the city to dig an immense trench; and the earth from it they threw up on their own side of the ditch. . . . At last the ditches were completed. Then, when he heard that a certain festival had come round in Babylon . . . Cyrus took a large number of men, just as soon as it was dark, and opened the heads of the trenches at the river. As soon as that was done, the water flowed down through the ditches in the night, and the bed of the river, where it traversed the city, became passable for men (*Cyr*. 7.5.10, 15-16).

Several canals already did flow east from the river, as did the city moat, so it is unlikely that cutting additional channels eastward to the north and south of the city could have so dramatically affected the river's depth.[287] Xenophon presumably knew of the Persian strategy from some source and set about to reconstruct as plausible a scenario as possible, but the details of the account do not inspire confidence.

It is not clear how lowering the river would have facilitated infiltration into the city. A clue, however, might come from an inscription of Nebuchadnezzar, which describes his fortification of the canal outlets. The terminology is opaque, but the text reads as follows:

> *aš-šum in* ÍD *mu-ṣe-e me-e-ša ḫa-ab-ba-a-tim mu-ut-ta-ḫa-li-lum la e-ri-bi in pa-ar-zi-il-lum e-lu-tim àṣ-ba-at mu-ṣa-a-ša in ḫu-qu gu-ul-la-tim pa-ar-zi-il-lum ú-uš-ši-im-ma*[288] *ú-uš-ši-iṭ ri-ki-is-sa*

---

[286] For a discussion of modern data concerning irrigation in southern Mesopotamia and the variation throughout the year in Euphrates water levels, see M. P. Charles, "Irrigation in Lowland Mesopotamia," *Bulletin on Sumerian Agriculture* 4 (1988): 1-39, esp. Table 5.

[287] The most up to date ground plan of the city can be had in George, *BTT*, 24, fig. 4; and for a plan including the defenses and moats, ibid., 141, fig. 7.

[288] *CAD* A/2 408, s.v. *ašābu* omits this reference to the verb *uššib* as corrupt, but it seems to be the most plausible derivation.

> so that robbers and thieves do not enter the canal's water outlet, I secured its outlet with pure iron. In crossbars I installed iron discs (?), and I reinforced its (the outlet's) joint(s).[289]

Although the text and terminology here are not transparent, the passage proves that the Babylonians were well aware that the city could be penetrated through the canal outlets or drains which entered the eastern half of the city. Iron structures were therefore set below the water level to protect against penetration. Wetzel noted that drains were in fact built into the foundations of the defensive towers along Nabonidus's quay wall; Wetzel speculated that these might have been the type that Herodotus linked to the Persian infiltration.[290] In any case, lowering the water level as the Persians are supposed to have done might very well have allowed for the circumvention, destruction, or removal of the type of installations described by Nebuchadnezzar.

The discussions above raise questions concerning the sufficiency of the cuneiform accounts about Babylon's submission to Cyrus. These accounts were all opposed to Nabonidus but favorable to Cyrus. Were Cyrus's Babylonian apologists drawing attention away from the fact that he conquered the city in order to have him appear instead as a peaceful liberator? It turns out that defensive flooding around Babylon did make it possible to lower the level of the Euphrates; that the Greek historians' narratives about Cyrus's ruse for penetrating Babylon are plausible in view of the physical geography, seasonal timing, and defensive architecture and installations around the city; and that the Babylonians themselves knew that the city could be penetrated through the canals entering from the Euphrates and took measures to prevent this. These possibilities do not verify the Greek accounts, but they suggest that they are at least plausible.

There may be additional information in Jeremiah 50-51 that bears on the problem of Babylon's fall. There is clear evidence that the prophet expected or described a military attack against the city. The writer mentions that a military officer and cavalry were to be arrayed against Babylon, and in one instance he uses an Akkadian loanword for

---

[289] VAB 4 84 (Nbk 5=Zyl II,5) ii 1-10.

[290] F. Wetzel, *Die Stadtmauern von Babylon*, WVDOG 48 (Leipzig: J. C. Hinrichs, 1930), 53, and for a plan of the fortification, pl. 49; see also Koldewey, *Wieder erstehende Babylon*, 179.

the military officer, טפסר, Akk. *ṭupšarru* (Jer 51:27).[291] It was noted above that the prophet urged celebration at the fall of Babylon's defenses, including its "turrets" and "wall," where turrets may again be a loanword (Jer 50:15).

The description of the city's capture in Jer 51:30-32 is suggestive in view of the classical sources. It reads as follows:

30. חדלו גבורי בבל להלחם ישבו במצדות
נשתה גבורתם היו לנשים הציתו משכנתיה נשברו בריחיה
31. רץ לקראת־רץ ירוץ ומגיד לקראת מגיד
להגיד למלך בבל כי־נלכדה עירו מקצה
32. והמעברות נתפשו ואת־האגמים שרפו באש
ואנשי המלחמה נבהלו

> 30. The warriors of Babylon have ceased fighting, they remain in the strongholds.
> Their strength has dried up, they have become women![292] Its dwellings are burned; its bars are smashed.
> 31. Runner runs to meet runner, messenger to meet messenger,
> to report to the king of Babylon that his city is taken from the outskirts:
> 32. "The fords are seized and they have burned the reed marshes, the soldiers are terrified."

The account of the messengers' report is rather precise, especially v. 32, and it is at least not obviously dependent upon traditional prophetic language. Does this passage preserve authentic traditions about Babylon's fall? The two Hebrew terms, מעברות and אגמים, may refer to the topography around Babylon. The Akkadian cognate of מעברות is *nēberu*, "crossings, fords"; these appear commonly in Akkadian texts that describe the capture of such fords as a military strategy.[293] The Hebrew term אגמים can mean "pools," or the like, but here probably refers to the reed marshes around Babylon.[294] The Akkadian cognate

---

[291] The Hebrew word appears also in Nah 3:17; see the discussion of Machinist, "Assyria and Its Image," 732, n. 79.

[292] Compare Nah 3:13.

[293] See *CAD* N/2, s.v. *nēberu* 1 a. On the physical characteristics of such fords, see Cole, "Marsh Formation," 93 and n. 62.

[294] This was noted by Bright, *Jeremiah*, 357; and Holladay, *Jeremiah 2*, 427; see also Isa 14:23, where an editorial addition brings the older poem in vv. 4b-21 into connection with the fall of Babylon and likewise mentions that the city will be turned into אגמי־מים.

agammu, "swamp, marsh," refers to a topographical item well-attested in the vicinity of Babylon. The term is in fact an Akkadian loan into Hebrew.[295] Akkadian texts, much like the report in Jeremiah, also refer to the burning of such marshes, usually in connection with curse formulas or as a military tactic for flushing out fugitives, although in these contexts the term used is *apu*, "reed thicket, canebrake," rather than *agammu* (the cognate of אגם). Thus, for example, in the curse section of the epilogue to Hammurapi's Laws, Nergal is requested to destroy his people *kīma išātim ezzētim ša apim*, "like a furious marshfire."[296] On the other hand, *agammū*, "marshes," are precisely where the Sargonid kings of Assyria frequently chased recalcitrant Babylonians, although there is apparently no reference to burning of *agammū*. Marshfires would of course be most easily ignited at the driest time of the year, which in southern Mesopotamia corresponds precisely with the time Babylon is said to have been captured, Tašrītu (September/October).

Is it possible that the two military tactics alluded to by the Babylonian messengers in Jer 51:31-32, seizing of fords and burning of reed marshes, were influenced by the Persian assault against Babylon in the autumn of 539? Perhaps the fords referred to in Jer 51:32 were the key points along the Euphrates where the river's flow could be diverted out of the main channel to lower its level. The seizure of fords could then refer to the Persian manipulation of the river's water level through such diversion. Burning of marshes is less obviously connected to the Persian strategy as narrated by the Greek historians, but we have seen that it is a practice well-known in Mesopotamian military tactics, one that may have been used against Babylon or its defenders. Ultimately, of course, these suggestions are only intriguing possibilities, but in view of the traditions preserved by the Greek historians they are possibilities that open the question whether the native cuneiform sources were intended as straightforward military accounts. In the aggregate, the Greek and biblical traditions caution the historian that cuneiform sources are not necessarily to be assigned greater value in such reconstruction merely because they are native.

---

[295] The date of the loan cannot be established since it is used elsewhere (e.g., Exod 7:19; 8:1; Isa 41:18; 42:15; Ps 107:35; 114:8). See the discussion of Mankowski, *Akkadian and Trans-Akkadian Loanwords*, 25-26.

[296] CH r. XXVIII 31-34; on marshfires generally, see *CAD* A/2, 200 s.v. *apum* A b.

We have argued, then, that the anti-Babylon oracles of Jeremiah 50-51 date to the end of the Babylonian imperial era, and that the author of the oracles had specific knowledge of Babylon's architecture and physical environment. In these oracles, however, Babylon is no longer an international force to be reckoned with, but stands under Yahweh's judgment and will finally be destroyed because of crimes against his people. The descriptions of the city's fall are not specific enough in every detail to allow for a reconstruction of that event, but there are some intriguing indications, most notably Jer 51:32, that suggest that the writer had already witnessed the fall of Babylon to the Persians. If this is correct, then these oracles, together with the more explicit classical accounts, provide an alternative tradition to the native cuneiform accounts about the fall of the great imperial city, and indeed of the Babylonian imperial state.

CHAPTER 4

SUMMARY AND CONCLUSIONS

I have attempted in this study to provide an analysis of the theory and practice of the Neo-Babylonian empire in its relationship to subjugated populations, and in particular to the population of Judah. I have also tried to investigate how the perspectives about empire that are preserved in a variety of passages from the biblical prophets, members of the subjugated Judean community, offer the historian useful information about the empire. Several conclusions derive from the study.

Analysis of the Neo-Babylonian royal inscriptions in the first chapter led to the conclusion that the Babylonian kings, and Nebuchadnezzar II in particular, attempted to formulate a coherent imperial creed. The inscriptions, however, do not expound this creed in a formal set of propositions: it finds expression in a particular recombination of traditional language about the king and the state and their relationship to the non-Babylonian world. The royal titulary, usually the first component of these inscriptions, indicates several characteristic ways in which the scribes conceived the king's role within the realm. First, the royal titulary is self-consciously Babylonian. That is, the selection of royal epithets is characteristic of the Babylonian tradition, and, with exceptions in the inscriptions of Nabonidus, avoids epithets not found in that tradition, especially Neo-Assyrian royal epithets. In fact, several archaic epithets that had been common in the Babylonian tradition from early on, but which became the sine qua non of the Neo-Assyrian titulary, *šarru rabû*, "great king," *šarru dannu*, "mighty king," *šar kiššati*, "king of the universe," and *šar kibrāt erbetti*, "king of the four corners (of the earth)," are avoided by the Neo-Babylonian kings in their titulary, again with several notable exceptions under Nabonidus. Furthermore, the titulary emphasizes the traditional role of the king as the caretaker of Babylon and the sanctuaries of the gods, and avoids epithets which are explicitly militaristic in tone or which lodge claims for the king's universal dominion. This contrasts with the general Neo-Assyrian titulary, and with the titulary claimed by the Assyrian kings in their Babylonian inscriptions, where such epithets are usual. Again, of the Neo-Babylonian kings only Nabonidus provides exceptions to this pattern. We concluded that, inasmuch as the titulary reflects a programmatic understanding of the king's role as ruler of the empire, the Neo-Babylonian tradition shows remarkable restraint in its portrait of the king as conqueror and warrior. The exceptions from Nabonidus do not suggest that he abandoned such restraint completely, but rather that he had a particular agenda which involved forging a link with the Assyrian tradition.

The expression of the king's role in the titulary, which avoids militaristic and expansionist epithets, is partially paralleled by the passages in the *inūma* clauses of the royal inscriptions that narrate the commissioning of the king by the gods. Under Nabopolassar, the perspective of these passages is parochial: although his defeat of the Assyrians receives emphasis, the texts do not ascribe him rule over the entire universe or all humanity; rather, the focus in his inscriptions is on Babylonia. This changes with Nebuchadnezzar, who is now said to rule over all humanity and the four corners of the earth, a claim that accords with his efforts to extend Babylonian domination beyond the Mesopotamian heartland. It is here—and not in the titulary, as with the Neo-Assyrian kings—that we see an effort to articulate the king's imperial dominion through the use of traditional language coupled with a newly conceived imperial geography. Nevertheless, even the passages describing Nebuchadnezzar's commission are restrained in expressing aspirations for conquest or expansion of the realm. In these passages, the gods do not command the king to conquer foreign peoples or to expand the borders, as is usual in Neo-Assyrian texts; rather, the gods simply "give" (*nadānu*) or "entrust" (*qepû*) the widespread peoples of the earth to the king, or they "fill (his) hands" (*qātī mullû*) with the responsibility to shepherd or rule them. The inscriptions, thus, portray the king as the protector and benefactor of the people whom the gods have granted him to rule. Further, according to the imperial creed, Babylon is the administrative and economic center of the world, and the king gathers all peoples "for good" (*ṭābiš*) into its "eternal shadow." The imperial portrait of the king depicts him as the benign agent of the gods on earth, and not, as in the Assyrian tradition, as the gods' agent of conquest.

After this description in the first chapter of Babylonian ideas about imperial rule, the second chapter described the complement of these ideas, the imperial bureaucracy in the west. It proved difficult to discern, however, precisely how the imperial theory found expression in the bureaucratic and administrative procedures implemented in the western periphery of the empire. In fact, while it was possible to determine some of the broad circumstances that influenced the military policy of Nebuchadnezzar in the west—particularly the persistent and competing Egyptian interest in the region—the mechanisms that sustained imperial domination, beyond regular military campaigns, remain opaque. The Babylonians apparently made no systematic effort to establish provincial units in the periphery, and it is not clear that they perpetuated those that the Assyrians had created. Among the royal inscriptions, only Nebuchadnezzar's Etemenanki inscription refers to the existence of *piḫātu* and *šakkanakkū* officials in Eber Nāri and Ḫatti (Syria-Palestine). Two additional administrative tablets from the Ebabbar temple in Sippar refer to the governor of Arpad, north of Aleppo, but none farther south; it remains difficult to determine with any precision at all the bailiwicks or functions of these few individuals.

Several lines of evidence converge to suggest, as well, that there was only minimal Babylonian oversight of the peripheral economies, including those of the Southern Levant. I followed Stager's view and argued that Babylonian policy under Nebuchadnezzar focused on the destruction of Egyptian client cities in the southern Levant; this rendered the economic advantage of conquest immediate rather than durative. A similar conclusion derives from the distribution of East Greek ceramics in the Levant. In the last third of the seventh century, prior to the arrival of the Babylonians in the Levant, the East Greek trade expanded throughout the region. This probably resulted in part from Egyptian patronage of the trade under Psammetichus I. Evidence for the East Greek trade in the Levant, however, declines precipitously in the first half of the sixth century, while it expands in the same period in the Egyptian Delta. Babylonian action against Egypt's clients in the Levant, including the Greeks, may explain this shift, and suggests either that Babylonian interests in the region did not extend to installation of an administrative bureaucracy and oversight of the local economies, or that the principal interest was the elimination of Egyptian control in the region. The Babylonians did make periodic, at first almost annual, incursions into the Levant for the purpose of obtaining tribute, and they seem also to have kept up some bilateral trade with the region, but they did not establish a systematic bureaucratic presence.

The material culture of Judah after the Babylonian invasions of 597 and 587-86 B.C.E. also shows a clear disjunction and a sharp contraction in demographic terms, as has long been argued. There is little evidence to support the view that the Babylonians implemented a bureaucratic system for exploiting the economy of the region. This conclusion is supported not only by the significant occupational gap at the large majority of urban sites in the region between the late Iron Age II and Persian periods. It is also indicated by a virtual absence, during the period, of Babylonian ceramics or other material culture in the territory of Judah and Benjamin. This is in contrast, for example, to the large assemblage of Neo-Assyrian materials from the first half of the seventh century that arrived as a direct consequence of Assyrian hegemony. Lehmann also emphasized in his analysis of pottery developments in this period farther north, in Syria and Lebanon, that a radical transformation of the repertoire takes place in the first half of the sixth century.[1] Clearly this marks a decisive break with previous patterns of production and distribution. On the whole, it would seem that the effort of the Babylonian imperial administration, such as it was, conformed to the hyperbole of the imperial creed: the principal imperial interest of the Babylonians under Nebuchadnezzar focused on the transformation of Babylon into an imperial megalopolis; creation of a bureaucratic provincial organization in the periphery was not a priority. This centripetal momentum accounts also for the mechanics of deportation of subjugated populations: unlike the Assyrians, the Babylonians did not transfer people into the depopulated periphery because they did not attempt to develop the economies of conquered kingdoms.

In the third chapter, I offered a select survey of contemporary biblical prophetic passages that concern Babylon, and attempted to categorize the language about empire in them. In surveying the relevant texts an effort was made to see how the biblical writers acquiesced in or, more often, resisted imperial ideas and practices. The assumption was that analysis of the prophetic texts about Babylon could furnish some independent information about the empire by providing the perspective of a subjugated community. The focus was, thus, not simply on

[1] Lehmann, "Local Pottery Development in Syria and Lebanon," 21, 29-30 and fig. 15.

demonstrating that the Judean writers were influenced by the empire. The point, rather, was to show how the prophetic responses that emerged from the imperial context can aid in better understanding the empire and its relationship to subject populations.

From this analysis of the prophetic writings, it became apparent that, on one level, the language about Babylon was generated typologically. In other words, the preexisting Israelite prophetic tradition relating in particular to imperial depredations under Assyria was appropriated in the Babylonian imperial context. This was the case for Micah 4:10, a passage interpolated into the book which asserts that the population of Judah would go into exile in Babylon, not Assyria. In Isaiah 14:4b-21, a poem that apparently referred originally to the fall of an Assyrian ruler was brought into explicit connection with "the king of Babylon," perhaps Nebuchadnezzar II (Isa 14:3-4a, 22-23). Jeremiah's frequent description of the foe from the north likewise draws on earlier prophetic traditions about the Mesopotamian imperial threat to describe the emergence of Babylon. Some of the prophetic texts have a tendency to speak of Babylon using a set of images mediated through the earlier tradition of contact with Assyria. This process receives concise expression in the mid-sixth century statement of Jer 50:17: "Israel is a scattered ewe, (which) lions deported; the first to devour it was the king of Assyria, and now this is the last to crush its bones, Nebuchadrezzar, king of Babylon." At this level, therefore, the contemporary prophetic response to the Babylonian empire was formulated in continuity with the earlier prophetic tradition. This shows that the prophetic language about empire was not wholly shaped by the new imperial circumstances, or solely by Babylonian imperial ideas and procedures.

There are other indications, however, that some texts were composed more directly in response to new imperial ideas and actions. In Habakkuk 1-2 the prophet challenges Yahweh to account for the violence perpetrated by the Chaldeans against Judah. Yahweh informs the prophet that the Chaldeans are his agents for bringing punishment, but that ultimately the empire will be destroyed. Habakkuk accepts this view, one with antecedents in the description of Assyria from the First Isaiah and his contemporaries. Habakkuk, however, delineates numerous particular crimes of the Chaldeans and the "arrogant man" (probably Nebuchadnezzar) which derive from observation of Babylonian imperial procedures. In the woe oracles of chapter 2 that describe the crimes for which the Chaldeans will be repaid, the prophet denounces several dominant imperial ideas: the king is a rapacious conqueror, and not the arbiter of universal justice as Nebuchadnezzar insisted in his titulary and elsewhere. The king gathers populations for forced labor and for their destruction; he does not assemble them "for good" under Babylon's eternal shadow. Tribute is violently plundered from subject people; it is not delivered in recognition of Babylon's preeminence. The stones and beams of the king's corrupt "house" serve as witnesses against the king in his abuse of the nations, not, as in the royal inscriptions, as intermediaries before his patron deities. Other crimes of the imperial king, including the plundering of the Lebanon, may be allusions to the concrete procedures of the imperial army. The perspective of Habakkuk provides a good example of how subjugated communities perceived the empire and struggled to assert that it would not finally prevail.

This is also true of the Second Isaiah, the anonymous prophet who was present in Babylon during the final years of the empire. The prophet's diatribes against the idols of the Babylonians and the vaunted expertise of Babylonian religious experts provide the most sustained effort to challenge the imperial worldview. His attacks clearly are intended to undermine the institutions and practices upon which the imperial worldview rests. The prophet's larger purpose, of course, is thus to demonstrate for the subjugated Judean community that Yahweh, the only true God, controls the affairs of humanity. It is noteworthy, however, that it is the imperial worldview and specific Babylonian procedures—the use of religious statuary in the cult, the affirmation of Marduk's universal sovereignty in the *akītu*-festival, the king's reliance upon expert interpretation of the movement of celestial bodies, and Babylonian divinatory procedures—that dictate the parameters of the prophet's polemic.

I have tried to show, then, that we can detect the traces of a relatively coherent Neo-Babylonian imperial worldview in the royal inscriptions, one which eschewed the militaristic and expansionist rhetoric characteristic of the Neo-Assyrian kings, and which attempted instead to adapt traditional Babylonian conceptions of the king's role to the new realities of empire. Although domination and expansion characterized the functioning of the empire on the ground, the imperial bureaucracy designed to exploit the periphery was minimally developed.

The reflections of the Judean prophets on Babylon and on Babylonian imperial theory and practice illuminate the responses to empire generated by a subjugated population. These responses clarify how the empire functioned inasmuch as those responses and their language were shaped by the empire itself. On one level, the new reality of Babylonian imperialism was quickly assimilated to the preexisting Israelite and Judean prophetic traditions, especially those which had formerly described imperial depredations under Assyria, and this assimilation suggests a nativist response to the phenomenon. On another level, the brute facts of subjugation elicited condemnations of imperial practice. Indeed the severity of these depredations give rise to an image of the conquering empire in the prophetic corpus that contrasts sharply with the modest propagandistic claims of the Babylonian imperial kings. On yet another level, perhaps best reflected by Habakkuk and the Second Isaiah, the practices and ideas that sustained the empire were scrutinized and attacked in order to demonstrate their transience and the ultimate sovereignty of Yahweh.

BIBLIOGRAPHY

Aaboe, A. "Babylonian Mathematics, Astrology, and Astronomy." In *CAH*, 2d ed. Vol. 3, part 2, *The Assyrian and Babylonian Empires and Other States of the Near East, from the Eighth to the Sixth Centuries B.C.*, ed. J. A. Boardman et al., 276-92. Cambridge: Cambridge University Press, 1991.

Aberbach, D. *Imperialism and Biblical Prophecy: 750-500 B.C.E.* New York: Routledge, 1993.

Abu Assaf, A., P. Bordreuil, and A. Millard. *La première bilingue assyro-araméenne: la statue de Tell Fekherye*. Paris: Editions Recherche sur les civilizations, 1982.

Ackroyd, P. R. *Exile and Restoration*. London: SCM, 1968.

________. *Israel Under Babylon and Persia*. Oxford: Oxford University Press, 1970.

Aharoni, Y. *The Land of the Bible: A Historical Geography*. 2d ed. Trans. and ed. by A. Rainey. Philadelphia: Westminster, 1979.

________. *Arad Inscriptions*. Jerusalem: Israel Exploration Society, 1981.

Albright, W. F. *From the Stone Age to Christianity*. 2d ed. Baltimore: Johns Hopkins University Press, 1946.

________. "Cilicia and Babylonia under the Chaldean Kings." *BASOR* 120 (1950): 22-25.

Al-Rawi, F. N. H. "Nabopolassar's Restoration Work on the Wall *Imgur-Enlil* at Babylon." *Iraq* 47 (1985): 1-13.

Alt, A. "Die Rolle Samarias bei der Entstehung des Judentums." In *Kleine Schriften zur Geschichte des Volkes Israel*. Vol. 2:316-37. Munich: C. H. Beck, 1959. Originally published in *Festschrift Otto Proksch zum 60. Geburtstag* (Leipzig: Dekhurt and Hinrich, 1934), 5-38.

Arcari, E. "La politica estera di Nabucodonosor in Siria-Palestina." *Rivista di Studi Fenici* 17 (1990): 159-72.

Avigad, N. *Discovering Jerusalem*. Oxford: Basil Blackwell, 1984.

________. *Hebrew Bullae From the Time of Jeremiah*. Jerusalem: Israel Exploration Society, 1986.

Barkay, G. "The Priestly Benediction on Silver Plaques from Ketef Hinnom in Jerusalem." *TA* 19 (1992): 139-92.

________. "Excavations at Ketef Hinnom in Jerusalem." In *Ancient Jerusalem Revealed*, ed. H. Geva, 85-106 (Jerusalem: Israel Exploration Society, 1994).

________. "The King of Babylonia or a Judaean Official?" *IEJ* 45 (1995): 41-47.

Barnett, R. D. "Xenophon and the Wall of Media." *JHS* 83 (1963): 1-26.

________. *Assyrian Sculpture in the British Museum*. Toronto and London: McClelland and Stewart, 1975.

Barstad, H. M. "On the So-called Babylonian Literary Influence in Second Isaiah." *Scandinavian Journal of the Old Testament* 2 (1987): 90-110.

________. *The Myth of the Empty Land*. Symbolae Osloenses Fasc. Suppl., 28. Oslo: Scandanavian University Press, 1996.

________. *The Babylonian Captivity of the Book of Isaiah*. Oslo: Novus, 1997.

Beaulieu, P.-A. *The Reign of Nabonidus King of Babylon, 556-539 B.C.* YNER 10. New Haven: Yale University Press, 1989.

________. "An Episode in the Fall of Babylon to the Persians." *JNES* 52 (1993): 241-61.

________. "The Impact of Month-lengths on the Neo-Babylonian Cultic Calendar." *ZA* 83 (1993): 66-87.

________. "A New Inscription of Nebuchadnezzar II Commemorating the Restoration of Emaḫ in Babylon." *Iraq* 59 (1997): 93-96.

Begg, C. T. "Babylon in the Book of Isaiah." In *The Book of Isaiah–Le Livre d'Isaïe: Les oracles et leur relectures. Unité et complexité de l'ouvrage*. BETL 81, ed. J. Vermeylen, 121-25. Leuven: Leuven University Press/Peeters, 1989.

Behr, J. W. *The Writings of Deutero-Isaiah and the Neo-Babylonian Royal Inscriptions*. Publications of the University of Pretoria, Series III, Arts, no. 3. Pretoria: University of Pretoria, 1937.

Beljawski, V. A. "Der politische Kampf in Babylon in den Jahren 562-556 v. Chr." In *In Memoriam Eckhard Unger. Beiträge zur Geschichte, Kultur und Religion des Alten Orients*, ed. M. Lurkner, 197-215. Baden-Baden: Koerner, 1971.

Bergamini, G. "Levels of Babylon Reconsidered." *Mesopotamia* 12 (1977): 111-52.

________. "Excavations in Shu-anna, Babylon 1987." *Mesopotamia* 23 (1988): 5-17.

Berger, P.-R. "Das Neujahrfest nach den Königsinschriften des ausgehenden babylonischen Reiches." In *Actes de la 17ᵉ RAI*, ed. A. Finet, 155-59. Ham-sur-Heure, Belgium: Comité belge de recherches en Mésopotamie, 1970.

________. *Die neubabylonischen Königsinschriften: Königsinschriften des ausgehenden babylonischen Reiches (625-539 a. Chr.)*. AOAT 4/1. Kevelaer: Butzon & Bercker; Neukirchen-Vluyn: Neukirchener, 1973.

________. "Der Kyros-Zylinder mit dem Zusatzfragment BIN II Nr. 32 und die akkadischen Personennamen im Danielbuch." *ZA* 64 (1974): 192-234.

Berger, P.-R., and J. Zablocka. "Ein vollständigeres Duplikat zur Nebukadnezar II-Inschrift VAB 4 Nr. 46." *Or* n.s. 38 (1969): 122-25.

Bergmann, E. *Codex Ḫammurabi: Textus Primigenius*, 3d ed. Rome: Pontifical Biblical Institute, 1953.

Berlejung, A. *Die Theologie der Bilder: Herstellung und Einweihung von Kultbildern in Mesopotamien und die alttestamentliche Bilderpolemik*. OBO 162. Freiburg, Schweiz: Universitätsverlag; Göttingen: Vandenhoeck & Ruprecht, 1998.

Bickerman, E. J. "The Babylonian Captivity." In *The Cambridge History of Judaism*. Vol. 1, *Introduction: The Perisan Period*, ed. W. D. Davies and L. Finkelstein, 342-58. Cambridge: Cambridge University Press, 1984.

Black, J. A. "The New Year Ceremonies in Ancient Babylon: 'Taking Bel By the Hand' and a Cultic Picnic." *Religion* 11 (1981): 39-59.

________. "Babylonian Textual Evidence." In *Ḥabl aṣ-Ṣaḫr 1983-85: Nebuchadnezzar II's Cross-country Wall North of Sippar*. *NAPR*, ed. J. A. Black, H. Gasche, et al., 1.15-25. Ghent: University of Ghent Press, 1987.

Blau, J. "*Hōberê Šāmayim* (Jes xlvii 13) = Himmelsanbeter?" *VT* 7 (1957): 183-84.

Boardman, J. *The Greeks Overseas: Their Early Colonies and Trade*. New and enl. ed. London: Thames and Hudson, 1980.

Boardman, J. A., et al., ed. *CAH*, 2d ed. Vol. 3, part 2, *The Assyrian and Babylonian Empires and Other States of the Near East, from the Eighth to the Sixth Centuries B.C.* Cambridge: Cambridge University Press, 1991.

________. *CAH*, 2d ed. Vol. 3, part 3, *The Expansion of the Greek World, Eighth to Sixth Centuries B.C.* Cambridge: Cambridge University Press, 1982.

Borger, R. *Die Inschriften Asarhaddons Königs von Assyrien*. *AfO* Beiheft 9. Graz: 1956.

________. "Der Aufstieg des neubabylonischen Reiches." *JCS* 19 (1965): 59-78.

________. *Babylonisch-Assyrische Lesestücke*. 2d ed. AnOr 54. Rome: Pontifical Biblical Institute, 1979.

________. *Beiträge zum Inschriftenwerk Assurbanipals*. Wiesbaden: Harrassowitz, 1996.

Bottéro, J. "Magie. A." *RLA* 7 (1987-1990): 200-34.

Braun, T. F. R. G. "The Greeks in the Near East." In *CAH*, 2d ed. Vol. 3, part 3, *The Expansion of the Greek World, Eighth to Sixth Centuries B.C.*, ed. J. A. Boardman et al., 1-31. Cambridge: Cambridge University Press, 1982.

________. "The Greeks in Egypt." In *CAH*, 2d ed. Vol. 3, part 3, *The Expansion of the Greek World, Eighth to Sixth Centuries B.C.*, ed. J. A. Boardman et al., 32-56. Cambridge: Cambridge University Press, 1982.

Bright, J. *Jeremiah*. AB. Garden City, N.Y.: Doubleday, 1965.

Brinkman, J. A. "Merodach-baladan II." In *Studies Presented to A. Leo Oppenheim*. 6-53. Chicago: University of Chicago Press, 1964.

________. *A Political History of Post-Kassite Babylonia, 1158-722 B.C.* AnOr 43. Rome: Pontifical Biblical Institute, 1968.

________. "Sennacherib's Babylonian Problem: An Interpretation." *JCS* 25 (1973): 89-95.

________. "The Early Neo-Babylonian Monarchy." In *Le Palais et la royauté*, ed. P. Garelli, 409-415. Paris: Geuthner, 1974.

________. *Prelude to Empire: Babylonian Society and Politics, 747-626 B.C.* Occasional Publications of the Babylonian Fund 7. Philadelphia: University Museum, 1984.

________. "The Akkadian Words for 'Ionia' and 'Ionian.'" In *Daidalikon: Studies in Memory of Raymond V. Schoder, S.J.*, ed. R. F. Sutton, 53-71. Wauconda, Ill: Bolchazy-Carducci, 1989.

________. "Political Covenants, Treaties, and Loyalty Oaths in Babylonia and Between Assyria and Babylonia." In *I Trattati nel mondo antico. Forma Ideologia Funzione*, ed. L Canfora, M. Liverani, and C. Zaccagnini, 81-112. Rome: Istituto Gramsci, 1990.

________. "Babylonia under the Shadow of Assyria (747-626 B.C.)." In *CAH*, 2d ed. Vol. 3, part 2, *The Assyrian and Babylonian Empires and Other States of the Near East, from the Eighth to the Sixth Centuries B.C.*, ed. J. A. Boardman et al., 1-70. Cambridge: Cambridge University Press, 1991.

________. "Meerland."*RLA* 8 (1993): 6-10.

Briquel-Chatonnet, F. *Les Relations entre les cités de la côte phénicienne et les royaumes d'Israël et de Juda.* Studia Phoenicia 12, OLA 46. Leuven: Peeters, 1992.

Brueggemann, W. "At the Mercy of Babylon: A Subversive Rereading of the Empire." *JBL* 110 (1991): 3-22.

Bunnens, G. "Til Barsib under Assyrian Domination: A Brief Account of the Melbourne University Excavations at Tell Ahmar." In *Assyria 1995*, ed. S. Parpola and R. M. Whiting, 17-28. Helsinki: Neo-Assyrian Text Corpus Project, 1997.

Burstein, S. M. *The Babyloniaca of Berossus.* SANE I/5. Malibu: Undena, 1978.

Caquot, A. "Une inscription araméene d'époque assyrienne." In *Hommages à André Dupont-Sommer*, ed. E. Bresciani, 9-16. Paris: Maisonneuve, 1971.

Cazelles, H. "Sophonie, Jérémie, et les Scythes en Palestine." *RB* 74 (1967): 24-44; reprinted as "Zephaniah, Jeremiah, and the Scythians in Palestine," in *A Prophet to the Nations, Essays in Jeremiah Studies*, ed. L.G. Perdue and B. Kovacs, 129-49. Winona Lake, Ind.: Eisenbrauns, 1984.

Charles, M. P. "Irrigation in Lowland Mesopotamia." *Bulletin on Sumerian Agriculture* 4 (1988): 1-39.

Childs, B. S. "The Enemy From the North and the Chaos Tradition." *JBL* 78 (1959): 185-98.

Clifford, R. "The Function of the Idol Passages in Second Isaiah." *CBQ* 42 (1980): 450-64.

Cogan, M. "Sentencing at the Gate in Jeremiah 1:15-16." *Gratz College Annual of Jewish Studies* 1 (1972): 3-6.

________. *Imperialism and Religion: Assyria, Israel and Judah in the Eighth and Seventh Centuries B.C.E.* SBLMS 19. Missoula: Scholars, 1974.

________. "Judah Under Assyrian Hegemony: A Re-examination of Imperialism and Religion." *JBL* 112 (1993): 403-14.

Cogan, M., and H. Tadmor. *II Kings.* AB. Garden City, N.Y.: Doubleday, 1988.

Cohen, C. *Biblical Hapax Legomena in the Light of Akkadian and Ugaritic.* SBLDS 37. Misoula: Scholars, 1978.

Cohen, M. *The Cultic Calendars of the Ancient Near East.* Bethesda, Md.: CDL, 1993.

Cole, S. W. "Marsh Formation in the Borsippa Region and the Course of the Lower Euphrates." *JNES* 53 (1994): 81-109.

________. *The Early Neo-Babylonian Governor's Archive from Nippur.* OIP 114. Chicago: The Oriental Institute of the University of Chicago, 1996.

________. *Nippur in Late Assyrian Times, c. 755-612 B.C.* SAAS 5 (Helsinki: Neo-Assyrian Text Corpus Project, 1996).

Collins, J. J., and A. Yarbro Collins. *Daniel.* Heremeneia. Philadelphia: Fortress, 1993.

Collon, D. *First Impressions: Cylinder Seals in the Ancient Near East.* Chicago: University of Chicago Press, 1987.

Coxon, P. "Nebuchadnezzar's Hermeneutical Dilemma." *JSOT* 66 (1995): 87-97.

Cross, F. M., Jr. "Epigraphic Notes on Hebrew Documents of the Eighth-Sixth Centuries B.C.: 2. The Murabbaʿât Papyrus and the Letter Found Near Yabneh-Yam." *BASOR* 165 (1962): 34-46.

________. "Epigraphic Notes on Hebrew Documents of the Eighth-Sixth Centuries B.C.: 3. The Inscribed Jar Handles from Gibeon." *BASOR* 168 (1962): 18-23.

________. "The Cave Inscriptions from Khirbet Beit Lei." In *Near Eastern Archaeology in the Twentieth Century: Essays in Honor of Nelson Glueck*, ed. J. A. Sanders, 299-306. Garden City, N.Y.: Doubleday, 1970.

________. "A New Aramaic Stele from Taymāʾ." *CBQ* 48 (1986): 387-94.

Cross, F. M., Jr., and D. N. Freedman. "Josiah's Revolt Against Assyria." *JNES* 12 (1953): 56-58.

Dalley, S. "Foreign Chariotry and Cavalry in the Armies of Tiglath-pileser III and Sargon II." *Iraq* 47 (1985): 31-48.

Dalley, S., and A. Goguel. "The Selaʿ Sculpture: A Neo-Babylonian Rock Relief in Southern Jordan." *ADAJ* 41 (1997): 169-76.

________. "Nineveh after 612 BC." *AoF* 20 (1993): 134-47.

Dandamayev, M. A. "Die Fischerei in neubabylonischen Texten des 6. und 5. Jahrhunderts v. u. Zeit." *Jahrbuch für Wirtschaftsgeschichte* IV (1981): 67-82.

________. *Slavery in Babylonia*. Trans. V. A. Powell. Ed. M. A. Powell and D. B. Weisberg. DeKalb, Il: Northern Illinois University Press, 1984.

________. "Neo-Babylonian Society and Economy." In *CAH*. 2d ed., Vol. 3, part 2, *The Assyrian and Babylonian Empires and Other States of the Near East, from the Eighth to the Sixth Centuries B.C.*, ed. J. A. Boardman, et al., 252-75. Cambridge: Cambridge University Press, 1991.

________. "The Neo-Babylonian *tamkārū*." In *Solving Riddles and Untying Knots, Biblical, Epigraphic, and Semitic Studies in Honor of Jonas C. Greenfield*, ed. Z. Zevit, S. Gitin and M. Sokoloff, 523-30. Winona Lake, Ind.: Eisenbrauns, 1995.

Delitzsch, F. *Babel und Bibel*. Stuttgart: Deutsche Verlags-Anstalt, 1905.

Der Manuelian, P. *Living in the Past: Studies in the Archaism of the Egyptian Twenty-sixth Dynasty*. New York: Routledge, 1994.

Dhorme, P. "Le désert de la mer (Isaïe XXI)." *RB* 31 (1922): 403-6.

Diakonoff, I. "Elam." In *The Cambridge History of Iran*. Vol. 2. *The Median and Achaemenian Periods*, ed. I. Gershevitch, 1-24. Cambridge: Cambridge University Press, 1985.

________. "Media." In *The Cambridge History of Iran*. Vol. 2, *The Median and Achaemenian Periods*, ed. I. Gershevitch, 36-148. Cambridge: Cambridge University Press, 1985.

________. "ערי מדי. The Cities of the Medes." In *Ah, Assyria . . .: Studies in Assyrian History and Ancient Near Eastern Historiography Presented to Hayim Tadmor*. ScrHier 33, ed. M. Cogan and I. Ephʿal, 13-20. Jerusalem: Magnes, 1992.

________. "The Naval Power and Trade of Tyre." *IEJ* 42 (1992): 168-93.

Diodorus of Sicily. *Bibliotheca Historica*. Trans. C. H. Oldfather. Loeb Classical Library. Cambridge: Harvard University Press, 1933-1967.

Dobbs-Allsopp, F. W. *Weep, O Daughter of Zion: A Study of the City-Lament Genre in the Hebrew Bible*. BibOr 44. Rome: Pontifical Biblical Institute, 1993.

Dothan, M. *Ashdod II-III*. *'Atiqot* (English Series) 9-10 (1971).

Dothan, M., and D. N. Freedman. *Ashdod I*. *'Atiqot* (English Series) 7 (1967).

Dothan, M., and Y. Porath. *Ashdod IV*. *'Atiqot* (English Series) 15 (1982).

Dougherty, R. P. *Nabonidus and Belshazzar: A Study of the Closing Events of the Neo-Babylonian Empire*. YOR 15. New Haven: Yale University Press, 1929.

Ebeling, E. "Fisch." *RLA* 3 (1957-1971): 66-67.

Edel, E. "Amasis und Nebukadrezar II." *GM* 29 (1978): 13-20.

Edens, C., and Bawden, G. "History of Tayma' and Hejazi Trade During the First Millennium B.C." *JESHO* 32 (1989): 48-103.

Edzard, D. O. "Kaldu." *RLA* 5 (1977): 291-97.

Eisenstadt, S. N. "Observations and Queries about Sociological Aspects of Imperialism in the Ancient World." In *Power and Propaganda: A Symposium on Ancient Empires*, Mesopotamia 7, ed. M.T. Larsen, 21-33. Copenhagen: Akademisk Forlag, 1979.

________. "Communication Patterns in Centralized Empires." In *Propaganda and Communication in World History*. Vol. 1, *The Symbolic Instrument in Early Times*, ed. H. D. Lasswell, D. Cerner, and H. Speier, 536-51. Honolulu: University Press of Hawaii, An East-West Center Book, 1979.

________. *The Political Systems of Empires*. London and New York: The Free Press of Glencoe, 1963. Reprint, with an introduction by the author, New Brunswick, N. J. and London: Transaction Publishers, 1993.

Eissfeldt, O. "Jeremias Drohorakel gegen Ägypten und gegen Babel." In *Verbannung und Heimkehr: Beiträge zur Geschichte und Theologie Israels im 6. und 5. Jahrhundert v. Chr., Wilhelm Rudolph zum 70. Geburtstage*, ed. A. Kuschke, 31-37. Tübingen: Mohr, 1961.

Elat, M. "Phoenician Overland Trade Within the Mesopotamian Empires." In *Ah, Assyria . . .: Studies in Assyrian History and Ancient Near Eastern Historiography Presented to Hayim Tadmor*. ScrHier 33, ed. M. Cogan and I. Eph'al, 21-35. Jerusalem: Magnes, 1991.

Elayi, J. "L'exploitation des cèdres du Mont Liban par les rois Assyriens et Néo-Babyloniens." *JESHO* 31 (1988): 14-41.

Ellis, R. S. *Foundation Deposits in Ancient Mesopotamia*. YNER 2. New Haven: Yale University Press, 1968.

Eph'al, I. "The Western Minorities in Babylonia in the 6th-5th Centuries B.C.: Maintenance and Cohesion." *Or* n.s. 47 (1978): 74-90.

________. "Israel: Fall and Exile." In WHJP Vol. 4/1, *The Age of the Monarchies: Political History*, ed. A. Malamat, 180-91. Jerusalem: Massada, 1979.

________. "Assyrian Dominion in Palestine." In WHJP Vol. 4/1, *The Age of the Monarchies: Political History*, ed. A. Malamat, 276-89. Jerusalem: Massada, 1979.

________. *The Ancient Arabs. Nomads on the Borders of the Fertile Crescent, 9th-5th Centuries B.C.* Leiden: Brill, 1982.

________. "Isa 40:19-20: On the Cultural and Linguistic Background of Deutero-Isaiah." *Shnaton* 10 (1986): 31-35 (Hebrew).

________. "Syria-Palestine under Achaemenid Rule." In *CAH*. Vol 4. *Persia, Greece and the Western Mediterranean c. 525 to 479 B.C.*, ed. J. A. Boardman et al., 139-64. Cambridge: Cambridge University Press, 1988.

________. "'You Are Defecting to the Chaldeans' (Jer 37:13)." *EI* 24 (Avraham Malamat Volume) (1993): 18-22 (Hebrew).

Erlandsson, S. *The Burden of Babylon: A Study of Isaiah 13:2-14:23*. Coniectanea Biblica Old Testament Series 4. Lund: Gleerup, 1970.

Fales, F. M. "West Semitic Names in the Šēḫ Ḥamad Texts." *SAAB* 7 (1993): 139-50.

Fales, F. M., and J. N. Postgate. *Imperial Administrative Records, Part II*, SAA 11. Helsinki: Helsinki University Press, 1995.

Feigin, S. I. "The Babylonian Officials in Jeremiah 39:3,13." *JBL* 45 (1926): 149-55.

Finkelstein, I. "*Ḥorvat Qiṭmīt* and the Southern Trade in the Late Iron Age II." *ZDPV* 108 (1992): 156-70.

Finkelstein, J. J. "Hebrew חבר and Semitic *ḪBR." *JBL* 75 (1956): 328-31.

________. "Bible and Babel: A Comparative Study of the Hebrew and Babylonian Religious Spirit." *Commentary* 26 (1958): 431-44; reprinted in *Essential Papers on Israel and the Ancient Near East*, ed. F. E. Greenspahn, 355-80. New York: New York University Press, 1991.

Fitzmyer, J. A. *The Aramaic Inscriptions of Sefire*. BibOr 19. Rome: Pontifical Biblical Institute, 1967.

Forrer, E. *Die Provinzeinteilung des assyrischen Reiches*. Leipzig: Hinrichs, 1920.

Frame, G. *Babylonia 689-627 B.C.: A Political History*. Nederlands Historisch-Archaeologisch Instituut te Istanbul 69. Istanbul: Nederlands Historisch-Archaeologisch Instituut, 1992.

________. *Rulers of Babylonia from the Second Dynasty of Isin to the End of Assyrian Domination (1157-612 B.C.)*. Royal Inscriptions of Mesopotamia, Babylonian Periods 2. Toronto: University of Toronto Press, 1995.

Franke, C. A. "The Function of the Satiric Lament over Babylon in Second Isaiah (47)." *VT* 41 (1991): 408-18.

________. *Isaiah 46, 47, and 48: A New Literary-Critical Reading*. Biblical and Judaic Studies, vol. 3. Winona Lake, Ind.: Eisenbrauns, 1994.

Freedy, K. S., and D. B. Redford. "The Dates in Ezekiel in Relation to Biblical, Babylonian and Egyptian Sources." *JAOS* 90 (1970): 462-85.

Funck, B. "Studien zur sozialökonomischen Situation Babyloniens im 7. und 6. Jahrhundert v.u.Z." In *Gesellschaft und Kultur im alten Vorderasien*, ed. H. Klengel, 45-67. Schriften zur Geschichte und Kultur der alten Orient 15. Berlin, 1982.

Gadd, C. J. "Inscribed Barrel Cylinder of Marduk-apla-iddina II." *Iraq* 15 (1953): 123-34.

________. "The Harran Inscriptions of Nabonidus." *AnSt* 8 (1958): 35-92.

________. "Hammurabi and the End of His Dynasty." In *CAH*, rev. ed., vol. 2, ch. 5. Cambridge: Cambridge University Press, 1965.

Galling, K. "Jesaia 21 im Lichte der neuen Nabonidtexte." In *Tradition und Situation: Studien zur alttestamentlichen Prophetie (Festschrift A. Weiser)*, ed. E. Würthwein and O. Kaiser, 49-62. Göttingen: Vandenhoeck & Ruprecht, 1963.

Garelli, P. "La conception de la royauté en Assyrie." In *Assyrian Royal Inscriptions: New Horizons in Literary, Ideological, and Historical Analysis*, ed. F. M. Fales, 1-11. Orientis Antiqui Collectio 17. Rome: Instituto per l'Oriente, 1981.

________. "The Achievement of Tiglath-pileser III: Novelty or Continuity?" In *Ah, Assyria . . .: Studies in Assyrian History and Ancient Near Eastern Historiography Presented to Hayim Tadmor*, ScrHier 33, ed. M. Cogan and I. Eph'al, 46-51. Jerusalem: Magnes, 1992.

Garelli, P., and V. Nikiprowetzky. *Le Proche-orient asiatique: les empires mésopotamiens, Israël*. Paris: Presses Universitaires de France, 1974.

Gasche, H. et al. "Ḥabl aṣ-Ṣaḫr 1986, nouvelles fouilles. L'ouvrage défensif de Nabuchodonosor II au nord de Sippar." *NAPR* 2 (1989): 23-69.

George, A. R. *Babylonian Topographical Texts*. OLA 40. Leuven: Peeters, 1992.

________. "Babylon Revisited: Archaeology and Philology in Harness." *Antiquity* 67/257 (1993): 735-46.

________. *House Most High: The Temples of Ancient Mesopotamia*. Winona Lake, Ind.: Eisenbrauns, 1993.

Gerardi, P. "Declaring War in Mesopotamia." *AfO* 33 (1986): 30-38.

Gershevitch, I., ed. *The Cambridge History of Iran*. Vol. 2. *The Median and Achaemenian Periods*. Cambridge: Cambridge University Press, 1985.

________. "Sissoo at Susa (OPers. *Yakā-* = *Dalbergia Sissoo* Roxb.)." *BSOAS* 19 (1957): 317-20.

Geva, H., ed. *Ancient Jerusalem Revealed*. Jerusalem: Israel Exploration Society, 1994.

Ginsberg, H. L. "Reflexes of Sargon in Isaiah after 715 B.C.E." *JAOS* 88 (1968): 47-53.

Gitin, S. "Tel Miqne-Ekron: A Type-Site for the Inner Coastal Plain in the Iron Age II Period." In *Recent Excavations in Israel: Studies in Iron Age Archaeology*. AASOR 49, ed. S. Gitin and W. G. Dever, 23-58. Winona Lake, Ind.: Eisenbrauns, 1989.

________. "Miqne, Tel." In *NEAEHL*, ed. E. Stern, 3.1051-59. Jerusalem: Israel Exploration Society, 1993.

________. "Tel Miqne-Ekron in the 7th Century B.C.E.: The Impact of Economic Innovation and Foreign Cultural Influences on a Neo-Assyrian Vassal City-State." In *Recent Excavations in Israel: A View to the West*. Archaeological Institute of America Colloquia and Conference Papers, no. 1, ed. S. Gitin, 61-79. Dubuque, Iowa: Kendall Hunt, 1995.

________. "The Neo-Assyrian Empire and its Western Periphery: The Levant, with a Focus on Philistine Ekron." In *Assyria 1995*, ed. S. Parpola and R. M. Whiting, 77-103. Helsinki: Neo-Assyrian Text Corpus Project, 1997.

Gitin, S., and T. Dothan. "Ekron of the Philistines, Part II: Olive-Oil Suppliers to the World," *BAR* 16 (1990): 32-42.

Gitin, S., T. Dothan, and J. Naveh. "A Royal Dedicatory Inscription from Ekron." *IEJ* 47 (1997): 1-16.

Goossens, G. "Les recherches historiques à l'époque néo-babylonienne." *RA* 42 (1948): 149-59.

Gosse, B. "Le 'Moi' prophétique de l'oracle contre Babylone d'Isaïe XXI, 1-10." *RB* 93 (1986): 70-84.

________. *Isaïe 13,1-14,23 dans la tradition littéraire du livre d'Isaïe et dans la tradition des oracles contre les nations*. OBO 78. Freiburg: Universitätsverlag; Göttingen: Vandenhoeck and Ruprecht, 1988.

Graham, J. N. "'Vinedressers and Plowmen': 2 Kings 25:12 and Jeremiah 52:16." *BA* 47 (1984): 55-59.

Grayson, A. K. "Chronicles and the Akītu-Festival." In *Actes de la 17e Rencontre assyriologique internationale*, ed. A. Finet, 160-70. Ham-sur-Heure, Belgium: Comité belge de recherches en Mesopotamie, 1970.

________. *Assyrian and Babylonian Chronicles*. Locust Valley, N.J.: J. J. Augustin, 1975.

________. *Babylonian Historical Literary Texts*. Toronto: University of Toronto Press, 1975.

________. "Assyria and Babylonia." *Or* n.s. 49 (1980): 140-94.

________. "Assyria 668-635 B.C.: The Reign of Assurbanipal." In *CAH*, 2d ed. Vol. 3, part 2, *The Assyrian and Babylonian Empires and Other States of the Near East, from the Eighth to the Sixth Centuries B.C.*, ed. J. A. Boardman, et al., 144-61. Cambridge: Cambridge University Press, 1991.

________. "Mesopotamia, History of (Babylonia)." In *ABD*, ed. D. N. Freedman, 4.755-77. Garden City, N.Y.: Doubleday, 1992.

Greenberg, M. *Ezekiel 1-20*. AB. Garden City, N.Y.: Doubleday, 1983.

________. "Nebuchadnezzar and the Parting of the Ways: Ezek. 21:26-27." In *Ah, Assyria . . .: Studies in Assyrian History and Ancient Near Eastern Historiography Presented to Hayim Tadmor*. ScrHier 33, ed. M. Cogan and I. Eph'al, 267-71. Jerusalem: Magnes, 1991.

Greenspahn, F. E. "A Mesopotamian Proverb and its Biblical Reverberations." *JAOS* 114 (1994): 33-38.

Groot A. de, and D. T. Ariel, ed. *Excavations at the City of David 1978-1985. Vol. 3*. Qedem 33. Jerusalem: Hebrew University Press, 1992.

Guinan, A. "Left/Right Symbolism in Mesopotamian Divination." *SAAB* 10 (1996): 5-10.

Hallo, W. W. *Early Mesopotamian Royal Titles: A Philologic and Historical Analysis*. AOS 43. New Haven: AOS, 1957.

________. "Biblical History in its Near Eastern Setting: The Contextual Approach." In *Scripture in Context: Essays on the Comparative Method*, ed. C. D. Evans, W. W. Hallo, J. B. White, 1-26. Pittsburgh Theological Monograph Series 34. Pittsburgh: Pickwick Press, 1980.

________. "Cult Statue and Divine Image: A Preliminary Study." In *Scripture in Context II: More Essays on the Comparative Method*, ed. W. W. Hallo, J. C. Moyer and L. G. Perdue, 1-17. Winona Lake, Ind.: Eisenbrauns, 1983.

________. "Compare and Contrast: The Contextual Approach to Biblical Literature." In *The Bible in the Light of Cuneiform Literature; Scripture in Context III*. Ancient Near Eastern Texts and Studies 8, ed. W. W. Hallo, B. W. Jones and G. L. Mattingly, 1-30. Lewiston, N.Y.: E. Mellen, 1990.

Halpern, B. "'Brisker Pipes than Poetry': The Development of Israelite Monotheism." In *Judaic Perspectives on Ancient Israel*, ed. J. Neusner, B. A. Levine, and E. S. Frerichs, 77-115. Philadelphia: Fortress, 1987.

________. "Jerusalem and the Lineages in the Seventh Century B.C.E.: Kinship and the Rise of Individual Moral Liability." In *Law and Ideology in Monarchic*

Israel, ed. B. Halpern and D. W. Hobson, 11-107. JSOTSup 124. Sheffield: Academic, 1991.

________. "The Baal (and the Asherah) in Seventh-Century Judah: Yhwh's Retainers Retired." In *Konsequente Traditionsgeschichte: Festschrift Klaus Baltzer zum 65. Geburtstag*, ed. R. Bartelmus, T. Kruge, and H. Utzschneider, 115-54. OBO 126. Freiburg: Universitätsverlag; Göttingen: Vandenhoeck and Ruprecht, 1993.

________. "Sybil, or the Two Nations? Archaism, Alienation and the Elite Redefinition of Traditional Culture in Judah in the 8th-7th Centuries B.C.E." In *The Study of the Ancient Near East in the Twenty-First Century*, ed. J. S. Cooper and G. Schwartz, 291-338. Winona Lake, Ind.: Eisenbrauns, 1996.

Hartberger, B. *An den Wassern von Babylon . . .: Psalm 137 auf dem Hintergrund von Jeremia 51, der biblischen Edom-Traditionen und babylonischer Originalquellen*. Bonner biblische Beiträge 63. Frankfurt: Hanstein, 1986.

Hayes, J. H. "The Usage of the Oracles Against Foreign Nations in Ancient Israel." *JBL* 87 (1968): 81-92.

Hayes J. H., and J. M. Miller. *A History of Ancient Israel and Judah*. Philadelphia: Westminster, 1986.

Held, M. "Studies in Biblical Lexicography in the Light of Akkadian" *EI* 16 (Harry Orlinsky Volume) (1982): 76-85 (Hebrew).

Heltzer, M. "An Old-Aramean Seal-Impression and Some Problems of the History of the Kingdom of Damascus." In *Arameans, Aramaic and the Aramaic Literary Tradition*, ed. M. Sokoloff. Ramat-Gan: Bar-Ilan University Press, 1983.

Hermisson, H.-J. *Deuterojesaja*. BKAT 11/2. Neukirchen-Vluyn: Neukirchener, 1987-.

Herodotus. *Works*. Trans. A. D. Godley. Loeb Classical Library 117. 1920. Cambridge: Harvard University Press, 1990.

Hiebert, T. *God of My Victory: The Ancient Hymn in Habakkuk 3*. HSM 38. Atlanta: Scholars, 1986.

Hillers, D. R. "A Convention in Hebrew Literature: The Reaction to Bad News." *ZAW* 77 (1965): 86-90.

________. *Treaty Curses and the Old Testament Prophets*. BibOr 16. Rome: Pontifical Biblical Institute, 1964.

________. *Micah*. Hermeneia. Philadelphia: Fortress, 1984.

Hinke, W. J. *A New Boundary Stone of Nebuchadrezzar I from Nippur*. Babylonian Expedition of the University of Pennsylvania. Series D., Researches and Treatises; vol. 4. Philadelphia: University of Pennsylvania, 1907.

Hoftijzer, J., and K. Jongeling. *Dictionary of the North-West Semitic Inscriptions*. 2 vols. Leiden: E. J. Brill, 1995.

Hoglund, K. *Achaemenid Imperial Administration in Syria-Palestine and the Missions of Ezra and Nehemiah*. SBLDS 125. Atlanta: Scholars, 1992.

Holladay, W. L. *Jeremiah 1*. Hermeneia. Philadelphia: Fortress, 1986.

________. *Jeremiah 2*. Hermeneia. Philadelphia: Fortress, 1989.

Huffmon, H. B. "*Babel und Bibel*: The Encounter between Babylon and the Bible." *Michigan Quarterly Review* 22 (1983): 309-20.

Hurowitz, A. *I Have Built You an Exalted House: Temple Building in the Bible in Light of Mesopotamian and Northwest Semitic Writings.* JSOTSup 115. Sheffield: Academic, 1992.

________. *Divine Service and Its Rewards: Ideology and Poetics in the Hinke Kudurru.* Beer-Sheva Studies by the Department of Bible and Ancient Near East, 10. Beer-Sheva, Israel: Ben-Gurion University of the Negev, 1997.

Hyatt, J. P. *The Treatment of Final Vowels in Early Neo-Babylonian.* YOR 23. New Haven: Yale University Press, 1941.

Jacobsen, T. "The Graven Image." In *Ancient Israelite Religion. Essays in Honor of Frank Moore Cross,* ed. P. D. Miller, P. D. Hanson, and S. D. McBride, 15-32. Philadelphia: Fortress, 1987.

James, T. G. H. "Egypt: the Twenty-fifth and Twenty-sixth Dynasties." In *CAH,* 2d ed. Vol. 3, part 2, *The Assyrian and Babylonian Empires and Other States of the Near East, from the Eighth to the Sixth Centuries B.C.,* ed. J. A. Boardman, et al., 677-747. Cambridge: Cambridge University Press, 1991.

Janssen, E. *Juda in der Exilszeit: Ein Beitrag zur Frage der Entstehung des Judentums.* Göttingen: Vandenhoeck and Ruprecht, 1956.

Japhet, S. *I & II Chronicles.* OTL. Louisville: Westminster/John Knox, 1993.

Jeppesen, K. "The Māśśā' Bābel in Isaiah 13-14." *Proceedings of the Irish Biblical Association* 9 (1985): 63-80.

Joannès, F. "La localisation de Ṣurru à l'époque néo-babylonienne." *Semitica* 32 (1982): 35-42.

________. "Trois texts de Ṣurru à l'époque néo-babylonienne." *RA* 81 (1987): 147-58.

________. "Une visite du gouverneur d'Arpad." *NABU* (March, no. 1, 1994): 21-22.

Johanning, K. *Der Bibel-Babel Streit: Eine Forschungsgeschichtliche Studie.* Europäische Hochschulschriften Reihe 23, Bd 343. Frankfurt: Peter Lang, 1988.

Kaiser, O. *Isaiah 13-39.* OTL. London: SCM, 1974.

Katzenstein, H. J. *The History of Tyre.* Jerusalem: Schocken Institute for Jewish Research, 1973.

________. "Nebuchadnezzar's Wars with Egypt." *EI* 24 (Avraham Malamat Volume) (1993): 184-86 (Hebrew).

Kaufman, S. A. *Akkadian Influences on Aramaic.* AS 19. Chicago: University of Chicago Press, 1974.

Kaufmann, Y. *The Religion of Israel: From its Beginnings to the Babylonian Exile.* Trans. and abridged by M. Greenberg. Chicago: University of Chicago Press, 1960.

Kelm, G. L., and A. Mazar. *Timnah: A Biblical City in the Sorek Valley.* Winona Lake, Ind.: Eisenbrauns, 1995.

Kennedy, D. A. "Documentary Evidence for the Economic Base of Early Neo-Babylonian Society: Part II: A Survey of Babylonian Economic Texts, 626-605 B.C." *JCS* 38 (1986): 172-244.

Kienitz, F. K. *Die politische Geschichte Ägyptens vom 7. bis zum 4. Jahrhundert vor der Zeitwende.* Berlin: Akademie, 1953.

________. "Die Saïtische Renaissance." In *Fischer Weltgeschichte*. Vol. 4. *Die altorientalische Reiche, III: Die erste Hälfte des I. Jahrtausends*, ed. E. Cassin et al., 256-82. Frankfurt: Fischer Taschenbuch, 1968.

King, L. W. *Bronze Reliefs from the Gates of Shalmaneser, King of Assyria, B.C. 860-825* London: British Museum, 1915.

________. *A History of Babylon, From the Foundation of the Monarchy to the Persian Conquest*. London, 1915. Reprint, New York: AMS, 1969.

King, P. J. *Jeremiah: An Archaeological Companion*. Louisville: Westminster/John Knox, 1993.

________. "Jeremiah and Idolatry." *EI* 25 (Joseph Aviram Volume) (1996), 31*-36*.

Kittel, R. "Cyrus und Deuterojesaja." *ZAW* 18 (1898): 149-62.

Koldewey, R. *Das wieder erstehende Babylon*, ed. B. Hrouda. 5th ed. Munich: C. H. Beck, 1990.

Kühne, H. et al. "Vier spätbabylonische Tontafeln aus Tell Šēḫ Ḥamad, Ost Syrien." *SAAB* 7 (1993): 75-86.

Kuhrt, A. "Nabonidus and the Babylonian Priesthood." In *Pagan Priests*, ed. M. Beard and J. North, 117-55. Ithica: Cornell University Press, 1990.

________. "The Assyrian Heartland in the Achaemenid Period." In *Dans les pas des Dix-Mille: Peuples et pays du Proche-Orient vus par un Grec*, ed. P. Briant, 239-54. Toulouse-le Mirail: Presses Universitaires du Mirail, 1995.

Kümmel, H. M. *Familie, Beruf und Amt in spätbabylonischen Uruk*. Abhandlungen der deutschen Orient-Gesellschaft 20. Berlin: Gebr. Mann, 1979.

Laato, A. "Zachariah [sic] 4,6b-10a and the Akkadian Royal Building Inscriptions." *ZAW* 106 (1994): 53-69.

Labat, R. "Assyrien und seine Nachbarländer (Babylonien, Elam, Iran) von 1000 bis 617 v. Chr; das neubabylonische Reich bis 539 v Chr." In *Fischer Weltgeschichte*. Vol. 4. *Die altorientalische Reiche, III: Die erste Hälfte des I. Jahrtausends*, ed. E. Cassin et al., 9-111. Frankfurt: Fischer Taschenbuch, 1968.

Lambert, W. G. "The Reign of Nebuchadnezzar I: A Turning Point in the History of Ancient Mesopotamian Religion." In *The Seed of Wisdom; Essays in Honour of T. J. Meek*, ed. W. S. McCullough, 3-13. Toronto: University of Toronto Press, 1964.

________. "Nebuchadnezzar King of Justice." *Iraq* 27 (1965): 1-11.

________. "A New Source for the Reign of Nabonidus." *AfO* 22 (1968): 1-8.

________. "The Babylonians and Chaldaeans." In *Peoples of Old Testament Times*, ed. D. J. Wiseman, 179-96. Oxford: Clarendon, 1973.

________. "Babylonien und Israel." in *Theologische Realenzyklopädie* Bd. V (1979): 67-69.

Lamprichs, R. *Die Westexpansion des neuassyrischen Reiches: Eine Strukturanalyse*. AOAT 239. Kevelaer: Butzon & Bercker; Neukirchen-Vluyn: Neukirchener, 1995.

Landsberger, B. Review of Unger, *Babylon*, in *ZA* 41 (1933): 292-99.

________. "Die Basaltstele Nabonids von Eski-Harran." In *Halil Edhem Hâtira Kitabi*. Vol 1, 115-51. Ankara: Türk Tarih Kurumu Basimevi, 1947.

________. *Brief des Bischofs von Esagila an König Asarhaddon*. Mededelingen der Koninklijke Nederlandse Akademie van Wetenschappen, Afd. Letterkunde.

N.R. 28, No. 6. Amsterdam: N.V. Noord-Hollandsche Uitgevers Maatschappij, 1965.

________. "Akkadisch-hebräische Wortgleichungen." VTSup 16 (1967):176-204.

Lang, B. "Ein babylonisches Motiv in Israels Schöpfungsmythologie (Jer 27,5-6)." *Biblische Zeitschrift* NF 27 (1983): 236-37.

Langdon, S. *Building Inscriptions of the Neo-Babylonian Empire; Part I, Nabopolassar and Nebuchadnezzar*. Paris: E. Laroux, 1905.

________. *Die neubabylonische Königsinschriften*. VAB 4. Trans. R. Zehnpfund. Leipzig: Hinrichs, 1912.

________. "New Inscriptions of Nabuna'id." *AJSL* 32 (1915): 102-17.

Lapp, N. *The Third Campaign at Tel el-Fûl: The Excavations of 1964*. AASOR 45. Cambridge, MA: ASOR, 1981.

Lapp, P. "The Pottery of Palestine in the Persian Period." In *Archäologie und Altes Testament, Festschrift für Kurt Galling*, ed. A. Kuschke and E. Kutsch, 179-98. Tübingen: Mohr, 1970.

Larsen, M. T., ed. *Power and Propaganda: A Symposium on Ancient Empires*. Mesopotamia 7. Copenhagen: Akademisk Forlag, 1979.

________. "The 'Babel/Bible' Controversy and its Aftermath." In *Civilizations of the Ancient Near East*, ed. J. M. Sasson et al., 1.95-106. New York: Macmillan, 1995.

Lehmann, G. "Trends in the Local Pottery Development of the Late Iron Age and Persian Period in Syria and Lebanon, ca. 700 to 300 B.C." *BASOR* 311 (1998): 7-37.

Lehmann, R. G. *Friedrich Delitzsch und der Babel-Bibel-Streit*. OBO 133. Freiburg: Universitätsverlag; Göttingen: Vandenhoeck and Ruprecht, 1994.

Leichty, E. "An Inscription of Aššur-etel-ilani." *JAOS* 103 (1983): 217-20.

Leuze, O. *Die Satrapieneinteilung in Syrien und im Zweistromlande von 520-320*. Halle, 1935. Reprint, Hildesheim: Gerstenberg, 1972.

Levenson, J. *Creation and the Persistence of Evil: The Jewish Drama of Divine Omnipotence*. New York: Harper and Row, 1987; reprint, Princeton: Princeton University Press, Mythos Series, 1994.

Lewy, J. "The Late Assyro-Babylonian Cult of the Moon and its Culmination at the Time of Nabonidus." *HUCA* 19 (1946): 405-89.

Liphschitz N., and G. Biger. "The Timber Trade in Ancient Palestine." *TA* 22 (1995): 121-27.

Liverani, M. "The Ideology of the Assyrian Empire." In *Power and Propaganda: A Symposium on Ancient Empires*. Mesopotamia 7, ed. M. T. Larsen, 297-317. Copenhagen: Akademisk Forlag, 1979.

________. *Prestige and Interest: International Relations in the Near East ca. 1600-1100 B.C.* Padova: Sargon, 1990.

________. "Nationality and Political Identity." *ABD*, ed. D. N. Freedman, 4.1031-37. Garden City, N.Y.: Doubleday, 1992.

________. *Studies on the Annals of Ashurnasirpal II, 2: Topographical Analysis*. Quaderni di Geografia Storica 4. Rome: Università di Roma "La Sapienza," 1992.

Liverani, M., ed. *Neo-Assyrian Geography*. Quaderni di Geografia Storica 5. Rome: Università di Roma "La Sapienza," 1995.

Loewenstamm, S. E. "*Yāpēaḥ, yāpiaḥ, yāpîaḥ.*" *Lešonénu* 26 (1962): 205-8, 280 (Hebrew); reprinted in S. E. Loewenstamm, *Comparative Studies in Biblical and Ancient Oriental Literatures*. AOAT 204. Neukirchen-Vluyn: Neukirchener, 1980 (English), 137-43.

________. "Further Additions to *yāpēaḥ, yāpiaḥ, yāpîaḥ.*" *Lešonénu* 27/28 (1964): 182 (Hebrew); reprinted in S. E. Loewenstamm, *Comparative Studies in Biblical and Ancient Oriental Literatures*. AOAT 204. Neukirchen-Vluyn: Neukirchener, 1980 (English), 144-45.

Macalister, R. A. S. *The Excavation at Gezer*. London: Palestine Exploration Fund, 1912.

Machinist, P. "Assyria and Its Image in the First Isaiah." *JAOS* 103 (1983): 719-37.

________. "The Assyrians and Their Babylonian Problem," *Wissenschaftskolleg zu Berlin Jahrbuch* (1984/85): 353-64.

________. "On Self-Consciousness in Mesopotamia." In *The Origins and Diversity of Axial Age Civilizations*, ed. S. N. Eisenstadt, 183-202, 511-18. Albany, N.Y.: State University of New York Press, 1986.

________. "The Question of Distinctiveness in Ancient Israel: An Essay." In *Ah, Assyria . . .: Studies in Assyrian History and Ancient Near Eastern Historiography Presented to Hayim Tadmor*. ScrHier 33, ed. M. Cogan and I. Eph'al, 196-212. Jerusalem: Magnes, 1991.

________. "Palestine, Administration of (Assyro-Babylonian)." *ABD*, ed. D. N. Freedman, 5:69-81. Garden City, N.Y.: Doubleday, 1992.

________. "Assyrians on Assyria in the First Millennium B.C." In *Anfänge politischen Denkens in der Antike, die nahöstlichen Kulturen und die Griechen*, ed. K. Raaflaub and E. Müller-Luckner, 77-104. Munich: R. Oldenbourg, 1993.

________. "The Fall of Assyria in Comparative Ancient Perspective." In *Assyria 1995*, ed. S. Parpola and R. M. Whiting, 179-95. Helsinki: Neo-Assyrian Text Corpus Project, 1997.

Machinist, P., and H. Tadmor. "Heavenly Wisdom." In *The Tablet and the Scroll. Near Eastern Studies in Honor of William W. Hallo*, ed. M. Cohen, D. Snell, and D. Weisberg, 146-51. Bethesda, Md.: CDL, 1993.

Macintosh, A. A. *Isaiah XXI: A Palimpsest*. Cambridge: Cambridge University Press, 1980.

Magen, Y., and I. Finkelstein. *Archaeological Survey of the Hill Country of Benjamin*. Jerusalem: Israel Antiquities Authority, 1993.

Malamat, A. "Josiah's Bid for Armegeddon: The Background of the Judean-Egyptian Encounter in 609 B.C." *JANES* 5 (1973 [Gaster Festschrift]): 267-79.

________. "The Twilight of Judah: In the Egyptian-Babylonian Maelstrom." VTSup 28 (1974): 123-45.

________. "The Last Years of the Kingdom of Judah." In WHJP. Vol. 4/1 *The Age of the Monarchies: Political History*, ed. A. Malamat, 205-21. Jerusalem: Massada, 1979.

________. "A Forerunner of Biblical Prophecy: The Mari Documents." In *Ancient Israelite Religion. Essays in Honor of Frank Moore Cross*, ed. P. D. Miller, P. D. Hanson, and S. D. McBride, 33-52. Philadelphia: Fortress, 1987.

________. "The Kingdom of Judah Between Egypt and Babylon: A Small State Within a Great Power Confrontation." In *Text and Context. Old Testament and Semitic Studies for F.C. Fensham*, ed. W. Classen, 117-29. JSOTSup 48. Sheffield: Academic, 1988.

Mankowski, P. V. "Akkadian and Trans-Akkadian Loanwords in Biblical Hebrew." Ph.D. diss., Harvard University, 1997.

Martin-Achard, R. "Esaïe 47 et la tradition prophétique sur Babylone." In *Prophecy: Essays Presented to Georg Fohrer on his 65th Birthday*, ed J. A. Emerton, 82-105. *BZAW* 150. Berlin: de Gruyter, 1980.

May, H."Some Cosmic Connections of *Mayim Rabbîm*." *JBL* 74 (1955): 9-21.

Mazar, A. *Archaeology of the Land of the Bible, 1000-586 B.C.E.* Garden City, N.Y.: Doubleday, 1990.

Mazar, B. et al. "En-Gedi: The First and Second Seasons of Excavations 1961-62." *'Atiqot* (English Series) 5 (1966).

McCarthy, D. J. *Treaty and Covenant*. AnBib 21, 2nd ed. Rome: Pontifical Biblical Institute, 1978.

McCown, C.C. *Tell en-Naṣbeh, I: Archaeological and Historical Results*. New Haven: ASOR, 1947.

Merrill, E. A. "The Literature of Isaiah 40-55 as Anti-Babylonian Polemic." Ph.D. diss., Columbia University Press, 1981.

Millard, A. *The Eponyms of the Assyrian Empire, 910-612 BC*. SAAS 2. Helsinki: Neo-Assyrian Text Corpus Project, 1994.

Miller, J. M., and J. J. M. Roberts. *The Hand of the Lord: A Reassessment of the "Ark Narrative" of I Samuel*. Johns Hopkins Near Eastern Studies. Baltimore: Johns Hopkins University Press, 1977.

Mitchell, T. C. "The Babylonian Exile and the Restoration of the Jews in Palestine (586-c.500 B.C.)." In *CAH*, 2d ed. Vol. 3, part 2, *The Assyrian and Babylonian Empires and Other States of the Near East, from the Eighth to the Sixth Centuries B.C.*, ed. J. A. Boardman et al., 410-60. Cambridge: Cambridge University Press, 1991.

Moran, W. L. "Notes on the New Nabonidus Inscriptions (Style and Composition H1B-H2, A and B)." *Or* n.s. 28 (1959): 130-40.

Moran, W. L., and G. F. Dole. "A Bowl of *alallu*-stone." *ZA* 81 (1991): 267-73.

Na'aman, N. "Chronology and History in the Late Assyrian Empire (631-619 B.C.)" *ZA* 81 (1991): 243-267.

________. "The Kingdom of Judah under Josiah." *TA* 18 (1991): 3-71.

________. "Nebuchadrezzar's Campaign in Year 603 B.C.E.." *Biblische Notizen* 62 (1992): 41-44.

________. "Province System and Settlement Pattern in Southern Syria and Palestine in the Neo-Assyrian Period." In *Neo-Assyrian Geography*, ed. M. Liverani, 103-15. Quaderni di Geografia Storica 5. Rome: Università di Roma "La Sapienza," 1995.

Na'aman, N., and R. Zadok. "Sargon II's Deportations to Israel and Philistia (716-708 B.C.)." *JCS* 40 (1988): 36-46.

Naveh, J. "A Hebrew Letter from the Seventh Century B.C." *IEJ* 10 (1960): 129-139.

________. "The Excavations at Meṣad Ḥashavyahu–Preliminary Report," *IEJ* 12 (1962): 89-113.

________. *The Development of the Aramaic Script*. Jerusalem: Israel Academy of Sciences and Humanities, 1970.

Neugebauer, O. *The Exact Sciences in Antiquity*. 2d ed. New York: Harper Torchbooks, 1962.

Oates, J. *Babylon*. 2d ed. London: Thames and Hudson, 1986.

________. "The Fall of Assyria." In *CAH*, 2d ed. Vol. 3, pPart 2, *The Assyrian and Babylonian Empires and Other States of the Near East, from the Eighth to the Sixth Centuries B.C.*, ed. J. A. Boardman et al., 162-193. Cambridge: Cambridge University Press, 1991.

Oded, B. "Judah and the Exile." In *Israelite and Judaean History*, ed. J. H. Hayes and J. M. Miller, 435-488. Philadelphia: Westminster, 1979.

________. *Mass Deportation in the Assyrian Empire*. Wiesbaden: Reichert, 1979.

Ofer, A. "Judean Hills Survey." In *NEAEHL*, ed. E. Stern, 3.814-15. Jerusalem: Israel Exploration Society, 1993.

Oppenheim, A. L. "'Siege-Documents' from Nippur." *Iraq* 17 (1955): 69-89.

________. "Essay on Overland Trade in the First Millennium B.C." *JCS* 21 (1967): 236-54.

________. *Ancient Mesopotamia: Portrait of a Dead Civilization*. 2d rev. ed. completed by E. Reiner. Chicago: University of Chicago, 1979.

________. "Neo-Assyrian and Neo-Babylonian Empires." In *Propaganda and Communication in World History*. Vol. 1, *The Symbolic Instrument in Early Times*, ed. H. D. Lasswell, D. Cerner, and H. Speier, 111-144. Honolulu: University Press of Hawaii, An East-West Center Book, 1979.

Oren, E. D. "Migdol: A New Fortress on the Edge of the Eastern Nile Delta." *BASOR* 256 (1984): 7-44.

________. "Sera', Tel." In *NEAEHL*, ed. E. Stern, 4.1333-34. Jerusalem: Israel Exploration Society, 1993.

Overholt, T. W. "King Nebuchadnezzar in the Jeremiah Tradition." *CBQ* 30 (1968): 39-48.

Parker, R. A., and W. H. Dubberstein. *Babylonian Chronology, 626 B.C.-A.D. 75*. Brown University Studies, vol. 19. Providence: Brown University Press, 1956.

Parpola, S. *Neo-Assyrian Toponymns*. AOAT 6. Kevelaer: Butzon & Bercker; Neukirchen-Vluyn: Neukirchener, 1970.

Parpola, S., and K. Watanabe. *Neo-Assyrian Treaties and Loyalty Oaths*. SAA 2. Helsinki: Helsinki University Press, 1988.

Paul, S. "Deutero-Isaiah and Cuneiform Royal Inscriptions." *JAOS* 88 (1968): 180-86.

________. "Fishing Imagery in Amos 4:2." *JBL* 97 (1978): 183-90.

________. *Amos*. Hermeneia. Minneapolis: Augsburg Fortress, 1991.

Pečírková, J. "The Administrative Organization of the Neo-Assyrian Empire." *ArOr* 45 (1977): 211-28.

________. "The Administrative Methods of Assyrian Imperialism." *ArOr* 55 (1987): 162-75.

Pongratz-Leisten, B. *Ina Šulmi Īrub: Die kulttopographische und ideologische Programmatik der akītu-Prozession in Babylonien und Assyrien im 1. Jahrtausend v. Chr.* Baghdader Forschungen 16. Mainz am Rhein: Philipp von Zabern, 1994.

Porten, B. "The Identity of King Adon." *BA* 44 (1981): 36-52.

Porter, B. N. *Images, Power, and Politics: Figurative Aspects of Esarhaddon's Babylonian Policy*. Philadelphia: American Philosophical Society, 1993.

Postgate, J. N. *Taxation and Conscription in the Assyrian Empire*. Rome: Pontifical Biblical Institute, 1974

________. "The Four 'Neo-Assyrian' Tablets from Šēḫ Ḥamad." *SAAB* 7 (1993): 109-24.

Preuss, H. D. *Verspottung fremder Religionen im Alten Testament*. BWANT 12. Stuttgart: Kohlhammer, 1971.

Pritchard, J. B. *Hebrew Inscriptions from Gibeon*. Philadelphia: University Museum, 1959.

Ravn, O. E. *Herodotus' Description of Babylon*. Copenhagen: NYT Nordisk Forlag, 1942.

Reade, J. E. "Assyrian Eponyms, Kings and Pretenders, 648-605 B.C." *Or* n.s. 67 (1998): 255-65.

Redford, D. B. *Egypt, Canaan, and Israel in Ancient Times*. New Jersey: Princeton University Press, 1992.

Reimer, D. J. *The Oracles Against Babylon in Jeremiah 50-51*. San Francisco: Mellen Research University Press, 1993.

Reiner, E. *"Your Thwarts in Pieces, Your Mooring Rope Cut": Poetry from Babylonia and Assyria*. Michigan Studies in the Humanities 5. Ann Arbor: Horace B. Rackham School of Graduate Studies, 1985.

Renger, J. "Königsinschriften. B. Akkadisch." *RLA* 6 (1980-1983): 65-77.

Riis, P. J. *Sūkās I. The North-East Sanctuary and the First Settling of Greeks in Syria and Palestine*. Det Kongelige Danske Videnskabernes Selskab Historisk-Filosofiske Skrifter 5,1. Copenhagen: Publications of the Carlsberg Expedition to Phoenicia 1, 1970.

Ringgren, H. *TDOT* 1.466-69, s.v. "Babhel."

Roberts, J. J. M. *Nahum, Habakkuk, and Zephaniah: A Commentary*. Louisville, Ky.: Westminster John Knox, 1991.

Röllig, W. "Zur historische Einordnung der Texte." *SAAB* 7 (1993): 129-32.

Rowlands, M., M. Larsen, and K. Kristiansen. *Centre and Periphery in the Ancient World*. Cambridge: Cambridge University Press, 1987.

Rowton, M. B. "The Role of Watercourses in the Growth of Mesopotamian Civilization." In *lišān mitḫurti. Festschrift Wolfram von Soden*, ed. W. Röllig, 307-16. AOAT 1. Kevelaer: Butzon & Bercker; Neukirchen-Vluyn: Neukirchener, 1969.

Rudolph, W. *Jeremia*. 3e Auflage. Handbuch zum alten Testament 12. Tübingen: Mohr, 1958.

Sack, R. H. *Awel-Marduk 562-560 B.C.* AOAT, Sonderreihe 4. Neukirchen-Vluyn: Neukirchener, 1972.

________. *Images of Nebuchadnezzar: The Emergence of a Legend*. Selinsgrove: Susquehanna University Press, 1991.

________. *Neriglissar: King of Babylon*. AOAT 236. Neukirchen-Vluyn: Neukirchener, 1994.

Saggs, H. W. F. "A Cylinder from Tell al Lahm." *Sumer* 13 (1957): 190-95.

________. "Assyriology and the Study of the Old Testament." Inaugural Lecture. Cardiff: University of Wales Press, 1969.

________. *The Greatness That Was Babylon*. 2d ed. London: Sidgwich and Jackson, 1988.
Sandmel, S. "Parallelomania." *JBL* 81 (1962): 1-13.
Schiff, L. "The Nur-Sin Archive: Private Entrepreneurship in Babylon, 603-507 B.C." Ph.D. diss., University of Pennsylvania, 1987.
Schmid, H. *Der Tempelturm Etemenanki in Babylon*. Baghdader Forschungen 17. Mainz am Rhein: Philipp von Zabbern, 1995.
Schrader, E. *Die Keilschriften und das Alten Testament*. 2d ed. Giessen: J. Ricker, 1883.
Seux, M.-J. *Épithètes royales akkadiennes et sumériennes*. Paris: Letouzey et Ané, 1967.
Smith, D. L. *The Religion of the Landless: The Social Context of the Babylonian Exile*. Bloomington: Meyer Stone, 1989.
Smith, S. *Babylonian Historical Texts Relating to the Capture and Downfall of Babylon*. London: Methuen, 1924.
________. "The Greek Trade at Al Mina." *The Antiquaries Journal* 22 (1942): 87-112.
________. *Isaiah Chapters 40-55: Literary Criticism and History*. Schweich Lectures of the British Academy, 1940. London: Oxford University Press, 1944.
Soden, W. von. "Der neubabylonische Funktionär *simmagir* und der Feuertod des Šamaš-šum-ukīn." *ZA* 62 (1972): 84-90.
________. "Die babylonischen Königsinschriften 1157-612 v. Chr. und die Frage nach der Planungszeit und dem Baubeginn von Etemenanki." *ZA* 86 (1996): 80-88.
Sommerfeld, W. *Der Aufstieg Marduks: Die Stellung Marduks in der babylonischen Religion des zweiten Jahrtausends v. Chr.* AOAT 213. Kevelaer: Butzon & Bercker; Neukirchen-Vluyn: Neukirchener, 1982.
Spalinger, A. "Psammetichus, King of Egypt I." *JARCE* 13 (1976): 133-47.
________. "Egypt and Babylonia: A Survey (c. 620 B.C.-550 B.C.)." *Studien zur Altägyptischen Kultur* 5 (1977): 221-244.
________. "Psammetichus, King of Egypt II," *JARCE* 15 (1978): 49-57.
________. "Egypt, History of (Dyn. 21-26)." In *ABD*, ed. D. N. Freedman, 2.353-64. Garden City, N.Y.: Doubleday, 1992.
Stager, L. E. "The Fury of Babylon: The Archaeology of Destruction," *BAR* 22 (1996): 56-69, 76-77.
________. "Ashkelon and the Archaeology of Destruction: Kislev 604 B.C.E.." *EI* 25 (Joseph Aviram Volume) (1996): 61*-74*.
Starr, I. *Queries to the Sungod: Divination and Politics in Sargonid Assyria*. SAA 4. Helsinki: The Neo-Assyrian Text Corpus Project, 1990.
Stern, E. *Material Culture of the Land of the Bible in the Persian Period, 538-322 B.C.* Warminster: Aris and Phillips, 1982.
________. "A Phoenician-Cypriote Votive Scapula from Tel Dor: A Maritime Scene." *IEJ* 44 (1994): 1-12.
________. "Israel at the Close of the Period of the Monarchy." *BA* 38 (1975): 26-54.
Stern, E., ed. *NEAEHL*. Jerusalem: Israel Exploration Society, 1993.
Strassmeier, J. N. "Inschriften von Nabopalassar." *ZA* 4 (1889): 144.

Tadmor, H. "Chronology of the Last Kings of Judah." *JNES* 15 (1956): 226-30.

________. "Three Last Decades of Assyria." *Proceedings of the 25th International Congress of Orientalists*, vol 1.240-41. Moscow, 1964.

________. "The Inscriptions of Nabunaid: Historical Arrangement." In *Studies in Honor of Benno Landsberger*, ed. H. Güterbock and T. Jacobsen, 351-64. AS 16. Chicago: University of Chicago, 1965.

________. "Philistia under Assyrian Rule." *BA* 29 (1966): 86-102.

________. "The Period of the First Temple, the Babylonian Exile and the Restoration." In *A History of the Jewish People*, ed. H. H. Ben-Sasson, 91-159. Cambridge: Harvard University Press, 1976.

________. "History and Ideology in the Assyrian Royal Inscriptions." In *Assyrian Royal Inscriptions: New Horizons in Literary, Ideological, and Historical Analysis*, ed. F. M. Fales, 13-33. Orientis Antiqui Collectio 17. Rome: Instituto per l'oriente, 1981.

________. *The Inscriptions of Tiglath-pileser III King of Assyria*. Jerusalem: Israel Academy of Sciences and Humanities, 1994.

________. "Propaganda, Literature, Historiography: Cracking the Code of the Assyrian Royal Inscriptions." In *Assyria 1995*, ed. S. Parpola and R. M. Whiting, 325-38. Helsinki: Neo-Assyrian Text Corpus Project, 1997.

________. "Nabopolassar and Sin-shum-lishir in a Literary Perspective." In *Festschrift für Rykle Borger zu seinem 65. Geburtstag am 24. Mai 1994: tikip santakki mala bašmu*. Cuneiform Monographs 10, ed. S. M. Maul, 353-57. Groningen: Styx, 1998.

Tadmor H., and B. Landsberger. "Fragments of Clay Liver-Models from Hazor." *IEJ* 14 (1964): 201-17.

Tallqvist, K. *Akkadische Götterepitheta*. Helsinki: Societas Orientalish Fennica, 1938. Reprint New York: Georg Olms, 1974.

Thureau-Dangin, F. "L'inscription des lions de Tel-Barsib." *RA* 27 (1930): 57-64.

Toorn, K. van der. "The Babylonian New Year Festival: New Insights from the Cuneiform Texts and their Bearing on Old Testament Study." VTSup 43 (1991): 331-44.

Tsevat, M. "The Neo-Assyrian and Neo-Babylonian Vassal Oaths and the Prophet Ezekiel." *JBL* 78 (1959): 199-204.

Tsumura, D. T. "Hab 2:2 in the Light of Akkadian Legal Practice." *ZAW* 94 (1982): 294-95.

Tuplin, C. "The Administration of the Achaemenid Empire." In *Coinage and Administration in The Athenian and Persian Empires*. British Archaeological Reports International Series 343, ed. I. Carradice, 109-66. Oxford: British Archaeological Reports, 1987.

Unger, E. A. "Nebukadnezar II. und sein Šandabakku (Oberkommissar) in Tyrus." *ZAW* 44 (1926): 314-17.

________. *Babylon: Die Heilige Stadt nach der Beschreibung der Babylonier*. 2. Auflage, ed. R. Borger. Berlin: de Gruyter, 1970.

Vaggione, R. P. "All Over Asia? The Extent of the Scythian Domination in Herodotus." *JBL* 92 (1973): 523-30.

Van Beek, G. "The Arch and the Vault in Ancient Near Eastern Architecture." *Scientific American* 257 (1987): 96-103.

________. "Jemmeh, Tell." *NEAEHL*, ed. E. Stern, 2.670-72. Jerusalem: Israel Exploration Society, 1993.

Van Driel, G. "Wood, Reeds and Rushes: A Note on Neo-Babylonian Practical Texts." *Bulletin on Sumerian Agriculture* 6 (1992): 171-76.

Voigtlander, E. von. "A Survey of Neo-Babylonian History." Ph.D. diss., University of Michigan, Ann Arbor, 1963.

Waldbaum, J. C. "Early Greek Contacts with the Southern Levant, ca. 1000-600 B.C.: The Eastern Perspective." *BASOR* 293 (1994): 53-66.

________. "Greeks *in* the East or Greeks *and* the East? Problems in the Definition and Recognition of Presence." *BASOR* 305 (1997): 1-17.

Waldbaum, J. C., and J. Magness. "The Chronology of Early Greek Pottery: New Evidence from Seventh-Century B.C. Destruction Levels in Israel." *AJA* 101 (1997): 23-40.

Waldman, N. M. "A Biblical Echo of Mesopotamian Royal Rhetoric." In *Essays on the Occasion of the Seventieth Anniversary of the Dropsie University*, ed. A. I. Katsh and L. Nemoy, 449-55. Philadelphia: The Dropsie University Press, 1979.

________. "The Wealth of Mountain and Sea: The Background of a Biblical Image." *JQR* 71 (1981): 176-80.

Walker, C. B. F. *Cuneiform Brick Inscriptions*. London: British Museum Publications, 1981.

Walker, C. B. F., and M. B. Dick. "The Induction of the Cult Image in Ancient Mesopotamia." In *Born in Heaven, Made on Earth: The Making of the Cult Image in the Ancient Near East*, ed. M. B. Dick. Winona Lake, Ind.: Eisenbrauns, forthcoming.

Wall-Romana, C. "An Areal Location of Agade." *JNES* 49 (1990): 205-45.

Weber, M. *Ancient Judaism*. Trans. H. H. Gerth and D. Martindale. New York: The Free Press, 1967.

Weidner, E. F. "Jojachin, König von Juda, in Babylonischen Keilschrifttexten." In *Mélanges Syriens offerts à Monsieur René Dussaud*, Academie des inscriptions et belles-lettres, 2.923-35. Paris: Geuthner, 1939.

Weinberg, S. S. "Post-Exilic Palestine." *Proceedings of the Israel Academy of Sciences and Humanities* 4/5 (1971): 78-97.

Weinfeld, M. "The Protest against Imperialism in Ancient Israelite Prophecy." In *The Origins and Diversity of Axial Age Civilizations*, ed. S. N. Eisenstadt, 169-82. Albany, N.Y.: State University of New York Press, 1986.

________. *Deuteronomy and the Deuteronomic School*. Oxford: Oxford University Press, 1972. Reprint, Winona Lake, Ind.: Eisenbrauns, 1992.

Weissbach, F. H. *Die Inschriften Nebuchadnezars II im Wâdī Brîsā und am Nahr el-Kelb*. WVDOG 5. Leipzig: J. C. Hinrichs, 1906.

________. Review of Unger, *Babylon*. *ZA* 41 (1933): 258-59.

Weissert, E. "Royal Hunt and Royal Triumph in a Prism Fragment of Ashurbanipal (82-5-22,2)." In *Assyria 1995*, ed. S. Parpola and R. M. Whiting, 339-58. Helsinki: Neo-Assyrian Text Corpus Project, 1997.

Westenholz, J. G. "Akkadian 'Therefore': An Example of Morpheme Substitution Among Pronouns." *Or* n.s. 54 (1985): 321-26.

Westermann, C. *Isaiah 40-66*. OTL. London: SCM, 1969.

Wetzel, F. *Die Stadtmauern von Babylon*. WVDOG 48; Leipzig: J. C. Hinrichs, 1930.

Wetzel, F., and Weissbach, F. H. *Das Hauptheiligtum des Marduk in Babylon, Esagila und Etemenanki*. WVDOG 59. Leipzig: J. C. Hinrichs, 1938.

Whiting, R. "The Post-Canonical and Extra-Canonical Eponyms." In *The Eponyms of the Assyrian Empire, 910-612 B.C.*, by A. Millard, 72-78. SAAS 2. Helsinki: The Neo-Assyrian Text Corpus Project, 1994.

Wildberger, H. *Jesaja*. BKAT 10. Neukirchen-Vluyn: Neukirchener, 1978.

Williamson, H. G. M. "Isaiah 40.20–A Case of Not Seeing the Wood for the Trees." *Biblica* 67 (1986): 1-20.

Winter, I. J. "Art *in* Empire: The Royal Image and the Visual Dimensions of Assyrian Ideology." In *Assyria 1995*, ed. S. Parpola and R. M. Whiting, 359-81. Helsinki: Neo-Assyrian Text Corpus Project, 1996.

Wiseman, D. J. *The Chronicles of the Chaldean Kings (625-556 B.C.)*. London: British Museum, 1956.

________. "A Late Babylonian Tribute List?" *BSOAS* 30 (1967): 495-504.

________. *Nebuchadrezzar and Babylon*. The Schweich Lectures, 1983. Oxford: Oxford University Press, 1985.

________. "Babylonia 605-539 B.C." In *CAH*, 2d ed. Vol. 3, part 2, *The Assyrian and Babylonian Empires and Other States of the Near East, from the Eighth to the Sixth Centuries B.C.*, ed. J. A. Boardman et al., 229-51. Cambridge: Cambridge University Press, 1991.

Wohl, H. "A Note on the Fall of Babylon." *JANES* 2 (1969): 28-38.

Woolley, C. L. *Carchemish*. London: British Museum, 1929.

________. "Excavations at Al Mina, Sueidia." *JHS* 58 (1938): 1-30, 133-70.

Xenophon. *Cyropaedia*. Rev. ed., trans. W. Miller. Loeb Classical Library 52. Cambridge: Harvard University Press, 1989.

Zablocka, J., and P.-R. Berger. "Ein vollständigeres Duplikat zur Nebukadnezar II-Inschrift VAB 4 Nr. 46." *Or* n.s. 38 (1969): 122-25.

Zadok, R. "Phoenicians, Philistines and Moabites in Mesopotamia in the First Millennium B.C.E. Chiefly according to Akkadian Sources." *BASOR* 230 (1978): 57-65.

________. "The Nippur Region during the Late Assyrian, Chaldean and Achaemenian Periods Chiefly According to Written Sources." *IOS* 8 (1978): 266-332.

________. "On Some Foreign Population Groups in First-Millennium Babylonia." *TA* 6 (1979): 164-81.

________. *The Jews in Babylonia during the Chaldean and Achaemenian Periods, According to the Babylonian Sources*. Studies in the History of the Jewish People and the Land of Israel, vol. 3. Haifa: University of Haifa Press, 1979.

________. "Notes on the Early History of the Israelites and Judeans in Mesopotamia." *Or* n.s. 51 (1982): 391-93.

________. "The Origin of the Name Shinar." *ZA* 74 (1984): 240-44.

________. *Geographical Names According to New- and Late-Babylonian Texts*. Répertoire géographique des textes cunéiforms 8. Beihefte zum Tübinger Atlas des vorderen Orients B7. Wiesbaden: L. Reichert, 1985.

________. "Notes on Syro-Palestinian History, Toponomy and Anthroponomy." *UF* 28 (1996): 721-49.

Zawadski, S. *The Fall of Assyria and Median-Babylonian Relations*. Adam Mickiewicz University, Poznán, Historical Series, 149. Poznán: Adam Mickiewicz University Press, 1988.

________. "A Contribution to the Last Days of the Assyrian Empire." *ZA* 85 (1995): 67-73.

Zimmerli, W. *Ezekiel 1*. Hermeneia. Philadelphia: Fortress, 1979.

Zimmern, H. *Akkadische Fremdwörter als Beweis für babylonischen Kultureinfluss*. 2e Auflage. Leipzig: Hinrichs, 1917.

Zorn, J. R. "Mesopotamian-style Ceramic 'Bathtub' Coffins from Tell en-Nasbeh." *TA* 20 (1993): 216-24.

________. "Tell En Naṣbeh: A Re-evaluation of the Architecture and Stratigraphy of the Early Bronze Age, Iron Age and Later Periods." Ph.D. diss., University of California at Berkeley, 1993.

________. "Mizpah: Newly Discovered Stratum Reveals Judah's Other Capital." *BAR* 23/5 (1997): 28-38; 66.

Zorn, J. R., J. Yellin, and J. Hayes. "The *m(w)ṣh* Stamp Impressions and the Neo-Babylonian Period." *IEJ* 44 (1994): 161-83.

Index of Textual Citations

1. Hebrew Bible

Genesis

1:2 138n
10:4 79n
10:8-9 1
10:10 123n
11:1-9 1
11:2 123n
14:2, 9 123n

Exodus

7:19 201n
8:1 201n
8:3, 14, 15 185n
9:11 185n
15 149
22:17 182n
22:25-26 79

Deuteronomy

1:5 158
9:21 158n
18:10 182n
24:10-13 79
27:8 158, 158n, 159
28:30 182n
28:33 143, 146
28:49 143, 143n, 146

Judges

5:4 138n

1 Samuel

5:3-4 177n
6:2 185n
30:14 104n

2 Kings

13:14-19 168n
15:29 146, 146n
17 128
17:6 118, 131
17:24, 30 118
19:23 154
19:25 121
20:12-19 118
20:14 126n
22:3 68
23:29-30 148n
23:33 81
24:1-17 161n
24:7 81, 98
24:12, 17 105
24:13 134
25:6-7 100
25:8, 11, 20 150n
25:22-23, 24 105
25:25 83n, 105

Isaiah

5:19 159n
8:7-8 147
10:5 148, 154
10:28-32 146n
11:11 123n

13:2-16 124, 126
13:7 126, 145
13:11 125, 125n
13:16-17 124
13:19 124, 126n, 134, 163
13:21-22 124
14:1-2, 4a 128
14:3-4, 22-23 128, 207
14:4b-21 134, 207
14:8 154
14:13b, 16b 138n
14:23 200n
18:7 167
19:8 155n
21 125, 129, 131, 132, 133
21:2 124, 131, 133
21:6-8 157
21:9 129, 132, 133, 177n
25:3-5 125n
30:8 159n
33:19 144n
37:24 154
39:1-8 118
39:3 126n
39:7 129n
40:12, 22 187
40:18-20 171, 172
40:20 174
41:18 201n
42:15 201n
44:14 174
44:25 183n, 184, 186
45:12 187
46:1 179
46:1-2 171, 175, 175n, 176nn, 179, 180
47 181
47:1 163
47:2 193
47:9, 10, 12 182
47:13 183, 184
47:15 184
47:11 185
48:13 187
50:3 187
60:5-13 46n

Jeremiah

1:13-16 137, 138, 139
1:15 139, 139n
2:10 79n
2:15 140
2:18, 36 136
4:5-8 140, 145
4:13 142
4:15 146
4:23-26 138n, 148
5:6 140, 142n.80
5:15 142, 143n, 144, 146, 171
6:1-5 145
6:1, 5 145
6:11-12 182n
6:22-26 126, 130n, 145
6:23 138n
8:14-16 145
9:10 127n
10:1-16 172, 184n
10:2 183n
10:22 127n, 145
10:25 138n
12:12 130n
15:14 142n
16:13 142
16:16 155n, 157
17:4 142
22:6 167
22:26, 28 143
23:21 158n
25:9 139
25:11-12 129n
26 120, 122
26:11 120
26:18 120-21
27:7 189
27:8-10 121
27:8, 11, 12 25n
28:2, 4, 11 25n
29:10 189
31:8 143

37:5-11 87
39:3, 13 139, 149-51
39:12-14 189
40:4-6 189
40:7 105
41:3 83n, 105
43:10-13 89
44:30 146
46:1-2, 13-14 82, 146
46:7-8 147
46:8 149
46:9 88n
46:20 146-47
47:2 147
48:8, 15, 18 130n
49 132
50:12 182n
50:13 192
50:14 191
50:15 190, 191, 200
50:17 122, 122n, 142, 207
50:28 117n, 189
50:36 183n
50:38 192
50:42 145n
50:43 145n
51:11b, 24, 35, 51 189
51:13 192, 194
51:27 200
51:29 117n
51:30-32 200, 201
51:34 149, 160n
51:36 192
51:38 140n, 192
51:42 192, 194
51:44 160
51:58 163n
51:59-64 189

Ezekiel

1:1 111
3:6 144n
3:15 110
12:21, 26 160n
16:30 169n
17:1-10 164
17:3, 4 167
17:12-16 165
17:13 165, 166
17:14, 19 166
20:32 138n
21:23-29 167
21:26, 27 168, 185n
23 136
23:14, 15 123n
24:6 162n
25:16 104n
26:7 148
27:6 79n
28:7 125n
30:11 125n
31:12 125n
32:3 155
32:2 140n
32:12 125n
32:11-12 89

Amos

4:2 155n, 157
7:17 182n

Micah

1:1 117
3:10 162n
3:11 121
3:12 120, 120n, 121, 122
4:10 117, 120, 122, 123, 144, 207
5:7 121n

Nahum

1:5 138n
2:7-9 194n
2:8 182n
2:12-14 141
2:15-16 182n
3:1 162n
3:4 138n, 182n

3:5 182n
3:8 194n
3:13 200n
3:17 200n

Habakkuk

1:2-3a 153
1:5 130n
1:6 153n
1:8-10 155
1:8 142
1:9 153, 160
1:11 156
1:13 130n
1:14-17 155
1:15-16 155
2:1 157
2:2-3 159
2:2 157-58, 158nn
2:3 159
2:5 130n, 160
2:6 161, 164n
2:6b-7 161
2:8a 157
2:8b, 2:17b 153
2:9-19 161
2:12 162
2:13 163
2:17a 153
2:18-19 156, 172

Zephaniah

2:4-15 154
2:5 104n
2:15 182

Zechariah

5:11 123n
14:17-18 138n

Malachi

3:5 182n

Psalms

7:3 140
17:12 140
18:18 138n
92:13-14 167
93:4 194
107:35 201n
114:8 201n
137:1 193

Lamentations

2:1a 126n
4:6 126n
5:8 126n
5:11 126n

Daniel

1:2 123n
1:20 185n
2:2, 12, 18, 24, 27, 48 182n
2:48, 49 117n
3:1, 12, 30 117n
9:1 133n
11:1 133n

Ezra

7:16 117n

2 Chronicles

34:3 68
36:13 166

2. Cuneiform Inscriptions

For explanation of the conventions used to cite NB inscriptions, see above p. 10, n. 4. Citations of texts published in VAB 4 are listed first for convenience.

VAB 4

Npl 1 i 29-31 25
Npl 1 ii 2-4 30
Npl 1 ii 47-48 32n
Npl 1 iii 1-5 22n

Npl 2 i 6-7 24
Npl 2 ii 1-4 25

Npl 3 i 1-ii 22 14-15
Npl 3 i 2 22n

Npl 4 11-12 31
Npl 4 12 23-24
Npl 4 17-21 25n
Npl 4 25 28n
Npl 4 31-41 24n

Nbk 1 i 11-14 35
Nbk 1 iii 48-49 49

Nbk 2 iii 37-44 49

Nbk 4 ii 28-32 49

Nbk 5 ii 23-29 49
Nbk 5 ii 1-10 198-99

Nbk 7 ii 31 49

Nbk 9 i 3 28n
Nbk 9 i 13-28 45n
Nbk 9 i 19, ii 29, iii 13 156n
193n

Nbk 9 iii 18-24 42n
Nbk 9 iii 51-55 46

Nbk 10 i 7-10 35
Nbk 10 ii 22-26 162

Nbk 11 i 13-14 43n
Nbk 11 ii 21-22 48-49

Nbk 12 i 17-24 35n
Nbk 12 iii 11 43n
Nbk 12 iii 13 43n
Nbk 12 iii 17 49n

Nbk 13 i 22-25 35n

Nbk 14 i 13-17 35
Nbk 14 i 16-17 42
Nbk 14 i 53 48
Nbk 14 ii 52-53 48
Nbk 14 iii 50-51 46
Nbk 14 iii 52-53 49n

Nbk 15 ii 17-23 10n
Nbk 15 i 40-46 35n
Nbk 15 i 44, ii 27 43n
Nbk 15 iv 61-62 184n
Nbk 15 vi 19-21 48
Nbk 15 ix 29-32 48n
Nbk 15 ix 54-56 48
Nbk 15 x 9-12 46n
Nbk 15 x 13-16 49n

Nbk 16 i 9 43

Nbk 17 see WVDOG 59 44-48

Nbk 18 21-22 35-36

Nbk 19 A ii 1 43n
Nbk 19 A iv 38 156n
Nbk 19 A iv 37-39 193n
Nbk 19 A iv 38-v 18 156n
Nbk 19 A iv 58-v 18 156n
Nbk 19 A vii 10 156n
Nbk 19 A vii 29-34 178n
Nbk 19 B vi 12-13 175

Nbk 19 B vii 19	156n
Nbk 19 B viii 26-35	42n
Nbk 19 B ix 23-24	87n
Nbk 19 B ix 51	141n
Nbk 19 B x 16	44n, 156n
Nbk 20 iii 61-64	48-49
Nbk 20 iii 90	49n
Nbk 21 ii 46	49n
Nbk 23 ii 8-15	49n
Nbk 26 13	48n
Nbk 42 7	49n
Nbk 46	*see Or* n.s. 38
Nbk 48	*see CCK*, xx-xxi
Ner 1 38-40	46n
Ner 2 i 33	31n
Ner 2 ii 3	41n
Nbn 1	21n, 53n
Nbn 1 i 39-41	39n
Nbn 1 ii 5	22n
Nbn 1 i 47-48	57n
Nbn 1 ii 3-4, 43-46	57n
Nbn 2 i 4	57n
Nbn 3	52n
Nbn 3 i 10	55n
Nbn 6	54n
Nbn 6 i 5	55n
Nbn 6 ii 45	25n
Nbn 7	52n, 53n
Nbn 7 i 17-19	54
Nbn 8 ix 31-32	11n
Nbn 8 viii 27	31n
Nbn 8 v 8-10	54
Nbn 8 i 26-34	57n
Nbn 8 x 32-37	57n
Al-Rawi, *Iraq* 47	
A Babylon 11 i 19-21	31
A Babylon 11 i 28-ii 5	24-25
A Babylon 11 ii 31	28
AnSt 8 H1, B i 29-30	57n
AnSt 8 H1, B i 41-43	39n, 56n
AnSt 8 H 1, B ii 6-7	14n
AnSt 8 H1, B ii 26	57n
AOB 1 38 2:3	17n
ARM XIII 23:6-15	156n
Bauer Asb. 42 Sm 671 20	18n
BBSt No. 5 i 31	30n
BE 8/1 no. 31:9	101
Berger, *Kyros-Zylinder*	133n
196:17	195
198:24-25	180n
BHLT 25 ii 17	133n
BHLT, 30 i 24	28n
BHLT, 82 ii 14	22n
BHT, 86 col. v 11	186n
BIWA 44 A iv 74-76	140n
BIWA 69 A ix 115-28	66n
BM 41649	37n
Borger Esarh.	
12 §11 Ep. 1:17	17n, 19n
14 §11 Ep. 7:38-42	194
15 §11 Ep. 9	143n
20 §11 Ep. 19 Fass. c	33n
22 §11 Ep. 28	33n
30 §13	20
30 §18 7	20
45 §27 Ep. 2:84	143n

58 §27 Ep. 18:6 140n
70 §39 17
73 §47 9 20
74 §47:24 17n.32
75 §48 6-9 20n
77 §50 20n
92 §63:7 18n
94 §64 Smlt vs. 23-29 48n
98 §65 32 43n

BRM 4 51 i 2 22n
BRM 4 51 i 7-13 31
BRM 4 51 i 14-19 30, 94n

BTT 66:64 178n

CT 36 21 53n
CT 36 21 i 25 55n
CT 37 pls. 5-20 15
CT 37 pls. 6-7 i 25-29 45n, 45-46
CT 37 pl. 7 i 42-43 154n
CT 37 pl. 8 38 175n
CT 37 pl. 12 ii 27 191n
CT 37 pl. 14 ii 51 191n
CT 46 45 91
CT 46 45 v 4-16 45n
CT 46 45 v 7 156n
CT 46 45 v 20-21 98
CT 51 75 18 31n
CT 56 439 13 99n, 100

CCK pl. xxi rev. 1 88n
CCK, pl. xxi rev. 2 88n

GCCI 94:11-12 100n
GCCI I 151:6 101n
GCCI I 169:3 101n

Gerardi, *AfO* 36
34 obv. 3, 36 rev. 3 26
35 obv. 14-15 31-32
36 rev. 5 26n
36 rev. 10-11 26

HSM 890.3.1 iii 6 38n
HSM 890.3.1 iii 8 38n

LIH no. 57: 3 17n
LIH no. 95: 3 17n
LIH no. 97: 13-19 36n

OECT 1 pls. 23-28 53n
OECT 1 32-37 54n
OECT 1 pl. 23 i 21 55

OIP 2 85: 5 43n
OIP 2 156 no. 25 139

Or n.s. 38 123 ii 8-9 96-97

PBS 15 79 i 22-28 46n
PBS 15 pl. 25 i 43-44 154n
PBS 15 79 i 75-76 178n

RA 11 110 i 1 53n
RA 11 110 i 24 55

RIMB 2 22, obv. 11 28n
RIMB 2 200 13 20n
RIMB 2 218 8 20n

ROM 2, no. 2:8-9 102n
ROM 2, no. 2:17 101n

TCS 5 chron 1 11n
TCS 5 chron 1 i 34 98n
TCS 5 chron 1 i 36 29n
TCS 5 chron 1 iii 3 98n
TCS 5 chron 2:14 27n
TCS 5 chron 2:19 27n
TCS 5 chron 2:25-32 27n
TCS 5 chron 3:2-8 28n
TCS 5 chron 3:10 29n, 80n
TCS 5 chron 3:25, 72 98
TCS 5 chron 3:27-28 29n
TCS 5 chron 3:38-45 132n
TCS 5 chron 3:54, 59 29
TCS 5 chron 4:3, 11 98
TCS 5 chron 5:1-8 82
TCS 5 chron 5 obv. 6 98
TCS 5 chron 5 obv. 11-13 161n
TCS 5 chron 5 obv.18 72n, 147
TCS 5 chron 5 rev.6-7 87n

TCS 5 chron 5 rev. 20	132n
TCS 5 chron 7 ii 10-12	179n
TCS 5 chron 7 iii 15-16	133n
TCS 5 chron 7 iii 5	179n
TCS 5 chron 7 iii 9-12	179n
TCS 5 chron 7 iii 17-22	180n
TCS 5 chron 7 iii 14, 15-16	195
TCS 12 84	47
Unger, *Babylon* 282 i 1-13	45n.
Unger, *Babylon* 282 i 8-9	156n
Unger, *Babylon* 283 ii 6-21	41-42
Unger, *Babylon* 283 ii 25	34n
Unger, *Babylon* 284 iii 16-18	46n
Unger, *Babylon* 284 iii 23-34	93
Unger, *Babylon* 284 iii 35	150
Unger, *Babylon* 285 iv 22	151
Unger, *Babylon* 286 v 7-8	37n
Unger, *Babylon* 286 v 23	101n
UVB 1 56	19n
WVDOG 5 pl. 35 29	41n
WVDOG 5 pl. 39 23-24	87n
WVDOG 5 pl. 39:26-30	10n
WVDOG 59 44 no. 2	26
WVDOG 59 46 3.9-13	40n
WVDOG 59 46 3.13-30	36-37
WVDOG 59 46 3.39-53	94
WVDOG 59 46 3.46	25n
WVDOG 59 46 3.55-56	37
WVDOG 59 46 4.8	38n
WVDOG 59 46 4.7-13	38
WVDOG 59 46 4.11-25	37n
YOS 1 39	187n
YOS 1 44 i 11-13	35
YOS 1 44 i 24-ii 8	50n
YOS 1 44 ii 27-29	49n
YOS 1 45 ii 39	184n
	186n
YOS 6 168	47
YOS 9 84	*see* BRM 4 51
ZA 4 144, no. 15, rev. 9	21n

General Index

Adad-Guppi, 53
Adon and Adon Letter, 75, 89, 102-3
Aharoni, Y., 79
Ahmar, Tell, 67
akītu
    festival, 177-80, 179n, 208
    temple, 178
Akkad, 16, 19, 24, 24n, 25, 27, 32, 38, 44, 95-96
Albright, W. F., 51n, 108, 109n
Al Mina, 76, 84, 86
Amasis, 85, 88, 89
Arpad, 99-100, 102, 104, 105, 205
Arwad, 70, 97
Ashdod, 70-72, 75, 79, 82, 97, 106
Ashkelon, 72, 73, 75, 78, 80, 82, 106, 147
Assur (city), 29
Assur (land), 38, 38n
Aššur (god), 41, 43, 45, 49,
Assurbanipal, 19, 20, 68, 131, 141
    Assyria's decline and, 63-66, 69, 136
    death of, 67-68, 81
    Nabonidus and, 11, 21, 52-53, 57n, 58
Aššur-etel-ilāni, 19, 20, 174-75
Aššur-šarru-uṣur, 67n
Aššur-uballiṭ II, 67, 91
Assyria(n), 117-18
    bureaucracy, 4, 61-62, 74, 109, 111, 119, 146, 205-6
    contraction of, 64-68, 69-70, 77, 80, 81, 136
    defeat by Nabopolassar, 24-29, 31
    empire, 2, 3, 7, 38-39, 51, 83, 90-92, 97-98, 99, 105, 108, 113, 119, 120-21, 161
    royal inscriptions, 9, 11, 32-33, 40-41, 43, 47-49, 126, 131, 139, 143
    royal titulary, 17-23, 203, 204
    See also deportation, NA procedures for; Nabonidus and the Assyrian tradition; Philistia and Assyria
Babylon (city)
    antiquity of in biblical descriptions, 142, 144, 171
    biblical use of name, 117n
    depicted as a shamed lady, 181
    fall of in Jeremiah, 193-201
    fortifications, 190-91
    imperial center, 45-49
    intellectual experts in, 182-84
    topography, 191-93
Babylonia
    foreign nation *par excellence* in Jeremiah, 142-44
    defensive walls in, 191-92
Barstad, H., 106, 110, 170
Batash, Tel. *See* Timnah
Beaulieu, P. A., 34n, 54n, 55, 58, 187n
Bel, 160, 175-77, 179. *See* Marduk
Belshazzar, 179,
Benjamin (tribal territory), 85n, 105-6, 108, 146n
Berger, P.-R., 15-16, 34, 44n, 50n, 88, 115
Boardman, J. A., 77-78, 84n, 85

Brinkman, J. A., 11, 123n, 131n, 165n
call report. *See* royal inscriptions, Neo-Babylonian, commission to rule in
Carchemish, 66, 67, 80, 81, 82, 104, 146
cedar. *See* Lebanon, cedars of
Chaldea, 24n, 123n
Chaldeans, 24n, 105, 123, 123n, 130, 142, 182n, 183n
  in Habakkuk, 142, 153, 153n, 154, 157, 160, 163, 207
Cilicia, 11n, 40, 67, 86, 92
Cimmerians, 64
Cogan, M., 82n, 105, 139n
Cole, S., vii, 38n, 113, 192, 193
Coogan, M. D., vii, 206n
Coniah. *See* Jehoiachin
Corinthian ceramics. *See* Greek ceramics
covenant, 164-66
  covenant curses, 140n, 143-44, 166n
  See also treaty
Cross, F. M., vii, 67n, 79, 108n, 138n, 149
Cush, 88, 114n
Cyrus, 90, 133, 170, 180, 195-99
Dan (city), 146
Dandamayev, M., 113, 155n
Daphnae, 77, 80, 85, 86
deportation
  of Marduk and Nabû, 179, 180
  NA procedures for, 43, 111, 118-19, 144
  NB procedures for, 43, 86, 97n, 99, 101, 110-12, 139, 143, 160-61, 206
  verbs for in Jeremiah, 122n
Deuteronomistic historian, 81, 98, 118
Diodorus of Sicily, 77-78, 85
Dobbs-Allsopp, F. W., 126n, 127n, 134
East Greek ceramics. *See* Greek ceramics
Ebabbar temple (Sippar), 21, 54, 54n, 99, 104, 162, 205
Eber Nāri, 38, 39, 40, 91-92, 96, 97, 99
Edel, E., 88, 89
Egypt, 28, 64
  Assyria and, 28, 64
  Babylonian defeat of, 82
  as border of NB empire, 40
  Greeks and, 76-78
  and the Levant, 69-81
  Nebuchadnezzar II's policy toward, 81-89
Eḫulḫul temple, 21, 56
Eichhorn, J. G., 137
Ein Gedi, 103, 106
Ekron (Tel Miqne), 73-75, 78, 82, 106
Elam, 64, 108, 113, 130-34
Elat, M., 100, 101n, 113
Enlil, 28, 30
Enlil-šāpik-zēri, 100
En-nigaldi-Nanna, 53, 184n
Enūma Anu Enlil, 186, 186n
Eph'al, I., 65, 66, 90, 101n, 111, 172, 174-75
eponym chronicles, 65-68
Esarhaddon, 19, 20, 33n, 48n, 127, 143n, 168, 194,
Etemenanki, 26
  Nabopolassar's inscriptions for, 30, 32n, 40, 40n
  Nebuchadnezzar II's E. inscription and imperial geography, 4, 36-40, 91, 92-93, 94-96, 104, 205
extispicy, 53, 168-69
Esagil (temple), 19, 20, 26, 46, 178
Ezida (temple), 19, 20, 26, 46, 178
fish and fishing
  as metaphor for imperial crimes in Habakkuk, 155-57
foe from the north, 136-49
  lion similes and, 140-42
Gaza, 39n, 97
Gedaliah, 83, 105, 108
Gerardi, P., 26, 29n, 123n
Gezer, 66, 83, 106
Gibeon, 107
Gitin, S., 73n, 74
Gozan (Tell Halaf), 118
Grayson, A. K., 9n, 25, 28n, 90

Greek ceramics,
in the Southern Levant, 76-80, 83-87, 106, 205-6
Habakkuk
Chaldean violence in, 153-63
Lebanon in, 153-54
legal idioms in, 158-60
Ḥabl-aṣ-Ṣaḫr, 132, 192
Ḥalaḫ, 118
Halpern, B., vii, 51n, 121n, 187
Ḫanunu, 62n
Hammurapi, 6, 17, 18, 20, 22, 44, 50-51
Hammurapi's Laws, 17n, 38n, 44, 50, 201
Ḫatti, 38-40, 91-92, 96, 99, 104, 205
Herodotus, 70, 71, 72, 75, 77, 85, 87, 137, 191n, 196, 197, 198, 199
Hezekiah, 118, 121, 126n
Hoglund, K., 91
Ḫumê, 11n, 92, 98. *See also* Cilicia, Qū'e
Imgur-Enlil
Nabopolassar's inscription for, 30, 31
imperialism, definition of, 5-6
Ionia and Ionians, 77, 79n, 86, 88
Jacobsen, T., 157n, 171n, 172n
Jehoiachin, 97n, 105, 142, 154n, 165
Jemmeh, Tel, 76n, 83, 106
Joannès, F., 99-100, 101n
Josiah, 29, 67-68, 79, 148
Katzenstein, H. J., 71, 89, 100
Ketef Hinnom, 108
Kidish, 101, 102
King, P. J., vii, 172n
Koldewey, R., 178n, 197n
Lachish, 106, 139
Lambert, W. G., 43, 44, 91, 98, 130
Landsberger, B., 21, 34n, 42n, 56, 92, 94, 100
Langdon, S., 10n, 13, 14, 15, 16, 30, 34, 38n, 52
Larsen, M., 5
Lebanon, 109, 153, 206
cedars of, 32, 70, 153-54
in political allegory, 164-65, 166-67
Nebuchadnezzar's campaign to, 10n, 87, 154
Zion as, 167
Lehmann, G., 109-110, 112, 206
Levenson, J., 148n
Liverani, M., 12n, 47, 112, 114
Libya, 88
Lydia, Lydians, 40, 64, 87, 88n, 98
Machinist, P., vii, 2, 40, 105, 129, 130, 141, 147
Magness, J., 78, 84
Malamat, A., 65, 80, 81n
Mannu-kī-aḫḫē, 66
Marduk
in *akītu* festival, 178-79, 208
demotion under Nabonidus, 52, 56
god of Babylon and Babylonia, 28, 30, 37, 39, 187, 195
in hymns, 46, 48
offerings for, 156, 174
patron of kings, 20, 26, 31, 35, 42, 49, 54, 55, 56, 57
patron of temples, 14, 26, 36, 91, 162, 178
statue, 175, 178, 179
See also Bel
Marduk-šarru-uṣur, 66n
Marduk-zākir-šumi, 30n
Medes, 29, 39, 58, 124, 125, 127, 131, 132, 133, 134
"cities of," 118
Meṣad Ḥashavyahu, 68, 78-80, 84, 106
Merneptah, 73
Merodach-baladan II, 18n, 25n, 118, 119, 131,
Micah
on exile to Babylon, 117-22
use of in Jeremiah, 120-21
Middle Gate, 139
Milki-eṭēri, 101
Miqne, Tel. *See* Ekron
mīs pî, 172, 172n
Mizpah (Tell en-Naṣbeh), 83, 105, 108
cuneiform inscription from, 108-9
m(w)ṣh stamps and, 108

musukkannu wood, 173-75
Na'aman, N., vii, 27, 65, 68n, 79, 82n, 137
Nabonidus, 11n, 47, 113, 173, 176, 182-83, 202
and the Assyrian tradition, 11, 21, 53-54, 56, 58, 58n, 59
innovations introduced in
cult, 52, 54
inscriptions, 53-55, 56-57
titulary, 21, 22, 22n, 23, 56n, 206-7
and the Second Isaiah, 187n, 188-90, 190n
Nabonassar, 11
Nabopolassar, 11, 14, 15, 23, 34, 63, 80, 98, 125n, 137, 200, 207
commission to rule, 23-24, 31-32, 32n, 42, 95n
conflict with Assyria, 24-29, 32, 50
titulary, 22
Nabû, 175, 179, 190
in *akītu* festival, 178
patron of kings, 10n, 14, 25, 30, 35, 42, 43n, 46
statue, 177, 178, 179, 180
See also Nebo
Nabû-da''inanni, 66n
Nabû-šar-aḫḫēšu, 66
Nabû-šarrūssu-ukīn, 151, 151n
Nabû-šezibanni, 151
Nabû-šuma-ukīn, 102n
Nabuzaradan (Nabû-zēra-iddinam), 153
Nabû-zēr-kitti-līšir, 102n
Naram-Sin, 23n, 37n, 50n, 144n
Naṣbeh, Tell en-. *See* Mizpah
Naucratis, 77, 80, 85, 86
Naveh, J., 78, 79, 103n, 107n
Nebo, 150, 175, 176, 179. *See also* Nabû
Nebuchadnezzar I, 18, 18n, 22, 28n, 52
Nebuchadnezzar II,
architect of NB empire, 4
Babylonian king *par excellence* in biblical tradition, 129
conflict with Egypt
depictions of, 141, 141n, 154, 167
as an eagle in political allegory, 164
NB empire under, 33-51 *passim*
See also, deportation, NB procedures for; Egypt, Nebuchadnezzar II's policy toward; Etemenanki, Nebuchadnezzar II's inscription and imperial geography; Lebanon, Nebuchadnezzar's campaign to; Philistia and Babylonia; royal inscriptions, Neo-Babylonian; treaty, between Nebuchadnezzar and Zedekiah
Necho II, 71, 71n, 79, 81, 83, 84, 146n, 148
nĕhar kĕbār, 110-11
Neo-Babylonian language, 9n
short final vowels in, 14n
Nergalśar'eṣer (Neriglissar), 150-51
Nineveh, 26n, 29, 66, 67, 90, 98, 118, 132, 139, 141, 162n, 182, 182n, 194n
Nippur, 17n, 27-29, 30, 100, 101n, 102, 111n, 113
Nitocris, 196-97
oath. *See* treaty
Opis, 192
Oppenheim, A. L., 3, 11, 12, 47, 62n, 94, 95n, 112-13
Oren, E., 85
Paul, S., 46n, 155n, 170, 171n
Philistia, 63, 84, 138
and Assyria, 82-83
and Babylonia, 82-83, 87, 111-12, 147
and Egypt, 70-76, 80
pīḫatu, 38n, 92, 98, 99, 101, 102, 103, 195, 104, 205
Piriddu, 87, 98
Psammetichus I, 64, 69, 70, 71, 72, 75, 77, 78, 79, 80, 81, 83, 84, 85, 205 80-81
Qadesh, 101, 102n
Qû'e, 66n, 92. *See* Cilicia, Ḫumê
Ramses VIII, 73

Reade, J., 66, 68
Redford, D. B., 71, 80
Reimer, D. J., 189
Riblah, 81, 100
riksātu, 44, 44n, 165, 165n
Roberts, J. J. M., 153n, 156n, 157n, 162n
royal inscriptions, Neo-Babylonian
 apolitical character of, 9-12
 archaic elements in, 16-18
 Assyrian elements in Nabonidus's, 53-54, 57n, 58, 204
 commission to rule in, 23-24, 31-32, 32n, 35-41, 42, 53-56, 95n, 161, 204
 form in, 13-16, 52-53
 precedents for, 50-51
 Second Isaiah's dependence on, 172-75
 See also titulary, royal
šakkanakku, 16, 38n, 91, 92, 104, 205
Samaria, 65n, 66, 68, 118
Šamaš, 14, 27, 28, 30, 36, 37, 39, 42n, 53, 54, 55n
Šamaš-šuma-ukīn, 19, 20, 64, 70, 132
šandabakku, 100, 101n, 102n
Sandmel, S., 1
Saqqara papyrus. *See* Adon Letter
Sargon of Agade, 21, 23, 144n, 182n
Sargon II, 19, 40, 44, 82n, 118, 128, 144
Scythians, 40, 136-38, 144, 148
Sealand, 24n, 123n, 130, 131
Second Isaiah
 attack on Babylonian divination, 181-88
 Babylonian context for, 169-70
 hope of restoration, 122
 polemics against images, 171-80
Sennacherib, 1, 19, 20n, 119, 121, 128, 132, 139, 146n, 194-95
Sera', Tel, 82, 83n, 106
Shinar, 123n
šibirru, 43, 44
Sidon, 71, 97
Sîn, 12, 39n, 52, 53, 56, 57n, 58, 184n, 185
Sin-magir, Simmagir, 151
Sin-šar-iškun, 67n
Sin-šum-lišir, 25, 27,
Sippar, 14, 15, 28, 30, 37, 39, 54, 99, 132, 192, 193, 205
Spalinger, A., 71
Stager, L. E., vii, 72, 73, 74, 82, 83, 91, 109, 111, 205
Subarian, 14, 25, 26, 29, 39n
Sūkās, Tell, 76, 83, 84, 85, 86
Šum-ukīn, 186
Ṣurru, 100-102
Tadmor, H., 18n, 21, 22n, 55, 70, 92, 105
Teima, 22n, 54, 56, 179
Tel Abib, 110-11
Tiglath-Pileser III, 146
Timnah (Tel Batash), 78, 82
titulary, royal, 16-23, 203-4
treaty
 between Nebuchadnezzar and Zedekiah, 164-66
 curses, 127, 140n, 143, 144, 146n, 165, 166n
 lack of NB examples, 161, 161n
 YHWH as witness to, 166, 166n
Tsevat, M., 165-66
Tyre, 66, 71, 73n, 97, 100, 101n, 113, 125n, 148
Unger, E., 34n, 93, 94, 97, 100
Uruk, 20, 27, 37, 95, 96n, 100, 101n, 102
Vaggione, R. P., 137
Via Maris, 70, 80, 146
Waldbaum, J., 76n, 77, 78, 80n, 84
Weinfeld, M., 122n, 127, 140n, 143
Weissbach, F. H., 28, 37, 93, 154
Wetzel, F., 199
Wiseman, D. J., 97n, 100,
Xenophon, 132, 192, 196, 198
Zadok, R., 30n, 101n, 111n, 119n, 123n
Zedekiah, 87, 105, 132, 164, 165, 166

Hebrew Words

אנמים, 200-1
אלה, 165
ארן, 174
אשיות, 190-91
באר, 158-59
ברית, 165-66
הברו, 183, 183n, 184, 184n
הדיח, 122n
חמס, 153-54
מגיד, 158n
מדבר־ים, 130-31
מסכן, 173-74
מעברות, 200-1
משפחה, 138n
עבוט, 161n
עד, 159, 159n
ערץ, 125n
רוץ, 158n
שַׁחְרָהּ, 185

www.ingramcontent.com/pod-product-compliance
Lightning Source LLC
Chambersburg PA
CBHW021122300426
44113CB00006B/252
9780788505799